The Genesis of Nineteenth-Century Civil Codes in the United States

Legal History Library

VOLUME 66

The titles published in this series are listed at *brill.com/lhl*

The Genesis of Nineteenth-Century Civil Codes in the United States

By

Julie Rocheton

BRILL | NIJHOFF

LEIDEN | BOSTON

Library of Congress Cataloging-in-Publication Data

Names: Rocheton, Julie, author.
Title: The genesis of nineteenth-century civil codes in the United States / by Julie Rocheton.
Description: Leiden ; Boston : Brill/Nijhoff, 2024. | Series: Legal history library; volume 66 | Includes index. | Summary: "Starting in Louisiana in the early nineteenth century, this book takes the reader on a journey through the USA and the development of their civil codes. From Georgia and New York, civil codes traveled to California and Dakota Territory; in the Great Plains, they made their way to Montana, North Dakota, and South Dakota by the end of the century. Unveiling the history of nineteenth-century civil codes in the USA, this book examines their origin stories, circulation, and usage by focusing on the social-historical context of their drafting and legal concepts. "Rocheton's work, published four decades after Cook's book on 'The American Codification Movement,' contains an exhaustive and insightful analysis of nineteenth-century civil codes. It thoroughly discusses their context, how they were conceived, discussed, drafted and approved, their main foreign influences and content, and their practical operation." – Aniceto Masferrer, University of Valencia "While there is a vast corpus of literature on codification and, more specifically, civil codes in the civil law tradition, it is much less known that six US states codified their private laws during the 19th century. This book tells the fascinating story. Spoiler alert: it's a family affair." – Stefan Vogenauer, Max Planck Institute for Legal History and Legal Theory"– Provided by publisher.
Identifiers: LCCN 2023052194 (print) | LCCN 2023052195 (ebook) | ISBN 9789004689961 (hardback) | ISBN 9789004689978 (ebook)
Subjects: LCSH: Civil law–United States. | Law–United States–Codification.
Classification: LCC KF434 .R63 2024 (print) | LCC KF434 (ebook) | DDC 340.5/6097309034–dc23/eng/20231117
LC record available at https://lccn.loc.gov/2023052194
LC ebook record available at https://lccn.loc.gov/2023052195

Typeface for the Latin, Greek, and Cyrillic scripts: "Brill". See and download: brill.com/brill-typeface.

ISSN 1874-1793
ISBN 978-90-04-68996-1 (hardback)
ISBN 978-90-04-68997-8 (e-book)
DOI 10.1163/9789004689978

This book is printed on acid-free paper and produced in a sustainable manner.

To all of you who got me through hell and back for a moment, often, or forever, yesterday, or today, with a simple smile or anything else,

MERCI

Contents

PART 3

Acknowledgements

First and foremost, I am grateful and thankful to Prof. Aniceto Masferrer, who supported and guided me with kindness and patience during my doctoral research on the subject. This work only exists thanks to him, and his expertise has been invaluable. This research was conducted thanks to his support and the support of the Faculty of Law of the Universitat de València.

The writing process for this book, turning my doctoral thesis into a manuscript, was conducted at the Max Planck Institute for Legal History and Legal Theory in Frankfurt am Main. The environment was perfect, and the result of this project is a combination of the generosity and dedication of many people. I particularly would like to thank Prof. Stefan Vogenauer for his advice during this process.

The contents of this book have been presented at various stages at several conferences throughout the years, each helping to add new depths to this work. During my doctoral years, I also had the privilege to be hosted as a visiting research scholar at the University of Michigan Law School. In addition to granting me access to their library filled with the sources and materials I required, the scholarly community there was instrumental in the development of my research. I especially would like to thank Prof. William J. Novak and Prof. Thomas A. Green for all the time they dedicated to me and my work. I also would like to express my thankfulness and appreciation to all the people and institutions I had the privilege to be part of—under various affiliations—during my Ph.D. for their invaluable assistance during this long process.

I am indebted to the defense committee of my Ph.D., consisting of Prof. María Magdalena Martínez Almira, Prof. Jean-Louis Halpérin, Dr. Juan B. Cañizares Navarro, Dr. Luisa Stella Coutinho Silva, Prof. Gabriela Cobo del Rosal Pérez, and Prof. Javier Plaza Penadés, who provided valuable insights on my work.

I am thankful to all of my colleagues and friends from places all over the globe who generously shared their time and knowledge, assistance, encouragement, support, and advice. This project would not exist without all of you. I also would like to thank Teresa and Grigorij for all their help in sharpening my writing and for spending countless hours proofreading the different versions of this work.

My appreciation also goes to the anonymous reviewers and the editors of the *Studies in Legal History* series, who, with their insights and feedback, aided in improving this book. Last but not least, I would like to express my gratitude to the amazing editorial team at Brill.

Illustrations

Figures

Tables

Diagrams

Appendices

Abbreviations

AL *C. 1852*	*The Code of Alabama*, eds. John J. Ormond, Arthur P. Bagby, George Goldthwaite, and Henry C. Semple, Montgomery (AL): Brittan and de Wolf, State Printers, 1852.
AK *C. 1900*	*Alaska Codes: Political, Civil and Civil Procedure, approved June 6, 1900*, San Francisco: Bancroft-Whitney Co., 1900.
AR *Rev. Stat. 1901*	*The Revised Statutes of Arizona Territory, containing also the Laws passed by the twenty-first Legislative Assembly, the Constitution of the United States, the Organic Law of Arizona and the Amendments of Congress relating thereto*, Columbia (MO): Press of E. W. Stephens, 1901.
CA *Civ. C. 1872*	*The Civil Code of the State of California, as enacted in 1872*, ed. Albert Hart, San Francisco: Sumner Whitney & Co., 1880.
DT *Rev. C. 1877*	*The Revised Codes for the Territory of Dakota*, ed. Geo. H. Hand, Yankton: Bowen & Kingsbury, 1877.
FR *C. Civ. 1804*	*Code civil des Français. Édition originale et seule officielle*, Paris: Imprimerie de la République, 1804.
GA *C. 1861*	*The Code of the State of Georgia*, eds. Richard H. Clark, Thomas R. R. Cobb, and David Irwin, Atlanta (GA): John H. Seals, 1861.
HI *Civ. C. 1859*	*The Civil Code of the Hawaiian Islands, passed in the Year of our Lord 1859*, Honolulu: Printed for the Government, 1859.
IN *Rev. Laws 1824*	*The Revised Laws of Indiana, adopted and enacted by the General Assembly at their eight Session*, Corydon (IN): Carpenter & Douglas, 1824.
LA *Civ. C. 1825*	*Code Civil de l'État de la Louisiane. Traité de Cession de cet État par la France, Constitution de cet État, Constitution des États-Unis d'Amerique*, unknown: Publié par un Citoyen de la Louisiane, 1825.
LA *Digest 1808*	*A Digest of the Civil Laws now in Force in the Territory of Orleans, with Alterations and Amendments adapted to its present System of Government*, New Orleans: Bradford & Anderson, Printers to the Territory, 1808.
LA *Rev. Civ. C. 1870*	*The Revised Civil Code of the State of Louisiana*, New Orleans: Printed at the Office of the Republican, 1870.
MT *C. & Stat. 1895*	*The Codes and Statutes of Montana, in force July 1, 1895, including the Political Code, Civil Code, Code of Civil Procedure and Penal Code*, 1st vol., Butte (MT): Inter Mountain Publishing Co., 1895.

ND Rev. C. 1895	*The Revised Codes of the State of North Dakota 1895 together with the Constitution of the United States and the State of North Dakota*, Bismarck (ND): Tribune Company, 1895.
NY Civ. C. 1865	*The Civil Code for the State of New York: Reported complete by the Commissioners of the Code*, eds. David Dudley Field et al, Albany: Weed, Parsons & Co., 1865.
NY Rev. Stat. 1829	*The Revised Statutes of New York passed during the Year one thousand eight hundred and twenty-seven and one thousand eight hundred and twenty-eight, printed and published under the Direction of the Revisers appointed for that purpose*, 4th vol., Albany: Printed by Packard and van Benthuysen, 1829.
SD Rev. C. 1903	*The Revised Codes 1903, State of South Dakota, comprising the Political Code, Civil Code, Code of Civil Procedure, Probate Code, Justices Code, Penal Code and Code of Criminal Procedure*, Pierre: Hipple Printing Company, 1904.
TN C. 1858	*The Code of Tennessee, enacted by the General Assembly of 1758–'8*, eds. J. Meigs and William F. Cooper, Nashville (TN): E. G. Eastman & Co., State Printers, 1858.

Codification[1]

A code, or not a code—that is the question!
Whether 'tis better in the law to suffer
The flaws and defects of numerous practiques
Or to take arms against a sea of troubles,
And, by revising, end them!—To prune—To change—
No more! Any by a code to say we end
Abuses, and the thousand natural pests
The law is heir to: 'tis a consummation
Devoutly to be wished.—To prune—To change—
To change, and perhaps destroy! Ay, there's the rub!
For in that sleep of law what ills may come,
When we have shuffled off the dreadful plague,
must give us a pause. There's the respect
That makes precedents of so long life;
For who would bear the whips and smarts of law,
The high judge's frown; the lawyer's charges;
The pangs of satisfying debts; the law's delay;
The insolence of sheriffs, and the spurns
That patient merit of the policemen takes,
When he himself might his quietus make
With a bare reform? Who would judges pay,
To groan and sweat under a weary life;
But that the dread of something after change—
(Those undiscovered evils, from whose ruin
no government returns)—puzzles the will,
And makes us rather bear those ills we have
Than fly to others that we know not of.
Thus wisdom does make cowards of us all,
And thus the native hue of resolution
Is sicklied o'er with the pale cast of thought;
And enterprizes of great pith and moment
With this regard their currents turn away,
And lose the name of action.

1 An unknown Lawyer, "Codification", 2 *United States Law Intelligencer and Review* 1830, p. 268.

Introduction

On October 23, 1860, the *Columbus Daily* of Georgia proclaimed the success of the state's codification efforts, noting that "the code will doubtless meet the approval of the legislature and be a textbook for every lawyer in the State". Sipping their favorite bourbon and reading the optimistic words of a trusted journalist, the men of Georgia were likely filled with a sense of pride. But not all of them had been in favor of a code. Indeed, just a year earlier, on February 3, 1859, the *Daily Morning News* had announced the creation of the code to the gentlemen readers of Savannah with a vehement warning that "within three years after its establishment its originator will be the best abused man in Georgia and those who voted for it will be saved from universal contempt only by their very universal obscurity". Meanwhile, in New York, David Dudley Field was working tirelessly to have his 1860 Draft of a Civil Code for the State of New York adopted. This draft in turn circulated from the Dakotas to California, taking with it the idea of codification and spreading an increasingly heated debate. "A code, or not a code—that is the question!" And it was a question that provoked increasingly passionate opinions amongst nineteenth-century Americans,[1] for whom codification became the subject of a heated debate in which convictions were strong and positions expertly defended. This was the case, at least, until the codes were adopted. Once enacted, they became an undeniable part of the adopting state's legal corpus, so accepted that it requires some effort to excavate their controversial origins.

Many countries have considered the question of codification at some point in their history, whether due to inherent issues in the law or from a drive to enter the age and vision of rationalization. The answers differed from one place to another, one tradition to another, one state to another, one legal matter to another. Some answered the call, while others rejected it. The beauty of codification is that it has been called upon nearly everywhere for discussion and decision. Wherever and whenever it has been proposed, codification has tended to provoke controversy, a fact that is especially true in the world governed by common law.[2] Strikingly, every attempt at codification in England—the common law state *par excellence*—has been rejected, a fact that is doubly notable given that the word "codification" was invented by an Englishman, Jeremy Bentham.

1 Whenever the term "American" is used in this book, it refers to the inhabitants of the United States or to some characteristics of the United States.

2 Maurice Eugen Lang, *Codification in the British Empire and America*, Clark (NJ): The Lawbook Exchange, 2005, p. 14.

 | DOI:10.1163/9789004689978_002

By contrast, though it inherited much of the English legal tradition, the United States has adopted its fair share of codes, many of which have been explored by scholars in depth. In the US case, the civil procedural codes have attracted particular attention, as have the criminal codes. Additionally, the Uniform Commercial Code,[3] which remains in use in the twenty-first century, has been described as, "one of the finest pieces of lawmaking in the history of the common law world".[4] Another notable example can be found in the Civil Codes of Louisiana, which have been extensively studied by scholars yet are often treated as marginal given Louisiana's particular historical ties to the civil law tradition. Yet the nature and extent of these examples prompts the question of their influence and spread to the rest of the United States. Were the Civil Codes of Louisiana really the only ones in the entire US territory? Pushing beyond works which have tended to study each state or case in isolation, this book excavates the history of private law codification in the United States as a whole. In doing so, it uncovers the extensive influence of the idea and practice of codification across states and territories often left out of earlier accounts.

Given that private law is the law of everyday life, including areas such as marriage, the family, contracts, and private property, the question of codification was one of paramount importance, especially as the nature and complexity of such relationships exploded in the nineteenth century.[5] Private law is mundane, focusing on relationships between individuals or organizations, but it is also everywhere and is the most practiced field of law. This importance is reflected in the broad extent of private law codification in the nineteenth-century United States. And yet no existing study has attempted a more global portrait of codification in the nineteenth century United States. Discovering the existence of so many civil codes, and learning how fundamental they were to the construction of numerous US states, highlighted the need for the comprehensive and comparative study that follows. Assumptions about common

3 Richard Danzing, "A Comment on the Jurisprudence of the Uniform Commercial Code", 27 *Stanford Law Review* 1975, pp. 621–635; Mitchell Franklin, "On the Legal Method of the Uniform Commercial Code", 16 *Law and Contemporary Problems* 1951, pp. 330–343; Gunther A. Weiss, "The Enchantment of Codification in the Common-Law World", 25 *Yale Journal of International Law* 2000, pp. 515–527; Robert Braucher, "The Legislative History of the Uniform Commercial Code", 58 *Columbia Law Review* 1958, pp. 798–814.

4 Roy Goode, "The Codification of Commercial Law", 14 *Monash University Law Review* 1988, pp. 135–157.

5 For a comprehensive study on the Code of Civil Procedure, its history, its impact, and its application, see Kellen Funk, *The Lawyer's Code: The Transformation of American Legal Practice, 1828–1938*, Princeton: Princeton University, 2018.

law versus civil law have profoundly shaped understandings of US legal history and have rendered codes invisible to all but the most specialized legal scholars.

By not adopting a unified Napoleonic Code, the individual state efforts might seem quixotic and unimportant even though they shaped key aspects of land law, commercial policy, family structure, etc ... Indeed the Napoleonic Code has distorted our sense of what a code should look like—and has made it impossible to see the centrality of codification to state building projects in the United States. This work also the demotes the Napoleonic model itself, showing that codification could take idiosyncratic and varied forms, and could involve hybrids between common law and civil law.

The research presented here tells the broad story of US private law codification, while also exploring the genesis of, and differences between, particular state's codes. Unveiling this hidden history of codification, and exploring the particular US-based definition and usage of civil codes, this study lays the groundwork for an array of new directions in the history of codification by opening the doorway to diversity and by desacralizing the Napoleonic Code.

In Search of a Definition of the Civil Code

Codification is often associated primarily with the civil law tradition, and is indeed regularly used to distinguish civil law from common law. Historically, they are presented as written law tradition versus unwritten law tradition, with each having their own peculiarities. And yet, as many earlier scholars have pointed out, the antagonism between the two traditions has been vastly overdrawn.[6] Like others before it, this book emphasizes the affinities between the two systems. The reality is that both traditions mutually influenced and borrowed from one another, a process that has become particularly salient within the current, globalized economy. Scholars nowadays recognize that if,

> codification has erroneously been considered a peculiarity of the civil law tradition, and hence somehow incompatible with the common law, this is because Napoleon's codifications have, unfortunately, been presented as the model of civil law codification, a mythical idea and prejudice that

6 Aniceto Masferrer, "French Codification and Codiphobia in Common Law Traditions", 34 *Tulane European & Civil Law Forum* 2019, pp. 1–31; Alain A. Levasseur, "Portalis and Pound: A Debate on 'Codification'", 81 *Louisiana Law Review* 2021, pp. 1113–1128.

> [has] constituted a remarkable obstacle for codification in many common law jurisdictions.[7]

Although codification is a familiar concept, it remains a slippery one that is constantly evolving.[8] The word "code" comes from the Latin *codex*. Early on, Roman documents had been contained in scrolls, while with the advent of the *codex* separate sheets of parchment came to be bound together on the left. In short, a *codex* was what we now know as a book. During the centuries that followed, the term *codex* referred to a formal way of presenting a document and did not necessarily have links with the law. The word entered the legal field with the Justinian Code,[9] the first document to gather distinct pieces of legal information and laws on a particular subject and the first to be given the title "code". The term continued to evolve: during the Middle Ages, for instance, the word *codex* referred to a compilation, *collectio*, a set of diverse alphabetically organized canon laws. It was only in the sixteenth century that the word "code" regained its Roman meaning as an arrangement of laws and came to be employed outside of canon law in a variety of countries on the European continent. At the time, lawmakers used the term "code" rather than "compilation", but both terms corresponded to the same idea. The word "code" only gained its modern meaning with the Napoleonic Code in the early nineteenth century.[10]

Since then, the concept of codification has had numerous definitions and meanings. Accordingly, the significance of codification, as well as the expected contents of a code, fluctuate depending on the specific meaning given to the term. In his book *Le Concept de Code en Europe Occidentale du XIIe au XIXe Siècle*,[11] Jacques Vanderlinden explains that the definition of codification differed from one state or time to another and is consequently more historical than generic. While in Ancient Rome, a code was just a document with no specified system of legal organization, in Napoleonic France a code came to signify the rationalization of law, becoming the ultimate source of law. In

7 Aniceto Masferrer, "French Codification and Codiphobia in Common Law Traditions", 34 *Tulane European & Civil Law Forum* 2019, pp. 1–31.

8 Jean Louis Bergel, "Principal Features and Methods of Codification", 48 *Louisiana Law Review* 1988, pp. 1073–1097.

9 Mathias Reimann, "The historical School against Codification: Savigny, Carter, and the defeat of the New York Civil Code", 37 *The American Journal of Comparative Law* 1989, pp. 95–119.

10 Shael Herman, "From Philosophers to Legislators, and Legislators to Gods: The French Civil Code as Secular Scripture", 597 *University of Illinois Law Review* 1984, p. 612.

11 Jacques Vanderlinden, *Le Concept de Code en Europe Occidentale du XIIe au XIXe Siècle: Essai de Définition*, Bruxelles: Éditions de l'Institut de Sociologie de l'Université libre de Bruxelles, 1967.

France, codification was tied to a national, top-down effort at legal, social and political unification.

Here my goal is not to list all the existing definitions of "civil code" and "codification" as these have been extensively covered by other scholars,[12] and because every time and place adds its specificities to the concept. For the purposes of this study, it is sufficient to note that there is no single model of codification, but rather only particular codes drafted according to distinct sets of rules.[13] Even so, this study required a working definition of codification. What defines a code in the specific context of this research? The Napoleonic Code was undoubtedly the main example of codification at the time. Despite the importance of this model, common law lawyers developed changing notions of codification in consonance with their legal training and education. Similarly, even the documents defining or explaining the different codification projects do not agree on a definition of codification, a fact which demonstrates the versatility of the notion.

Though definitions vary, some specific elements recur in most of them. This work relies on the academic consensus[14] defining codification. Scholars have been writing profusely on what exactly makes a codification. This consensus identifies four key components to codification as it occurred in different times and places. Those are particularly poignant in the context of nineteenth-century codification. The first concerns its origins, as—without any room for deviation or exception—a code must originate from the state, meaning that any private compilation or codification has been excluded from the analysis. The second component is its exclusivity, in the sense that a true code must contain all the law related to a particular legal field. Hence, a code must include all legal sources on its subject. Documents given the title "code", but which did not include all sources of law, whether statutes, common law or customs, have been excluded even where they were enforceable by the state. In order to get a clear picture of the different codifications of private law, all partial codifications were disregarded. The third element builds on the second and pertains to the form of the code, which requires that a collection of legal rules be brought

12 On this subject, see Rémy Cabrillac, *Les Codifications* (*Droit, Éthique, Société*), Paris: Presses Universitaires de France, 2002.

13 Aniceto Masferrer, "French Codification and Codiphobia in Common Law Traditions", 34 *Tulane European & Civil Law Forum* 2019, pp. 1–31.

14 For an overview of the evolution and consensus on codification, see J. M. Milo, J. H. A. Lokin, and J. M. Smiths, *Tradition, Codification and Unification: Comparative-Historical Essays on the Development in Civil Law* (*Ius Commune Europeum*), Cambridge: Intersentia, 2014, pp. 3–11.

together in a single document. Finally, the fourth key element of codification is the intent, which is found in codification efforts worldwide and in all the US codifying states. At their core, codes are intended to allow a better understanding of the law. These components put together establish the following definition: codification is the gathering of all legal rules on a particular legal field in one document created by the state with the aim of better understanding the law. This standard definition of codification is also quite traditional.[15] Utilizing this definition, I was able to find civil codes based on objective, quantifiable and identifiable elements.

In the timeframe covered by my research—the broad nineteenth century—only a few of the fifty current US states had a document called a "civil code" or even a "code". Even among these, not all of them conform to the definition of a civil code as a document that collects legislation, contains all of a territory's private law, and enables a better understanding of the law.[16] In total, fourteen states had documents called "civil codes" or "codes". However, the Codes of Alabama,[17] Arizona,[18] Indiana,[19] and Tennessee,[20] contain all the legislation and statutes concerning private law, but do not include the common law and are, therefore, not exhaustive. They thus lack an essential element necessary to be counted as codes.

Additionally, some codes had to be excluded due to the selected timeframe. The study focused on the nineteenth century; the century known for its codification endeavors worldwide. Starting with the first civil code in 1808, the study spans the nineteenth century, ending in 1903. It thus extends the century by three years to include the last civil code resulting from the Dakota Division. During this timeframe, two other codes existed in the territories which later

15 Joseph Dainow, "The Civil Law and the Common Law: Some Points of Comparison", 15 *The American Journal of Comparative Law* 1966, pp. 419–435; Aniceto Masferrer, "French Codification and Codiphobia in Common Law Traditions", 34 *Tulane European & Civil Law Forum* 2019, pp. 1–31; Eva Steiner, "Codification in England: The Need to move from an ideological to a functional Approach—A Bridge too far?", 25 *Statute Law Review* 2004, pp. 209–222; Rémy Cabrillac, *Les Codifications* (*Droit, Éthique, Société*), Paris: Presses Universitaires de France, 2002; Jacques Vanderlinden, *Le Concept de Code en Europe Occidentale du XIIe au XIXe Siècle: Essai de Définition*, Bruxelles: Éditions de l'Institut de Sociologie de l'Université libre de Bruxelles, 1967.

16 Jacques Vanderlinden, *Le Concept de Code en Europe Occidentale du XIIe au XIXe Siècle: Essai de Définition*, Bruxelles: Éditions de l'Institut de Sociologie de l'Université libre de Bruxelles, 1967, pp. 15–16.

17 *AL C. 1852.*

18 *AR Rev. Stat. 1901.*

19 *IN Rev. Laws 1824.*

20 *TN C. 1858.*

became part of the United States. The Codes of Hawaii[21] and Alaska[22] were excluded, as both of them only became states in 1959. While both had codes, they were not part of the United States at the time of codification, leaving them outside of the geographical boundaries of this research. Consequently, the nineteenth-century US civil codes included, in chronological order, the following: the 1808 and 1825 Civil Codes of Louisiana; the 1862 Code of Georgia; the 1866 Civil Code of the Dakota Territory; the 1870 Revised Civil Code of Louisiana; the 1872 Civil Code of California; the 1895 Revised Code of North Dakota; the 1895 Civil Code of Montana; and the 1903 Revised Code of South Dakota. Another code this study considers was the Field Civil Code, also known as the 1860 Draft of a Civil Code for the State of New York. Although it was never adopted, it had a significant impact on subsequent civil codes.

Throughout this work, some terms are used interchangeably to refer to the civil codes in the United States: "US civil codes", "civil codes", "codes", "nineteenth-century US civil codes", and "nineteenth-century codes". These terminologies have to be understood as synonyms, covering the aforementioned set of codes respectively. When specifications are required, qualifications such as "common law codes" for all the nineteenth-century codes except the Civil Codes of Louisiana, or "New York tradition codes" for all the nineteenth-century codes except for the Civil Codes of Louisiana and the Code of Georgia are being utilized.

Methodology

A notable feature of all the US civil codes is that they came from diverse backgrounds and cultures, and each one had its own history, particular codifiers and distinctive style of codification. As a result, every code was different and fulfilled a multilayered agenda that included a wide range of objectives. These objectives are at the heart of the codification endeavor, and they are the reason why it was essential to explore the origins of the different codification efforts. Indeed, a code would be drafted differently if it responded to a perceived need to modernize the law than if it was simply designed to make the law more accessible by consolidating it into a single document. A code driven by politics was not the same as one originating from popular demands. Emphasis on such fundamentals of the codes means that this research does not aim to cover

21 *HI Civ. C. 1859.*

22 *AK C. 1900.*

and compare every article of every code, for the results would be impossible to present in one volume. Instead, this book focuses on each code's genesis while also presenting their main features. A comparative approach is key here in highlighting the particularities of codification across distinct jurisdictions. I have traced differences and similarities by exploring the law, history, politics, culture, and economy of the different spaces in which codification took place. This book focuses on events that happened in eight territories—Louisiana, Georgia, New York, California, Dakota Territory, North Dakota, Montana, and South Dakota—all situated across the United States. The rich legal historiography of these states not only allows the usage of comparative legal history methodology, but also invites methodological approaches drawn from social history and law as well. This mixed methodology enables the book to apprehend the genesis of US civil codes and to explore the way they worked together in creating what I see as an US codification tradition. This tradition emerged when the idea of codification was transplanted into common law states with quite different backgrounds, history and appreciation of the law. Nineteenth-century lawyers in the United States could have simply imported codification whole cloth. Instead, they chose the more practical route of adapting codification to fit the distinctive needs and cultures of the US states.

Drawing on this range of methodologies, this volume aims to offer a more comprehensive understanding of the legal historiography of these states. Since law is a cultural product rooted in time and a place, this book considers the studied sources in light of factors both internal and external to the law. The study follows a broadly chronological arc, with historical events taking precedence as driving forces in the history of codification. Problematizing codification requires the reconstruction of events and institutions which played a role in the process, while also keeping in mind that codification is a matter both of mentalities and individual agency. Understanding the spirit of a certain time and place helps one to grasp the full extent of the project, while key actors often exerted a decisive influence in shepherding codification efforts to completion. In short, this book focuses on showing how the codification of private law in the United States evolved around the interplay of different actors in particular contexts. This research started out searching for a monocausal explanation for codification in those particular states, examining the traditional factors that shape codification—political power, a crisis in the sources of law, discontentment with the state of the law, a need for geographical unity and so forth. Each of these factors was indeed present in all of the states examined, but my research turned up no single driver of codification. Instead, it was the conjunction of these factors that made codification a reality in the eight different states studied, coupled with the existence of a network of interconnected legal professionals who made codification their panacea. Nineteenth-century US civil codes did not originate from a single agency dedicated to codification but rather from a network of privately connected legal professionals, all of them men, who tied their reputations to the idea of a code. The civil codes were above all an innovation resulting from personal convictions and familial connections.

While reliance on historical, comparative, and legal methodologies was a given, most of my methodological choices were dictated by the sources. The main methodological concern was to let the codes themselves tell their story, and to follow them wherever they led. This included, first, the codes, discourses, and American legal scholarship on codification during the set research timeframe. Second, I drew on secondary sources surrounding the codes. Studying the codes in their local context led me to seek out an array of secondary sources that helped to make sense of each code's particularity. "Similar to nineteenth-century codifiers, comparative legal historians must embark in treasure trove activities, seeking the most authoritative and useful sources that might help them answer their research questions".[23]

The sources also shaped the relevant timeframe, with most codes being written within the broad nineteenth century. This frame in turn dictated that the research strives to distance itself from a twenty-first century mindset rooted in the view of codes as the sole source of law so as to grasp the essence of the codes.[24] On the early end, however, moving beyond the nineteenth century into an examination of colonial law was necessary to grasp the origins of the codes in each state's particular legal culture.

Additionally, this work is a study of the translation and acculturation of a legal concept—the civil code—in a predominantly common law country. The fact that this defining notion of a civil law system was exported to another country with an "opposite" tradition proves the versatility of this legal practice and of the concept of codification. This transposition also demonstrates how a strong legal concept can evolve and adapt to different circumstances. The nineteenth century, known worldwide as the golden age of the code, has been depicted as one of stark opposition between the common law tradition and civil law tradition, with the existence of a code serving as a pivotal element in defining the opposition between the two legal systems. Thus, it is important to examine the ways in which a new country such as the United States navigated

23 Agustín Parise, *Ownership Paradigms in American Civil Law Jurisdictions: Manifestations of the Shifts in the Legislation of Louisiana, Chile, and Argentina (16th–20th Centuries)*, Leiden and Boston: Brill Nijhoff, 2017, p. 22.

24 *Ibid*, p. 3.

these waters. What was the decision-making process for the states? How did former common law colonies resolve their shift towards codes? And how did civil law colonies fight to keep their legal traditions intact? Using each code and place as a case study—almost like comparing case law—allows one to understand the interaction of relevant factors while showcasing the workings of different legal mechanisms, social, political and economic concerns, and a variety of actors. This study emphasizes the transposition of the concept of a civil code into a common law country, while also demonstrating what emerged as inherently US codification patterns and concepts.

This research is organized into three parts. The first focuses on contextualizing the codes. In order to understand the codes themselves, this part lays the foundational knowledge necessary, while also providing key background on codification. The first chapter presents the national theoretical debate over codification and explores its key arguments. It considers both proponents of codification, who underscored the legal clarity a code would bring, and the opponents who highlighted the legal flexibility of the common law system in adapting to a changing society. The second chapter is a chronicle of the nineteenth-century US civil codes, giving an overview of the codes, their origins and their immediate context. The second part of the book focuses on explaining and understanding the codes themselves. The third chapter asks why the codification of private law was ultimately successful in specific states. Using a comparative methodology, the chapter explores an array of possible factors leading to the success or failure of codification efforts and shows that, at key moments, chance, family ties and networking were more influential than political will or broad social acceptance. The fourth chapter examines the sources and forms of the civil codes, apprehending the different conceptions of codification that emerged in different states. The third and final part of the book examines how the codes worked concretely in the fifth chapter, with the sixth chapter dealing with their practical aspects from the adoption process to the rules of interpretation. Some concluding remarks provide a brief summary of the main findings and offer key questions for future research.

Bibliography

Bergel, Jean Louis: "Principal Features and Methods of Codification", 48 *Louisiana Law Review* 1988, pp. 1073–1097.

Braucher, Robert: "The Legislative History of the Uniform Commercial Code", 58 *Columbia Law Review* 1958, pp. 798–814.

Cabrillac, Rémy: *Les Codifications* (*Droit, Éthique, Société*), Paris: Presses Universitaires de France, 2002.

Dainow, Joseph: "The Civil Law and the Common Law: Some Points of Comparison", 15 *The American Journal of Comparative Law* 1966, pp. 419–435.

Danzing, Richard: "A Comment on the Jurisprudence of the Uniform Commercial Code", 27 *Stanford Law Review* 1975, pp. 621–635.

Franklin, Mitchell: "On the Legal Method of the Uniform Commercial Code", 16 *Law and Contemporary Problems* 1951, pp. 330–343.

Funk, Kellen: *The Lawyer's Code: The Transformation of American Legal Practice, 1828–1938*, Princeton: Princeton University, 2018.

Goode, Roy: "The Codification of Commercial Law", 14 *Monash University Law Review* 1988, pp. 135–157.

Herman, Shael: "From Philosophers to Legislators, and Legislators to Gods: The French Civil Code as Secular Scripture", 597 *University of Illinois Law Review* 1984, pp. 597–620.

Lang, Maurice Eugen: *Codification in the British Empire and America*, Clark (NJ): The Lawbook Exchange, 2005.

Levasseur, Alain A.: "Portalis and Pound: A Debate on 'Codification'", 81 *Louisiana Law Review* 2021, pp. 1113–1128.

Masferrer, Aniceto: "French Codification and Codiphobia in Common Law Traditions", 34 *Tulane European & Civil Law Forum* 2019, pp. 1–31.

Parise, Agustín: *Ownership Paradigms in American Civil Law Jurisdictions: Manifestations of the Shifts in the Legislation of Louisiana, Chile, and Argentina* (*16th–20th Centuries*), Leiden and Boston: Brill Nijhoff, 2017.

Reimann, Mathias: "The historical School against Codification: Savigny, Carter, and the defeat of the New York Civil Code", 37 *The American Journal of Comparative Law* 1989, pp. 95–119.

Steiner, Eva: "Codification in England: The Need to move from an ideological to a functional Approach—A Bridge too far?", 25 *Statute Law Review* 2004, pp. 209–222.

Vanderlinden, Jacques: *Le Concept de Code en Europe Occidentale du XIIe au XIXe Siècle: Essai de Définition*, Bruxelles: Éditions de l'Institut de Sociologie de l'Université libre de Bruxelles, 1967.

Weiss, Gunther A.: "The Enchantment of Codification in the Common-Law World", 25 *Yale Journal of International Law* 2000, pp. 435–532.

PART 1

Introduction to Part 1. Contextualizing Codification

Telling the full history of codification and of the various codification efforts is a task that would take more than one book. While not taking on that herculean task, some foundational elements have to be kept in mind in order to understand the subject of this book, the nineteenth-century civil codes that existed in some US states. My goal in this brief addendum is to underscore some of the elements and examples of codification that will help the reader understand and situate the history of these particular civil codes.

Nineteenth-Century Codification—Paradigm Shifts

The history of codification and civil codes is the history of the rationalization of law. It pertains most importantly to the question of law as a science. It is also a history of the state's efforts to take charge of private law. In both senses, the history of codification is a history of the search to establish the sources of law. This ever-changing concept of codification had its golden age in the last quarter of the eighteenth and nineteenth centuries following a wave of codification whose most well-known product was the Napoleonic Code. The concept existed before this period, and it persisted after, but it shone most brightly during the nineteenth century.[1] During that time, codes multiplied in almost all the European states.[2]

The first movement of civil codification in Europe started with the Bavarian Code of 1756,[3] the "Codex Maximilianeus Bavaricus Civilis", followed by the Prussian Code of 1794,[4] titled "Allgemeines Landrecht". After these came the

1 Csaba Varga, *Codification as a socio-historical Phenomenon*, Budapest: Szent István Társulat, 2011, pp. 71–90; Denis Tallon, "Reforming the Codes in a Civil Law Country", 15 *Journal of the Society of Public Teachers of Law, New Series* 1980, pp. 33–41.

2 John Henry Merryman, *The Civil Law Tradition. An Introduction to the Legal Systems of Western Europe and Latin America*, 2nd ed., Stanford (CA): Stanford University Press, 1985, pp. 26–33; Csaba Varga, *Codification as a socio-historical Phenomenon*, Budapest: Szent István Társulat, 2011, pp. 91–142; Pierre Legrand, "Strange Power of Words: Codification Situated", 9 *Tulane European & Civil Law Forum* 1994, pp. 1–34.

3 *Codex Maximilianeus Bavaricus Civilis*, ed. Wiguläus Xaver Alois von Kreittmayr, Munich: Johann Jacob Vötter, 1759.

4 *Allgemeines Landrecht für die Preussischen Staaten*, 2nd ed., Berlin: Joachim Pauli, 1794.

 | DOI:10.1163/9789004689978_003

French Civil Code of 1804,[5] known as "Code civil des Français", followed by the Austrian Civil Code of 1811,[6] named "Allgemeines Bürgerliches Gesetzbuch", the Dutch Civil Code of 1838,[7] called "Burgerlijk Wetboek", and those of the Italian peninsula prior to unification, where the Civil Codes of the Kingdom of Two Sicilies[8] and Kingdom of Sardinia[9] were partially influenced by the French Civil Code. With the Napoleonic conquest, the French Civil Code model was imposed in several parts of Europe, making it the model for codifying private law in the nineteenth century.[10]

Before the civil codes, European private law was characterized by legal pluralism, or the multiplication of different sources of law within a particular legal field.[11] In cases of legal pluralism, the various sources of law might complement one another, while in others they might clash or compete with one another. Legal pluralism can result from a territorial situation in which numerous official actors have the power to create norms. It can also result from contexts in which ethnic and class divisions result in different laws for different categories of people. These factors often overlapped, and the intersection of different legal sources was quite common in pre-code Europe. The nineteenth-century civil codifications aimed to change this pluralism within private law by replacing it with one unique source of law; their aim was to create a common law for a specific territory that could be applied to all its residents in order move beyond custom, territorial legislation, canon law, Roman law, and all of the

5 *Code civil des Français. Édition originale et seule officielle*, Paris: Imprimerie de la République, 1804.

6 *Allgemeines Bürgerliches Gesetzbuch für die deutschen Erbländer der österreichischen Monarchie*, Vienna: k.k. Hof- und Staatsdruckerei, 1811.

7 *Het Nederlandsch Burgerlijk Wetboek, vergeleken met het Wetboek Napoleon*, ed. Carel Asser, 's Gravenhage and Amsterdam: De Gebroeders van Cleef, 1838.

8 *Codice per lo Regno delle Due Sicilie*, Naples: Stamperia Reale, 1836.

9 *Codice civile per gli stati di Su Maestà il re di Sardegna*, Turin: Stamperia Reale, 1837.

10 Yves Lequette, *1804–2004, Le Code Civil. Un passé, un Présent, un Avenir*, Paris: Dalloz, 2004; Sylvain Soleil, *Le Modèle juridique français dans le Monde. Une Ambition, une Expansion* (*XVIe–XIXe siècle*), Paris: IRJS Editions, 2014; Antoine Leca, *Le Code était presque parfait. Introduction historique au Droit*, Paris: Lexis Nexis, 2013; *De l'Armorique a l'Amérique de l'indépendance. Deuxième partie du colloque du bicentenaire indépendance américaine 1796–1976* (*Annales de Bretagne et des Pays de l'Ouest, 84th vol.*), Rennes: Linarmor, 1977.

11 John Griffiths, "What is Legal Pluralism", 24 *Journal of Legal Pluralism and Unofficial Law* 1986, pp. 1–56; Sally Engle Merry, "Legal Pluralism", 22 *Law & Society Review* 1988, pp. 869–896; Franz von Benda-Beckmann, "Who's afraid of Legal Pluralism", 47 *Journal of Legal Pluralism and Unofficial Law* 2002, pp. 37–82.

multiple sources of law then in effect.[12] This was the paradigm shift brought about by the nineteenth-century civil codifications.

These civil codes were not the first attempt to put the different sources of private law in writing. The need to know the law, to fix it in a document, can be seen in the multiplication of customs books across the centuries. Customs books are a written testimony of legal regionalism providing a drafted source of law that nonetheless did not cover the entirety of a territory the way later codes would but the territories upon which specific customs were enforceable. In parallel, commentaries on Roman law were numerous before the nineteenth century, as were statute books compiling state legislation. The idea of writing the law was always in the jurist's mind, but codification differed in that it was rooted in a broader theory and in practices whose aim was universality. Once enacted, civil codes became a legislative source with official state sanction, one that aimed to encompass an entire legal field. In the nineteenth century, codification aimed to become a synthesis of the plural sources of law drafted into articles and organized rationally. Codification in the nineteenth century was also a key part of state building projects, whether as a tool for developing territorial unity or as an instrument for enforcing the political project of an old or newly established or unified state political project.[13] Inasmuch as it involves a selection of laws and their different sources, a private code governing many aspects of everyday life naturally lends itself to enforcing an array of political agendas. These can be as simple as imposing unity on a territory, but they can also include the creation of a specific state culture, or the reinforcement of an existing one. Civil codes are thus, by their very nature, political, and will vary according to the different political agenda they encompass. And yet they have effects beyond specific political agendas: a civil code can serve an individual or an ideology while also having a role in creating social, cultural, or geographical unity. Put differently, while furthering a political agenda, a civil code also reinforces a states' central power. By nature, civil principles are understood as a

---

12 Jacques Vanderlinden, *Le Concept de Code en Europe Occidentale du XIIe au XIXe Siècle: Essai de Définition*, Bruxelles: Éditions de l'Institut de Sociologie de l'Université libre de Bruxelles, 1967; Bruno Oppetit, *Essai sur la Codification* (*Droit, Éthique, Société*), Paris: Presses Universitaires de France, 1998; Rémy Cabrillac, *Les Codifications* (*Droit, Éthique, Société*), Paris: Presses Universitaires de France, 2002; J. M. Milo, J. H. A. Lokin, and J. M. Smiths, *Tradition, Codification and Unification: Comparative-Historical Essays on the Development in Civil Law* (*Ius Commune Europeum*), Cambridge: Intersentia, 2014.

13 Rémy Cabrillac, *Les Codifications* (*Droit, Éthique, Société*), Paris: Presses Universitaires de France, 2002, pp. 68–70.

creation of the state; they cannot exist without a state strong enough to impose them and, in turn, they tend to bolster its power.[14]

Returning to the specific subject of this research, the nineteenth-century US civil codes cannot be understood without a more general understanding of codification. However, it is also necessary to situate the nineteenth-century US civil codes within the global context of the nineteenth century to apprehend their uniqueness, while also grasping why they were overshadowed by other codes in the century of codification. This is the task of the next section, while the following one places the US state codes in the context of European and the broader US codification efforts, which illustrate that, contrary to popular belief, codification was not an unknown legal tool in the United States. Rather, it was an object of constant concern.

Civil Codes in a Global Context

Outside of the theoretical frame of codification and its aims and goals, it is important to extend the geographical scope of the research to understand the diversity of codification efforts that have existed. Among the many civil codes in the world, some are central to understanding the US state codes.

Despite other codification models in Europe, like the German Civil Code,[15] or the Austrian Civil Code,[16] the French model prevailed during the nineteenth century. The French Civil Code of 1804,[17] also known as the Napoleonic Code or "Code Napoléon", was widely adopted in various parts of Europe and beyond.[18]

---

14 John W. Head, "Codes, Cultures, Chaos and Champions: Common Features of legal Codification Experiences in China, Europe, and North America", 13 *Duke Journal of Comparative & International Law* 2003, pp. 2–93; Rémy Cabrillac, *Les Codifications (Droit, Éthique, Société)*, Paris: Presses Universitaires de France, 2002; Gunther A. Weiss, "The Enchantment of Codification in the Common-Law World", 25 *Yale Journal of International Law* 2000, pp. 451–470.

15 "Bürgerliches Gesetzbuch", 21 *Deutsches Reichsgesetzblatt* 1896, pp. 195–603.

16 *Allgemeines Bürgerliches Gesetzbuch für die deutschen Erbländer der österreichischen Monarchie*, Vienna: k.k. Hof- und Staatsdruckerei, 1811.

17 *Code civil des Français. Édition originale et seule officielle*, Paris: Imprimerie de la République, 1804.

18 Régine Beauthier and Isabelle Rorive, *Le Code Napoléon, un Ancêtre vénére? Mélanges offerts à Jacques Vanderlinden*, Bruxelles: Bruylant, 2005; Aristides N. Hatzis, "The Short-Lived Influence of the Napoleonic Civil Code in 19th Century Greece", 14 *European Journal of Law and Economics* 2002, pp. 253–263; Gerrit Meijer, "Influence of the Code Civil in the Netherlands", 14 *European Journal of Law and Economics* 2002, pp. 227–236; Francisco J. Andrés Santos, "Napoleon in America? Reflections on the Concept of 'Legal Reception' in the Light of the Civil Law Codification in Latin America", in *Entanglements in Legal*

It was imposed throughout the French empire, including annexed territories, and enforced in the Kingdom of Italy and Kingdom of Holland.[19] The member states of the Confederation of the Rhine, the Kingdom of Naples,[20] and the Kingdom of Westphalia,[21] among others, also adopted the French Civil Code. A civil code modelled on the French code similarly came to symbolize national unity for the newly unified Italy.[22] Making a list of all the places over the world influenced during the nineteenth century by the French Civil Code would be tedious. Suffice it to say that its influence was undeniable and has been studied in detail by many brilliant scholars who have shown its near-sacred status and worldwide reception.[23] Looking at the Napoleonic Code as a model

---

History: Conceptual Approaches (*Global Perspectives on Legal History, 1st vol.*), ed. Thomas Duve, Frankfurt am Main: Max Planck Institute for European Legal History, 2014, pp. 297–313; M. C. Mirrow, "The Power of Codification in Latin America: Simón Bolívar and the Code Napoléon", 8 *Tulane Journal of International and Comparative Law* 2000, pp. 83–116; M.C. Mirrow, "Borrowing Private Law in Latin America: Andres Bello's Use of the Code Napoléon in Drafting the Chilean Civil Code", 61 *Louisiana Law Review* 2001, pp. 291–330; M. C. Mirrow, "The Code Napoléon: Buried but ruling in Latin America", 33 *Denver Journal of International Law and Policy* 2005, pp. 179–194; Alejandro Guzmán Brito, "La Influencia del Código Civil francés en las Codificaciones americanas", in *De la Codificación a la Descodificación. Code Civil (1804–2004), Código de Bello (1855–2005)*, ed. Alejandro Guzmán Brito, Santiago de Chile: Ediciones Universidad Diego Portales, Escuela de Derecho, 2005, pp. 27–60.

19 Paul-Ludwig Weinacht, "The Sovereign German States and the Code Napoléon. What spoke for its Adoption in the Rhine Confederation?", 14 *European Journal of Law and Economics* 2002, pp. 205–213; Hans A. Schmitt, "Germany without Prussia: A closer Look at the Confederation of the Rhine", 6 *German Studies Review* 1983, pp. 9–39; Desmond Gregory, *Napoleon's Italy*, London: Associated University Press, 2001, pp. 119–143; Riccardo Ferrante, "Los Orígenes del Modelo de Codificación entre los Siglos XIX y XX en Europa, con particular Atención al Caso italiano", 25 *Revista de Derecho Privado* 2013, pp. 29–56; John Stanley, "The Adaptation of the Napoleonic Political Structure in the Duchy of Warsaw (1807–1813)", 31 *Canadian Slavonic Papers / Revue Canadienne des Slavistes* 1989, pp. 128–145; Piotr Z. Pomianowski, *Napoleonic Divorce Law in Poland (1808–1852)*, Leiden and Boston: Brill Nijhoff, 2022, pp. 1–9, 51–56; Gerrit Meijer, "Influence of the Code Civil in the Netherlands", 14 *European Journal of Law and Economics* 2002, pp. 227–236.

20 *Codice di Napoleone il Grande pel Regno d'Italia. Edizione originale e la sola ufficiale*, Milan: Dalla Reale Stamperia, 1806.

21 *Napoleons Gesetzbuch. Einzig offizielle Ausgabe für das Königreich Westphalen*, Strasbourg: F. G. Levrault, 1808.

22 Paolo Cappellini, "Voyage en Italie. Code Napoléon et Historiographie: Une Esquisse inachevée", in *Le Code Napoléon, un Ancêtre vénére? Mélanges offerts à Jacques Vanderlinden*, eds. Régine Beauthier and Isabelle Rorive, Bruxelles: Bruylant, 2005, p. 71.

23 For a study on the general history and overall impact of the Napoleonic Code, see Jean-Louis Halpérin, *The French Civil Code*, London: UCL Press, 2006; see further Duncan Fairgrieve, *The Influence of the French Civil Code on Common Law and beyond*, London: British Institute of International and Comparative Law, 2007.

also highlights the circulation of traditional conceptions of private law. The myth about the French Civil Code being revolutionary law has been debunked throughout the years, and scholars have exposed its multiple origins, defining it as a mixture of the *Ancien Régime* and the revolutionary principles.[24] In the case of the nineteenth-century US civil codes, however, the influence of the Napoleonic Code, especially as a primary model, is questionable. This point will be explored in detail in the book.

Looking at geographical spaces closer to the United States, the American continent has its fair share of civil codes. Indeed, all Latin-American jurisdictions adopted civil codes between 1826 and 1916.[25] Among the earliest cases, Haiti adopted its civil code in 1825,[26] followed by Peru in 1852,[27] Chile in 1855,[28] Ecuador in 1861, Argentina in 1869,[29] Mexico in 1870,[30] Colombia in 1887,[31] and Brazil in 1916.[32]

> The structure of most codes followed the model provided by the Code Napoléon. At the turn of the century, the [German Civil Code] and other European civil codes also had a considerable impact on first generation codes, though the impact was mainly recognized later in second generation texts.[33]

All of them drew, sometimes extensively, on the Napoleonic Code.[34] One notable example of a civil code outside of Europe and Latin America was the Civil

24 James Gordley, "Myths of the French Civil Code", 42 *The American Journal of Comparative Law* 1994, pp. 459–505.

25 J. M. Milo, J. H. A. Lokin, and J. M. Smiths, *Tradition, Codification and Unification: Comparative-Historical Essays on the Development in Civil Law* (*Ius Commune Europeum*), Cambridge: Intersentia, 2014, pp. 183–193.

26 *Code Civil d'Haïti*, Port-au-Prince: L'Imprimerie du Gouvernment, 1826.

27 *Código Civil de la República del Perú*, Lima: Imprenta del Gobierno, 1852.

28 *Código Civil de la República de Chile*, Santiago: Imprenta Nacional, 1855.

29 *Código Civil de la República Argentina*, ed. Dalmacio Vélez Sársfield, Buenos Aires: Pablo Coni, 1869.

30 *Código Civil del Distrito Federal y Territorio de la Baja-California*, México: Jose Batiza, 1870.

31 *Código Civil Nacional expedido por el Congreso de los Estados Unidos de Colombia*, Bogotá: Imprenta de Gaitán, 1873.

32 *Codico Civil da Republica dos Estados Unidos do Brasil*, Rio de Janeiro: Imprensa Nacional, 1915.

33 J. M. Milo, J. H. A. Lokin, and J. M. Smiths, *Tradition, Codification and Unification: Comparative-Historical Essays on the Development in Civil Law* (*Ius Commune Europeum*), Cambridge: Intersentia, 2014, p. 185.

34 Olivier Moréteau and Agustín Parise, "Recodification in Louisiana and Latin America", 83 *Tulane Law Review* 2009, pp. 1103–1162; Bernardo Bravo Lira, "La Codification en

Code of Lower Canada,[35] which was adopted in 1866 and was similarly based on the French Civil Code model.[36]

In the century of codification, one has to keep in mind that the case of the United States is a case among many others in a century of codification in which many polities were busy implementing, translating, acculturating, and understanding the new legal tool that was the civil code. To quote Alan Watson, "a successful transplant—like that of a human organ—will grow in its new body, and become part of that body just as the rule or institution would have continued to develop in its parent system."[37] Codification's spread was a legal transfer in that it was, "the movement of a rule or system of law from one country to another, or from one people to another".[38]

Chile (1811–1907), Dentro del Marco de la Codification Europea e Hispanoamericana", 12 *Revista Estudios Histórico-Jurídicos* 1987, pp. 51–109; Alejandro Guzmán Brito, *Andres Bello, Codificador. Historia de la Fijación y Codificación del Derecho Civil en Chile*, 1st & 2nd vol., Santiago de Chile: Ediciones de la Universidad de Chile, 1982; Alejandro Guzmán Brito, *La Codificación civil en Iberoamérica*, Santiago de Chile: Editorial Juridica de Chile, 2000; Alejandro Guzmán Brito, *Historia de la Codificación civil en Iberoamérica*, Cizur Menor: Thomson Aranzadi, 2006; C. F. Amunátegui Perelló, "Some Thoughts on the Codification Process in Latin America. Andrés Bello, from America to Japan", 2 *Acta Universitatis Sapientiae: Legal Studies* 2013, pp. 5–21; Ramón Domínguez A., "La Influencia de la Doctrina francesa en el Derecho chileno", in *De la Codificación a la Descodificación. Code Civil (1804–2004), Código de Bello (1855–2005)*, ed. Alejandro Guzmán Brito, Santiago de Chile: Ediciones Universidad Diego Portales, Escuela de Derecho, 2005, pp. 61–80; Fabricio Mantilla E., "La Influencia del Code Civil y la Doctrina francesa en el Derecho de las Obligaciones colombiano", in *De la Codificación a la Descodificación. Code Civil (1804–2004), Código de Bello (1855–2005)*, ed. Alejandro Guzmán Brito, Santiago de Chile: Ediciones Universidad Diego Portales, Escuela de Derecho, 2005, pp. 81–92; Agustín Parise, *Historia de la Codificación civil del Estado de Luisiana y su Influencia en el Código Civil argentino*, Buenos Aires: Eudeba, 2009.

35 *Code Civil du Bas-Canada*, ed. Edouard Lefebvre de Bellefeuille, Montréal: Beauchemin & Valois, 1866.

36 H. Patrick Glenn, "Napoleon's Civil Code 'outre-mer': A Québec Perspective", in *The Influence of the French Civil Code on Common Law and beyond*, ed. Duncan Fairgrieve, London: British Institute of International and Comparative Law, 2007, pp. 401–406; Jean-Louis Beaudouin and Pierre-Gabriel Jobin, "Le Code Civil Français et les Codes Civils Québécois", in *The Influence of the French Civil Code on Common Law and beyond*, ed. Duncan Fairgrieve, London: British Institute of International and Comparative Law, 2007, pp. 407–428; David Gilles, "Les Lois Civiles de Jean Domat, Premices a la Codification. Du Code Napoléon au Code Civil du Bas Canada", 43 *Revue Juridique Themis* 2009, pp. 1–50; C. Mark Macneill, "Expanding the Exploration of Civil Law in New France, beyond Québec to Acadie: 1608–1867", 12 *Beijing Law Review* 2021, pp. 1215–1251.

37 Alan Watson, *Legal Transplants: An Approach to Comparative Law*, 2nd ed., Athens (GA): University of Georgia Press, 1993, p. 27.

38 *Ibid*, p. 21.

Codification in the US Context

From the global focus of the preceding section, this section turns to the broader context of codification in the United States. The history of codification endeavors in the United States demonstrates that codification was a long-standing national concern, even in a place closely associated with the common law tradition. Codification of private law was not just a subject of debate in the codifying states; some states like South Carolina[39] or Pennsylvania[40] debated the idea of a code without embarking on an official codification process.

The first codes existing in the US territory can be traced back to colonial times. Even if they are not related to private law, the Massachusetts Body of Liberties of 1641,[41] the Connecticut Code of Laws of 1650,[42] the Code of Virginia of 1661,[43] the Pennsylvania Charter of Privileges of 1701,[44] and the Carolina Fundamental Constitutions of 1669,[45] to just cite a few, are in themselves a form of codification. Most are a form of codification in that they are compilations of statutes. One of the most well-known is the Code of Virginia,[46] based on English common law, and which included laws related to land ownership, criminal law, and legal procedures. The Code of Virginia had many different versions and evolved through time, with the first compilation taking place in 1733. After a first draft by a committee of advisors appointed by the General Assembly of Virginia, the Code of Virginia went through nine different versions or revisions over the course of the nineteenth century.[47] The colonial codes

39 Charles M. Cook, *The American Codification Movement: A Study of Antebellum Legal Reform* (*Contributions in Legal Studies*), Westport (CT): Greenwood Press, 1981, pp. 121–131.

40 George M. Hezel, "The Influence of Bentham's Philosophy of Law on the early nineteenth Century Codification Movement in the United States", 22 *Buffalo Law Review* 1972, pp. 253–268.

41 *The General Laws of the Massachusetts Colony, revised and published by Order of the General Court*, Boston: General Court, 1648.

42 *The Code of 1650, being a Compilation of the earliest Laws and Orders of the General Court of Connecticut*, Hartford: Silas Andrus, 1822.

43 *The Laws of Virginia now in Force: Collected out of the Assembly Records, and digested into one Volume. Revised and confirmed by the Grand Assembly held at James City, by Prorogation, the 2nd of March 1661 in the 13th Year of the Reign of our Sovereign Lord King Charles II.*, London: E. Cotes, for A. Seile, 1662.

44 *The Charter of Privileges, granted by William Penn Esq. to the Inhabitants of Pennsylvania and Territories*, Philadelphia: Benjamin Franklin, 1741.

45 *The Fundamental Constitutions of Carolina*, London: John Locke, 1670.

46 *A Collection of all the Acts of Assembly, now in Force in the Colony of Virginia*, Williamsburg: William Parks, 1733.

47 William E. Ross, "History of Virginia Codification", 11 *The Virginia Law Register* 1905, pp. 87–96; Robert W. Kerns, "The History of the West Virginia Code", 120 *West Virginia Law*

were generally exercises in compilation and those who wrote them lacked the legal knowledge to turn them into formal codes. However, in some instances, they went so far as to declare common law principles as the foundation of the law, which was nonetheless more of a formal profession than a real one.[48]

During the nineteenth century, codification was also at the heart of debates over civil procedure. In his book *Codification in the British Empire and America*, Maurice Eugen Lang summarizes the process leading to the adoption of the Code of Civil Procedure of New York in 1848.[49] This code was then exported to more than thirty-one states.[50] Adopting the Code of Civil Procedure of New York led to a change in the system of civil procedure, from common law pleading to code pleading.

In parallel to the civil and civil procedure codes, the different US states also developed criminal or penal codes and criminal procedure codes. Among the notable example are the Revised Statutes of New York of 1829,[51] which included a compilation of criminal offenses and procedures, the Illinois Criminal Code of 1827,[52] the Ohio Criminal Code of 1841,[53] the Code of Virginia of 1849,[54] most of them codifying criminal offenses and procedure, and the Alabama Criminal Code of 1852, which consolidated and revised existing criminal law. California also adopted a penal code the same year as it enshrined a civil code, 1872.[55] It can generally be said that, by the end of the nineteenth century, all the US states had some form of criminal code, the extent, and scope of which varied depending on the jurisdiction.

Review 2017, pp. 169–171; Warren M. Billings and Brent Tarter, *'Esteemed Bookes of Lawe' and the Legal Culture of early Virginia*, Charlottesville: University of Virginia Press, 2017.

48 William E. Ross, "History of Virginia Codification", 11 *The Virginia Law Register* 1905, p. 93.

49 Maurice Eugen Lang, *Codification in the British Empire and America*, Clark (NJ): The Lawbook Exchange, 2005, p. 100.

50 For a comprehensive study on the Code of Civil Procedure, its history, its impact, and its application, see Kellen Funk, *The Lawyer's Code: The Transformation of American Legal Practice, 1828–1938*, Princeton: Princeton University, 2018.

51 *NY Rev. Stat. 1829*.

52 *The Revised Code of Laws of Illinois, enacted by the fifth General Assembly at their Session held at Vandalia, commencing on the fourth Day of December 1826, and ending the Nineteenth of February 1827*, Vandalia: Robert Blackwell, Printer to the State, 1827.

53 *Statutes of the State of Ohio, of a general Nature, in Force December 7, 1840*, Columbus: Samuel Medary, State Printer, 1841.

54 *The Code of Virginia with the Declaration of Independence and Constitution of the United States*, Richmond: William F. Ritchie, Public Printer, 1849.

55 *The Penal Code of California*, eds. Creed Haymond, John C. Burch, and John H. McKune, Sacramento (CA): T. A. Springer, State Printer, 1872.

Further fleshing out the history of codification in the US territory, the *Code Noir*,[56] a codification of slavery laws in Louisiana, is another code that needs to be cited. King Louis XIV of France decreed the *Code Noir* as the law governing slavery in all the French colonies. It was first introduced in Louisiana in 1724, and partially integrated into the state's 1808 Digest, remaining in place until the enactment of the post-Civil War Civil Code of 1870, which removed all articles pertaining to slavery.

Beyond the timeframe of this research, it is also worth mentioning the US codification of commercial law undertaken in the 1950s. The Uniform Commercial Code[57] aimed to provide consistency and uniformity in commercial laws across the various states and covered commercial law and commercial practices. It is often presented as one of the most famous examples of codification in the United States. This code was drafted by the American Law Institute and the National Conference of Commissioners on Uniform State Laws as a model code that each state could adopt as a whole or in part through the legislative process.[58] Most states have adopted it with minor variations. While providing a framework, it does not cover all areas of commercial law. It is centered on business law because it was created to develop a country-wide usage of the commercial practices and laws.

One final form of codification that needs to be mentioned here, even if it is outside of the timeline, is the United States Code.[59] The latter is a compilation of federal statutes enacted by the US Congress and first published in 1926. The

56 *Le Code Noir, ou Édit du Roy*, Paris: Claude Girard, 1735.

57 *Uniform Commercial Code*, Philadelphia: The American Law Institute and National Conference of Commissioners on Uniform State Laws, 1952. For more information on the Uniform Commercial Code, see Robert E. Scott, "The Uniform Commercial Code and the ongoing Quest for an efficient and fair Commercial Law", in *The American Law Institute. A Centennial History*, eds. Andrew S. Gold and Robert W. Gordon, Oxford: Oxford University Press, 2023, pp. 273–292.

58 Richard Danzing, "A Comment on the Jurisprudence of the Uniform Commercial Code", 27 *Stanford Law Review* 1975, pp. 621–635; Mitchell Franklin, "On the Legal Method of the Uniform Commercial Code", 16 *Law and Contemporary Problems* 1951, pp. 330–343; Gunther A. Weiss, "The Enchantment of Codification in the Common-Law World", 25 *Yale Journal of International Law* 2000, pp. 515–527; Robert Braucher, "The Legislative History of the Uniform Commercial Code", 58 *Columbia Law Review* 1958, pp. 798–814.

59 *The Code of the Laws of the United States of America of a general and permanent Character in Force December 7, 1925, and Appendix with Laws to December 6, 1926*, Washington: United States Government Printing Office, 1926. For the current list of titles, see the Office of the Law Revision Counsel available at »https://uscode.house.gov/« and last retrieved August 1, 2023. For a brief overview on the United States Code, see Peter G. LeFevre, "The United States Code: Its Accuracy, Accessibility, and Currency", 38 *Administrative and Regulatory News* 2013, pp. 10–12.

idea behind the project was to consolidate and organize federal law into one single document. Since its initial publication, it has been regularly amended and updated. Nevertheless, though the United States Code is an official compilation initiated by the Federal Government, it is not in itself an official enactment of law, serving instead as a tool for organizing and making the law more accessible.

As these examples of codification efforts in other legal fields show, the question of codifying the law was at the forefront of legal debate in US history. All legal fields asked themselves the question at some point, and a number of them answered it with some type of code. In the nineteenth century especially, the golden age of codification also found its place in the United States territory.

Bibliography

Beaudouin, Jean-Louis; Jobin, Pierre-Gabriel: "Le Code Civil Français et les Codes Civils Québécois", in *The Influence of the French Civil Code on Common Law and beyond*, ed. Duncan Fairgrieve, London: British Institute of International and Comparative Law, 2007, pp. 407–428.

Beauthier, Régine; Rorive, Isabelle: *Le Code Napoléon, un Ancêtre vénére? Mélanges offerts à Jacques Vanderlinden*, Bruxelles: Bruylant, 2005.

Billings, Warren M.; Tarter, Brent: *'Esteemed Bookes of Lawe' and the Legal Culture of early Virginia*, Charlottesville: University of Virginia Press, 2017.

Braucher, Robert: "The Legislative History of the Uniform Commercial Code", 58 *Columbia Law Review* 1958, pp. 798–814.

Brito, Alejandro Guzmán: "La Influencia del Código Civil francés en las Codificaciones americanas", in *De la Codificación a la Descodificación. Code Civil (1804–2004), Código de Bello (1855–2005)*, ed. Alejandro Guzmán Brito, Santiago de Chile: Ediciones Universidad Diego Portales, Escuela de Derecho, 2005, pp. 27–60.

Brito, Alejandro Guzmán: *Andres Bello, Codificador. Historia de la Fijación y Codificación del Derecho Civil en Chile*, 1st & 2nd vol., Santiago de Chile: Ediciones de la Universidad de Chile, 1982.

Brito, Alejandro Guzmán: *Historia de la Codificación civil en Iberoamérica*, Cizur Menor: Thomson Aranzadi, 2006.

Brito, Alejandro Guzmán: *La Codificación civil en Iberoamérica*, Santiago de Chile: Editorial Juridica de Chile, 2000.

Cabrillac, Rémy: *Les Codifications (Droit, Éthique, Société)*, Paris: Presses Universitaires de France, 2002.

Cappellini, Paolo: "Voyage en Italie. Code Napoléon et Historiographie: Une Esquisse inachevée", in *Le Code Napoléon, un Ancêtre vénére? Mélanges offerts à Jacques*

Vanderlinden, eds. Régine Beauthier and Isabelle Rorive, Bruxelles: Bruylant, 2005, pp. 61–76.

Cook, Charles M.: *The American Codification Movement: A Study of Antebellum Legal Reform* (*Contributions in Legal Studies*), Westport (CT): Greenwood Press, 1981.

Danzing, Richard: "A Comment on the Jurisprudence of the Uniform Commercial Code", 27 *Stanford Law Review* 1975, pp. 621–635.

Domínguez A., Ramón: "La Influencia de la Doctrina francesa en el Derecho chileno", in *De la Codificación a la Descodificación. Code Civil (1804–2004), Código de Bello (1855–2005)*, ed. Alejandro Guzmán Brito, Santiago de Chile: Ediciones Universidad Diego Portales, Escuela de Derecho, 2005, pp. 61–80.

Fairgrieve, Duncan: *The Influence of the French Civil Code on Common Law and beyond*, London: British Institute of International and Comparative Law, 2007.

Ferrante, Riccardo: "Los Orígenes del Modelo de Codificación entre los Siglos XIX y XX en Europa, con particular Atención al Caso italiano", 25 *Revista de Derecho Privado* 2013, pp. 29–56.

Franklin, Mitchell: "On the Legal Method of the Uniform Commercial Code", 16 *Law and Contemporary Problems* 1951, pp. 330–343.

Gilles, David: "Les Lois Civiles de Jean Domat, Premices a la Codification. Du Code Napoléon au Code Civil du Bas Canada", 43 *Revue Juridique Themis* 2009, pp. 1–50.

Glenn, H. Patrick: "Napoleon's Civil Code 'outre-mer': A Québec Perspective", in *The Influence of the French Civil Code on Common Law and beyond*, ed. Duncan Fairgrieve, London: British Institute of International and Comparative Law, 2007, pp. 401–406.

Gordley, James: "Myths of the French Civil Code", 42 *The American Journal of Comparative Law* 1994, pp. 459–505.

Gregory, Desmond: *Napoleon's Italy*, London: Associated University Press, 2001.

Griffiths, John: "What is Legal Pluralism", 24 *Journal of Legal Pluralism and Unofficial Law* 1986, pp. 1–56.

Halpérin, Jean-Louis: *The French Civil Code*, London: UCL Press, 2006.

Hatzis, Aristides N.: "The Short-Lived Influence of the Napoleonic Civil Code in 19th Century Greece", 14 *European Journal of Law and Economics* 2002, pp. 253–263.

Head, John W.: "Codes, Cultures, Chaos and Champions: Common Features of legal Codification Experiences in China, Europe, and North America", 13 *Duke Journal of Comparative & International Law* 2003, pp. 2–93.

Hezel, George M.: "The Influence of Bentham's Philosophy of Law on the early nineteenth Century Codification Movement in the United States", 22 *Buffalo Law Review* 1972, pp. 253–268.

Kerns, Robert W.: "The History of the West Virginia Code", 120 *West Virginia Law Review* 2017, pp. 166–183.

Lang, Maurice Eugen: *Codification in the British Empire and America*, Clark (NJ): The Lawbook Exchange, 2005.

Leca, Antoine: *Le Code était presque parfait. Introduction historique au Droit*, Paris: Lexis Nexis, 2013.

LeFevre, Peter G.: "The United States Code: Its Accuracy, Accessibility, and Currency", 38 *Administrative and Regulatory News* 2013, pp. 10–12.

Legrand, Pierre: "Strange Power of Words: Codification Situated", 9 *Tulane European & Civil Law Forum* 1994, pp. 1–34.

Lequette, Yves: *1804–2004, Le Code Civil. Un passé, un Présent, un Avenir*, Paris: Dalloz, 2004.

Lira, Bernardo Bravo: "La Codification en Chile (1811–1907), Dentro del Marco de la Codification Europea e Hispanoamericana", 12 *Revista Estudios Histórico-Jurídicos* 1987, pp. 51–109.

Macneill, C. Mark: "Expanding the Exploration of Civil Law in New France, beyond Québec to Acadie: 1608–1867", 12 *Beijing Law Review* 2021, pp. 1215–1251.

Mantilla, E. Fabricio: "La Influencia del Code Civil y la Doctrina francesa en el Derecho de las Obligaciones colombiano", in *De la Codificación a la Descodificación. Code Civil (1804–2004), Código de Bello (1855–2005)*, ed. Alejandro Guzmán Brito, Santiago de Chile: Ediciones Universidad Diego Portales, Escuela de Derecho, 2005, pp. 81–92.

Meijer, Gerrit: "Influence of the Code Civil in the Netherlands", 14 *European Journal of Law and Economics* 2002, pp. 227–236.

Merry, Sally Engle: "Legal Pluralism", 22 *Law & Society Review* 1988, pp. 869–896.

Merryman, John Henry: *The Civil Law Tradition. An Introduction to the Legal Systems of Western Europe and Latin America*, 2nd ed., Stanford (CA): Stanford University Press, 1985.

Milo, J.M.; Lokin, J.H.A.; Smiths, J.M.: *Tradition, Codification and Unification: Comparative-Historical Essays on the Development in Civil Law (Ius Commune Europeum)*, Cambridge: Intersentia, 2014.

Mirrow, M. C.: "Borrowing Private Law in Latin America: Andres Bello's Use of the Code Napoléon in Drafting the Chilean Civil Code", 61 *Louisiana Law Review* 2001, pp. 291–330.

Mirrow, M. C.: "The Code Napoléon: Buried but ruling in Latin America", 33 *Denver Journal of International Law and Policy* 2005, pp. 179–194.

Mirrow, M. C.: "The Power of Codification in Latin America: Simón Bolívar and the Code Napoléon", 8 *Tulane Journal of International and Comparative Law* 2000, pp. 83–116.

Moréteau, Olivier; Parise, Agustín: "Recodification in Louisiana and Latin America", 83 *Tulane Law Review* 2009, pp. 1103–1162.

Oppetit, Bruno: *Essai sur la Codification (Droit, Éthique, Société)*, Paris: Presses Universitaires de France, 1998.

Parise, Agustín: *Historia de la Codificación civil del Estado de Luisiana y su Influencia en el Código Civil argentino*, Buenos Aires: Eudeba, 2009.

Perelló, C. F. Amunátegui: "Some Thoughts on the Codification Process in Latin America. Andrés Bello, from America to Japan", 2 *Acta Universitatis Sapientiae: Legal Studies* 2013, pp. 5–21.

Pomianowski, Piotr Z.: *Napoleonic Divorce Law in Poland (1808–1852)*, Leiden and Boston: Brill Nijhoff, 2022.

Ross, William E.: "History of Virginia Codification", 11 *The Virginia Law Register* 1905, pp. 79–101.

Santos, Francisco J. Andrés: "Napoleon in America? Reflections on the Concept of 'Legal Reception' in the Light of the Civil Law Codification in Latin America", in *Entanglements in Legal History: Conceptual Approaches (Global Perspectives on Legal History, 1st vol.)*, ed. Thomas Duve, Frankfurt am Main: Max Planck Institute for European Legal History, 2014, pp. 297–313.

Schmitt, Hans A.: "Germany without Prussia: A closer Look at the Confederation of the Rhine", 6 *German Studies Review* 1983, pp. 9–39.

Scott, Robert E.: "The Uniform Commercial Code and the ongoing Quest for an efficient and fair Commercial Law", in *The American Law Institute. A Centennial History*, eds. Andrew S. Gold and Robert W. Gordon, Oxford: Oxford University Press, 2023, pp. 273–292.

Soleil, Sylvain: *Le Modèle juridique français dans le Monde. Une Ambition, une Expansion (XVIe–XIXe siècle)*, Paris: IRJS Editions, 2014.

Stanley, John: "The Adaptation of the Napoleonic Political Structure in the Duchy of Warsaw (1807–1813)", 31 *Canadian Slavonic Papers / Revue Canadienne des Slavistes* 1989, pp. 128–145.

Tallon, Denis: "Reforming the Codes in a Civil Law Country", 15 *Journal of the Society of Public Teachers of Law, New Series* 1980, pp. 33–41.

Vanderlinden, Jacques: *Le Concept de Code en Europe Occidentale du XIIe au XIXe Siècle: Essai de Définition*, Bruxelles: Éditions de l'Institut de Sociologie de l'Université libre de Bruxelles, 1967.

Varga, Csaba: *Codification as a socio-historical Phenomenon*, Budapest: Szent István Társulat, 2011.

von Benda-Beckmann, Franz: "Who's afraid of Legal Pluralism", 47 *Journal of Legal Pluralism and Unofficial Law* 2002, pp. 37–82.

Watson, Alan: *Legal Transplants: An Approach to Comparative Law*, 2nd ed., Athens (GA): University of Georgia Press, 1993.

Weinacht, Paul-Ludwig: "The Sovereign German States and the Code Napoléon. What spoke for its Adoption in the Rhine Confederation?", 14 *European Journal of Law and Economics* 2002, pp. 205–213.

Weiss, Gunther A.: "The Enchantment of Codification in the Common-Law World", 25 *Yale Journal of International Law* 2000, pp. 435–532.

CHAPTER 1

Not a Movement, but a Discussion—the National Codification Framework

> Are we not as capable of performing a great act of legislation as Romans or Germans, as Frenchmen or Italians?
>
> DAVID DUDLEY FIELD, 1855.[1]

The possible transition from common law to civil law would marked a significant change, yet supporters of codification believed they should, and could, embark on this journey. So sure were they of the necessity of codification that they expressed surprise that the switch had not yet been made.[2] An 1886 quote from Edmond Kelly perfectly summarizes the problems critics saw in the common law:

> When Mr. Carter asserted that the common law is reasonably well settled, easily accessible, harmonious, and fixed, he fairly took our breath away. Every lawyer at the table knew that it is no such thing, but that it is obscure, contradictory, inconveniently scattered and fluctuating.[3]

Commonly referred to as "the American Codification Movement", this nineteenth-century debate over the possibility of codifying US law rested on an elementary question: which legal system best fit the special conditions of the newly founded United States? Those involved in the debate were intimately familiar with the workings of the law, both in theory and through daily

1 David Dudley Field, *An Address to the graduating Class of the Law School of the University of Albany, delivered on March 23, 1856*, Albany: W.C. Little & Co., 1856, p. 26.
2 Morton J. Horwitz, *The Transformation of American Law, 1780–1860* (*Studies in Legal History*), Cambridge (MA): Harvard University Press, 1977, p. 16.
3 Andrew P. Morriss, "Codification and right Answers", 74 *Chicago-Kent Law Review* 1999, p. 369.

 | DOI:10.1163/9789004689978_004

practice.[4] Lawyers trained in English and US common law argued for legal freedom and flexibility, while supporters of the civil law system, preferred a formal code, rigid interpretation, and legal certainty. This debate arose at two specific moments in the nineteenth century. It was particularly heated during the antebellum period, from the 1820s to the 1830s, and then resurfaced during the postbellum period, between the 1870s to the 1880s.[5] However, most of the literature has focused on only one of these two periods,[6] overwhelmingly privileging the postbellum debate.[7] By contrast, the foundational early debate over

---

4 Nuno Garoupa and Andrew P. Morriss, "The Fable of the Codes: The Efficiency of the Common Law, legal Origins, and Codification Movements", 5 *University of Illinois Law Review* 2012, pp. 1443–1498.

5 Perry Miller, *The Life of the Mind in America from the Revolution to the Civil War*, New York (NY): Harcourt, Brace & World, 1965, pp. 105–109; Charles M. Cook, *The American Codification Movement: A Study of Antebellum Legal Reform* (*Contributions in Legal Studies*), Westport (CT): Greenwood Press, 1981, pp. 96–120; Gunther A. Weiss, "The Enchantment of Codification in the Common-Law World", 25 *Yale Journal of International Law* 2000, pp. 435–532; John W. Head, "Codes, Cultures, Chaos and Champions: Common Features of legal Codification Experiences in China, Europe, and North America", 13 *Duke Journal of Comparative & International Law* 2003, pp. 2–93; David Gruning, "Vive la difference? Why no Codification of Private Law in the United States?", 39 *Revue Juridique Themis* 2005, pp. 153–194; Maurice Eugen Lang, *Codification in the British Empire and America*, Clark (NJ): The Lawbook Exchange, 2005, pp. 114–158; Sylvain Soleil, *Aux Origines de l'Opposition entre Systèmes de Common Law et de Droit codifié—Les Controverses anglo-américaines des Années 1820–1835*, Paris: Société de Législation Comparé, 2021.

6 Lewis Grossman, "Langdell Upside-Down: The Anticlassical Jurisprudence of Anticodification", 19 *Yale Journal of Law & Humanities* 2007, pp. 1–67; Aniceto Masferrer, "The passionate Discussion among Common Law Lawyers about postbellum American Codification: An Approach to its legal Argumentation", 40 *Arizona State Law Journal* 2008, pp. 173–256; Aniceto Masferrer, "Defense of the Common Law against postbellum American Codification: Reasonable and fallacious Argumentation", 50 *The American Journal of Legal History* 2008, pp. 355–430.

7 Marion Smith, "The first Codification of the substantive Common Law", 4 *Tulane Law Review* 1929, pp. 178–189; David Dudley Field, *Centenary Essays: Celebrating One Hundred Years of Legal Reform*, New York (NY): Alison Reppy, 1949; Wienczyslaw J. Wagner, "Codification of Law in Europe and the Codification Movement in the Middle of the nineteenth Century in the United States", 2 *Saint Louis University Law Journal* 1952, pp. 335–359; Morton J. Horwitz, *The Transformation of American Law, 1780–1860* (*Studies in Legal History*), Cambridge (MA): Harvard University Press, 1977; Stephen Subrin, "David Dudley Field and the Field Code: A historical Analysis of an earlier procedural Vision", 6 *Law and History Review* 1988, pp. 311–373; Mathias Reimann, "The historical School against Codification: Savigny, Carter, and the defeat of the New York Civil Code", 37 *The American Journal of Comparative Law* 1989, pp. 95–119; Lewis Grossman, "Codification and the California Mentality", 45 *Hastings Law Journal* 1994, pp. 617–639; Andrew P. Morriss, "Codification and right Answers", 74 *Chicago-Kent Law Review* 1999, pp. 355–391; Lawrence M. Friedman, *A History of American Law*, 3rd ed., New York (NY): Simon & Schuster, 2005.

US law is barely depicted in US literature. Only one book, written by Charles M. Cook, is dedicated specifically to the study of the American codification movement as a whole.[8] There are also some brief references in chapters of general volumes on law in the United States that deal with US legal history or the nineteenth-century American legal profession.[9] In addition to Cook's work, Aniceto Masferrer has written two important articles on the debate,[10] summarizing its core issues while highlighting the special role of New York as the epicenter of legal controversy. The remainder of the available literature on this subject is limited to several scholarly articles.[11]

---

8 Charles M. Cook, *The American Codification Movement: A Study of Antebellum Legal Reform* (*Contributions in Legal Studies*), Westport (CT): Greenwood Press, 1981.

9 Francis R. Aumann, *The changing American Legal System: Some selected Phases*, New York (NY): Da Capo Press, 1969; Maxwell Bloomfield, *American Lawyers in a changing Society, 1776–1876* (Studies in Legal History), Cambridge (MA): Harvard University Press, 1976; Charles Warren, *A History of the American Bar* (*Historical Writings in Law and Jurisprudence*), Buffalo: W.S. Hein, 1980; Bernard Schwartz, *Main Currents in American legal Thought*, Durham (NC): Carolina Academic Press, 1993; Perry Miller, *The Life of the Mind in America from the Revolution to the Civil War*, New York (NY): Harcourt, Brace & World, 1965; Kunal Madhukar Parker, *Common Law, History, and Democracy in America, 1790–1900: Legal Thought before Modernism* (*Cambridge Historical Studies in American Law and Society*), New York (NY): Cambridge University Press, 2011; David M. Rabban, *Law's History: American legal Thought and the transatlantic Turn to History* (*Cambridge Historical Studies in American Law and Society*), Cambridge: Cambridge University Press, 2013.

10 Aniceto Masferrer, "The passionate Discussion among Common Law Lawyers about postbellum American Codification: An Approach to its legal Argumentation", 40 *Arizona State Law Journal* 2008, pp. 173–256; Aniceto Masferrer, "Defense of the Common Law against postbellum American Codification: Reasonable and fallacious Argumentation", 50 *The American Journal of Legal History* 2008, pp. 355–430.

11 Roscoe Pound, *The Spirit of the Common Law*, Francestown (NH): Marshall Jones Co., 1921; James Brierly, "The Future of Codification", 12 *British Yearbook of International Law* 1931, pp. 1–12; George L. Haskins, "De la Codification du Droit en Amérique du Nord au XVIIe Siècle. Un Étude de Droit comparé", 23 *Tijdschrift voor Rechtsgeschiedenis* 1955, pp. 311–332; Maxwell Bloomfield, "William Sampson and the Codifiers: The Roots of American Legal Reform, 1820–1830", 11 *The American Journal of Legal History* 1967, pp. 234–252; H. R. Hahlo, "Codifying the Common Law: Protracted Gestation", 38 *The Modern Law Review* 1975, pp. 23–30; Christian Atias and Alain A. Levasseur, "American Legal Culture and traditional scholarly Order", 46 *Louisiana Law Review* 1986, pp. 1117–1136; Morell E. Mullins, "An academic Perspective on Codification and the Arkansas Code of 1987 annotated", 11 *University of Arkansas at Little Rock Law Journal* 1988, pp. 288–294; Mathias Reimann, "The historical School against Codification: Savigny, Carter, and the defeat of the New York Civil Code", 37 *The American Journal of Comparative Law* 1989, pp. 95–119; Barbara C. Salken, "To codify or not to codify—That is the Question: A Study of New York's Efforts to enact an evidence Code", 58 *Brooklyn Law Review* 1992, pp. 641–704; Shael Herman, "The Fate and the Future of Codification in America", 40 *The American Journal of Legal History* 1996, pp. 407–437; Andrew P. Morriss, "Codification and right Answers", 74 *Chicago-Kent Law Review* 1999,

Nonetheless, it is possible to gain a clear picture of the debate by drawing on the original sources. In fact, the controversy was highly visible, involving dramatic harangues at legal events and polemical newspaper articles in the local or national press. The debate was fueled by public discontent over the state of the law, as the United States faced a broad crisis of the sources of law. Between 1783 and 1815, some politicians had already broached the possibility of abolishing the common law due to its inherent flaws, although in that early debate codification was not offered as a remedy.[12] It was only in the 1820s, influenced by the Napoleonic Code, that jurists began to point to codification as a solution to the problems of the common law. Indeed, supporters of codification saw it as the only remedy to these problems, declaring that:

> Among the many subjects, of a general and local nature, that will occupy your deliberations, there are none of such vital importance as the undigested state of our written and unwritten laws.[13]

Opponents, on the other hand, argued that,

> to codify what is only half understood, […] is to perpetuate a mass of errors and shallow ambiguities; it is to begin at the wrong end.[14]

Obviously, codification elicited passionate convictions, eliciting controversial partisan statements intended to provoke reaction and to push for change. However, one of the peculiarities of this theoretical debate was that, even as it became increasingly heated, it had no concrete effect on actual codification efforts, beyond granting them a distant conceptual framework. The axes of

---

pp. 355–391; Norman W. Spaulding, "The Luxury of the Law: The Codification Movement and the Right to Counsel", 73 *Fordham Law Review* 2004, pp. 983–996; Catherine Skinner, "Codification and the Common Law", 11 *European Journal of Law Reform* 2009, pp. 225–258; Sylvain Soleil, "'On the Vocation of our Age for Codes.' Le Recours à Savigny lors de la Controverse anglo-américaine sur la Codification du Common Law (1820–1835)", 18 *Historia et Ius* 2020, pp. 1–31.

12 Maxwell Bloomfield, "William Sampson and the Codifiers: The Roots of American Legal Reform, 1820–1830", 11 *The American Journal of Legal History* 1967, pp. 234–252; Joseph Hopkinson, *Considerations on the Abolition of the Common Law in the United States*, Philadelphia: William P. Farrand & Co., 1809.

13 Pishey Thompson, *Sampson's Discourse and Correspondence with various Learned Jurists upon the History of the Law with the Addition of several Essays, Tracts, and Documents relating to the Subject*, Washington: Gales & Seaton, 1826, p. 95.

14 James Bradley Thayer, "The Teaching of English Law at Universities", 9 *Harvard Law Review* 1895, p. 181.

that debate, as I lay them out below, revolved around two main topics arising from the US experiment with the common law: its inherent problems on one hand, and the need for an alternative on the other.

1.1 Grasping the Common Law

Those assessing the common law experiment during the nineteenth century examined it from every angle, evaluating its practicality and usage. The first complaint was that the legal profession tended to view the common law as sacred, instead of as a science. The discussion then moved to the archaic remnants that had accrued within the long-evolving matrix of the common law. Finally, these assessments focused on the uncertainty inherent to common law, whether in terms of content or shape. Most of the time, defenders of common law countered arguments in favor of codification with the argument that, as a flexible legal source, common law was capable of generating internal mechanisms of control and equilibrium.

1.1.1 *Common Law versus Rationalization Science*

One of the first criticisms of common law was that it was not a science. In a century where science was perceived to be at the center of life, it was a major issue that the main source of law was considered by some to function unscientifically. In his 1823 *Anniversary Discourse* to the Historical Society of New York, William Sampson[15] inaugurated the national debate over the practicability of codification with a stinging critique of the common law. Due to his own life experience, Sampson was from the start a fervent opponent of the common law, which he saw as an obstacle in his principled pursuit of civil liberties and their protection. In his speech he depicted common law as an evil eroding US

15 William Sampson (1764–1836) was an Irish Lawyer who was forced to emigrate to the United States. Born in Londonderry in 1764 to a family of Anglo-Irish churchmen and landowners, his early education was uneventful. He started to work as a lawyer in Ireland during the time of political crisis, which turned him into a radical. He became an advocate of liberty, predominantly between 1790 and 1798. Due to his activism, he came to be suspected of treason and had to live in hiding in Portugal and France for seven years from 1799 to 1806. In May 1805, he left France, not without first having witnessed the reconstruction of the country and the creation of the Napoleonic Code, an event which influenced his legal opinions thereafter. Unable to return to Ireland, he arrived in New York in May 1806, and began his legal career in the United States. See Maxwell Bloomfield, "William Sampson and the Codifiers: The Roots of American Legal Reform, 1820–1830", 11 *The American Journal of Legal History* 1967, pp. 234–252.

law.[16] Drawing together a concern for civil liberties with belief in the scientific nature of the law, his speech denounced common law as archaic and as unsuited to the scientific field of law. Instead, the foundation of the rights and duties of men should be rational and easily knowable. For Sampson, the common law was only understandable thanks to *Blackstone Commentaries*:

> In soliciting admission for the common law into the seats of academic learning, where its rival, the civil law, had long been favored inmate no advocate ever pleaded his cause with more eloquence and grace; but he could not make that a science, which was reducible to no fixed rules, or general principles; and the more he brought it into light, the more the sunny rays of his bright genius fell upon it; the more its grotesque forms became defined, the more they proved to be the wild result of chance and rude convulsions.[17]

He regretted the fact that the law hidden within the common law was not understandable on its own. It was neither rational nor was it a science, and it did not arise from logical reasoning. This vision of the common law, as an inchoate mixture of principles and decisions resulting from random circumstances, became widespread in the early nineteenth century.[18] Consonant with the nineteenth-century thinking that praised rationalism and scientific reasoning, critics considered it impossible to reduce the common law to universal rules understandable by everyone.[19] The rationality argument was the main point which codifier David Dudley Field used to push codification endeavors in New York during the second part of the nineteenth century.[20]

Aside from the fact that the common law was not a science in the pure sense of the term, codification supporters condemned what they saw as its "holiness". Undeniably, the law cannot be effectively developed if it is seen as a sacred object exempt from criticism. Sampson bemoaned that,

16 Kunal Madhukar Parker, *Common Law, History, and Democracy in America, 1790–1900: Legal Thought before Modernism* (*Cambridge Historical Studies in American Law and Society*), New York (NY): Cambridge University Press, 2011, p. 125.

17 William Sampson, *An Anniversary Discourse delivered before the New-York Historical Society on the Common Law*, New York (NY): E. Bliss and E. White, 1824, p. 9.

18 Charles M. Cook, *The American Codification Movement: A Study of Antebellum Legal Reform* (*Contributions in Legal Studies*), Westport (CT): Greenwood Press, 1981, pp. 96–120.

19 Nathan Crystal, "Codification and the Rise of the Restatement Movement", 54 *Washington Law Review* 1979, p. 248.

20 David Dudley Field, "A Third of a Century given to Law Reform", 1873.

> These people, long after they had set the great examples of self-government upon the principles of perfect equality, [...] had still one pagan idol to which they daily offered up much smokey incense. They called it by the mystical and cabalistic name of common law. A mysterious essence. Like the Dalai Lama, not to be seen or visited in open day; of most indefinite antiquity; sometimes in the decrepitude of age, and sometimes in the bloom of infancy, yet still the same that was to be, and evermore to sit cross-legged and motionless upon its antique altar, for no use of purpose but to be praised and worshipped by ignorant and superstitious votaries.[21]

For those in support of codification, a formal codification of the common law was required to overcome its sanctity. The law was not be considered to be an unchanging divine entity, but instead a fallible human creation.[22] On the other side of the spectrum, common law's defenders pointed to the Napoleonic Code as a counterargument: as the most famous code in the world, the latter was regarded as more sacred than the common law.[23] In the twentieth century, authors actually went so far as to declare that the Napoleonic Code had replaced the holy scriptures in the wake of the French Revolution.[24] Therefore, the debate at hand was centered around the appreciation, indeed reverence, given to what was considered the main legal source. Both sides thought the other too steeped in the sacred to produce an efficient system of law.

To critics, in drawing on centuries of unwritten precedent, the common law produced rulings that were both outdated and contradictory.[25] David Dudley Field and William Sampson, both ardent advocates of codification, considered that these oral roots precluded the creation of a legal science comprehensible to all. As a matter of fact, most supporters of codification saw the origin of the common law as its greatest weakness, for it prevented it from being accessible and understandable from a single document. Some authors in favor of common law saw this as spurious criticism. As Joseph Hopkinson, judge, member of the House of Representatives of the State of Pennsylvania, and

21 William Sampson, *An Anniversary Discourse delivered before the New-York Historical Society on the Common Law*, New York (NY): E. Bliss and E. White, 1824, pp. 17–18.

22 David Dudley Field, Codification: *An Address delivered before the Law Academy of Philadelphia, April 18, 1886*, Philadelphia: Printed for the Law Academy, 1886.

23 Francis Barlow, *Facts for Mr. David Dudley Field*, Albany: Weed, Parsons & Co., 1871.

24 James Gordley, "Myths of the French Civil Code", 42 *The American Journal of Comparative Law* 1994, pp. 488–489.

25 Konrad Zweigert and Hein Kötz, *Introduction to Comparative Law*, 3rd ed., Oxford and New York (NY): Oxford University Press and Clarendon Press, 1998, pp. 256–285.

fervent defender and promoter of the common law, wrote, "the term unwritten refers to its origin, not to its present form".[26] As a fervent proponent of the common law, Hopkinson also believed that redrafting the law would not necessarily mean greater certainty, as law is always open to interpretation.[27] In fact, defenders of common law considered its origins in oral tradition to be a strength; in written law, "a word inadvertently used or carelessly omitted; a comma misplaced by accident or ignorance shall change the whole meaning of the clause",[28] whereas the common law was far more versatile. The deep roots of the current law were seen by one side as a defect, requiring evolution to create a more rational science, while the opposing side deemed these roots as a time-honored source of flexibility.

1.1.2 *Archaisms within the Common Law*

One of the central points of the discussion about the common law was the question of its archaic content. Many authors criticized the fact that common law still contained enforceable principles dating back to the "barbarians" and "Norman invaders" as well as to feudal times.[29] They viewed these principles as inappropriate for modern society. For the supporters of codification, the common law was:

> An irregular mass of usage and statutes derived partly from traditions of various and discordant tribes and races, partly from the enactments of tyrannical kings and struggling parliaments, and partly, it may be added, from interpolations by judges and chancellors from the civil or canon law.[30]

However, in the eyes of its advocates it was precisely this ancestral component that constituted the virtue of common law, which they viewed as the fruit of the wisdom of previous generations. Hopkinson declared that,

26 Joseph Hopkinson, *Considerations on the Abolition of the Common Law in the United States*, Philadelphia: William P. Farrand & Co., 1809, p. 18.

27 *Ibid*, pp. 25–26.

28 *Ibid*, p. 31.

29 William Sampson, *An Anniversary Discourse delivered before the New-York Historical Society on the Common Law*, New York (NY): E. Bliss and E. White, 1824, p. 29.

30 David Dudley Field, *An Address to the graduating Class of the Law School of the University of Albany, delivered on March 23, 1856*, Albany: W.C. Little & Co., 1856, p. 19.

> The common law of England is 'a collection of maxims and customs' which have been preserved in various authentic ways, 'and handed down from times of highest antiquity' it is in the truth the common sense of mankind, it is human wisdom, corrected and taught by experience.[31]

> Common law is but another name for common sense, tested and systematically arranged by long experience.[32]

Hence, the two visions collided in their views of the common law's origins. On one side were those who viewed longevity as a strength,[33] while on the other codifiers called for detachment from the past and its customs. While those in favor of codification wanted to strip the common law of its archaic legacies, common law's advocates considered age as a token of truth and wisdom. However, even common law supporters struggled to defend those feudal provisions, particularly regarding private property, which were still enforceable—though rarely, if ever, applied—in the United States.[34] Instead common law proponents fell back on the argument that feudal legacies were proof of the system's ability to function through the centuries while readapting itself to societal developments. The question of archaic remnants was especially strong in the domain of procedure, where the call for codification was particularly forceful and well received.[35] Both the public and jurists lamented the existence of laws that were not attuned to modern times or jurisprudence. They particularly condemned fluctuations of procedural rules and jurisdictional uncertainties which made the enforcement of the law unpredictable.[36] As for the opponents of codification, even if they recognized the obsolescence of certain procedural rules, they argued that, much like feudal remnants in the law, those outdated rules would disappear over time and through court usage. For them, it was a false problem, and their opponents just had to be patient.[37]

31 Joseph Hopkinson, *Considerations on the Abolition of the Common Law in the United States*, Philadelphia: William P. Farrand & Co., 1809, p. 16.

32 *Ibid*, p. 21.

33 James C. Carter, *The proposed Codification of our Common Law*, New York (NY): Evening Post Job Printing Office, 1884, p. 87.

34 *Association of the Bar of the City of New York, Report of the Special Committee to 'Urge the Rejection of the proposed Civil Code' reappointed November 1, 1881*, New York (NY): Evening Post Job Printing Office, 1882.

35 Kellen Funk, *The Lawyer's Code: The Transformation of American Legal Practice, 1828–1938*, Princeton: Princeton University, 2018, p. 83.

36 Maurice Eugen Lang, *Codification in the British Empire and America*, Clark (NJ): The Lawbook Exchange, 2005.

37 Charles M. Cook, *The American Codification Movement: A Study of Antebellum Legal Reform (Contributions in Legal Studies)*, Westport (CT): Greenwood Press, 1981, p. 13.

1.1.3 *The Uncertainty of Common Law Rules*

The uncertainty of common law rules was one of the most passionately discussed questions arising from the US experience with common law.

> The present state of the law, both in theory and in practice, is so complicated that its best-informed professors are at a loss on very many important questions, to pronounce what is law, and what is not law.[38]

Codification's supporters insisted that common law and common law jurisprudence evolved according to the cases before the courts,[39] and they wondered, "how can there be anything like certainty in the law, while the whole of common law is the mere creature of judicial legalization, changing its character as the bench of judges changes its occupants".[40] It was this problem of legal uncertainty that pushed the opponents of common law to praise the idea of a code:

> Our law is in a state of chaos. Nothing will bring it out of chaos but a code. [...] The chaotic state of the law arises, of course, from the vast mass of disarranged, and sometimes discordant, material.[41]

To summarize this indictment of the common law, codification supporters' main arguments were that:

> With regards to the advantages to be derived from reducing the law to a written code, [...] it would render law, as a science, more level of understanding of all. To strip it of its unnecessary intricacy, absurd fictions, obsolete and inapplicable maxims, rules, and forms, cannot be doubted.[42]

---

38 Pishey Thompson, *Sampson's Discourse and Correspondence with various Learned Jurists upon the History of the Law with the Addition of several Essays, Tracts, and Documents relating to the Subject*, Washington: Gales & Seaton, 1826, pp. 68–69.

39 Albert Mathews, "Thoughts on Codification of the Common Law", 1887, p. 23.

40 Pishey Thompson, *Sampson's Discourse and Correspondence with various Learned Jurists upon the History of the Law with the Addition of several Essays, Tracts, and Documents relating to the Subject*, Washington: Gales & Seaton, 1826, pp. 68–69.

41 David Dudley Field, "Correspondence between the California Bar and Mr. David Dudley Field", 1870, p. 465.

42 Pishey Thompson, *Sampson's Discourse and Correspondence with various Learned Jurists upon the History of the Law with the Addition of several Essays, Tracts, and Documents relating to the Subject*, Washington: Gales & Seaton, 1826, p. 87.

Moreover, critics faulted judges for changes and uncertainties within the common law at both the state and federal levels. Codification, by contrast, would create legal continuity and certainty. By making the law fixed, the power of judicial interpretation would be limited, and litigants would no longer be dependent on the good will of a judge.[43]

> If it be asked upon what principles a chancellor or a judge would decide a case for which the common law has made no provision, experience shows that to prevent a failure of justice, as it is called, he resorts to the English act of parliament, the civil law, or his own idea of convenience, and borrows, or makes a rule, which he thinks will answer the purpose. This is afterwards precedent and law—judges become legislators, and a law is imposed to the community without their knowledge or consent, and frequently with slender deliberation and with little wisdom.[44]

To counter the emphasis codification advocates placed on the uncertainty of common law, supporters highlighted common law's flexibility[45] in adapting to new conditions outside of those in which laws were originally established.[46] Legal rules, they argued, should be adaptable to changing circumstances, even as they remained the law of the land.[47] For these supporters, it was the common law's strong suit that it developed in parallel to society. In their opinion, a code was too formal and could not remain up-to-date over time. Instead, it would be forced to rely on interpretation and amendment, resulting in a mass of incomprehensible, written law incapable of fulfilling its promise of legal certainty. In an article in the *Evening Post*, Thomas Cooper explained that:

---

43 Charles M. Cook, *The American Codification Movement: A Study of Antebellum Legal Reform* (*Contributions in Legal Studies*), Westport (CT): Greenwood Press, 1981, p. 113.

44 Pishey Thompson, *Sampson's Discourse and Correspondence with various Learned Jurists upon the History of the Law with the Addition of several Essays, Tracts, and Documents relating to the Subject*, Washington: Gales & Seaton, 1826, p. 90.

45 Reinhard Zimmermann, "Statuta sunt stricte interpretanda? Statutes and the Common Law: A continental Perspective", 56 *The Cambridge Law Journal* 1977, pp. 315–328.

46 David M. Rabban, *Law's History: American legal Thought and the transatlantic Turn to History* (*Cambridge Historical Studies in American Law and Society*), Cambridge: Cambridge University Press, 2013, p. 356.

47 James C. Carter, *The Provinces of the written and unwritten Law*, New York (NY): Banks & Brothers, Law Publishers, 1889, p. 37.

> The Code Napoléon itself, the great model of all schemes, is already beginning to be superseded and lost sight of in the multiplicity of judicial decisions which have arisen under it.[48]

In response, Sampson argued that,

> as to the Napoleonic Code, so far from being superseded, or lost sight of, as is gratuitously asserted, it is so firmly fixed that, in France, and in most of the extensive territories where it governed, it is still looked to as the North Star.[49]

For the supporters of codification, a code was a permanent, yet flexible legal tool, allowing just the right amount of balance between flexibility and certainty. Moreover, its use of broad, general language, allowed sufficient room for interpretation by judges.[50]

1.1.4 *A Common Law of Uncertain Shape*

One other focal point in questioning the common law was its shape and accessibility. Codification defenders emphasized this point, while their opponents were unable to fully counter the criticism and had to propose alternative solutions.

The first element of criticism of the form of the common law was its material inaccessibility. Indeed, legal doctrine was only available to those willing to consult a significant number of documents and who had access to specialized libraries.

---

48 Pishey Thompson, *Sampson's Discourse and Correspondence with various Learned Jurists upon the History of the Law with the Addition of several Essays, Tracts, and Documents relating to the Subject*, Washington: Gales & Seaton, 1826, p. 58; David Dudley Field, *An Address to the graduating Class of the Law School of the University of Albany, delivered on March 23, 1856*, Albany: W.C. Little & Co., 1856, p. 59.

49 Pishey Thompson, *Sampson's Discourse and Correspondence with various Learned Jurists upon the History of the Law with the Addition of several Essays, Tracts, and Documents relating to the Subject*, Washington: Gales & Seaton, 1826, p. 66.

50 Nuno Garoupa and Andrew P. Morriss, "The Fable of the Codes: The Efficiency of the Common Law, legal Origins, and Codification Movements", 5 *University of Illinois Law Review* 2012, pp. 1443–1498.

> The yearly reports of decided cases are now so voluminous that our lawyers can neither afford the money to purchase them, nor the time to pursue them.[51]

> That portion of us, who are to spend our lives in the course of professional employment, find that our labors are severely increased, by the multiplication of books, which we are forced to examine. Our duty seems to be comprised rather in distinction making among adjudged cases than in applying general and acknowledged principles, to the case to be decided.[52]

The legal profession acutely felt the need for certainty and easier access to the law. In addition to the existence of a large number of cases, not all of them were published, making large parts of the law materially inaccessible.[53] Advocates of common law argued that this was not an issue in common law *per se*, but one unique to the US context. In the United States, even statutes were difficult to obtain because of their large number, constant reprinting, and the limited number of copies in each printing. Usually published with considerable delay, statutes sometimes changed on a daily basis and their variations accumulated over the years. As such, the statutes were considered as inaccessible as the common law.[54] In the eyes of the legal profession, this created an urgent need to reduce the amount of legally enforceable material, while also accentuating the necessity of making the law more easily accessible.[55]

---

51 Pishey Thompson, *Sampson's Discourse and Correspondence with various Learned Jurists upon the History of the Law with the Addition of several Essays, Tracts, and Documents relating to the Subject*, Washington: Gales & Seaton, 1826, p. 68.

52 William Sullivan, *Address to the Members of the Bar of Suffolk, Mass at their stated Meeting on the first Tuesday of March 1824*, Boston: Press of the North America Review, 1825, pp. 54–55.

53 Charles M. Cook, *The American Codification Movement: A Study of Antebellum Legal Reform (Contributions in Legal Studies)*, Westport (CT): Greenwood Press, 1981, p. 8.

54 Pishey Thompson, *Sampson's Discourse and Correspondence with various Learned Jurists upon the History of the Law with the Addition of several Essays, Tracts, and Documents relating to the Subject*, Washington: Gales & Seaton, 1826, p. 89.

55 *NY Civ. C. 1865*, pp. III–IX. See also David Dudley Field, *Speeches, Arguments, and miscellaneous Papers*, New York (NY): D. Appleton & Co., 1884, p. 377. "There is as much reason why the American people should have their laws or five pocket-volumes as there is why the French people should have theirs ... But not alone to people would it be convenient; it would be a greater one to the lawyers and the judges." See also William B. Fisch, "The Dakota Civil Code: More Notes for an uncelebrated Centennial", 45 *North Dakota Law Review* 1967, pp. 13–14; Andrew P. Morriss, "Decius S. Wade's Necessity for Codification", 61 *Montana Law Review* 2000, pp. 407–433.

During discussion of the possibility of codification, critics also attacked the common law inasmuch as it derived its form from oral tradition. Consequently, in order to establish enforceable law, the lawyer or layman would sometimes have to consult hundreds of at-times opposing rulings on the subject, with changes accruing from one decision to another and from one judge to another. In litigants' minds, a day in court ended up being more of a battle between rival cases than a dispute over law and justice. This problem pointed towards the need for a common law code, as it would make the law accessible and involve some decision-making regarding previously diverging judgments.[56] The undeniable advantage of a code was that all rules on a particular subject could be found in a single document. A code would also bring unity to the national and the state levels. As one critic wrote,

> is the common law the law of the United States? On the first formation of the colonies, the founders brought with them the common law, which every Englishman regards as his birthright; but each colony judged for itself, what parts of it were fit to its new situation, and either by legislative provisions or judicial decisions, or usage and practice, adopted certain parts and rejected the others; so that in no State of the Union was the whole of it received, [...] the common law of one state, is not the common law of another, much less of the United States.[57]

The question of the form of law and its material inaccessibility was also easily grasped by laymen who supported the idea of a common law codification in order to improve its clarity and applicability.[58] It would also make the law less of an elite tool, providing broad, unrestricted access to all segments of the population.[59] A code would make rights and obligations explicit, creating a law

56 Hugh Henry Brackenridge, *Considerations on the Jurisprudence of the State of Pennsylvania*, Philadelphia: W. Duane, 1808, p. 5–7.

57 Pishey Thompson, *Sampson's Discourse and Correspondence with various Learned Jurists upon the History of the Law with the Addition of several Essays, Tracts, and Documents relating to the Subject*, Washington: Gales & Seaton, 1826, pp. 55–56.

58 Charles M. Cook, *The American Codification Movement: A Study of Antebellum Legal Reform* (*Contributions in Legal Studies*), Westport (CT): Greenwood Press, 1981, pp. 12–13.

59 David Dudley Field, *The Completion of the Code. Five Articles*, New York (NY): Evening Post, 1850. "The people of this state have determined, and in their future fundamental law have declared, that they will have a complete code of all their law, and however it may be delayed, it cannot be prevented." David Dudley Field, *Speeches, Arguments, and miscellaneous Papers*, New York (NY): D. Appleton & Co., 1884, p. 383. "As an American, speaking to Americans, I venture to predict that the instincts of our people and the inexorable logic of events will hasten the completion of the work here and sooner than in England." George

that was more comprehensible and granting easier and less expensive access to justice. Codification would allow litigants to predict a judge's ruling and to place limits on judges' power. Common law decisions are usually exhaustive in terms of facts and include a long analysis of prior applicable cases. The judge bases their decision on previous decisions under the principle of *stare decisis*. The requirement to have precedents, which are numerous and often contradictory, gives the judge liberty to adapt his decision and on occasion to ignore precedents viewed as troublesome. In 1886, a *New York Times* editorial in favor of codification summarized this point with the following tale:

> An earnest debate over a decision occurred between two judges, one of whom said to the other, 'I tell you this is the law' and the other replied, it may be the law now, but it will not be the law after this case is decided.[60]

It was exactly this kind of judicial freedom that was disturbing to defenders of codification even while being praised by common law advocates. Common law supporters did not ignore issues of access, though they offered another solution: an extensive statute law revision. They believed that the common law had to keep its versatility and could be balanced with statutes which dealt with particular subjects about which certainty was needed. "What is a statute? It is the express or written will of the legislature, rendered authentic by certain prescribed forms and solemnities", wrote James Kent.[61] James C. Carter, one of the most ardent defenders of common law, believed that "while codification of the statutes may be good, codification of the common law is bad"[62] because,

> judge-made law, on the whole, tends to conform itself to the principles of common sense, right reason and justice. Statutory law, on the other hand, tends to become technical and arbitrary. [...] There is this much of truth on the side of those who favor elasticity of the common law. Elasticity in itself is not an advantage, but a disadvantage. [...] But the opposite extreme of rigidity and technicality is also a disadvantage, and we are

---

Hoadly, *Codification in the United States: An Address delivered before the Graduating Class at the Sixtieth Anniversary of the Yale Law School on June 24, 1884*, New Haven: Published by the Law Department of Yale College, 1884, p. 496. "But the American people are not the English people, or of exclusively English descent. Germans, Celts, Scandinavians, Spaniards, Frenchmen, Italians enter into our midst and become American citizens."

60 "Common Law Fetichism", *New York Times*, April 19, 1895.

61 James Kent, *Commentaries on American Law*, 1st vol., New York (NY): O. Halsted, 1827, p. 58.

62 David Dudley Field, "A short Response to a long Discourse, an Answer to Mr. James C. Carter's Pamphlet on the proposed Codification of our Law", 1884.

> thus left to a choice of evils. My own opinion is that if this were the only objection to codification, the balance of expediency would be in favor of the codifiers. It seems to me that certainty would be a gain, even if the law became more rigid and technical, since it is better in most cases that the law should be certain and ascertainable than it should be theoretically just.[63]

To its proponents, common law was a flexible tool, especially in opposition to statutes. In fact, a statute in the common law tradition should not be interpreted and must be applied strictly. Hence, the common lawyer believed that the civil law, and by consequence the code, was rigid, imbuing all legislation with the same rigidity as the common law statutes. Whereas each tradition had its own "methods of calibrating the law",[64] the fact that civil law judges had room to interpret the code was lost in translation, leading common law lawyers to depict their tradition as the only one capable of flexibly applying the law.[65]

Despite the opinions of the strongest advocates for codification, the first practical step taken towards legal certainty was usually a revision of the statutes, for example a review of legislative acts in force in the territory. The construction and / or revision of a statute was performed according to a defined technique:

> The construction of a statute indeed, like the operation of a device, depends upon the apparent intention of the maker, to be collected either from particular provisions or the general context; acts of parliament and will ought to be alike constructed, according to the intention of the parties that make them; [...] In the exposition of a statute, then, the leading clue to the construction to be made, is the intention of the legislator. [...] If a statute makes use of a word, the meaning of which is well known, and has a certain definite sense at the common law, the word shall be

63 William Hornblower, "Is Codification of the Law expedient? An Address delivered before the American Social Science Association", 1888, p. 9.

64 Kunal Madhukar Parker, *Common Law, History, and Democracy in America, 1790–1900: Legal Thought before Modernism* (*Cambridge Historical Studies in American Law and Society*), New York (NY): Cambridge University Press, 2011, p. 239.

65 Reinhard Zimmermann, "Statuta sunt stricte interpretanda? Statutes and the Common Law: A continental Perspective", 56 *The Cambridge Law Journal* 1977, pp. 315–328.

> expounded and received in the same sense in which it is understood in the common law.[66]

The Revised Statutes of New York are a potent illustration of how statute revision worked. In fact, it was considered such an important example that the Revised Statutes of New York were exported and adopted in all the other states. Between 1800 and 1820, both New York's population and the number of laws on its books almost tripled, creating an incomprehensible mass of statutes without any rational organization. Consequently, in order to know the law on a given subject, it was necessary to examine the statutes from one year to the next, rendering the law almost impossible to understand. The first report of the revision committee, delivered to the legislature in March 1826, explained that the statutes were classified as follows: 1) internal civil administration and policy of the state, 2) substantial law in terms of private property rights or personal relationships, 3) the judicial system and civil procedure, 4) criminal law, and 5) public law. The new organization provided a classification similar to the *Blackstone Commentaries*. It allowed legislation to be grouped by subject rather than by date. The legislature approved this organization and unreservedly supported the commissioners until the completion of their work three years later. The Revised Statutes of New York were published in 1829.[67] In the context of the time, this total reclassification of the statutes was considered to be the first step towards a comprehensive codification of the law. It was also touted as a partial codification, solving the problem of the incomprehensible mass of statutes. On the one hand, it was seen as an example of how codification could resolve an array of legal issues, while it also provided a model for how the common law might be both reformed and preserved. The Revised Statutes of New York worked for both conflict parties and added fuel to the debate, all while leaving the common law itself in place.

1.2 Emancipation from Common Law

The idea that codification could bring greater freedom circulated in many countries,[68] and the United States was no exception. Codification promised

66 Fortunatus Dwarris, *A general Treatise on Statutes and their Rules of Construction*, Philadelphia: John S. Littell, 1835, pp. 39–44.

67 *NY Rev. Stat. 1829*.

68 Rémy Cabrillac, *Les Codifications* (*Droit, Éthique, Société*), Paris: Presses Universitaires de France, 2002, p. 53.

liberation for two precise reasons. First, a code offered liberation from the former colonial regime while, second, a code would allow liberation from the legal profession itself.

1.2.1 *Liberation from English Legacy*

During the nineteenth century, the argument for geographical unity and liberation from the English legacy took on a new weight. The common law was inherited from the former colonial empire and became a standing symbol of dependency.[69] After the American Revolution, all the states either implicitly or explicitly declared the preservation of the laws in force, meaning English laws, in their territories. As David Dudley Field notes, "the revolution, of course, brought an immense change in the official machinery; but it made at first very little change in the laws beside".[70] In fact, the earliest call for revision of the law's English content occurred during the period from 1783 to 1815.[71] As Benjamin Austin noted:

> Can the monarchical and aristocratical [sic] institutions of England be consistent with the republican principles of our Constitution? We may as well adopt the law of the Medes and Persians.[72]

However, the practicability of English common law as an already known and enforceable legal system prevailed over calls for legal independence.[73] The first challenges to common law arose early on, but it was only after the War of 1812[74] that criticisms became more widespread, as state legislatures adopted

---

69 *Ibid*, p. 62; Maurice Eugen Lang, *Codification in the British Empire and America*, Clark (NJ): The Lawbook Exchange, 2005, p 103.

70 David Dudley Field, *An Address to the graduating Class of the Law School of the University of Albany, delivered on March 23, 1856*, Albany: W.C. Little & Co., 1856, p. 20.

71 Maxwell Bloomfield, "William Sampson and the Codifiers: The Roots of American Legal Reform, 1820–1830", 11 *The American Journal of Legal History* 1967, p. 234.

72 Perry Miller, *The Life of the Mind in America from the Revolution to the Civil War*, New York (NY): Harcourt, Brace & World, 1965, p. 106.

73 Kunal Madhukar Parker, "Law and Regime Change: The Common Law, Knowledge Regimes, and Democracy between the nineteenth and twentieth Century", 3 *Critical Analysis of Law* 2016, pp. 363–369.

74 The War of 1812, fought between the United States and the British Empire, started in June 1812 and continued until early 1815. The United States declared war on the United Kingdom on June 18, 1812, invading the British-Canadian territories with which they maintained numerous commercial relationships. The resentment attached to this war was the resentment of Americans facing forced recruitment as sailors, the weakening of trade with the Native Americans and, of course, the resentment against the British Empire as former oppressors. The war took place on three fronts: the Atlantic Ocean,

acts prohibiting the reception of new jurisprudence coming from England.[75] Paired with the wish to move away from English law was a desire to have a distinctly US law. These desires were the beginnings of US legal nationalism. It was difficult, however, to undo years of English common law usage through common law practice itself. Codification seemed to be the perfect solution, as it would allow the law to be stripped of its English contents. William Sampson was again one of the leading early thinkers in this vein. In his *Anniversary Discourse*,[76] he preached abandonment of the legal tradition inherited from the United Kingdom,[77] as

> we should have had laws suited to our condition and high destinies; and our lawyers would have been the ornaments of our country [...] we must either be governed by laws made for us or made by us.[78]

He went on to develop his argument and criticism of English law on three grounds, which would be reiterated during the entire subsequent debate: men should be equal before the law; the English statutes created inequalities; and the common law and the statutes should be passed through the filter of democracy.[79] More broadly, Sampson did not see the usefulness of maintaining foreign law that did not correspond to the fundamental principles of the United States. English judges who created and developed the common law were appointed by the king,[80] and applying and using laws established by a monarchy went against the founding principles of the United States: freedom,

---

the Southern States, and the Great Lakes region. At the beginning of the conflict, the United States attempted to invade the British colonies, but were pushed back (Capture of Detroit, Battle of Queenstown Heights). Consequently, the Royal Navy imposed a blockade along the coast, weakening the US economy due to subsequent reductions of US agricultural exports. Domination of the sea allowed the British to conduct coastal raids and to burn Washington in August 1814. The naval battles of the Great Lakes though turned to the advantage of the United States. The war ended on February 17, 1815, with no frontiers changed.

75 The first state to adopt such an act was New Jersey in 1799, while other states, such as Kentucky, Delaware, and Pennsylvania, followed in the 1820s.

76 William Sampson, *An Anniversary Discourse delivered before the New-York Historical Society on the Common Law*, New York (NY): E. Bliss and E. White, 1824, p. 65.

77 Charles M. Cook, *The American Codification Movement: A Study of Antebellum Legal Reform* (*Contributions in Legal Studies*), Westport (CT): Greenwood Press, 1981.

78 William Sampson, *An Anniversary Discourse delivered before the New-York Historical Society on the Common Law*, New York (NY): E. Bliss and E. White, 1824, p. 52.

79 *Ibid*, p. 59–61.

80 *Charles M. Cook, The American Codification Movement: A Study of Antebellum Legal Reform* (*Contributions in Legal Studies*), Westport (CT): Greenwood Press, 1981, pp. 58–61.

and democracy. From 1820 on, the debate over codification became more powerful as it came to be linked to liberation from the former colonial regime and to the desire for a US-created law. To give more strength to their argument, lawyers used the French example and explained how the Napoleonic Code helped to overcome the monarchial laws of the past. "French jurisprudence has been improved by the substitution of a single and uniform code [...] instead of the fifty systems of the former government".[81] At the same time, the desire for liberation through the creation of a US law, could also work to the disadvantage of codification. For many, the law would be made clearer, less technical, and more American not by a code, but through the development of US legal literature, such as treatises, digests, and textbooks.[82] In practice, the courts followed this trend in legal Americanization, gradually detaching themselves from the old, established jurisprudence. Judges initiated their own law and jurisprudence, creating a unique US common law. Doing so provided a double fix: the common law not only became US-based, but also more certain as lawyers would have to rely less on inaccessible English precedent.

1.2.2 *Codification as Liberation from the Legal Profession*

Advocates of codification also saw it as a move that would liberate the country from the rule of legal professionals. The first argument in this vein related to judges themselves. In fact, the debate over codification took place in a broader context of controversy within American legal thought, as scholars disagreed on the role of the judge as a maker or finder of the law.[83]

One point stressed in favor of a code was that, unlike the members of the legislature who would make the law in a code system, common law judges did not receive authority through the democratic process. The US legal system instead awarded positions on the bench as the prize for a long career in the legal field. Appointment as a judge was linked to legal, political, or academic success, rather than to the express will of the people.[84] As a matter of fact, during the nineteenth century, rules governing access to the judiciary differed

81 *Ibid*, p. 73.

82 US legal literature is not without problems. The use of legal treatises only provides access to outlines of set principles on a topic or a branch of a law. Moreover, they are often incomplete and evoke more what the law should be. The book most useful to lawyers would be the digest, for it is a collection of basic legal elements enforceable in the territory.

83 David M. Rabban, *Law's History: American legal Thought and the transatlantic Turn to History* (*Cambridge Historical Studies in American Law and Society*), Cambridge: Cambridge University Press, 2013, pp. 356–361.

84 Jean Blondel, "La Common Law et le Droit Civil", 3 *Revue internationale de Droit Comparé* 1951, p. 587.

from one state to another; a judge could be appointed by the legislature or the governor, and might even be elected in rare cases. In most cases then, they were not chosen by the people, yet they still had the ability to create law without any democratic or popular sanction. Judges had the power to determine rights and duties, but no legitimacy to do so. Critics argued that codification would allow the people to have rights and duties defined and decided by more legitimate democratic actors. This argument was well received and could only be criticized or ignored with difficulty. Over time, it was resolved through the development of an elective procedure for judges in all states, wresting momentum from arguments for codification.

The second argument for codification as a tool of liberation from legal actors held that codification would make the law more understandable, thereby lessening the need for a lawyer. Like the common law itself, the American legal profession was in a phase of development. During the nineteenth century, law schools were not yet widespread. In order to become a lawyer, the student had to become an apprentice in a law firm and be educated by experienced lawyers. The lawyer-in-training kept the records of his supervisor and undertook jurisprudential research. It was a very concrete and practical education, allowing the future lawyer to get used to the law and its ways.[85] This system also ensured the centrality of lawyers to legal education, a fact supported by the belief that, "justice is attainable only through lawyers". [...] "The science of the law is so vast in its extent that they alone can master it they who make it their principal study".[86] Here David Dudley Field implies that the law is complicated and requires specialized knowledge to understand. But the quote also highlights the importance of lawyers as guardians of family secrets, suggesting that *only* lawyers could grasp the ramifications of the law. Field went even further, stating that:

> The importance of the lawyer is always in proportion to the importance of the law. [...] Tell me the freedom of a state, and I will tell you the strength of its bar. [...] In our country the legal profession has every element of strength and preeminence. Our only sovereign is the law, and lawyers are its only ministers and interpreters.[87]

---

85 *Ibid*, p. 588.

86 David Dudley Field, *An Address to the graduating Class of the Law School of the University of Albany, delivered on March 23, 1856*, Albany: W.C. Little & Co., 1856, p. 11.

87 *Ibid*, p. 4.

This preponderant place of the lawyer was not much criticized by the main architects of the debate—either for or against codification—as most of them were lawyers themselves. Instead, it took the rise of a populist political movement, and the rise of the Jacksonian Party (forerunner to the Democratic Party) to spur broad concern with the role of legal professionals.[88] In the 1830s, a wind of change worked its way through the United States. Andrew Jackson, a man of modest upbringing, succeeded John Quincy Adams as President of the United States in 1829. In the process he created *Jacksonianism*, a political movement built around the figure of Jackson, his conception of popular government and his presidency. This movement was primarily focused on his democratic doctrine: the extension of the vote to all white men and the extension of US influence across the continent to the Pacific. He also defended the idea of a Federal Government with limited powers, economic laissez-faire, and opposition to the monopoly of banks, in particular that of a central bank.[89] Through this movement a new criticism of the legal profession surfaced: on the one hand, lawyers' monopoly of the law was considered undemocratic,[90] while on the other critics argued that the dominance of legal professionals made the exercise of justice slow and unaffordable.[91] This monopoly and the need for legal representation therefore had to disappear to free the population. A code would limit the need for representation in litigation, while allowing all, particularly laymen, to understand the law. Of course, none of these critics proposed dispensing with the legal profession altogether. In some rare cases, there would no longer be a need for a legal representative to face the courts, but the belief that,

> the reduction of law to a code can dispense with the necessity of the profession, and enable every man to be his own lawyer, is an idea which everyone who understands the organization of society will pronounce weakly theoretical, and if practicable, would never be practiced. The subdivision of labor, which is found so advantageous to all classes, forbids it.[92]

---

88 Kunal Madhukar Parker, *Common Law, History, and Democracy in America, 1790–1900: Legal Thought before Modernism* (*Cambridge Historical Studies in American Law and Society*), New York (NY): Cambridge University Press, 2011, pp. 124–139.

89 Charles M. Cook, *The American Codification Movement: A Study of Antebellum Legal Reform* (*Contributions in Legal Studies*), Westport (CT): Greenwood Press, 1981, pp. 158–166.

90 *Ibid.*

91 *Ibid*, p. 13.

92 Pishey Thompson, *Sampson's Discourse and Correspondence with various Learned Jurists upon the History of the Law with the Addition of several Essays, Tracts, and Documents relating to the Subject*, Washington: Gales & Seaton, 1826, p. 87.

Through this quote one is reminded, that, in reality, this utopia could never be achieved. The Jacksonian presidency, and the anti-elitist movement that accompanied it, would not bring codification to the United States. Nonetheless, Jacksonians kept working for change within the legal profession. The main goal was to lower bar admission standards, allowing those who were less educated to be able to learn the craft. By making the profession more accessible to a broad swath of the population, such efforts ultimately made the pro-codification argument of deliverance from lawyers irrelevant.

1.3 Codifier Jeremy Bentham and the United States

The national codification framework could not be complete without looking at the codifier Jeremy Bentham. Bentham,[93] a philosopher, jurist, and English reformer, is considered to be the inventor of the term "codification".[94] He was the nineteenth century writer who dedicated the most numerous works to codes and codification, intervening on both the theoretical and practical levels. His theory of codification was centered on criticism of the common law and the disadvantages of unwritten law in general, which he viewed as unstable and erratic in its judicial development. In this context, Bentham saw codification as the only way to save the law. For him, a code always had to be succinctly, clearly, and precisely written. It had to match the doctrine of utilities and should be protected from the interpretation of the courts. In his writings he even proposed a specific period—one hundred years—after which a code should be revised.[95] Though this conception of a code seemed revolutionary, the problem was that it was primarily theoretical. Indeed, Bentham was primarily a theoretician, an academic, who therefore had no practical vision of codification.[96] Living his reclusive life, Bentham and his ideas appeared utopian to the practitioners of the American codification movement.

Bentham's first attempt at a codification occurred in England, but he quickly realized that it was an impossible task; the English culture was neither ready, nor willing to take the path of codification. He thus decided to turn his efforts

93 For biographical information on Jeremy Bentham, see Christophe Chauvet, *Jeremy Bentham: Vie, Oeuvres, Concepts*, Paris: Ellipses, 2010.

94 Jeremy Bentham, *Oeuvres Complètes*, Bruxelles: Louis Hauman et Comp, 1830, pp. 87–126.

95 Jeremy Bentham, *Treatise on Civil and Criminal Legislation*, Paris: Bossange, Masson et Besson, 1802.

96 *Ibid*, pp. 77–78.

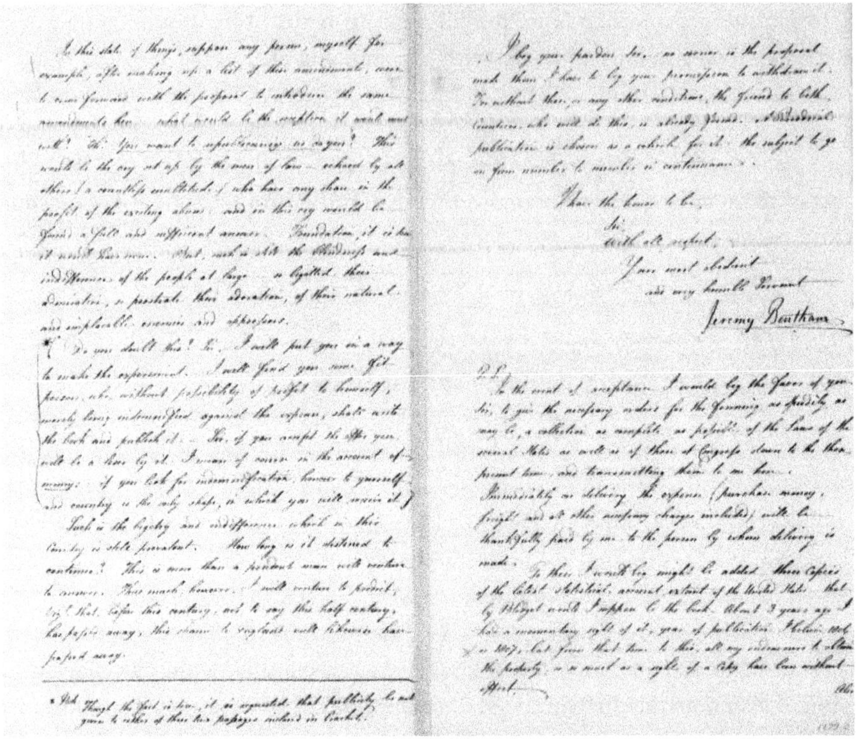

FIGURE 1 Letter of Jeremy Bentham to James Madison, October 30, 1812
COURTESY OF THE LIBRARY OF CONGRESS, AVAILABLE AT »HTTPS://WWW.LOC.GOV/ITEM/MJM016752/« AND LAST RETRIEVED AUGUST 1, 2023

and ambitions to other countries.[97] In awe of the fledgling democracy—even if he had not and would never set foot on US soil—he imagined giving this new nation a code based on its own common law.[98] Accordingly, he first wrote to President James Madison in October 1812,[99] offering to write a set of codes, called *Pannomion*, for the United States. In his letter (Figure 1), he developed all the pro-codification arguments that would be used a few years later during the national debate. His message continued with a request for a letter of endorsement, so that he could persist in the endeavor that he had already begun, and it ended with a request that the president respond promptly.

97 Maurice Eugen Lang, *Codification in the British Empire and America*, Clark (NJ): The Lawbook Exchange, 2005, pp. 33–39.

98 Jeremy Bentham, *The Works of Jeremy Bentham*, 4th vol., Edinburgh: William Tait, 1843, pp. 451–533.

99 *Ibid*, pp. 433–467.

The reply took five years coming. Bentham's letter was received on the eve of the War of 1812, and the president had neither time nor interest in codification, especially for proposals from a British citizen.[100] The response, finally composed on May 5, 1816, was brief and negative.[101] Even while recognizing Bentham as more competent than a lawyer in the United States to undertake such work, the president deemed codification unnecessary and remained a staunch believer in the common law. The Englishman's response was immediate and refuted all the arguments advanced by the American.[102] In parallel, convinced of the imperative of his project, Bentham wrote a circular letter to the governors of all the US states, similarly offering them his *Pannomion*.[103] Once again, he received only negative replies, with the sole exception of the State of Pennsylvania. But even there, codification failed after several attempts due to inadequate support from the legislature ... [104] Besides these letters to governors, Bentham composed and sent an open letter to all US citizens. The letter consisted of eight parts, and summarized Bentham's thoughts on codification. The main argument he developed was that the Americans had freed themselves from the British colonial regime, yet tied themselves to an arbitrary and dangerous legal system:

> Yes, my friends, if you love each other, if you value your safety, close the door to the common law as you would the plague. Let us with the sad privilege to be governed by this tissue of imposture by this gang of lawmakers [...]. Never forget this lesson: wherever the common law landed, security has disappeared.[105]

To Bentham's dismay, these public letters had few readers in the United States, and exerted no significant influence over public debate. Hence, receiving no support or even authorization to undertake such a work, he never wrote a

100 Andrew P. Morriss, Scott J. Burnham, and Hon. James C. Nelson, "Debating the Field Civil Code 105 years late", 371 *Montana Law Review* 2000, p. 372.

101 *Ibid*, pp. 467–468.

102 Philippe Gérard, François Ost, and Michel Van de Kerchove, *Actualité de la Pensée juridique de Jeremy Bentham* (*Travaux et Recherches*), Bruxelles: Presses de l'Université Saint-Louis, 1987, pp. 192–197.

103 Jeremy Bentham, *The Works of Jeremy Bentham*, 4th vol., Edinburgh: William Tait, 1843, pp. 478–507.

104 Charles M. Cook, *The American Codification Movement: A Study of Antebellum Legal Reform* (*Contributions in Legal Studies*), Westport (CT): Greenwood Press, 1981, pp. 98–101.

105 Jeremy Bentham, *The Works of Jeremy Bentham*, 4th vol., Edinburgh: William Tait, 1843, pp. 478–507.

code, let alone a *Pannomion*, for the United States. Even so, Bentham had an undeniable—if ambivalent—influence on the codification debate, at least in its theoretical aspects.

To American eyes, Bentham's ideas were problematic for two reasons. Not only was he English, but his codification projects and his theoretical approach lacked pragmatism.[106] Indeed, very few US codifiers recognized Bentham as an influence. Only Edward Livingston, one of the authors of the Civil Code of Louisiana, and Thomas Cooper, a lawyer and defender of codification in South Carolina, viewed themselves as successors of the English philosopher, although Cooper only admitted his affiliation with Bentham after the failure of codification in his state.[107] The preface of the Civil Code of North Dakota also proclaimed the commission's status as heirs to Jeremy Bentham,[108] being the only commission in the United States to have done so. Still, it was undeniable that many US authors were influenced by his ideas even if they did not consider themselves to be his heirs.

Why did so few lawyers admit Bentham's influence? In his book on codification, Charles M. Cook speculated that the reason might lie in animosity towards the British, who were seen as former oppressors. However, there are other plausible explanations. First, Bentham's theses on codification were not only purely theoretical, but also virtually unenforceable, making his ideas anathema to the very pragmatic and application-centered discussion in the United States.[109] As a result, Bentham's theories on codification only seemed to confuse and hinder debate, and they were used mainly by critics of codification to highlight its inapplicability and lack of practicality.[110] This rejection of Bentham's codification proposal extended to the very terms of the debate. All defenders of codification up to 1830 refused to employ the word "codification",

106 George M. Hezel, "The Influence of Bentham's Philosophy of Law on the early nineteenth Century Codification Movement in the United States", 22 *Buffalo Law Review* 1972, pp. 253–268.

107 Charles M. Cook, *The American Codification Movement: A Study of Antebellum Legal Reform* (*Contributions in Legal Studies*), Westport (CT): Greenwood Press, 1981, pp. 74–75.

108 *ND Rev. C. 1895*, p. III.

109 Samuel Williston, "Written and unwritten Law", 17 *American Bar Association Journal* 1931, p. 39. "Field did not take the absurd view of Jeremy Bentham that a code would do everything, but he did say, in Carter's words, that whatever was clearly understood could be clearly stated, and if that was true, it was possible to enact a code which should cover everything that was clearly known. It would not be possible to cover all possible cases that might arise in the future; but the answer to that was that the code should not attempt to do so, and that as to such matters, you would be not worse off than you would be if there were no code, and as to other matters you would be better off."

110 *Ibid*, p. 39.

so tied was the word to the man who coined it. They preferred the term "codified law".[111] However, Bentham's commitment to codification as a means of developing law and bettering the administration of justice made its way into the ideas of the leading supporter of codification in New York, David Dudley Field.[112]

1.4 Concluding Remarks: Was There an American Codification Movement?

In discussing the codification question in the nineteenth century, one has to bear in mind that the idea of an organized American codification movement is a scholarly invention. Codification was indeed of interest to the legal profession throughout the nineteenth century, and its proponents produced a rich literature, the peak of which was reached with the adoption of Field's Code of Civil Procedure of New York. However, the debate never took the form of a specific and organized movement. Thus, the different actors of the "movement" had no common political leanings, nor did they share training or geographical location. They consequently had no tangible connection to one another beyond an interest in codification and the fact that they were for most of them members of the legal profession. This last point explains the specialized arenas in which the debate over codification took place.

It is historians, not participants in the debate, who collected disparate speeches and opinions to make them into a movement. In truth, no formal organization or agency has been devoted to the defense and implementation of codification in the United States. While posing as a practical debate, the question of codification remained primarily a theoretical or rhetorical one. Like Field, some individuals attempted to enact concrete codification projects. As mostly private actors, however, their attempts had no direct ties with the national conversation. Even the Louisiana codifiers were not linked to this national debate, as the implementation of the Civil Code of Louisiana took place in the early nineteenth century —before the broader conversation began. After the war, various codification efforts took place, but they were modeled on the Field Civil Code and did not draw directly on the national discussion. As for the Code of Georgia, it was undertaken at a state level, without

111 *Ibid*, p. 165.

112 George L. Haskins, "De la Codification du Droit en Amérique du Nord au XVIIe Siècle. Un Étude de Droit comparé", 23 *Tijdschrift voor Rechtsgeschiedenis* 1955, p. 312.

any participation in the general conversation, and would remain an isolated case among its fellow civil codes.

Bibliography

Atias, Christian; Levasseur, Alain A.: "American Legal Culture and traditional scholarly Order", 46 *Louisiana Law Review* 1986, pp. 1117–1136.

Aumann, Francis R.:*The changing American Legal System: Some selected Phases*, New York (NY): Da Capo Press, 1969.

Barlow, Francis: *Facts for Mr. David Dudley Field*, Albany: Weed, Parsons & Co., 1871.

Bartlett, Roger: *The Bentham Brothers and Russia. The Imperial Russian Constitution and the St Petersburg Panopticon*, London: UCL Press, 2022.

Bentham, Jeremy: *Oeuvres Complètes*, Bruxelles: Louis Hauman et Comp, 1830.

Bentham, Jeremy: *The Works of Jeremy Bentham*, 4th vol., Edinburgh: William Tait, 1843.

Bentham, Jeremy: *Treatise on Civil and Criminal Legislation*, Paris: Bossange, Masson et Besson, 1802.

Blondel, Jean: "La Common Law et le Droit Civil", 3 *Revue internationale de Droit Comparé* 1951, pp. 585–598.

Bloomfield, Maxwell: "William Sampson and the Codifiers: The Roots of American Legal Reform, 1820–1830", 11 *The American Journal of Legal History* 1967, pp. 234–252.

Bloomfield, Maxwell: *American Lawyers in a changing Society, 1776–1876* (*Studies in Legal History*), Cambridge (MA): Harvard University Press, 1976.

Brackenridge, Hugh Henry: *Considerations on the Jurisprudence of the State of Pennsylvania*, Philadelphia: W. Duane, 1808.

Brierly, James: "The Future of Codification", 12 *British Yearbook of International Law* 1931, pp. 1–12.

Cabrillac, Rémy: *Les Codifications* (*Droit, Éthique, Société*), Paris: Presses Universitaires de France, 2002.

Carter, James C.: *The proposed Codification of our Common Law*, New York (NY): Evening Post Job Printing Office, 1884.

Chauvet, Christophe:*Jeremy Bentham: Vie, Oeuvres, Concepts*, Paris: Ellipses, 2010.

Cook, Charles M.: *The American Codification Movement: A Study of Antebellum Legal Reform* (*Contributions in Legal Studies*), Westport (CT): Greenwood Press, 1981.

Crystal, Nathan: "Codification and the Rise of the Restatement Movement", 54 *Washington Law Review* 1979, pp. 239–274.

Dwarris, Fortunatus: *A general Treatise on Statutes and their Rules of Construction*, Philadelphia: John S. Littell, 1835.

Field, David Dudley: "A short Response to a long Discourse, an Answer to Mr. James C. Carter's Pamphlet on the proposed Codification of our Law", 1884.

Field, David Dudley: "A Third of a Century given to Law Reform", 1873.
Field, David Dudley: "Correspondence between the California Bar and Mr. David Dudley Field", 1870.
Field, David Dudley: *An Address to the graduating Class of the Law School of the University of Albany, delivered on March 23, 1856*, Albany: W.C. Little & Co., 1856.
Field, David Dudley: *Centenary Essays: Celebrating One Hundred Years of Legal Reform*, New York (NY): Alison Reppy, 1949.
Field, David Dudley: *Codification: An Address delivered before the Law Academy of Philadelphia, April 18, 1886*, Philadelphia: Printed for the Law Academy, 1886.
Field, David Dudley: *Speeches, Arguments, and miscellaneous Papers*, New York (NY): D. Appleton & Co., 1884.
Field, David Dudley: *The Civil Code for the State of New York: Reported complete by the Commissioners of the Code*, Albany: Weed, Parsons & Co., 1865.
Field, David Dudley: *The Completion of the Code. Five Articles*, New York (NY): Evening Post, 1850.
Fisch, William B.: "The Dakota Civil Code: More Notes for an uncelebrated Centennial", 45 *North Dakota Law Review* 1967, pp. 9–55.
Friedman, Lawrence M.: *A History of American Law*, 3rd ed., New York (NY): Simon & Schuster, 2005.
Funk, Kellen: *The Lawyer's Code: The Transformation of American Legal Practice, 1828–1938*, Princeton: Princeton University, 2018.
Garoupa, Nuno; Morriss, Andrew P.: "The Fable of the Codes: The Efficiency of the Common Law, legal Origins, and Codification Movements", 5 *University of Illinois Law Review* 2012, pp. 1443–1498.
Gérard, Philippe; Ost, François; Van de Kerchove, Michel: *Actualité de la Pensée juridique de Jeremy Bentham* (*Travaux et Recherches*), Bruxelles: Presses de l'Université Saint-Louis, 1987.
Gordley, James: "Myths of the French Civil Code", 42 *The American Journal of Comparative Law* 1994, pp. 459–505.
Grossman, Lewis: "Codification and the California Mentality", 45 *Hastings Law Journal* 1994, pp. 617–639.
Grossman, Lewis: "Langdell Upside-Down: The Anticlassical Jurisprudence of Anticodification", 19 *Yale Journal of Law & Humanities* 2007, pp. 1–67.
Gruning, David: "Vive la difference? Why no Codification of Private Law in the United States?", 39 *Revue Juridique Themis* 2005, pp. 153–194.
Hahlo, H. R.: "Codifying the Common Law: Protracted Gestation", 38 *The Modern Law Review* 1975, pp. 23–30.
Haskins, George L.: "De la Codification du Droit en Amérique du Nord au XVIIe Siècle. Un Étude de Droit comparé", 23 *Tijdschrift voor Rechtsgeschiedenis* 1955, pp. 311–332.

Head, John W.: "Codes, Cultures, Chaos and Champions: Common Features of legal Codification Experiences in China, Europe, and North America", 13 *Duke Journal of Comparative & International Law* 2003, pp. 2–93.

Herman, Shael: "The Fate and the Future of Codification in America", 40 *The American Journal of Legal History* 1996, pp. 407–437.

Hezel, George M.: "The Influence of Bentham's Philosophy of Law on the early nineteenth Century Codification Movement in the United States", 22 *Buffalo Law Review* 1972, pp. 253–268.

Hoadly, George: *Codification in the United States: An Address delivered before the Graduating Class at the Sixtieth Anniversary of the Yale Law School on June 24, 1884*, New Haven: Published by the Law Department of Yale College, 1884.

Hopkinson, Joseph: *Considerations on the Abolition of the Common Law in the United States*, Philadelphia: William P. Farrand & Co., 1809.

Hornblower, William: "Is Codification of the Law expedient? An Address delivered before the American Social Science Association", 1888.

Horwitz, Morton J: *The Transformation of American Law, 1780–1860* (*Studies in Legal History*), Cambridge (MA): Harvard University Press, 1977.

Kent, James: *Commentaries on American Law*, 1st vol., New York (NY): O. Halsted, 1827.

Lang, Maurice Eugen: *Codification in the British Empire and America*, Clark (NJ): The Lawbook Exchange, 2005.

Masferrer, Aniceto: "Defense of the Common Law against postbellum American Codification: Reasonable and fallacious Argumentation", 50 *The American Journal of Legal History* 2008, pp. 355–430.

Masferrer, Aniceto: "The passionate Discussion among Common Law Lawyers about postbellum American Codification: An Approach to its legal Argumentation", 40 *Arizona State Law Journal* 2008, pp. 173–256.

Mathews, Albert: "Thoughts on Codification of the Common Law", 1887.

Miller, Perry: *The Life of the Mind in America from the Revolution to the Civil War*, New York (NY): Harcourt, Brace & World, 1965.

Morriss, Andrew P.: "Codification and right Answers", 74 *Chicago-Kent Law Review* 1999, pp. 355–391.

Morriss, Andrew P.: "Decius S. Wade's Necessity for Codification", 61 *Montana Law Review* 2000, pp. 407–433.

Morriss, Andrew P.; Burnham, Scott J.; Nelson, Hon. James C.: "Debating the Field Civil Code 105 years late", 371 *Montana Law Review* 2000, pp. 371–405.

Mullins, Morell E.: "An academic Perspective on Codification and the Arkansas Code of 1987 annotated", 11 *University of Arkansas at Little Rock Law Journal* 1988, pp. 285–327.

Parker, Kunal Madhukar: "Law and Regime Change: The Common Law, Knowledge Regimes, and Democracy between the nineteenth and twentieth Century", 3 *Critical Analysis of Law* 2016, pp. 362–384.

Parker, Kunal Madhukar: *Common Law, History, and Democracy in America, 1790–1900: Legal Thought before Modernism* (*Cambridge Historical Studies in American Law and Society*), New York (NY): Cambridge University Press, 2011.

Pound, Roscoe: *The Spirit of the Common Law*, Francestown (NH): Marshall Jones Co., 1921.

Rabban, David M.: *Law's History: American legal Thought and the transatlantic Turn to History* (*Cambridge Historical Studies in American Law and Society*), Cambridge: Cambridge University Press, 2013.

Reimann, Mathias: "The historical School against Codification: Savigny, Carter, and the defeat of the New York Civil Code", 37 *The American Journal of Comparative Law* 1989, pp. 95–119.

Salken, Barbara C.: "To codify or not to codify—That is the Question: A Study of New York's Efforts to enact an evidence Code", 58 *Brooklyn Law Review* 1992, pp. 641–704.

Sampson, William: *An Anniversary Discourse delivered before the New-York Historical Society on the Common Law*, New York (NY): E. Bliss and E. White, 1824.

Schwartz, Bernard: *Main Currents in American legal Thought*, Durham (NC): Carolina Academic Press, 1993.

Skinner, Catherine: "Codification and the Common Law", 11 *European Journal of Law Reform* 2009, pp. 225–258.

Smith, Marion: "The first Codification of the substantive Common Law", 4 *Tulane Law Review* 1929, pp. 178–189.

Soleil, Sylvain: "'On the Vocation of our Age for Codes.' Le Recours à Savigny lors de la Controverse anglo-américaine sur la Codification du Common Law (1820–1835)", 18 *Historia et Ius* 2020, pp. 1–31.

Soleil, Sylvain: *Aux Origines de l'Opposition entre Systèmes de Common Law et de Droit codifié—Les Controverses anglo-américaines des Années 1820–1835*, Paris: Société de Législation Comparé, 2021.

Spaulding, Norman W.: "The Luxury of the Law: The Codification Movement and the Right to Counsel", 73 *Fordham Law Review* 2004, pp. 983–996.

Subrin, Stephen: "David Dudley Field and the Field Code: A historical Analysis of an earlier procedural Vision", 6 *Law and History Review* 1988, pp. 311–373.

Sullivan, William: *Address to the Members of the Bar of Suffolk, Mass at their stated Meeting on the first Tuesday of March 1824*, Boston: Press of the North America Review, 1825.

Thayer, James Bradley: "The Teaching of English Law at Universities", 9 *Harvard Law Review* 1895, pp. 169–184.

Thompson, Pishey: *Sampson's Discourse and Correspondence with various Learned Jurists upon the History of the Law with the Addition of several Essays, Tracts, and Documents relating to the Subject*, Washington: Gales & Seaton, 1826.

Wagner, Wienczyslaw J.: "Codification of Law in Europe and the Codification Movement in the Middle of the nineteenth Century in the United States", 2 *Saint Louis University Law Journal* 1952, pp. 335–359.

Warren, Charles: *A History of the American Bar* (*Historical Writings in Law and Jurisprudence*), Buffalo: W.S. Hein, 1980.

Weiss, Gunther A.: "The Enchantment of Codification in the Common-Law World", 25 *Yale Journal of International Law* 2000, pp. 435–532.

Williston, Samuel: "Written and unwritten Law", 17 *American Bar Association Journal* 1931, pp. 39–41.

Zimmermann, Reinhard: "Statuta sunt stricte interpretanda? Statutes and the Common Law: A continental Perspective", 56 *The Cambridge Law Journal* 1977, pp. 315–328.

Zweigert, Konrad; Kötz, Hein: *Introduction to Comparative Law*, 3rd ed., Oxford and New York (NY): Oxford University Press and Clarendon Press, 1998.

CHAPTER 2

The Development of Private Law Codification in the US States

> Ceux qui veulent acquérir une connaisance exacte de la manière dont il font établir ou abroger les lois ne le peuvent puiser que dans l'histoire.
>
> KING FREDERICK II of Prussia, 1744.[1]

The eight nineteenth-century US civil codes arose from different histories and were shaped by the unique legal needs of the particular states implementing them. Though in each case participants claimed they were the first to accomplish codification, the story of US civil codes started in Louisiana (2.1). It then continued with a series of common law codes ending with South Dakota in 1903 (2.2). Most of the US states' codification history has been covered separately by the legal historiography. The purpose of this section is to provide a chronological overview of the codes, and to reconstruct the story of codification of private law in the United States.

2.1 The Most Famous US Civil Codes: the Civil Codes of Louisiana

Whenever the subject of civil codification arises in the context of the United States, the first response is usually, "Louisiana, of course". Considered to be the only state to have a civil code, the Civil Codes of Louisiana have become the symbol of codification in the United States. Though not the only state to codify its laws, Louisiana's codification efforts became famous[2] while preceding other

1 "Those who want to gain an accurate knowledge of how one must establish or abolish laws can only draw it from history." King Frederick II of Prussia, *Œuvres Philosophiques de Frédéric II, Roi de Prusse*, 2nd vol., Berlin: Rodolphe Decker, Imprimeur du Roi, 1848, p. 11.

2 David Gruning, "Mapping Society through Law: Louisiana Civil Law recodified", 26 *Lex Electronica* 2021, pp. 34–77.

 | DOI:10.1163/9789004689978_005

codification projects. The 1800s were the century of codification in Louisiana. Between the post-independence period and the Civil War, the question of legal codification was key to political and legislative debates in the state, and three civil codes were implemented. The first appeared before statehood (2.1.1), followed by a first revision in 1825. Finally, the last nineteenth-century code was created 1870 to incorporate the changes brought about by the Civil War (2.1.2).

2.1.1 *The Survival of Civil Law in Louisiana*

Civil law is a fundamental part of Louisiana's culture;[3] indeed, it has become both a symbol of the state's colonial legacy and a deeply ingrained element of Louisiana's cultural identity (2.1.1.1). This fight for the preservation of Louisiana's legal heritage helped bring the 1808 Digest into existence (2.1.1.2).

2.1.1.1 Louisiana, the Civil Law State

Following in the footsteps of Juan Ponce de Léon, Hernando de Soto[4] decided to embark upon the quest for the "fountain of youth" in 1537. According to Native American legend, this miraculous fountain, which could give eternal life to anyone who drank from it, was situated in the territory that we now know as Florida. This quest for fame and eternal life did not come to fruition, but it did secure de Soto a place in history. By finding the mouth of the Mississippi, he became the first European to discover what would become Louisiana.[5] In 1677, Robert Cavelier de LaSalle, from the French town of Rouen, explored the Mississippi from its source to its northern end. Upon arriving at its mouth on the Gulf of Mexico in 1681, he decided to name the territory he discovered Louisiana, in honor of King Louis XIV of France and the king's mother, Anne of Austria.[6]

---

3 For an overview of the civil codes' history in Louisiana, see John W. Cairns, *Codification, Transplants and History. Law Reform in Louisiana (1808) and Quebec (1866)*, Clark (NJ): Talbot Publishing, 2015; Olivier Moréteau, "Les Codes Civils de Louisiana dans leurs Ordre naturel", 7 *Les Cahiers Portalis* 2020, pp. 207–223. See also Agustín Parise, "Private Law in Louisiana: An Account of Civil Codes, Heritage, and Law Reform", in *The Scope and Structure of Civil Codes* (*Ius Gentium, 32nd vol.*), ed. Julio César Rivera, Dordrecht: Springer, 2013, pp. 429–454; John H. Wigmore, "Louisiana: The Story of its Legal System", 1 *Southern Law Quarterly* 1916, p. 1, reprinted in 90 *Tulane Law Review* 2016, p. 529.

4 Appointed by King Charles I of Spain as governor of Cuba island and all the lands he was able to discover.

5 Victor Debouchel, *Histoire de la Louisiane: Depuis les premières Découvertes jusqu'en 1840*, New Orleans: J. F. Leleivre, 1841, pp. 17–24.

6 For a complete history of colonial Louisiana, see Victor Debouchel, *Histoire de la Louisiane: Depuis les premières Découvertes jusqu'en 1840*, New Orleans: J. F. Leleivre, 1841; Charles Gayarré, *Histoire de la Louisiane*, New Orleans: Imprimé par Magne & Weisse,

This French colony was ruled by the *Coutume de Paris* and the royal decrees.[7] The *Coutume de Paris* was a collection of laws which had governed Paris since the first such compilation in 1510. The version enforceable in the colonies was the one from 1579, which contained 362 articles. Louisiana was mostly flourishing during its first years and started to be administered separately from the other French colonies in 1712.[8] After France's defeat during the Seven Years War, Louisiana was ceded to Spain by the Treaty of Fontainebleau, also called the Treaty of Paris, in 1762. Spain took possession of the territory on November 25, 1769.[9] This change of dominion was not well received by the inhabitants. In fact, it took seven years for Spain to complete the transfer of power, leaving the territory under French dominion and rule during this time.[10] It was only in 1769, with the arrival of the Spanish colonial governor Don Alejandro O'Reilly, that the end of French rule became publicly visible. Spain exercised dominion over this territory for thirty-four years. However, as Jacques Vanderlinden shows in a study of legal documents from the era of Spanish rule, the inhabitants were still attached to French law, and most cases were settled privately using the earlier French customs.[11] On September 1, 1800, the Territory of Louisiana was re-ceded to France by Article 3 of the Treaty of San Ildefonso, between the Court of Madrid and the Republic of France. The territory was ceded in exchange for the Duchies of Tuscany and Parma, which Napoleon gave to the Spanish King's son-in-law.[12] In fact, Napoleon was convinced that a stronghold

1846; Bernard de la Harpe, *Journal historique de l'Établissement des Français à la Louisiane*, New Orleans: Paul Renouard, 1831; François-Xavier Martin, *The History of Louisiana from the Earliest Period*, New Orleans: Lyman and Beardslee, 1827; Bennett H. Wall, *Louisiana: A History*, 6th ed., Hoboken (NJ): Wiley-Blackwell, 2013.

7 Alain A. Levasseur, *Louis Casimir Elisabeth Moreau-Lislet: Foster Father of Louisiana Civil Code*, Baton Rouge: LSU Law Center Publications Institute, 1996, p. 3; A. N. Yiannopoulos, "The Civil Codes of Louisiana", 1 *Civil Law Commentaries* 2008, p. 2; Victor Debouchel, *Histoire de la Louisiane: Depuis les premières Découvertes jusqu'en 1840*, New Orleans: J. F. Leleivre, 1841.

8 H. Ward Fontenot, "The Louisiana Judicial System and the Fusion of Cultures", 63 *Louisiana Law Review* 2002, p. 1149.

9 Jacques Vanderlinden, "Origins of the French Legal Culture in North America", 2 *LSU Law Center Journal of Civil Law Studies* 2008, p. 9; Alain A. Levasseur, "The major Periods of Louisiana Legal History", 41 *Loyola Law Review* 1995, p. 590.

10 H. Ward Fontenot, "The Louisiana Judicial System and the Fusion of Cultures", 63 *Louisiana Law Review* 2002, pp. 1149–1160.

11 Jacques Vanderlinden, "Origins of the French Legal Culture in North America", 2 *LSU Law Center Journal of Civil Law Studies* 2008, p. 7.

12 H. Ward Fontenot, "The Louisiana Judicial System and the Fusion of Cultures", 63 *Louisiana Law Review* 2002, pp. 1155–1157; Alain A. Levasseur, *Louis Casimir Elisabeth Moreau-Lislet: Foster Father of Louisiana Civil Code*, Baton Rouge: LSU Law Center Publications Institute, 1996, p. 13.

adjacent to the territory of the United States would give him a strategic advantage in developing his commercial relations with the new American republic. The treaty between France and Spain included a confidentiality clause: as long as the war against Britain continued, the cession of the territory had to remain a secret. In June 1801, word of the secret clause reached the American ambassador to England, who promptly informed his superiors in Washington. Given the imperatives of western expansion and fears of imperial neighbors, this discovery set off a push for negotiations with France in the hopes of gaining Louisiana for the United States. These negotiations took two years and were led on the US side by Robert Livingston,[13] the brother of Edward Livingston, who would become one of Louisiana's champions of codification in the ensuing years. France's return to governing the territory lasted only twenty days. Nevertheless, in this short time, some major changes were undertaken: the creation of a municipal council,[14] a remodeling of the judicial system, and the adoption of the *Code Noir*, a code on slavery.[15] However, the law was still Spanish,[16] now joined with old and new French law.

The United States took possession of 828,000 square miles of territory on December 20, 1803,[17] eight months after purchasing Louisiana from France for 15 million dollars.[18] The agreement was sealed in the Treaty of Paris,[19] signed on May 20, 1803, which declared that:

> Article 1. § 2—[…] the First Consul of the French Republic, desiring to give to the United States a strong proof of his friendship hereby cede to the United States in the name of the French Republic forever and in full sovereignty the said territory with all its rights and appurtenances as

13 Alain A. Levasseur, *Louis Casimir Elisabeth Moreau-Lislet: Foster Father of Louisiana Civil Code*, Baton Rouge: LSU Law Center Publications Institute, 1996, pp. 13–14.

14 "Décret du 30 Novembre 1803 pour l'Établissement de l'Autorité municipale à la Nouvelle Orleans", 20 *Louisiana Historical Quarterly* 1937, p. 170.

15 H. Ward Fontenot, "The Louisiana Judicial System and the Fusion of Cultures", 63 *Louisiana Law Review* 2002, p. 1156.

16 *Ibid*, p. 1155.

17 Everett Somerville Brown, *The Constitutional History of the Louisiana Purchase 1803–1812*, Union (NJ): The Lawbook Exchange, 2000; Agustín Parise, "Codification of the Law in Louisiana: Early nineteenth-century Oscillation between Continental European System and Common Law Systems", 27 *Tulane European & Civil Law Forum* 2012, p. 138.

18 The sum of the purchase would correspond to 233 million dollars currently. Even if the amount sounds small, it in fact corresponded to 1.5 times the GDP of the United States at that time.

19 Alain A. Levasseur, *Louis Casimir Elisabeth Moreau-Lislet: Foster Father of Louisiana Civil Code*, Baton Rouge: LSU Law Center Publications Institute, 1996, p. 28.

fully and in the same manner as they have been acquired by the French Republic.[20]

Napoleon's intentions were very clear: "the ceding of this territory strengthens indefinitely the power of the United States, and I have just given England a maritime enemy that sooner or later will make them lose their pride".[21] The American congressional act allowing the possession of the territory established a provisional government and nominated two commissioners in charge of taking possession of the territory and signing the treaty with the French commissioners. One of the American commissioners was William Charles Cole Claiborne (Figure 2), who would later be named the first governor of Louisiana, thus taking over the administration of the territory.

Claiborne's first act as governor was to "maintain the law in force thus far".[22] Concretely, he maintained existing French and Spanish laws, justifying the move as a practical decision. Aware of the civil law legacy, he knew he did not have time to change the legal system while still allowing the law to function. Maintaining the existing legal system also gave him some time to get his bearings and learn about the new territory and its culture. He assumed that, once he had settled in, the inhabitants would become accustomed to American government and would want to adopt the common law.

He quickly realized that he had made a mistake. The legal system he inherited was chaotic and unlike what he was used to. The Spanish and French legislation in force in Louisiana involved more than eleven different codes, from the Spanish *Ordenanzas e Instrucciones* to the *Coutume de Paris,* as well as more than 20,000 laws, a number of them obsolete and/or contradictory.[23] In

20 "Article 1. § 2—[...] le Premier Consul de la République, désirant donner un témoignage remarquable de son amitié auxdits États-Unis, il leur fait, au nom de la République française, cession, à toujours et en pleine souveraineté, dudit territoire, avec tous ses droits, appurtenances, ainsi et de la même manière qu'ils ont été acquis par la République française."

21 Victor Debouchel, *Histoire de la Louisiane: Depuis les premières Découvertes jusqu'en 1840*, New Orleans: J. F. Leleivre, 1841, p. 93; M. Barbé-Marbois, *Histoire de la Louisiane et de la Cession de cette Colonie par la France aux États-Unis de l'Amérique septentrionale*, Paris: Imprimerie de Firmin Didot, Imprimeur du Roi, 1829, p. 317. "Cette cession de territoire affermit pour toujours la puissance des États-Unis, et je viens de donner à l'Angleterre une ennemie maritime qui tôt ou tard abaissera son orgueil."

22 "Proclamation of the Surrender of Louisiana, December 20, 1803", 1 *Louisiana Legal Archives* 1937.

23 Agustín Parise, "Codification of the Law in Louisiana: Early nineteenth-century Oscillation between Continental European System and Common Law Systems", 27 *Tulane European & Civil Law Forum* 2012, pp. 137–138.

FIGURE 2 William Charles Cole Claiborne
COURTESY OF THE LIBRARY OF CONGRESS, AVAILABLE AT »HTTPS://WWW.LOC.GOV/ITEM/2007675942/« AND LAST RETRIEVED AUGUST 1, 2023

his first report to the President of the United States, Claiborne explained his discomfort:

> Louisiana, like most other countries which have undergone a change of masters, is directed by many municipal customs and regulations from different sources; by what kinds of laws the French formally govern the province is unknown to me.[24]

---

24 "Letter of Governor Claiborne to the President [Thomas Jefferson], Natchez, August 24, 1803." Clarence Edwin Carter, *The Territorial Papers of the United States. Volume IX. The*

As a result, he quickly tried to introduce common law in the territory. Born in Virginia and trained in common law, Claiborne was a strong supporter of the common law system. He was deeply convinced that adopting common law in Louisiana would bring more ease and certainty to the legal process. Common law also had the advantage of providing the territory with a directly enforceable working legal system. To his surprise, however, he encountered considerable resistance from the Louisiana population and its notables.[25] In a letter to President James Madison, dated October 29, 1804, he explained:

> In the course of my efforts to introduce the American system of jurisprudence into the ceded territory, I experienced many difficulties, and excited some dissatisfaction among the people—I sincerely wish, that judges may find their duties agreeable; and that the happiest result may attend their exertions for the public good.[26]

The leaders of the opposition were two lawyers: Edward Livingston and Daniel Clark, two legal practitioners well-versed in Louisiana law. The fight over the state's legal system would make the three men enemies for life. At its height, an 1805 conspiracy charge brought against Claiborne by Clark led to a duel in which Clark shot Claiborne in the thigh, an injury that would leave him with a permanent limp.[27]

Aware of these tensions in Louisiana, on March 26, 1804, the US Congress extended an olive branch, in an act that had two major consequences. First, it divided the Territory of Louisiana into two parts. One, the District of Louisiana, later became the District of Missouri; the other, the Territory of Orleans, is now known as Louisiana. This geographical redefinition allowed the territory's administration to be divided, while also reducing the territory governed by each administration. The Territory of Orleans was ruled by a legislative council with thirteen members presided over by the governor, in this case, Claiborne.

Territory of Orleans 1803–1812, Washington: United States Government Printing Office, 1940, p. 19.

25 George Dargo, *Jefferson's Louisiana: Politics and the Clash of Legal Traditions*, Clark (NJ): The Lawbook Exchange, 2009, p. 219.

26 "Letter of Governor Claiborne to the Secretary of State [James Madison], New Orleans, October 29, 1804." Clarence Edwin Carter, *The Territorial Papers of the United States. Volume IX. The Territory of Orleans 1803–1812*, Washington: United States Government Printing Office, 1940, p. 317.

27 John T. Hood Jr., "The History and Development of the Louisiana Civil Code", 19 *Louisiana Law Review* 1958, p. 21.

The second goal of the congressional act was to ease tensions over the shape of the law. Section 11 stated that:

> The laws in strength in said territory, at the beginning of this act, and not inconsistent with the provisions thereof, shall continue in force up to altered, modified, or repealed by the legislature.

This was an attempt at appeasement, with the US Congress promising to safeguard existing laws, but it would not last long. Indeed, Claiborne was waiting impatiently for the meeting of the legislative council to address the issue of the adoption of the common law, which he viewed as a matter of urgency. To this end, he sought out the support of the major political figures in the region. The meeting, however, was repeatedly postponed due not only to a series of unforeseen events (a slave revolt, hurricanes, and the yellow fever epidemic), but also to the refusal of those key figures to participate in the council and therefore to implement Claiborne's vision.[28] Meanwhile, opposition to the common law persisted, spearheaded by Livingston and supported by the state's inhabitants, especially the major landowners. Opponents of common law drafted a *memorial*, adopted in public session in New Orleans in October 1804, whose signatories complained about having a governor unfamiliar with their laws and customs. They also challenged the introduction of the English language in the courts and the fragmentation of Louisiana into disparate territories.[29] They called for statehood, which would resolve their concerns by providing an elected government and control over the law of the territory. The hope was that the state could avoid the introduction of common law by electing individuals acquainted and accustomed to civil law and Louisiana's culture. The petition was addressed to the US Congress, but still arrived after the meeting of the first legislative council on December 5, 1804. Despite understanding the tension in the territory, the US Congress granted only half of the document's requests. In early 1805, the Federal Government refused to grant statehood to Louisiana. However, they removed the legislative council and replaced it with an elected legislature[30] along the lines of other US states.

28 *Ibid*, pp. 19–20; Agustín Parise, "Codification of the Law in Louisiana: Early nineteenth-century Oscillation between Continental European System and Common Law Systems", 27 *Tulane European & Civil Law Forum* 2012, pp. 133–164.

29 Victor Debouchel, *Histoire de la Louisiane: Depuis les premières Découvertes jusqu'en 1840*, New Orleans: J. F. Leleivre, 1841, p. 95.

30 The legislature was comprised of a Chamber of Representatives and a Senate elected by the local population, and therefore had the power to create and revise the laws and statutes of the state.

Though partial, these concessions were early victories for civil law proponents in Louisiana. While still refusing statehood, they granted the most politically important demand: the ability to hold elections and to achieve greater control over decision-making. Success was tainted by Claiborne, however, who refused to yield.

With a majority of delegates in support of civil law, the Louisiana Congress met for the first time in 1806. Its first decision was to approve an act declaring that the law in force prior to the Louisiana Purchase—meaning French and Spanish law—was to remain in force. However, Claiborne vetoed this decision. He justified his veto with pragmatic arguments: to his mind the current law with its overlay of Spanish and French law seemed confusing and unworkable. However, in truth his veto had ideological undertones, as he still hoped to establish common law in the territory. In reaction to the governor's veto of an act considered foundational for the territory, the legislature adjourned its session and published a manifesto declaring the dissolution of the General Assembly.[31] In this manifesto, they developed several arguments in favor of civil law and against the implementation of the common law:

> Now, what are the laws that Congress intended to preserve to us by this provision? What are the laws that must be subject to review and correction by the legislature of this territory? [...] Now, since we have the power to keep our old laws in so far as they do not conflict with the Constitution of the United States and the special acts passed for our provisional government, no one can deny the advantage to us of remaining under a system we are accustomed to and who can say anything contrary to the affection we owe to our government. [...] What difference does it make here that such an act should be governed by civil law while in the other States of the Union they are governed by common law?
>
> Certainly, we do not attempt to draw any parallels between civil law and the common law; but the wisdom of the civil law is recognized by the whole of Europe; and this law is the one that nineteen twentieths of the population of Louisiana are accustomed to since childhood, one of which they could not be deprived without falling into despair. [...]

31 The Chamber of Representatives and the Senate collectively, referred to as the General Assembly during joint meetings.

> The debate in the Chamber of Representatives and even the refusal of the sanction of the governor, do they not seem—both of them—to justify its prudence, by raising the presumption that there is a secret intention of throwing us, despite ourselves, into the frightful chaos of common law?[32]

This manifesto's importance lay in bringing to light the arguments and the political strength of supporters of civil law in Louisiana. The first argument had to do with political legitimacy. Drafters of the manifesto reminded the governor that, as an elected body, it was they—the legislature—who held the power to decide. There was an evident comparison to the governor's own status as an appointed—and therefore imposed—official. The second argument was that of tradition. The manifesto suggested that the governor rejected this system because he did not know it. By contrast, the entire population of the territory was accustomed to the civil law system. Third, the manifesto highlighted the wisdom of civil law and stressed that this system was a model for Europe. The fourth point criticized the common law in unstinting terms, depicting it as an uncertain and chaotic legal tool. Finally, the authors concluded by explaining that their commitment to civil law did not make them any less American suggesting that allegiance to the United States could coexist with a multiplicity of territorial legal forms. Bolstered by these arguments and confident of its power, the legislature met again on June 7, 1806, and adopted an act providing for the drafting of a civil code.[33]

2.1.1.2 The 1808 Digest, the First US Civil Code

In the June 7, 1806, act which authorized the drafting of a civil code, the legislature also appointed a commission tasked with doing so. It consisted of James Brown, Louis Moreau-Lislet and his assistant Joseph Villars, and Etienne Boré, and John Watkins as legal advisors. They were appointed to "write and organize an adequate civil code for this territory".[34] Moreau-Lislet, who had a

32 "Le Telegraphe, New Orleans, Tuesday, June 3, 1806. Excerpt from the session of the Legislative Council of May 26, 1806." Clarence Edwin Carter, *The Territorial Papers of the United States. Volume IX. The Territory of Orleans 1803–1812*, Washington: United States Government Printing Office, 1940, pp. 651–652. See also John A. Lovett, "On the Principle of Legal Certainty in the Louisiana Civil Law Tradition: From the Manifesto to the Great Repealing Act and Beyond", 63 *Louisiana Law Review* 2003, pp. 1397–1448.

33 "Letter of the Secretary of the Treasury Department to Hore Browse Trist, New Orleans, February 27, 1804." Clarence Edwin Carter, *The Territorial Papers of the United States. Volume IX. The Territory of Orleans 1803–1812*, Washington: United States Government Printing Office, 1940, p. 193.

34 *Acts passed at the first Session of the Legislative Council of the Territory of Orleans*, New Orleans: James M. Bradford, Printers to the Territory, 1805, pp. 214–218.

major role in drafting the civil code, was not initially included on the list. He was appointed after the fact to replace Livingston, because Claiborne used his influence as governor to prevent the latter from participating.[35]

Louis Casimir Elizabeth Moreau-Lislet is now considered the father of the Civil Code of Louisiana. His official name had been Louis Casimir Moreau, however the Lislet was added to distinguish him from his brother, Benjamin Moreau, who died.[36] The details of Moreau-Lislet's life are somewhat vague. He was born sometime between 1767 and 1769 in St. Martin of Dondon.[37] He completed his secondary education in France or in Cap Haïtien and received the title of "Lawyer in Parliament" in 1788. On September 10, 1789, the twenty-three-year-old Moreau-Lislet married Anne Elisabeth Philippine de Peters in Paris,[38] and the couple moved to Saint Domingue then to Cap-Français (Cap Haïtien). They stayed in Saint Domingue until 1803. During this time, Moreau-Lislet worked in several capacities, but always within the legal field. He then spent about a year in Santiago, Cuba, before emigrating to Louisiana.[39] His arrival in Louisiana was facilitated by knowledge of the laws of the territory as well as his language skills; as a speaker of French, Spanish and English he was able to integrate into the different circles of the new territory. He built a reputation as a translator of legal documents and then resumed his work in the legal profession. His reputation as a virtuous man with solid experience in the legal field led, eventually, to his appointment as one of the drafters of the civil code. In addition to these honors, he was appointed judge for the Parish of Orleans in May of 1807.[40]

According to the initial act, the drafters were supposed to be paid 800 dollars each year for five years after the completion of their work. However, a payment was authorized by the legislature in 1807 giving each the sum of 2,000 dollars in full compensation for their service.[41] While it is unclear whether the

35 John T. Hood Jr., "The History and Development of the Louisiana Civil Code", 19 *Louisiana Law Review* 1958, p. 20.

36 Alain A. Levasseur, *Louis Casimir Elisabeth Moreau-Lislet: Foster Father of Louisiana Civil Code*, Baton Rouge: LSU Law Center Publications Institute, 1996, Annex, Testament of Moreau-Lislet.

37 *Ibid*, pp. 80–82. Generally, it is accepted that he was born in 1767 as indicated on his tombstone, however, other documents—such as his marriage lines—address him as being born in 1768 or 1769.

38 Alain A. Levasseur, "A 'Civil Law' Lawyer: Louis Casimir Elisabeth Moreau Lislet", 42 *Loyola Law Review* 1996, p. 207.

39 *Ibid*, pp. 80–82, 95–113.

40 *Ibid*, pp. 114–118.

41 John T. Hood Jr., "The History and Development of the Louisiana Civil Code", 19 *Louisiana Law Review* 1958, p. 26.

change came from the legislature or at the drafters' request, it allowed them to have access to the money more swiftly while halving the total sum. The code was written in two years and finally adopted on March 31, 1808, by an "act that provides for the enactment of the digest of civil laws currently in force in the Territory of Orleans".[42] This code was called *A Digest of the Civil Law now in force in the Territory of Orleans, with Alterations and Amendments adapted to its present System of Government*.[43] The choice of the term "digest" rather than "code" might seem puzzling, especially as the legislature and commissioners of the code spoke in their work of a "civil code".[44] One explanation might be that the term "digest" implied a tribute to the Roman codes, while allowing this code to be distinguished from the Napoleonic Code. Another explanation is found in the definition of the term "digest". A digest is a compilation of existing laws, while codification entails an act of change and creation within the law. The Louisiana project was a compilation and selection of existing enforceable law; therefore, the term "digest" seems quite appropriate. Indeed, the term "digest" might have been chosen to emphasize the nature of the legal project behind the document.

Claiborne was not opposed to the civil code; even if its enactment constituted a personal political failure, it at least had the merit of clarifying the state's laws. Indeed, in the words of the legislature:

> Given the state of confusion in which the civil laws of this territory were plunged by the effect of the changes that took place in its government, it had become essential to know which of these laws are conserved after the repeal of all those that were contrary to the US Constitution; or incompatible with its principles, and to collect, in one book, which can offer the courts and lawyers, a sure guide to inform their decisions, without resorting to the multitude of volumes, mostly written in foreign languages who have their interpretations, inexhaustible resources at chicane.[45]

---

42 Louis Moreau-Lislet and Henry Carleton, *Digeste général des Actes de la Législature de la Louisiane passés depuis l'Année 1804 jusqu'en 1827, inclusivement, en force de Loi à cette dernière Époque: Suivi d'un Appendix et d'une Table de Matières*, 1st vol., New Orleans: Benjamin Levy, 1828, pp. 207–208.

43 *LA Digest 1808*.

44 Vernon Valentine Palmer, "The Quest to implant the Civilian Method in Louisiana: Tracing the Origins of judicial Methodology", 73 *Louisiana Law Review* 2013, pp. 804–805; Asya Ostroukh, "The Mystery of the Mixité around the Title of the Louisiana Digest of the Civil Laws of 1808", 62 *Loyola Law Review* 2016, pp.725–748.

45 Louis Moreau-Lislet and Henry Carleton, *Digeste général des Actes de la Législature de la Louisiane passés depuis l'Année 1804 jusqu'en 1827, inclusivement, en force de Loi*

The 1808 Digest, the first existing civil code in the United States, consisted of three books, divided into titles, chapters, and 2,121 articles. It essentially reproduced the Napoleonic Code and Spanish law in force in the territory.[46] It was, as a result, a hybrid, containing the two colonial legal traditions in the territory.[47] When the digest came into force, it was indeed accompanied by an English translation.[48]

After its adoption, the code came to be widely revered within the state.[49] Indeed, the digest seemed to fit perfectly with the political and cultural demands of the territory's inhabitants. By making the civil law system official, thereby preserving Louisiana's legal culture through a code rooted in the Roman tradition, it fulfilled the demands of the 1804 manifesto. However, this code remained unwieldy for lawyers from other US states who emigrated to the territory and were not educated in the civil tradition.[50] The legislature, recognizing the importance of the code and the innovation it introduced, decided to clarify the code's status as supreme territorial law:

> Section 2. All that in ancient civil laws of that territory or in the territorial statutes contrary to the provisions contained in the digest, or incompatible with it, are and remains repealed by this.[51]

The act was clear: the central impetus behind the code was to establish a core set of laws capable of superseding any earlier legislation that contradict them. With it, the legislature met one of the central criteria for codes according to nineteenth-century theory: a code had to be the primary source of law. However, what the section did not specify was what to do with the provisions

---

à cette dernière Époque: Suivi d'un Appendix et d'une Table de Matières, 1st vol., New Orleans: Benjamin Levy, 1828, pp. 207–208.

46 LA *Digest 1808*.

47 Olivier Moréteau, "De Revolutionibus: The Place of the Civil Code in Louisiana and in the Legal Universe", 5 *Journal of Civil Law Studies* 2012, pp. 31–66.

48 Vernon Valentine Palmer, *The lost Translators of 1808 and the Birth of Civil Law in Louisiana*, Athens (GA): University of Georgia Press, 2021, p. 10.

49 Warren M. Billings, "Louisiana Legal History and its Sources: Needs, Opportunities, and Approaches", in *Louisiana's Legal Heritage*, ed. Edward F. Haas, Pensacola (FL): The Perdido Bay Press, 1983, p. 199.

50 Mack E. Barham, "La Méthodologie du Droit civil de l'État de Louisiane", 27 *Revue internationale de Droit comparé* 1975, p. 800.

51 Louis Moreau-Lislet and Henry Carleton, *Digeste général des Actes de la Législature de la Louisiane passés depuis l'Année 1804 jusqu'en 1827, inclusivement, en force de Loi à cette dernière Époque: Suivi d'un Appendix et d'une Table de Matières*, 1st vol., New Orleans: Benjamin Levy, 1828, pp. 207–208.

that were neither contrary to nor included in the code. Practice would show that they remained enforceable.

2.1.2 *The Evolution of the Civil Codes of Louisiana during the Nineteenth Century*

The 1808 Digest did not remain static after its adoption. Instead, it evolved over the course of the nineteenth century to become, first, the 1825 Civil Code of Louisiana and then the 1870 Revised Civil Code of Louisiana.

Following the adoption of the digest in 1811, the Constitutional Convention convened in Louisiana to establish the first state constitution. The constitution came into force in January 1812, finally cementing Louisiana's statehood.[52] In parallel, the legal provisions not contrary to the code remained in force despite the digest, and this continued to create legal confusion. In an effort to make the law more understandable, the legislature authorized a translation of the *Siete Partidas,* a Spanish code still in force in Louisiana. The *Siete Partidas* was a legislative compendium written in Castile in the thirteenth century and imported, along with an array of other Spanish legal texts, into the territories colonized by Spain. The idea behind the translation was to have a document outlining the Spanish law still applicable in the territory after the code's enactment so as to have a comprehensive account of Louisiana law.[53] Moreau-Lislet, who by then was no longer serving as a judge, began the translation of the *Siete Partidas* into French. The translation was published in 1820 after authorization by the legislature.[54] Residual confusion over the scope of enforceable law pushed the Louisiana legislature to adopt a resolution in March 1822 appointing Edward Livingston, Louis Moreau-Lislet, and Pierre Derbigny[55] to,

52 Alain A. Levasseur, *Louis Casimir Elisabeth Moreau-Lislet: Foster Father of Louisiana Civil Code*, Baton Rouge: LSU Law Center Publications Institute, 1996, p. 127.

53 Louis Moreau-Lislet and Henry Carleton, *The Laws of Las Siete Partidas which are still in Force in the State of Louisiana*, 1st vol., New Orleans: James McKaraher, 1820, p. 493; David Gruning, "Bayou State Bijuralism: Common Law and Civil Law in Louisiana", 81 *University of Detroit Mercy Law Review* 2003, pp. 437–464.

54 Alain A. Levasseur, *Louis Casimir Elisabeth Moreau-Lislet: Foster Father of Louisiana Civil Code*, Baton Rouge: LSU Law Center Publications Institute, 1996, p. 130.

55 *Ibid*, p. 140. Among those offering their service for the writing of the code the votes were distributed as follows: 43 votes for Moreau-Lislet, 25 votes each for Livingston and Derbigny, 23 votes for Workman, 22 votes for Mazureau, 3 votes for Smith, 2 votes each for Morel and Carleton.

> revise the civil code by amending in such manner as they will deem it advisable, and by adding unto […] [it] […] such of the laws that are still in force and not included therein.[56]

At the same time, the three jurists worked to create a comprehensive Commercial Code and to draft a Judicial Code of Practice that would eventually become the Code of Civil Procedure. Derbigny was a nobleman and lawyer born in France, who emigrated to the United States during the French Revolution. Arriving in Louisiana at the age of thirty, he was, alongside Livingston, a strong advocate for codification. Moreau-Lislet, meanwhile, had seen his reputation grow as a lawyer, to the point of being appointed Attorney General of the State of Louisiana, a position he held for two years. Subsequently, he was elected as a Representative in the House of Representatives in 1818 and 1820.[57] On March 22, 1823, one year after their appointment, the commissioners sent a report outlining their plan for the complete revision of the code and including the main sources they relied on in determining Louisiana law. First among these was,

> [t]he Napoleonic Code, that rich legacy that the expiring Republic gave to France and to the world, we have a system approaching nearer to perfection than any that preceded it.[58]

Their report also explained their method, which consisted in rendering the civil code as exhaustive as possible. This included adding to the digest the new measures taken by the legislature since the adoption of the code, as well as the Spanish law that had not been integrated into the preliminary compilation. The head of the code revision committee in the House, who gave his full support to this project, was no other than one of Livingston's trainees and his protégé, Auguste Davezac.[59] Their plan was adopted by the legislature, which requested that the new code should be prepared and printed as soon as possible. This was also the year the three lawyers proposed a series of *Additions and Amendments to the Civil Code of the State of Louisiana, in Obedience to the*

56 "Preliminary Reports of the Code Commissioners, Project of the Civil Code of 1825", 1 *Louisiana Legal Archives* 1937, p. 29.

57 Alain A. Levasseur, *Louis Casimir Elisabeth Moreau-Lislet: Foster Father of Louisiana Civil Code*, Baton Rouge: LSU Law Center Publications Institute, 1996, pp. 113–141.

58 "Preliminary Reports of the Code Commissioners, Project of the Civil Code of 1825", 1 *Louisiana Legal Archives* 1937, p. 28.

59 Vernon Valentine Palmer, *The lost Translators of 1808 and the Birth of Civil Law in Louisiana*, Athens (GA): University of Georgia Press, 2021, p. 43.

Proposed Resolution of the Legislature of March 14, 1822, by the Jurists commissioned for that Purpose. As the title suggests, this project included both new articles to be added to the code and amendments to existing articles.

While the legislature accepted the updated code, the drafted Commercial Code was rejected. According to a federal directive aimed at simplifying interstate commerce, commercial law was meant to be uniform within the territory of the United States, thus preventing the adoption of state-level trade laws. The Judicial Code of Practice, on the other hand, was adopted on April 12, 1824. It consisted of 1,161 articles divided into two parts: *Of Civil Action*, and *Rules to be Observed in the Prosecution of Civil Action*. The Civil Code was adopted the same day as the Judicial Code of Practice. For the writing and distribution of texts regarding the Civil Code, Moreau-Lislet was the main author of Book I and of the first three chapters of Book III, as well as the likely author of Book II,[60] while Livingston was responsible for the remainder of Book III.[61] As for the printing of the code, it took time and delays were approved in February 1825. Printing was completed on May 20, 1825, three years after the appointment of the revision board.

The code was published under the title *Civil Code of the State of Louisiana*, and went into effect a month later, on June 20, 1825. It consisted of 3,522 articles, a full 1,401 more than the 1808 Digest. Though the authors claimed inspiration from the Napoleonic Code, the amendments and changes to the code served to render its content more Spanish.[62] The 1825 Civil Code was such a success that the legislature of Lower Canada—that is, Québec—in 1857 ordered the drafting of a civil code modeled on the 1825 Civil Code. The Canadian Civil Code ended up as primarily a repeat of the code, though freed of its Spanish provisions.[63]

The 1825 Civil Code was meant to endure in time, but the Civil War was to forever change the morals and social customs of the United States, particularly

60 Agustín Parise, "A Translator's Toolbox: The Law, Moreau-Lislet's Library, and the Presence of multilingual Dictionaries in nineteenth-century Louisiana", 76 *Louisiana Law Review* 2016, pp. 1163–1184.

61 Valentine Vernon Palmer, "The French Connection and the Spanish Perception: Historical and contemporary Debates Evaluation of French Influence in Louisiana Civil Law", 63 *Louisiana Law Review* 2003, pp. 1067–1126.

62 Rodolfo Batiza, "Origins of modern Codification of the Civil Law: The French Experiences and its Implications for Louisiana Law", 56 *Tulane Law Review* 1981, pp. 477–601; Olivier Moréteau and Agustín Parise, "Recodification in Louisiana and Latin America", 83 *Tulane Law Review* 2009, pp. 1103–1162.

63 Edouard Fabre-Surveyer, "The Civil Law in Québec and Louisiana", 1 *Louisiana Law Review* 1939, pp. 649–657.

Southern States such as Louisiana, which had to adapt to changing circumstances. These shifts mandated a revision of the 1825 Civil Code during the period of reconstruction. Before the Civil War, Louisiana had a state economy based primarily on the production of cotton through plantation slavery. The adoption of the 13th Amendment in 1865 abolished slavery and forced the Southern States to revise their laws.[64] After the war, Louisiana was under federal occupation and had to establish new legislation and a new organization of state government. The first step was to revise the state constitution. In 1868, a new constitution in accordance with the principles of the Union was adopted. The legislature then appointed a legislative committee, including Senator John Ray, to complete a revision of state statutes. The act declared that,

> [s]ome suitable person or persons, whose duty it shall be, under the supervision and leadership of said committee, to revise the statutes of the state in a general sense, to simplify their language, to make proper their incongruities, to make up for their deficiencies, to arrange them into a clear order, and to reduce them down to one text, with the view to adopting them as the Revised Statutes of the State.[65]

The order of priority—with statutory revision preceding attention to the code—was surprising in a territory previously dominated by civil law. This was particularly striking since the code sat above the statutes in Louisiana's legal hierarchy. The choice to review the statutes first demonstrated the growing influence of the US government, a common law government, which sought to impose order without attending to Louisiana's unique legal history. Louisiana was seen as just another Southern State that had to be "molded" into the image of the North. The military government therefore chose to ignore the civil law tradition and treat Louisiana like any other common law state.

The revision of the law continued on October 21, 1868, when the legislature approved an act to revise the Civil Code and the Code of Judicial Practice.[66] This revision was necessary to remove the provisions on slavery[67] from the

64 For an overview of the history of American law, see Lawrence M. Friedman, *A History of American Law*, 3rd ed., New York (NY): Simon & Schuster, 2005, pp. 226–235.

65 *1868 Louisiana Act No. 31*. See also A. N. Yiannopoulos, "Two critical Years in the Life of the Louisiana Civil Code: 1870 and 1913", 53 *Louisiana Law Review* 1992, p. 8.

66 Called Code of Practice.

67 In Louisiana, provisions on slavery are found in the Civil Code, but also in the Black Code adopted on June 7, 1806. For more information on the Black Code and Louisiana, see Thomas N. Ingersoll, "Slave Codes and Judicial Practice in New Orleans", 1718–1807, 13 *Law*

codes. John Ray was once more appointed to spearhead the revision. A native of Missouri, Ray became a member of the Louisiana Bar in 1839. He was elected to the House of Representatives in 1844, remaining in office until 1850, and was then elected to the Senate where he served until 1854. From 1854 to 1864, he left politics to take care of his plantation, and it was not until emancipation in 1854 that he became a full-time politician. In 1867 he became a member of the Executive Committee of the National Reconstruction Party of Louisiana, an organization composed only of radical Republicans. The following year, he gained a Senate seat and was nominated for various committees tasked with legal revision, such as that of the civil code. To assist in the revision of the civil code, Ray appointed three lawyers. Isaiah Garrett was responsible for helping to draw up the revision plan, while Franklin Garrett assisted Ray in reviewing the content of the provisions, and Colonel F. A. Hall was brought on mainly as a proofreader.[68] The project was accepted at the general meeting held on December 27, 1869. Ray's salary was defined by the adoption act. He was paid 25,000 dollars for the Revised Statutes, 15,000 dollars for the Civil Code, and 10,000 for the Code of Judicial Practice, signaling his status as the main architect of the Civil Code of 1870.[69]

The report proposing the civil code revision, a rather brief document, was representative of the various problems encountered during the revision process:

> This work has required much labor and thorough acquaintances with the civil code, the statutes of the state, and the decisions of the Supreme Court. It was found impossible to preserve the numbers of the articles of the code as they now exist. Since the adoption of the Code of 1825, the legislature has from time to time not only amended, but also repealed many articles of the code. The abolition of slavery also repealed many more. The provision of the constitution requiring the registry of all privileges and legal mortgages, before they can affect third persons, also introduced important changes. All articles which had been repealed, have been suppressed. It becomes necessary also to correct the translation of

---

and History Review 1995, pp. 23–62; Vernon Valentine Palmer, "The Origins and Authors of the Code Noir", 56 *Louisiana Law Review* 1996, pp. 363–407.

68 John Ray, "Report to the Joint Committee on the Revision of the Civil Code, dated December 27, 1869", in *The Civil Code of the State of Louisiana*, ed. John Ray, Monroe (LA): Office of the 'Louisiana Intelligencer', 1869.

69 A. N. Yiannopoulos, "Two critical Years in the Life of the Louisiana Civil Code: 1870 and 1913", 53 *Louisiana Law Review* 1992, p. 9.

> many articles derived from the Code Napoléon. Many new articles have been introduced, drawn from the legislative enactments since the adoption of the Code of 1825.[70]

The first subject the commissioners underscored was the issue of the sources used to carry out the code's revision. In this civil law state, one of the main innovations was to add the jurisprudence of the Supreme Court as one of the main sources of the new civil code. The Supreme Court's decisions had been reported, used as precedent and studied since 1813, but they had never been used officially as a legal source for the civil code. The incorporation of Supreme Court decisions showcased the slow emergence of what became Louisiana's characteristic hybrid system melding common and civil law. The second important point involved the nature of revisions to the code. The commissioners recognized that it was impossible to keep certain articles, in particular those relating to slavery, as these were not constitutionally authorized. Beyond removing these articles, the code was brought up to date by including amendments passed since 1825. No major legal innovation was announced, and as a result the revision of 1870 is generally regarded as a "technical revision".[71] The Revised Civil Code of Louisiana was adopted without discussion or amendments on March 14, 1870. Though a major change to state law, the revised code garnered scant attention in the major newspapers of the day.[72]

To understand this peculiar revision, it is important to take into consideration the changes that occurred between the 1808 Digest and the Revised Civil Code of Louisiana. For more than 60 years, French culture and heritage had withered. From 1865 on, the vast majority of the population spoke English, not French. To this one must add the influence of common law, which gradually found its way into Louisiana to the point that 1,275 of the 3,556 articles of 1870 are found neither in the Napoleonic Code nor in French doctrine.[73] These changes were long-lasting: the development of law from this code remained stable in the territory without major innovation thereafter. The civil code was

70 John Ray, "Report to the Joint Committee on the Revision of the Civil Code, dated December 27, 1869", in *The Civil Code of the State of Louisiana*, ed. John Ray, Monroe (LA): Office of the 'Louisiana Intelligencer', 1869.

71 A. N. Yiannopoulos, "Two critical Years in the Life of the Louisiana Civil Code: 1870 and 1913", 53 *Louisiana Law Review* 1992, pp. 9–10.

72 *Ibid*, p. 17.

73 A. N. Yiannopoulos, "Requiem for a Civil Code: A commemorative Essay", 78 *Tulane Law Review* 2003, p. 394.

enshrined as the first source of private law in the state. In the words of Mack Barham, despite a growing Americanization of the law,

> Louisiana is proud of its tradition of Roman law not merely by historical loyalty, but because it believes sincerely that the Roman law tradition serves the interests of the people of Louisiana. We also believe that our Romanist system had an influence on the development of US law as a whole.[74]

Indeed, after the establishment of the Revised Civil Code of Louisiana, five states drafted codes during the second half of the nineteenth century.

2.2 Common Law Civil Codes in Nineteenth-Century United States

On the eve of the Civil War, discussion of codification went from a national level to a federal one. Across the United States, several states opted for codification of their private laws with a civil code. At the beginning of the Civil War in 1860, two states—Georgia and New York—undertook this process (2.2.1). Then, following the Civil War, several other states—California, Dakota Territory, Montana, North Dakota, and South Dakota—jumped on the civil code bandwagon (2.2.2).

2.2.1 *The States of Georgia and New York: One Year, Two Civil Codes, Two Models*

In terms of both geography and ideology, Georgia and New York were two diametrically opposed states, each of which stood for a different tradition. However, the two converged on one particular point: they opted for a civil code at the same time without any connection to or communication with one another. The implementation of these projects in the 1860s varied profoundly from one state to the other, in large part because they did not pursue the same type of codification. In Georgia, the code was more a compilation of the law and passed unhindered by the legislature (2.2.1.1), whereas in New York, despite numerous attempts at codification, a civil code was never adopted (2.2.1.2).

---

74 Mack E. Barham, "La Méthodologie du Droit civil de l'État de Louisiane", 27 *Revue internationale de Droit comparé* 1975, pp. 815–816; Olivier Moréteau, "The Future of Civil Codes in France and Louisiana", 2 *Journal of Civil Law Studies* 2009, pp. 39–60.

2.2.1.1 A Successful Codification Compilation: the Code of Georgia

The Georgia Territory was discovered by Sir Walter Raleigh and became an English royal province in 1752. As the largest state in the South, Georgia was meant to block the Spaniards' expansion northward and westward out of Florida.[75] During the colonial period, legislation in the state remained rudimentary, as its development was not a priority. In fact, between 1732 and 1752, only three statutes were adopted in the territory, and, before 1752, only one resident of the state was a lawyer, and he was the governor.[76] The law was also handwritten, as Georgia had no public printers before 1762. Georgia was one of the first US states to obtain statehood on January 2, 1788, becoming the fourth State of the Union. After joining the Union, Georgia's legal development was characterized by a distinctive and continual concern for harmonization of the law. Starting in 1799, the legislature requested that all of the judges in the state should meet yearly to homogenize enforceable law in the territory.[77] This exceptional approach created great stability in Georgia's laws; from an early date, statutes and common law were applied uniformly across the territory, a groundbreaking feat for a young state.[78]

The first gestures towards codification appeared in 1832. Likely influenced by the national codification debate and by the decades-long effort to homogenize the state's law, in that year judge Joseph Lumpkin proposed a general review of the statutes in force in the territory. Nevertheless, at that early date he failed to obtain a majority in support of the initiative.[79] This request for harmonization of the law was repeated many times during the following years by different legal figures, but it was never taken up by the legislature. Despite legislative deadlock, an independent group, including Thomas R. R. Cobb, future editor of the civil code, composed and prepared a digest of statutes, listing the legislation enforceable in the state. These endeavors provided a valuable tool for the

75 Hugh McCall, *History of Georgia, containing brief Sketches of the most remarkable Events, up to the present Day*, Savannah (GA): William T. Williams, 1811. For a complete history of the State of Georgia, see Kenneth Coleman, *A History of Georgia*, 2nd ed., Athens (GA): University of Georgia Press, 1991; Trevor Richard Reese, *Colonial Georgia: A Study in British Imperial Policy in the eighteenth Century*, Athens (GA): University of Georgia Press, 2010; Buddy Sullivan, *Georgia: A State History*, Mount Pleasant (SC): Arcadia Publishing, 2010.

76 *GA C. 1861*, p. iv.

77 Jefferson James Davis, "The Georgia Code of 1863: America's first comprehensive Code", 4 *Journal of Southern Legal History* 1995, p. 8.

78 Warren M. Billings, "Law in colonial America: The Reassessment of early American Legal History", 81 *Michigan Law Review* 1983, pp. 953–962.

79 Joseph Lumpkin, "Law Reform in Georgia—Judge Lumpkin's Report on Law Reform", 7 *Western Law Journal* 1850, pp. 383–391.

legal professions, but they did not solve the core problem.[80] The push for codification was renewed in 1847, when the legislature asked the state's Supreme Court judges to send a report on what they viewed as the defects of the law, and to suggest solutions and give their views on a possible codification of the law.[81] The judges responded by proposing a commission to undertake a revision of the law in order to clarify and streamline its provisions.[82] This request was left unanswered until eleven years later (November 9, 1858) when, under the leadership of assemblyman George A. Gordon, the General Assembly of Georgia passed an act for the drafting of:

> A code, which shall as near as practicable, embrace in a condensed form, the laws of Georgia, whether derived from the common law, the constitution of the state, the statutes of the state, the decisions of the Supreme Court, or the statutes of England of force in this state; and shall be modeled, if practicable, upon the present Code of Alabama. Said code shall be completed within twenty months from the passage of this act; and shall be reported to the General Assembly at its session in eighteen hundred and sixty, in order that when ratified and adopted by them, it may supersede all other laws and decisions and establish fixed and uniform law in the State of Georgia.[83]

The Georgian project was quite ambitious, particularly because it was the first time a common law code had been contemplated. This initiative was not an easy exercise for the drafters of the code, as they were not accustomed to the workings of civil law, in which statutes predominated over common law. The act ordering the drafting of the code also mandated that the Code of Georgia be based on the 1852 Code of Alabama.[84] An early response to the question of choice of this particular model is found in the report to the Bar Association by Richard H. Clark, one of the drafters:

> The law required the commissioners to adopt as a model the [1852] Code [of Alabama]. Alabama is the daughter of Georgia. All her territory was

80 Jefferson James Davis, "The Georgia Code of 1863: America's first comprehensive Code", 4 *Journal of Southern Legal History* 1995, p. 11.

81 *1847 Georgia Laws No. 312.*

82 Erwin J. Surrency, "The Georgia Code of 1863 and its Place in the Codification Movement", 11 *Journal of Southern Legal History* 2003, p. 81.

83 *1858 Georgia Laws No. 95.*

84 *AL C. 1852.*

> derived from Georgia. Georgia furnished much of her early population, and among them some of the leading statesmen.[85]

In addition to the historical connection, this choice is explained by the fact that the Code of Alabama was a document the drafters and Georgia legal population knew well. Even if it had the title of "code", the Code of Alabama was a collection of statutes and revised statutes, and thus the type of work they were used to consulting and implementing in their daily work. The solution suggested a kind of hybrid: as much as the idea of codification was appealing, Georgia's codifiers did not opt for more traditional models such as the Napoleonic Code or the Civil Code of Louisiana. Instead, they chose as their model a code that was not exhaustive like the Napoleonic model, but was nonetheless more closely related to the state's existing laws. Even so, the Georgians pushed the project much further than their Alabaman counterparts.[86] As in Alabama, the statutes had to be organized, rationalized, and selected for the code, but in addition, and in contrast to the Code of Alabama, all the sources of law had to find a place in the code. The sources of law for the code hence were the statutes, the common law, the customs and the legal doctrine. Together, these sources made the Code of Georgia the primary legal source on the matter of private law, and it was this push for comprehensiveness that pushed Georgia to opt for codification over revised statutes. The benefit of building on the Code of Alabama was that the latter provided an improved and more exhaustive version of a model code, without having to refer to Louisiana or Europe and therefore to the Napoleonic Code or the civil tradition. This choice also gave the Code of Georgia its distinctive and innovative format. What was known as the *Code of the State of Georgia* was in fact one document divided into four codes: the Political and Public Organizations of the State, the Civil Code, the Code of Practice, and the Penal Laws.

The act of 1858 appointed three commissioners to draft the code with a compensation maximum of 4,000 dollars. Finding three competent men to volunteer for this project was not easy, and several eminent jurists refused the appointment as they did not support the project.[87] Ultimately, the three men

---

85 Richard H. Clark, "The History of the first Georgia Code", in *Report of the Seventh Annual Meeting of the Georgia Bar Association*, ed. unknown, Atlanta (GA): Jas. P. Harrison & Co., 1890, p. 154.

86 Erwin J. Surrency, "The Georgia Code of 1863 and its Place in the Codification Movement", 11 *Journal of Southern Legal History* 2003, p. 81.

87 In this case, Judge Iverson L. Harris, former Governor Herschel Vespasian Johnson, and Judge John C. Nicoll. See Richard H. Clark, "The History of the first Georgia Code", in

who were appointed were Richard H. Clark, Thomas R. R. Cobb, and David Irwin. Irwin,[88] a 52-year-old lawyer, who had been a judge until 1855, had spent only six months of his life at school. A self-taught lawyer from a poor family, Irwin was first a shoemaker before being elected to the post of court clerk, allowing him to pass the bar. He was then elected senator and judge in 1835. Clark was 35 years old and a county judge at the time of his appointment.[89] He was a recognized lawyer and was admired by members of the legal profession despite his youth. Cobb was also 35 years old, and a brilliant intellectual. Coming from a wealthy family and having grown up on the family plantation, he had graduated with degrees in French and Latin. After a financial setback in the family, however, he turned to law and opened his own law office while also working as a legal journalist. His family fortunes recovered, and, alongside his legal activities, he remained a wealthy plantation owner. In 1859, he opened the doors of his own law school, in Athens, Georgia, which became the University of Georgia Law School.[90] To fellow lawyers, the commissioners appeared pragmatic men, with solid practical sense and the ability to undertake so innovative a project as the creation of the first common law code.

Having other obligations which they refused to abandon, the draftsmen only worked part-time on the code. They first met in Atlanta in 1858 to divide up the work,[91] deciding to work separately on the different parts of the code so they could cover all aspects of the law: civil law, civil procedure, criminal law, and administrative organization. The section on administrative organization was written by Clark and that on civil procedure by Irwin. Cobb, meanwhile, drafted not only the civil code, but also the preliminary remarks and the criminal code.[92] After dividing the work, they had to choose a type of codification for the project. Clark later set out the different forms of codification they had identified before embarking on drafting the code.[93] The first was a

Report of the Seventh Annual Meeting of the Georgia Bar Association, ed. unknown, Atlanta (GA): Jas. P. Harrison & Co., 1890, p. 152.

88 *GA C. 1861*, p. XI.

89 *GA C. 1861*, p. X.

90 Jefferson James Davis, "The Georgia Code of 1863: America's first comprehensive Code", 4 *Journal of Southern Legal History* 1995, pp. 15–17.

91 Erwin J. Surrency, "The Georgia Code of 1863 and its Place in the Codification Movement", 11 *Journal of Southern Legal History* 2003, p. 89.

92 Jefferson James Davis, "The Georgia Code of 1863: America's first comprehensive Code", 4 *Journal of Southern Legal History* 1995, pp. 1–44; Thos F. Green, "Georgia's next Code", 2 *Georgia Bar Association Journal* 1939, p. 16.

93 *Report of the Seventh Annual Meeting of the Georgia Bar Association*, ed. unknown, Atlanta (GA): Jas. P. Harrison & Co., 1890, p. 142.

compilation, which they ultimately chose. This type of codification involved grouping the different sources of law and laws regarding a single legal field within one document, with the goal of being as exhaustive as possible without changing any of the law's content. It was a kind of compilation that affected the shape, rather than the content of the law The second type of codification was "the same as the first in form but going further and making such amendments as are deemed necessary to harmonize and perfect the existing system".[94] The third type of codification allowed them,

> to take a yet greater latitude, and without changing the existing system of laws to add new laws, and to repeal old laws, both in harmony with it, so that the code will meet present exigencies, and so far as possible provide for the future; and this is a real codification.[95]

Then the fourth and last form:

> To these three may be added a fourth, which has been proposed by many Solons of modern times. This is to disregard at will the existing laws, and make a system substantially new, evolved from the brain and conscience of the author, being such as he thinks will be best and wisest for the state.[96]

The Code of Georgia's draftsmen chose the most relevant to them, which was the first one: a classification with the fewest changes possible, as the enabling act requested. This fact explains why the Code of Georgia is not seen as a full codification, as is the case for some of the other codes such as those of New York or Louisiana. One other specificity of this code is that contrary to all the others, it did not reject the common law, but rather the opposite: it was a tool meant to embrace and further cement common law. For all these reasons, there is an ideological gap between the Code of Georgia and the other US codes, because, to use Clark's words, "a code is essentially an organized collection of legal rules",[97] nothing more, nothing less. This vision of a code as a digest ties the Code of Georgia to the first Civil Code of Louisiana, the 1808 Digest. On October 23, 1860, a *Columbus Daily* journalist commented on the

---

94 *Ibid.*

95 *Ibid.*

96 *Ibid.*

97 Jefferson James Davis, "The Georgia Code of 1863: America's first comprehensive Code", 4 *Journal of Southern Legal History* 1995, p. 1.

code "as a most perfect digest of the laws",[98] one comprehensive enough that, "the book will be about as large as Cobb's Digest, now used". In thus arranging and codifying the laws of the state the commissioners endeavored "to keep in view the interest and policy of the legislature".[99]

The change wrought by the civil code did not address the content of the law, but rather its form. The idea was to go further than any other common law states in fortifying written law, while barely altering the substance of existing law.[100] The drafters of the Code of Georgia, and hence of the civil, criminal, political and procedural codes therefore remained cautious when it came to content and legal change. In fact, the civil code was the part of the Code of Georgia which included most of the code's legal innovations. These consisted in minimal changes and mostly pertained to the removal of obsolete legislation in light of new and more current legal rules.[101] At the same meeting in Atlanta in 1858, the commissioners also decided on the following working methodology:

> As each commissioner finished a title, he had two copies sent to each other, so each could examine the work of each, to be prepared with suggestions of changes when we met to pass upon the whole work.[102]

This method of operation, although effective, was exhausting and difficult to achieve, in the words of Clark:

> This making of the first draft, and then two copies, was very laborious, and I had to employ an assistant to make the copies as I proceeded, so that when I was done [with] the original the copies would also be done. We had no shorthand or typewriting then, and every word had to be written in full and with a pen.[103]

---

98 "The Code of Georgia", *Columbus Daily Times*, October 23, 1860, available via the Georgia Historical Newspapers by the Digital Library of Georgia at »https://gahistoricnewspapers.galileo.usg.edu/« and last retrieved August 1, 2023.

99 Jefferson James Davis, "The Georgia Code of 1863: America's first comprehensive Code", 4 *Journal of Southern Legal History* 1995, p. 1.

100 *Ibid*, p. 22.

101 Erwin J. Surrency, "The Georgia Code of 1863 and its Place in the Codification Movement", 11 *Journal of Southern Legal History* 2003, p. 92.

102 *Report of the Seventh Annual Meeting of the Georgia Bar Association*, ed. unknown, Atlanta (GA): Jas. P. Harrison & Co., 1890, p. 153.

103 *Ibid.*

It was in August 1860 that the commissioners met for a second time in Atlanta to review the code as a whole, section by section, working from early morning to late evening.[104] They then presented their work to the legislative oversight committee in Milledgeville, the state capital, in October. The oversight committee was so pleased by the commissioners' work that they issued a report unanimously asking the legislature to adopt the code and advising a global rather than section by section vote. The legislature followed these recommendations, with the House of Representatives adopting the code on November 29 and the Senate on December 18, 1861. The Code of Georgia was set to come into force on January 1, 1862, and a public call for bids went out to printers in January 1861.

With the advent of the Civil War, a revision of the code was required to bring it into line with the new Constitution of the Confederation, as Georgia seceded from the Union in January 1861. These events pushed back the date on which the code would come into force to January 1863.[105]

The *Code of the State of Georgia* was a complete set of codes, together producing a single document divided into four codes: the Political and Public Organizations of the State, the Civil Code, the Code of Practice, and the Penal Laws. The Civil Code itself consisted of 1,575 articles and was divided into nine titles: of people, domestic relations, relations from other contracts, ownership and tenure, property and rights attached thereto, title and transfer mode, offenses or insults to the person or property, and equity.[106]

During the nineteenth century, the 1862 Code of Georgia was revised following the Civil War, first in 1867, and again in 1873. These versions were known as "Irwin's Code", as they were developed by David Irwin, the lawyer and Georgian judge. The code was then revised once more in 1882.[107]

2.2.1.2 An Attempt of Codification Innovation: the Civil Code of New York

The New York Bay was discovered in 1524 by explorer Giovanni da Verrazano, accompanied by Jacques Cartier, both sent by the King of France to explore the Americas. It was, however, only in 1624 that the Dutch settled on the island of Manhattan, founding the New Netherland colony two years later. The

104 Erwin J. Surrency, "The Georgia Code of 1863 and its Place in the Codification Movement", 11 *Journal of Southern Legal History* 2003, p. 90.

105 Jefferson James Davis, "The Georgia Code of 1863: America's first comprehensive Code", 4 *Journal of Southern Legal History* 1995, pp. 21–22.

106 *GA C. 1861.*

107 Archibald Hunt Davis, *An Analysis of the Law of Georgia since the Code of 1882*, Atlanta (GA): Constitution Publishing Company, 1888.

administration of the colony was established with the creation of a government council. As for the administration of justice, the judges were members of the council as well as the captains of the ships present in the harbor when the court was in session. It was in 1664 that the British conquered the New York area. They took the territory from the Dutch and renamed the colony New York in honor of the Duke of York. By winning the territory, the English also repealed Dutch law, replacing it with *The Duke of York's Laws*, a legal compilation prepared specifically for the colony of New York based on English common law and statutes. However, for ten years, the battle for dominion over New York continued, and the territory passed back and forth between the Dutch to the English. It was not until 1674 that New York became a permanent British colony, which it would remain until the war of independence. England's colonial administration of this territory did not differ significantly from that of other colonies. From 1685 on, New York was governed as a Royal Colony, with a governor at its head accompanied by a council, both appointed by the British crown. It also had a representative assembly elected by the people. As for the courts, from 1735 on, they all applied the English common law and legal principles.[108]

After independence and the creation of the United States in 1788, the city of New York became the leading American city virtually overnight. The city served as the US capital from 1785–1790, with George Washington being sworn in as president on the steps of Federal Hall, on Wall Street in April of 1789.[109]

Despite the repeal of the English statutes from the State of New York's legal corpus in 1788, the English common law remained in force, and the 1822 Constitution declared that, "such parts of the common law and the acts of the legislature of the colony of New York would continue unless altered or repealed or found unconstitutional".[110] Despite this conscious choice to keep the English law, dissatisfaction with the law grew,[111] making New York lawyers and New York City the epicenter of the national debate on codification. During the last years of the debate, while interest was decreasing across the rest of the United States, in New York it persisted and thrived. This was likely because the two central participants in the debate were New York lawyers. David Dudley

108 For a complete history of colonial New York, see Michael G. Kammen, *Colonial New York: A History (A History of the American Colonies)*, New York (NY): Scribner, 1975.

109 For a complete history of the State of New York, see Milton M. Klein, *The Empire State: A History of New York*, Ithaca (NY): Cornell University Press, 2005.

110 *Constitution of the State of New York*, 1821.

111 Charles Lincoln, *The Constitutional History of New York from the Beginning of the colonial Period to the Year 1905: Showing the Origin, Development, and Judicial Construction of the Constitution*, Rochester: The Lawyers co-operative Pub. Co., 1906.

Field and James C. Carter kept the debate alive there even after it had petered out elsewhere.[112] After years of discussion on the subject, the Constitutional Convention of 1846 decided to include provisions on codification in the 1846 Constitution of the State of New York, Article 1, Section 17. The article first contained the provisions of the 1822 Constitution on the law enforceable in the territory, while adding that in the next meeting of the legislature they were to appoint a committee of three people,

> to reduce into a written and systematic code the whole body of the law of this state, or so much and such parts thereof as to the said commissioners shall seem practicable and expedient.[113]

So strong was the support for reform of the law and codification among constitutional commission members that they managed to have the codification project included in the part of the constitution devoted to the judiciary. The vote this section of the constitution was far from unanimous. It was adopted with 60 votes in favor and 45 votes against.[114] Small margins in favor of codification at the congressional level reflected broader divisions over codification amongst New Yorkers, also evident in the many subsequent obstacles that arose during the codification effort. The literature produced in the context of the debate about the Field Civil Code was extensive,[115] as the subject elicited heated controversy.

112 Aniceto Masferrer, "The passionate Discussion among Common Law Lawyers about post-bellum American Codification: An Approach to its legal Argumentation", 40 *Arizona State Law Journal* 2008, pp. 173–256.

113 *Constitution of the State of New York*, 1846, Article 1 Section 17.

114 Charles Lincoln, *The Constitutional History of New York from the Beginning of the colonial Period to the Year 1905: Showing the Origin, Development, and Judicial Construction of the Constitution*, Rochester: The Lawyers co-operative Pub. Co., 1906, p. 164.

115 James Carter wrote an emotionally charged pamphlet against the Civil Code in 1884, see James C. Carter, *The proposed Codification of our Common Law*, New York (NY): Evening Post Job Printing Office, 1884. The same year, David Dudley Field answered with his own pamphlet, see David Dudley Field, "A short Response to a long Discourse: An answer to Mr. James C. Carter's Pamphlet on the proposed Codification of our Common Law", 1884. He devoted himself intensively to the codification enterprise, publishing David Dudley Field, *Codification: An Address delivered before the Law Academy of Philadelphia, April 18, 1886*, Philadelphia: Printed for the Law Academy, 1886; *NY Civ. C. 1865*, pp. iii–ix; David Dudley Field, "Codification", 20 *American Law Review* 1886, pp. 1–7; David Dudley Field, *Speeches, Arguments, and miscellaneous Papers*, New York (NY): D. Appleton & Co., 1884; David Dudley Field, "Codification in the United States", 1 *The Juridical Review* 1889, pp. 18–25; David Dudley Field, "Codification—Mr. Field's Answer to Mr. Carter", 14 *Virginia Law Journal* 1890, pp. 1–9. Scholars joined the debate on both sides, Albert Mathews on Carter's

By an act on April 8, 1847, the *Committee for the Codification of New York State Law* was nominated. Two commissions were formed: The *Commissioners on Practice and Pleadings*, working from 1847 to 1850, and the *State Commissioners of the Code*, working from 1847 to 1865. Priority was given to the first commission, which was the one in charge of drafting a code of civil procedure.[116] The leading member of this commission was David Dudley Field (Figure 3), considered the father of the Codes of New York.

Field was the oldest son of a pastor who had lived in Massachusetts since 1819. He began his apprenticeship as a lawyer in 1825 in his hometown before continuing his training six months later in New York, where he was admitted to the bar in 1828. In 1829, he married Lucinda Jane Hopkins, with whom he had two children. In 1836, shortly after the birth of his third child, the newborn and its mother's died. Affected by this tragedy, Field left his children with

---

behalf, see Albert Mathews, "Thoughts on Codification of the Common Law", 1887; and Ludlow Fowler on Field's behalf, see Ludlow Fowler, *Codification in the State of New York*, 2nd ed., New York (NY): Martin B. Brown, 1884. Five years after Field's "short response", Carter delivered an address at the annual meeting of the Virginia Bar Association, see James C. Carter, *The Provinces of the written and unwritten Law*, New York (NY): Banks & Brothers, Law Publishers, 1889; and in 1890, Carter set forth a detailed portrait of the common law in an anti-codification language in another address to the American Bar Association, see James C. Carter, "The Ideal and the Actual in the Law", in *Thirteenth Annual Meeting, August 21, 1890*, ed. American Bar Association, Philadelphia: Dando Printing and Publishing Company, 1890. See also James C. Carter, *Argument of James C. Carter in Opposition to the Bill to Establish a Civil Code before the Senate Judiciary Committee*, Albany: Senate Judiciary Committee, 1887; see further his posthumously published work, James C. Carter, *Law: Its Origin, Growth and Function*, New York (NY): Putnam's Sons, 1907. Many Commentators also took part in the discussion, see George Hoadly, *Codification in the United States: An Address delivered before the Graduating Class at the Sixtieth Anniversary of the Yale Law School on June 24, 1884*, New Haven: Published by the Law Department of Yale College, 1884; Samuel F. Miller, "Codification", 20 *American Law Review* 1886, pp. 315–322; John F. Dillon, "Codification", 20 *American Law Review* 1886, pp. 29–47; George Hoadly, "Codification of the Common Law: Address at the Convention of the American Bar Association", 1888; William Hornblower, "Is Codification of the Law expedient? An Address delivered before the American Social Science Association", 1888; Leonard A. Jones, "Uniformity of Laws through National and Interstate Codification", 28 *American Law Review* 1894, pp. 547–567; R. Floyd Clarke, "The Science of Law and Lawmaking", 1898.

116 *Constitution of the State of New York*, 1846, Article 6 Section 24. This commission has its very own section dedicated to it in the Constitution of 1846, "§24 [Commissioners to revise procedures]—The Legislature, at its first session partner after the adoption of this Constitution, shall provide for the appointment of three commissioners, whose duty it shall be to revise, reform, simplify, and abridge the rules of practice, pleadings, forms and proceedings of the courts of record of this state, and to report thereon to the Legislature, subject to their adoption and modification from time to time."

some close family friends, and left to tour Europe for a year, living in various European capitals and acquiring a close knowledge of European culture which would shape his ideas and opinions. In January of 1837, he left Paris to return to New York, bringing with him the deep influence of his time in France. Soon after, he opened a law practice—specialized primarily in commercial law—that he ran with his brother, Stephen Johnson Field, until the latter departed for California. Fortified by his travels and the European civil law culture he discovered, Field quickly became a supporter of codification. In 1841 he tried unsuccessfully to be elected to the House of Representatives of the State of New York, running on a platform that included strong advocacy for codification.[117] He never stopped practicing law, even as he dedicated his life to codification, as evidenced by the epitaph on his grave:

> He devoted his life to the reform of the law:
> To codify the common law;
> To simplify legal procedure;
> To substitute arbitration for war;
> To bring justice within the reach of all men.[118]

Following his nomination to the commission for drafting the Code of Civil Procedure in 1846, it took him two years to propose a code to the legislature, which he finally did on February 29, 1848. His project was approved on April 12, 1848, coming into force on July 1 of the same year. The Code of Civil Procedure became the emblem of the movement in favor of codification, to the point that, by 1900, more than half of the US states had adopted this Code of Civil Procedure, also known as the Field Code.[119]

The State Commissioners of the Code were responsible for drafting the substantive law codes. A legislative act adopted on April 8, 1847, nominated Reuben H. Walworth, Alvah Worden and John A. Collier as Commissioners to the Code and allocated them 2,000 dollars a year for the duration of the drafting process,

---

117 Philip J. Bergan, Owen M. Fiss, and Charles W. McCurdy, *The Fields and the Law: Essays*, New York (NY): Federal Bar Council, 1986, pp. 21–28.

118 Maurice Eugen Lang, *Codification in the British Empire and America*, Clark (NJ): The Lawbook Exchange, 2005, p. 114.

119 For a comprehensive study on the Code of Civil Procedure, its history, its impact, and its application, see Kellen Funk, *The Lawyer's Code: The Transformation of American Legal Practice, 1828–1938*, Princeton: Princeton University, 2018.

FIGURE 3 David Dudley Field
COURTESY OF THE LIBRARY OF CONGRESS, AVAILABLE AT »HTTPS://WWW.LOC.GOV/ITEM/2017895289//« AND LAST RETRIEVED AUGUST 1, 2023

which was set to take two years.[120] Walworth refused the position and Antony L. Robertson replaced him on May 13, 1847.[121] Collier resigned in January 1848 and was replaced by Seth C. Hawley.[122] All members of the commission were lawyers and were fully acquainted with the law and its shortcomings. The mission entrusted to this commission, however, was not straightforward. In their report to the legislature on April 8, 1849, they explained that the common law and statutes "are distinct in their character and cannot really be assimilated in their general and leading features".[123] Accordingly, they decided to focus only on statutes, undertaking a revision of the first six chapters of the Revised Statutes. The initiative was useful, to a point, as it allowed the statutes to be updated. However, it did not fulfill the mission statement. The commissioners, who were not trained according to the civil law tradition and had no codification experience, found themselves at an impasse and decided to abandon what they felt was an impossible task.[124]

Accordingly, on April 10, 1849, the legislature appointed a new commission, this time comprised by Hawley, Worden, and John C. Spencer. Again, they had to complete their work in a maximum period of two years, that is, by April 8, 1851.[125] This commission would also fail due to the resignation of all of its members. State Governor Hamilton Fish explained the difficulty in his inaugural address in 1850.[126] Aware of the difficulty of the task, he had "offered

120 *Laws of the State of New York, passed at the first Meeting of the seventieth Session of the Legislature, begun and held the fifth Day of January, 1847, at the City of Albany*, 1st vol., Albany: Charles van Benthuysen, 1847, Chapter 59, passed April 8, 1947, at pp. 66–68.

121 *Laws of the State of New York, passed at the first Meeting of the seventieth Session of the Legislature, begun and held the fifth Day of January, 1847, at the City of Albany*, 1st vol., Albany: Charles van Benthuysen, 1847, Chapter 289, passed May 13, 1847, at p. 354.

122 *Laws of the State of New York, passed at the second Meeting of the seventieth Session of the Legislature, begun and held the eight Day of September, 1847, at the City of Albany*, 2nd vol., Albany: Charles van Benthuysen, 1847, Chapter 453, passed December 14, 1847, at p. 579.

123 *First Report of the Commissioners of the Code*, 1st vol., Albany: Weed, Parsons & Co., 1849, p. 3.

124 Maurice Eugen Lang, *Codification in the British Empire and America*, Clark (NJ): The Lawbook Exchange, 2005, p. 135.

125 *Laws of the State of New York, passed at the seventy-second Session of the Legislature, begun the second Day of January, 1849, at the City of Albany*, Albany: Charles van Benthuysen, 1849, Chapter 312, at pp. 453–454.

126 Charles Lincoln, *Messages from the Governors, comprising executive Communications to the Legislature and other Papers relating to Legislation from the Organization of the first Colonial Assembly in 1683 to and including the Year 1906, with Notes*, Albany: J. B. Lyon Company, State Printers, 1909, pp. 488–489. "A law passed last winter, appointed three commissioners of the code to perform the duties specified in the seventeenth section of Article 1 of the Constitution. [...] Two of these commissioners have resigned. The resignation of Mr. Spencer was on the twenty-fifth of June last; that of Mr. Worden took effect on

the appointments to a number of the most eminent jurists of the state. The vacancies, however, still existed".[127] Indeed, he found himself in an impossible situation:

> The principal difficulty in filling the existing vacancies, arises from the inadequacy of the compensation allowed, and the limitation of time compared with the magnitude of the labor to be accomplished. The restriction of time imposed by the existing law is fatal to the accomplishment of the work. The undertaking 'to reduce into a written and systematic code the whole body of the law of this state', is too vast to be accomplished under the pendency of such a pressure, or to be completed by the labors of three men within two years.[128]

The operation and composition of the commission had to be reworked to grant the commissioners more time. Additionally, better financial compensation was required to allow the members to work full time on the project. In reaction to this speech, on April 10, 1850 a law was passed to remove the commission appointed in 1849.[129] The project remained on hold until April 1855, when the Senate tried but failed to approve the appointment of a new commission.[130] In the two subsequent years, Field repeatedly tried to push through the appointment of a new commission for a civil code, not succeeding until 1857.[131] On April 6 of that year, a new law appointed Field, William Curtis Noyes, and Alexander W. Bradford as *Commissioners to the Code*. Having learned from previous failures, the legislature granted them five years, but no remuneration, and requested an annual report to the legislature. The legislature also lay out a plan for the organization of the commissioners' work. They had to divide their work into three parts in order to establish a Political Code, a Criminal Code and a Civil Code, and their work was not to contain

---

the first day of November. Under the power conferred by the law, I have endeavored to fill the vacancies."

127 *Ibid*, p. 489.

128 *Ibid*, pp. 488–489.

129 *Laws of the State of New York, passed at the seventy-third Session of the Legislature, begun the first Day of January, and ended the tenth Day of April, 1850, at the City of Albany*, Albany: Little & Co., Law Booksellers, 1850, Chapter 281, passed April 10, 1850, at pp. 618–619.

130 Mildred V. Coe and Lewis W. Morse, "Chronology of the Development of the David Dudley Field Code", 27 *Cornell Law Quarterly* 1942, p. 244.

131 Maurice Eugen Lang, *Codification in the British Empire and America*, Clark (NJ): The Lawbook Exchange, 2005, p. 136.

any provisions found in the Codes of Procedure.[132] This time, the codification venture succeeded, and on April 10, 1860, the Political Code[133] was presented to the legislature. The lawmakers rejected this first effort, requesting changes to several of the articles which were not to their liking. The arrival of the Civil War did not stop codification and it remained a relevant concern during those troubled times. During his annual address to the legislature in 1861, Governor Reuben E. Fenton reminded lawmakers that,

> The codification of the laws of the state, which was initiated under the state constitution of 1846, and pursued under various acts of the legislature since that time, has been in charge of two boards of commissioners, who have cooperated in the task. I am informed that all the codes, as prepared by the commissioners, will be ready for examination and adoption during your present session.[134]

In 1861, fourteen years after the appointment of the first commission, the first draft project—including a civil code—was presented to the legislature,.[135] After examining the draft codes, the legislature decided in April 1862 to extend the commission until April 1, 1865, to allow the necessary time to adapt and rewrite the codes based on the legislature's concerns. The Penal Code was presented on February 13, 1865, but only adopted in 1881,[136] in parallel with the Code of Criminal Procedure.

As for the Civil Code, the first project was completed on April 5, 1862, and the full version was presented to the legislature on February 13, 1865.[137] It consisted of 2,034 sections and was adopted that same day. However, the governor vetoed it. Researchers suggest that he was under pressure from the Bar Association of

---

132 *Laws of the State of New York, passed at the eightieth Session of the Legislature, begun January sixth, and ended April eighteenth, 1857, at the City of Albany*, 1st vol., Albany: Charles van Benthuysen, 1857, Chapter 266, passed April 6, 1857, at pp. 552–553.

133 *The Political Code of the State of New York: Reported complete by the Commissioners of the Code*, Albany: Weed, Parsons & Co., 1860.

134 Charles Lincoln, *Messages from the Governors, comprising executive Communications to the Legislature and other Papers relating to Legislation from the Organization of the first Colonial Assembly in 1683 to and including the Year 1906, 5 Volumes, with Notes*, 5th vol., Albany: J. B. Lyon Company, State Printers, 1909, pp. 596–597.

135 Shael Herman, "The Fate and the Future of Codification in America", 40 *The American Journal of Legal History* 1996, p. 422.

136 *Laws of the State of New York, passed at the one hundred and fourth Session of the Legislature, begun January fourth, and ended July twenty-third, 1881, at the City of Albany*, 3rd vol., Albany: Weed, Parsons & Co., 1881, Chapter 676, passed July 26, 1881, at p. 1.

137 *NY Civ. C. 1865*.

New York, which itself was under the influence of James C. Carter, the main opponent of Field and his codification project. Field, however, did not give up, fighting ceaselessly for the adoption of the Civil Code. He encouraged the New York representatives to take a leadership role in instituting modern legal reform through codification, which he viewed as a matter,

> of public benefit and state pride. We boast justly that we have inherited from our fathers that English law which proclaims and enforces the rights of men. Let us give ourselves cause to boast also that we have enriched the great inheritance.[138]

It was only in 1878 that he managed to convince the legislature to vote once more on the adoption of his code, but the same scenario repeated itself: the governor vetoed the code, apparently for the same reasons.[139] In 1879, he continued to believe that "despite all [...] obstacles, [...] a codification of our law is not far off".[140] The Civil Code again went before the legislature in 1882, passing for a third time only to be once more blocked by the governor. The Civil Code of New York was rejected definitively on the fourth try in 1887. After years of struggle, Field's optimism finally dimmed, and he warned in 1890 that if his "codes are not accepted, there will be none enacted within this generation".[141] The Civil Code was never again presented to the legislature.

The cause of this "failure" of the Civil Code is still uncertain. Indeed, "the precise cause of the substantial failure of the nineteenth-century codification has been much speculated over".[142] The same pattern occurred each time: the Civil Code was adopted by the legislature, but each time a governor's veto blocked its implementation and final adoption, though none of New York's governors officially explained their decision:[143]

138 David Dudley Field, *Speeches, Arguments, and miscellaneous Papers*, New York (NY): D. Appleton & Co., 1884, p. 374.

139 Maurice Eugen Lang, *Codification in the British Empire and America*, Clark (NJ): The Lawbook Exchange, 2005, pp. 147–148.

140 David Dudley Field, *Speeches, Arguments, and miscellaneous Papers*, New York (NY): D. Appleton & Co., 1884, p. 383.

141 David Dudley Field, "Codification—Mr. Field's Answer to Mr. Carter", 14 *Virginia Law Journal* 1890, p. 9.

142 William B. Fisch, "The Dakota Civil Code: More Notes for an uncelebrated Centennial", 45 *North Dakota Law Review* 1967, p. 53.

143 William Draper Lewis, *Great American Lawyers: The Lives and Influence of Judges and Lawyers who have acquired permanent national Reputation, and have developed Jurisprudence of the United States*, 5th vol., Philadelphia: John C. Winston Co., 1908, p. 125.

> Different explanations have been given to explain why Field's proposed civil code failed: the historical reluctance in American law to enact civil-style codification with the dichotomous structure of the common law; the insufficient methods of developing legislative texts and interpretation; lack of the historical and political circumstances typical of European countries; no need to clarify and to systematize the common law at that moment, since the writings of James Kent and Joseph Story had provided a more stable basis for the common law in the mid-nineteenth century; and, finally, the conservatism of the legal profession.[144]

The best-known and most accepted explanation for this repeated veto was hostility towards codification among members of the New York Bar and the Bar Association of New York.[145] The leaders of the Bar Association and most prominent members of the New York Bar were against codification, and were often common law enthusiasts. It would appear that they used all of their influence and leverage to ensure the Civil Code would never be adopted.[146] Indeed, the supposed failure of the code is usually blamed on Field's most famous opponent, Carter,[147]

144 Aniceto Masferrer, "Defense of the Common Law against postbellum American Codification: Reasonable and fallacious Argumentation", 50 *The American Journal of Legal History* 2008, pp. 416–418; Gunther A. Weiss, "The Enchantment of Codification in the Common-Law World", 25 *Yale Journal of International Law* 2000, pp. 435–532.

145 As demonstrated by this citation, for which see William Hornblower, "Report of the Committee on the Amendment of the Law upon the proposed Civil Codes, Association of the Bar of the City of New York", 1881, pp. 17–18. "This work [the Civil Code] is a good example of what a code ought to be and illustrates on every page the defects and dangers of codification. Thus far our state has been spared the disaster of its enactment into law, for disaster it would be. Defective in arrangement, crude and inconsistent in its statement of principles, glaringly deficient in its definitions, ambiguous and often unintelligible in its language, revolutionary in its changes of existing law, grossly incomplete in some branches, absurdly minute in others, it has all the vices of a code with none of its virtues. There are severe words, but they are not used lightly or without due consideration. Every one of these criticisms could be abundantly justified by quotations and references to the proposed code had I time to give them, or had you patience to hear them."

146 Maurice Eugen Lang, *Codification in the British Empire and America,* Clark (NJ): The Lawbook Exchange, 2005, p. 146.

147 See Chapter Three at 3.4.1. See also Lewis Grossman, "James Coolidge Carter and Mugwump Jurisprudence", 20 *Law and History Review* 2002, pp. 595–598, 614–626; Lewis Grossman, "'From Savigny through Sir Henry Maine': Roscoe Pound's flawed Portrait of James Coolidge Carter's Historical Jurisprudence", 21 *WCL Research Paper Series* 2009, pp. 1–50; Mathias Reimann, "The historical School against Codification: Savigny, Carter, and the defeat of the New York Civil Code", 37 *The American Journal of Comparative Law* 1989, p. 103; Mathias Reimann, *Historische Schule und Common Law. Die deutsche*

> the defeat of Field's Civil Code was due most directly to Carter's ability to persuade [others of] the inexpediency of such legal reform in the context of the examined legal debate. [...] the codification debate was more passionate than scientific. The essence of the matter is that Carter was more persuasive than Field.[148]

One interpretation is that Field expended his political capital on opposition to the Code of Civil Procedure. Another, more theoretical, hypothesis is that, for the adoption of a code to be successful, it needed to be part of a broader political agenda. The Civil Code of New York was advocated by a prominent lawyer, but it was not tied to any major political agenda in the state. Hence, Field did not have enough political weight to carry his code to the finish line. Charles M. Cook[149] thus writes that the burden of codification in New York was shouldered by Field alone. And one man alone could not carry a code. The time demands of the codification process may also have played a role. The code was presented to the legislature eighteen years after the formation of the first commission. In the nearly two decades that had passed, codification had lost some of the appeal and urgency that it possessed in 1846.[150] Part of the issue was that the adoption of the Code of Civil Procedure had resolved many of the main procedural and practical issues of private law facing the state. Private law had indeed become more usable and was governed by clearer rules. Even if the content of private law remained somewhat chaotic, fixing the problem of form seemed to have made reforming content less of a pressing matter. Even in 1846, codification had been a controversial subject, but support only waned in the ensuing years. Finally, one has to bear in mind that the legal profession was trained in common law, and conservatism likely made practitioners reticent to change the system in which they worked on a day-to-day basis.

Whatever the reasons for the failure to adopt the Civil Code of New York, its effect was remarkable in large part because of its exportation to other states. The code was a substantial innovation, able to bridge the traditional divide between common law and civil law so as to make the entire body of statutes

Rechtswissenschaft des 19. Jahrhunderts im amerikanischen Rechtsdenken (Comparative Studies in Continental and Anglo-American Legal History, 4th vol.), Berlin: Duncker & Humblot, 1993, pp. 206–215.

148 Aniceto Masferrer, "Defense of the Common Law against postbellum American Codification: Reasonable and fallacious Argumentation", 50 *The American Journal of Legal History* 2008, p. 419.

149 Charles M. Cook, *The American Codification Movement: A Study of Antebellum Legal Reform (Contributions in Legal Studies)*, Westport (CT): Greenwood Press, 1981, p. 197.

150 "Mr. Justice Brown on Codification", 28 *American Law Review* 1894, p. 258.

clearer and more accessible. Even though this code was rejected repeatedly in Field's home state, it was adopted in other states, with some modifications to suit local characteristics.

2.2.2 *The Afterlives of the Civil Code of New York*

The novelty of the Civil Code of New York was that it created a compelling model of a common law code. Contrary to the Code of Georgia, the codification process in New York was widely publicized and was followed closely by observers in other states, especially after the success of the Code of Civil Procedure. Lawyers in other states saw the code as an effective tool for linking common law and statute law. After the governor's first veto in New York, Field made sure to circulate the code widely across US states and territories. Many of the new states, who were in the process of building their own governing structures, admired the document, and some of them did not hesitate to adopt it. In California, the code was adopted with amendments (2.2.2.1), while in the Dakota Territory and the states that resulted from its division, it was first imported without amendment and later amended, all while building upon the earlier versions (2.2.2.2).

2.2.2.1 The Unanimous Adoption of a Revised Civil Code of New York in California

California was a region only belatedly colonized. Considered a vast and arid territory, it was only in 1765, under the leadership of King Charles III of Spain, that the Spanish made significant inroads up the coast. They assigned these new lands first to the Jesuits, then, after the latter were expelled, to Franciscan monks.[151] In addition to their spiritual mission of conversion, the Spaniards brought Spanish and canon law to the territory.[152] The province known as Alta California[153] came under Mexican rule in 1821, with a consequent shift to Mexican law—an adaptation of Spanish law.[154] During this period, trade developed in the region, resulting in conflicts between the Anglo-American population, who were active in business and accustomed to their own legal tradition, and the local population attached to the Mexican law. To illustrate the difference in traditions between the new tradesmen and the locals, one only

151 Franklin Tuthill, *History of California*, San Francisco: H. H. Bancroft & Co., 1866, pp. 68–69.

152 *Ibid.*

153 Alta California, meaning "High California", was the territory corresponding to the southwest coast of California between San Diego and Los Angeles.

154 John Frost, *History of the State of California, from the Period of the Conquest by Spain, to her Occupation by the United States of America*, Auburn: Derby and Miller, 1853, p. 11.

has to look at how they expected to have conflicts resolved: for the locals, conflicts were resolved by conciliation, with meditation by a village elder, while many residents of other states conducting business in California expected a professional judge.[155] This double standard was detrimental to the development of commerce in the state. California became a US territory following the Mexican-American War. The Treaty of Guadalupe Hidalgo, signed on February 2, 1848, transferred a vast territory in what is now the American Southwest to the United States—including present-day California, New Mexico, and Arizona.[156] California became a US state without ever being under British rule. It was a territory with a strong civil tradition that had never experienced official common law.

In 1849, a committee was appointed by the California legislature to consider the choice of legal system—common or civil law—and, in 1850, in the process of obtaining statehood, California decided to adopt the common law and its provisions insofar as they were in agreement with the state constitution and prior legislative decisions. The "act adopting the common law" declared that,

> [t]he people of the State of California, represented in [the] Senate and Assembly, do enact as follows: The common law of England, so far as it is not repugnant to or inconsistent with the Constitution of the United States, or the constitution or laws of the State of California, shall be the rule of decision in all the courts of this state.[157]

While the Hispanic Bar petitioned for adoption of the civil law system and sought implementation of the Civil Code of Louisiana, the legislature took the route of common law. The common law was chosen for practical as much as ideological reasons: it was not feasible in a single year to draft a complete set of codes which could make the link between the two legal traditions. Having an urgent need for definitive and enforceable legislation to obtain state status, common law appeared to be the easier choice at this time.[158] Some authors

155 Arthur Rolston, "An Uncommon Common Law: Codification and the Development of California Law 1849–1874", 2 *California Legal History Journal* 2007, p. 150.

156 Lawrence M. Friedman, *A History of American Law*, 3rd ed., New York (NY): Simon & Schuster, 2005, p. 236.

157 *The Statutes of California, passed at the first Session of the Legislature, begun the fifteenth Day of December, 1849, and ended the twenty-second day of April, 1850, at the City of Pueblo de San José*, San José: J. Winchester, State Printer, 1850, Chapter 95, passed April 13, 1850, at p. 219.

158 Ralph N. Kleps, "The Revision and Codification of California Statutes", 42 *California Law Review* 1954, p. 766.

also explain the reasoning behind the Constitutional Convention's decision as an expedient way to be recognized as Americans, by choosing a legal framework applied by almost all US states.[159] The common law thus became evidence of a desire to integrate into the new country. However, the adoption of common law did not remove preexisting law, and some Mexican law provisions continued to apply within the State of California. Indeed, no action or act was taken to explicitly remove provisions already in force in the territory.[160] This situation appears to be very similar to what occurred in Louisiana at the time of its purchase by the United States. Similar situations pushed both states to opt for the same solution: a civil code.

In a state accustomed to civil law, adjusting to the common law posed significant difficulties and the traditional problems of the common law system quickly arose: uncertainty, in terms of both content and form, the accumulation of decisions and a lack of accessibility to both practitioners and the public. Added to this was the rapidly increasing population of the state, especially due to the arrival of the "forty-niners", who arrived in mass to prospect for gold after its discovery in 1849. They settled in California, making it the receptacle of a heterogeneous American population. More than 300,000 people decided to emigrate to California after the discovery of the first gold nugget.[161] As a result, no legal tradition was predominant in the state, as the population grew so large and diverse that the question of "pre-existing law" came to be muddied by the overlay of competing legal traditions.[162] Cultural diversity, the continued power of the civil law tradition, and the problems inherent to the newly adopted common law framework, increasingly militated in favor of codification. In this case, experimentation with common law itself created a sense of urgency around the project of codification. The will for a code also reflected the intellectual ambition of California's inhabitants. Californians wanted recognition as more than a wild gold frontier, seeking instead to showcase the state's status as an intellectual center. The population of California was considered to be ruthless, and California was perceived by other US states as a land populated by uncivilized savages without culture. The American philosopher Josiah Royce, at the time a professor at Berkeley, went so far as to proclaim that there was "no philosophy" in California:

---

159 Lewis Grossman, "Codification and the California Mentality", 45 *Hastings Law Journal* 1994, p. 635.

160 *LA Digest 1808.*

161 Lawrence M. Friedman, *A History of American Law*, 3rd ed., New York (NY): Simon & Schuster, 2005, pp. 236–237.

162 *Ibid.*

> From Siskiyou to Ft. Yuma, and from the Golden Gate to the summit of the Sierras there could not be found brains enough [to] accomplish the formation of a single respectable idea that was not a manifest plagiarism.[163]

This vision was shared by other intellectuals, both within and outside of the state, some of whom even blamed the intellectual poverty of the state on its arid climate.[164] Despite these criticisms of California and the "forty-niners", initiatives to improve security proliferated in the state. Local "vigilance committees" emerged, which were responsible for safety and punished behaviors that were harmful to society.[165] Despite these initiatives, California was in need of an intellectual product to prove that it was not a "barbaric" place, but a state that could influence its neighbors and the world. There could be no better proof of Californian culture and intellectual prowess than a common law code showcasing mastery of scientific understanding, rationality, and literary art. Codification appeared as the best way to show their sophistication.[166]

The endeavor began on March 28, 1868, when the legislature appointed a commission to revise the statutes. It consisted of J. B. Harmon, John Currey, and Henry P. Barber,[167]

> whose duty it shall be to meet in the city of San Francisco within three months after the approval of this act and proceed to revise and compile all the law of this state now in force or which may be passed at the seventeenth session of the legislature.[168]

If Section 1 of Chapter 365 seemed only to involve a compilation of statutes, the rest of the act showed a real desire to codify. Indeed, Section 2 states that:

163 Josiah Royce, *The Letters of Josiah Royce*, ed. John Clendenning, Chicago and London: University of Chicago Press, 1970, p. 135.

164 Lawrence M. Friedman, *A History of American Law*, 3rd ed., New York (NY): Simon & Schuster, 2005, p. 624.

165 *Ibid*, pp. 237–240; see also Franklin Tuthill, *History of California*, San Francisco: H. H. Bancroft & Co., 1866, pp. 432–454.

166 Lawrence M. Friedman, *A History of American Law*, 3rd ed., New York (NY): Simon & Schuster, 2005, p. 629.

167 See Appendix 3.

168 *The Statutes of California, passed at the seventeenth Session of the Legislature, 1867–1868*, Sacramento (CA): D. W. Gelwicks, State Printer, 1868, Chapter CCCLXV, approved March 28, 1868, at p. 435.

> Said commission shall continue its session from day to day and from time to time until a complete and thorough revision and compilation of said law [has] been effected and a comprehensive and concise system is prepared and arranged.[169]

In consequence, the commissioners had not only the ability to repeal all provisions they considered inadequate, but also the power to adapt the law. Sections 7 to 9 of the act establishing the commission[170] set out the practical details of the initiative, giving the commissioners until July 1 of the following year to perform their work, for which they were to receive the sum of 400 dollars per month of work, up to a limit of 3,000 dollars. The report of the commissioners was to be final, given the limited time available for revisions. Having worked from April 1868 to December 1869 it was impossible for the commission to complete the task it had been assigned. However, they proposed some amendments to the constitution and an alphabetical arrangement of statutes on about thirty topics.[171] In 1870, the legislature again appointed a specific commission

169 *Ibid.*

170 *Ibid.*

"Sec. 7—Said Commissioners shall receive for their service compensation at the rate of four hundred dollars per month for the time actually engaged in the revision and compilation of the laws as hereinbefore directed; provided, no compensation whatsoever shall be allowed to the Commissioners exceeding the sum of three thousand dollars each until the duties devolving upon them under the provisions of this Act shall have been fully performed and completed by them and reported to the Legislature."

"Sec. 8—On the sworn certificate of all of the Commissioners that the services have been performed, office rent or stationery furnished, the Controller is hereby directed to draw his warrant on the Treasurer at the end of each month for the amount of said certificate so appearing to be due to the parties as above provided, and the Treasurer is directed to pay the same out of any money in the Treasury not otherwise appropriated."

"Sec. 9—The said work of revision and compilation shall be completed by said Commissioners prior to the first day of July, eighteen hundred and sixty-nine, and the Secretary shall deliver the manuscript copy to the State Printer as soon as practicable thereafter. The State Printer shall furnish and deliver four hundred and eighty copies thereof, in bill form, to the Secretary of State, and the Secretary of State shall be and is hereby required to forward one copy thereof to each member of the Senate holder over and each member elect of the Legislature, to each Justice of the Supreme Court, District Judge, County Judge, and District Attorney of this State, prior to the first day of November, eighteen hundred and sixty-nine."

171 Ralph N. Kleps, "The Revision and Codification of California Statutes", 42 *California Law Review* 1954, p. 768.

in charge of drafting a code.[172] The man behind this resolution was none other than Stephen Johnson Field, brother of the New York codifier, David Dudley Field. Led by Charles Lindley,[173] this commission wrote several drafts attempting to reconcile the diverse legal legacy of the California territory. Two years after the first project, in 1872, and after several revisions of the various civil code projects, the most recent version was adopted by both houses without discussion and with a unanimous vote.[174] Strikingly, the code was adopted on March 21,[175] the same date as the Napoleonic Code sixty-eight years earlier. It is unlikely that this date was a coincidence, considering California's desire to prove itself on the national and international stage.

The Civil Code of California[176] fulfilled its role in this regard: it was the first legal-intellectual product to come out of the state. Contemporary Californian authors even went so far as to say that California was the first common law state to adopt a comprehensive set of codes. This claim is questionable given the existence of the Code of Georgia, which was adopted in 1860, preceding California by twelve years. Nevertheless, it was certainly not in California's interest to recall former codes, given its search for intellectual recognition. However, it was the first state to adopt a civil code that was inspired by the Civil Code of New York.

Indeed, the Californian commissioners did not create a code based exclusively on Californian law, instead adapting the Civil Code of New York to their local particularities. The Civil Code of California contained 3,543 provisions, an increase of 1,509 articles over the Field Civil Code. Among those, 385 articles focused directly on issues inherent to California, such as the issues of civil and

---

172 *The Statutes of California, passed at the eighteenth Session of the Legislature, 1869–1870*, Sacramento (CA): D. W. Gelwicks, State Printer, 1870, Chapter DXVI, approved April 4, 1870, at pp. 774–776.

173 Charles Lindley was a judge of Yuba County in 1860. His appointment by Governor Haight as code commissioner would be supported by a list of distinguished Californian lawyers, see Ralph N. Kleps, "The Revision and Codification of California Statutes", 42 *California Law Review* 1954, p. 773.

174 Lewis Grossman, "Codification and the California Mentality", 45 *Hastings Law Journal* 1994, pp. 625–626.

175 *Code civil des Français. Édition originale et seule officielle*, Paris: Imprimerie de la République, 1804; "The Civil Code of the State of California", in *The Codes of California, as amended and in force at the close of the thirty-sixth Session of the Legislature, 1905*, 2nd vol., ed. James M. Kerr, San Francisco: Bender Moss Co., 1908.

176 On the matter, see John Norton Pomeroy, *The true Method of Interpreting the Civil Code*, San Francisco: Bancroft, 1884; John Norton Pomeroy, *The "Civil Code" in California*, New York (NY): West Coast Reporter, 1885; W. H. H. Russel, "California System of Codes", 2 *Michigan Law Journal* 1893, pp. 279–295.

commercial companies, water rights and hydraulic drilling laws.[177] It was as a result of these changes, associated with the need for a code dealing with concrete matters of interest to the state, that the code was adopted unanimously by both houses of the legislature.[178]

Fervor for the code, however, decreased quickly after its implementation. Its death was sealed by a series of articles by Professor John Norton Pomeroy on the code's application. The articles focused specifically on the rules of interpretation of the civil code and argued that the continental vision of a code—as a main source of law—was inapplicable to this code[179] and to the State of California. To Pomeroy, the code must be treated as a mere supplement to the common law system. This rule of interpretation was discussed and expressly adopted by the California Supreme Court in 1888. Immediately after the adoption of the code, a commission was appointed in June 1872 to revise it, and it was amended in 1874.[180] The Civil Code of California was revised again in 1895, following the adoption of the new 1879 Constitution of California, but its rule of interpretation never changed.

2.2.2.2 The Model of the Civil Code of New York in the Dakota Territory

The study of the Dakota Territory and its later subdivisions is challenging due to the scarcity of available sources on this period. Indeed, the "reports" of cases defended before territorial courts are not available before 1867,[181] and only a few sources, such as the Journal of the legislature and that of the Council are available, and even then not for all years.[182]

The Dakota Territory[183] sat at the northern reaches of the Great Plains.[184] This territory became part of the United States by way of the Treaty of Paris,

---

177 *CA Civ. C. 1872*. Division First, Part IV, "Corporations"; Division Second, Part IV, Title VIII, "Water Rights".

178 Lewis Grossman, "Codification and the California Mentality", 45 *Hastings Law Journal* 1994, p. 628.

179 *Ibid.* The question of the rule of interpretation of the Code defined by Pomeroy will be studied fully in Chapter Six at 6.3.2.

180 *The Statutes of California, passed at the twentieth Session of the Legislature, 1873–1874*, Sacramento (CA): G. H. Springer, State Printer, 1874.

181 *Reports of Cases, argued and determined in the Supreme Court of the Territory of Dakota*, Yankton: Bowen & Kingsbury, available for the years 1867–1889.

182 *Council Journal of the Legislative Assembly of the Territory of Dakota*, Yankton: Bowen & Kingsbury, available for the years 1862–1889.

183 For a complete history of the Dakota Territory, see Howard Roberts Lamar, *Dakota Territory 1861–1889: A Study of Frontier Politics*, New Haven and London: Yale University Press, 1956.

184 William Blackburn, "A History of Dakota", 1897, p. 44.

also known as the Louisiana Purchase, in 1803. In fact, the sale included not only the Louisiana Territory, but all French possessions on what is today a US territory. This comprised 2,144,476 square kilometers, corresponding to 529,911,680 acres, at a price of 3 cents per acre, for a total of more than 15 million dollars at the time, or 80 million French francs.[185] This territory was subsequently populated by immigrants from Europe, the US, and Canada in the second half of the nineteenth century. The surge of immigration happened after the Homestead Act of 1862, which opened millions of acres for settlement in the Great Plains. Immigration from Europe was quite varied, with people coming from the British Isles, Germany—including German speaking people from Eastern Europe and the Russians domains, Scandinavia, the Slavic countries and France.[186] The portion of the plains made up by the Dakota Territory saw its population grow from a smattering of Canadians, French, German, and Scandinavian inhabitants to a point where, in 1870, 34% of its population was foreign-born.[187] By 1900, 14% of South Dakota and 10% of North Dakota inhabitants were of German descent, whether first or second generation.[188]

The uncertain context of early settlement created a strong need for codification and for enforceable legislation to unite the distinct cultures. On December 22, 1863, a committee was appointed to examine the 1860 Draft of a Civil Code for the State of New York which had just been sent to the territory.[189] On December 9, 1865, a the legislature consulted the judiciary on any necessary or advisable changes required to adapt the Code of New York to the Dakota Territory.[190] Finally, after the judiciary advised no changes, the Code of New York was adopted unanimously in its original form,[191] and titled *The*

185 Treaty of Paris of May 20, 1803, between France and the United States.

186 William C. Sherman, Playford V. Thorson, and Warren A. Henke, *Plains folk: North Dakota's ethnic History* (*North Dakota centennial Heritage Series*), Fargo (ND): North Dakota Institute for Regional Studies at North Dakota State University, 1986.

187 Frederick C. Luebke, "Ethnic Group Settlement on the Great Plains", 8 *Western Historical Quarterly* 1977, p. 406.

188 *Ibid*, pp. 411–412.

189 "December 22, 1863", in *House Journal, Third Session of the Legislative Assembly of the Territory of Dakota*, Yankton: G. W. Kingsbury, 1864, p. 86.

190 "Judiciary Consultation about Amendments necessary on the Civil Code of New York, December 9, 1865", in *Council Journal, Fifth Session of the Legislative Assembly of the Territory of Dakota*, Yankton: G. W. Kingsbury, 1866, pp. 43–44; "Committee Nomination for judiciary Consultation, December 9, 1865", in *House Journal, Fifth Session of the Legislative Assembly of the Territory of Dakota*, Yankton: G. W. Kingsbury, 1866, p. 48.

191 *Laws, Memorials and Resolutions of the Territory of Dakota, passed at the fifth Session of the Legislative Assembly*, Yankton: G. W. Kingsbury, 1866, pp. 1–2.

Code of the Dakota Territory. The first civil code of the plains went into effect on January 12, 1866.

> A printed copy of the report of the commission containing the civil and penal codes, and also the maritime code, came into the possession of the Supreme Court of the Territory of Dakota, [...] all favorably impressed by the codes prepared by Mr. Field. [...] the legislature of Dakota being the first legislative body to enact and put in operation these excellent laws.[192]

The peculiarity of codification in the Dakota Territory was that the impetus for codification came from judges, especially the Supreme Court, which was the opposite of what happened in New York, where a part of the legal profession pitted itself against codification. A small but influential French heritage, the need for clear legislation and the availability of the existing Code of New York seems to have prompted the legislature to adopt the code without making any changes. Indeed, the new territory showed its emancipation from France by adopting the Civil Code of New York instead of the Napoleonic Code, as had been done in Louisiana. The Code of New York, with its inclusion of common law, was likely chosen to honor population diversity in the territory. However, the problem with the code was precisely that it was adopted without change and was therefore difficult to apply. At the same time, Dakota was in its formative era as a state, and was still engaged in writing a proliferation of new legislation. Thus in 1870, Governor John Burbank requested the creation of a board of review because,

> [r]evision and codification has become a matter of greatest importance, and the difficulty and uncertainty growing out of the present systematic arrangement is well known to all who have occasion to refer to the statutes.[193]

Still undergoing a period of construction, in the years following the adoption of the code the legislature promulgated numerous new laws that were not integrated into the code. This legislative effervescence created confusion in the law. The call of the governor remained unanswered, and the situation worsened. It was not until 1885 that a commission was appointed for the revision of the civil code. The committee worked from 1885 to 1887. It was composed of

192 George W. Kingsbury, *History of Dakota Territory*, 1st vol., Chicago: S. J. Clarke Publishing Co., 1915, p. 430.

193 *Ibid.*

Chief Justice Peter Shannon, Associate Justice Granville Bennett and a lawyer, Bartlett Tripp, assisted by a layman secretary, W. H. H. Beadle. The men were considered a "distinguished array of legal talent".[194]

The Revision of the civil code was almost entirely the responsibility of Judge Shannon.[195] Hailing from Pennsylvania, this son of Irish immigrants was a successful lawyer who was offered and respectfully declined the position of foreign secretary by President Abraham Lincoln before he settled in Dakota. His move to the Dakota Territory was the result of his appointment by President Ulysses S. Grant as Chief Justice of the Dakota Supreme Court in 1873,[196] a position he accepted hoping the Dakotan climate would help him regain his health.[197] He was known as a thoughtful man with great knowledge of the law.

The secretary of the commission confirmed in his memoirs the procedure followed by the commission:

> We had the report of the New York Code Commission upon the entire subject. There was much study and discussion towards a clear understanding of the whole subject, and upon some points, such as corporations, some differences, but all sessions and all final acts where harmonious [...] thus from the former incomplete Code of Dakota, from the Field Report in New York, [Civil] Code of California [...] and original work, grew the full civil code ... Judge Shannon had nearly full charge of the civil code.[198]

Accordingly, the revision of the code changed its source from the New York version to the Californian, one adapted to the local specificities of the territory. The commissioners tasked with the revision were willing to engage in legal innovation which allowed them to effectively tailor the code to the territory. This new version consisted of 2,133 articles, 99 more than the Civil Code of New York and 1,410 fewer than the Civil Code of California. This revised code also adopted recommendations regarding the application of the code. In short, the code had to be understood and interpreted in light of existing law at the time of its adoption. Therefore, this rule of interpretation did not completely

194 *Bismarck Weekly Tribune*, September 23, 1887.

195 William B. Fisch, "The Dakota Civil Code: More Notes for an uncelebrated Centennial", 45 *North Dakota Law Review* 1967, p. 37.

196 Wayne Fanebust, *Outlaw Dakota: The murderous Times and criminal Trials of Frontier Judge Peter C. Shannon*, Sioux Falls: The Center for Western Studies, 2016, p. 54.

197 Estelline Bennett, *Old Deadwood Days*, Santa Barbara: The Narrative Press, 2001, p. 61.

198 *Ibid.*

remove case law or its strength and was thus closer to the Californian rule of application than the European rule.

2.2.2.3 The Continuity of the Civil Code after the Division of Dakota

In 1889 the Federal Government decided to create new states from the Dakota Territory. The Enabling Act of February 22, 1889, was,

> [a]n act to provide for the Division of Dakota into two states [...] Be it enacted by the Senate and House of Representatives of the United States of America in Congress assembled, that the inhabitants of the area of the United States now constituting the territories of Dakota, Montana, and Washington, as to the present described may become the States of North Dakota, South Dakota, Montana, and Washington, respectively, as hereinafter provided.[199]

More precisely, the Dakota Territory was divided at the seventh parallel, creating two states, North Dakota and South Dakota, and adding land to one other state, Montana. The creation of these new states might have provoked discussion of potential changes to the law. However, the new states[200] decided to maintain the law of the Dakota Territory and it took several years for them to acquire their own civil codes.

In North Dakota, the question of drafting a North Dakotan code specific to the new state was central, and as soon as January 1891, the governor stressed its importance. In his inaugural address on January 7, 1891, before the second legislative assembly—and in comments reprinted in multiple newspapers—Governor Andrew H. Burke noted that:

> I am aware that the proper revision and codification of the laws will require much arduous and conscientious labor, demanding the expenditure of a considerable sum of money; but If it be a duty which we owe the people of this state to provide for them a code of laws consistent with our constitution and in harmony with its provisions, I submit that no time

199 "The Enabling Act" [Approved February 22, 1889], in *Laws passed at the second Legislature of the State of South Dakota*, Pierre: Free Press & Co. Publishing, 1891, pp. iii–xiv.

200 Except for the State of Washington, which was mentioned and included in the Enabling Act, but had no territorial link with the Dakota Territory, and simply receiving their statehood under the same act at the same moment.

> should be lost in considering the means by which this obligation may be most effectively and economically discharged.[201]

A first commission was appointed in 1891 to review the statutes. On March 1, 1893, Burke Corbett, George. W. Newton and Charles F. Amidon were asked to, "to codify the laws adopted and revise excluding securities available and other formalities unnecessary the various parts of statutes".[202] Corbett and Amidon were both lawyers who then became judges in Grand Forks and Fargo, respectively, while Newton was an attorney at law who became a poet after his retirement from the law. The committee in question therefore undertook a general revision of codes inherited from the Dakota Territory. The preface of the Code of North Dakota also proclaimed the commission's status as heirs to Jeremy Bentham,[203] being the only commission in the United States to have done so. In their introduction, the commissioners also highlighted the originality and importance of Bentham's work:

> In preparing this revision the commission has undertaken a task of great magnitude and difficulty. It involved much more than a mere compilation or rearrangement of preexisting statutes. Not only have many changes been made in the form of existing law, but in each of the new codes a large number of provisions wholly new in this jurisdiction has been added.[204]

Indeed, the commission went way beyond its powers and did not hesitate to create new provisions while suppressing others, in large part because the commissioners had been tasked with adapting the code to the peculiarities of the territory. The draft was presented to the legislature, which adopted the *Revised Code of the State of North Dakota* in 1895. It consisted of 2,476 Sections, 343 more than in the Revised Civil Code of the Dakota Territory on which they based their work.

For South Dakota, the procedure for revising the Civil Code of the Dakota Territory was longer because the legislature temporarily adopted the Revised Civil Code of the Dakota Territory. Then in 1887, after the adoption by North Dakota of its "revised" code, this code was included in the legislation of the

201 *Bismarck Weekly Tribune*, January 9, 1891; *The Wahpeton Times*, January 15, 1891; *The Hope Pioneer*, January 16, 1891; *Griggs Courier*, January 16, 1891.

202 ND *Rev. C. 1895*, pp. IX–XI.

203 ND *Rev. C. 1895*, p. III.

204 ND *Rev. C. 1895*, p. VII.

State of South Dakota as a replacement for that of the Dakota Territory. It was only in 1901 that a commission was appointed in South Dakota for the revision of the civil code in order to incorporate the changes brought about by the Revised Code of North Dakota and the new South Dakota common law. The committee worked for 2 years and, in 1903, the *Revised Code of the State of South Dakota* was adopted. It consisted of 2,477 Sections, only one more than the Civil Code of North Dakota.

If the States of North Dakota and South Dakota were the result of the Dakota Division in 1889, the case of Montana was more complex.[205] The Montana Territory was created in 1864. It was first carved out of Idaho, and its borders continued to evolve until statehood in 1889,[206] most notably expanding to include the northeastern part of the Dakota Territory in 1872. Montana was governed by the common law, but codification efforts in neighboring Dakota prompted Montanan officials to follow suit. The successive incorporation of parts of Dakota Territory into Montana encouraged this initiative. The idea of codification spread, and during the last meeting of the territorial legislature in 1889, lawmakers voted for codification of the law.[207] At this time codification appeared desirable for two reasons: First, the state of the law was chaotic, and second, Montanan statehood was long overdue. Montanan authorities believed that codification was their chance to show how modern they were, and, as in California, they hoped they could impress the other states with their code.[208] In February 1892 the commission reported on four codes, the Civil Code, Code of Civil Procedure, Political Code, and Penal Code, but the next legislature did not adopt them, occupied as it was by other pressing political matters.[209] The need for a set of code was not urgent as the state had adopted the Codes of the Dakota Territory in 1889, when first granted statehood. In 1894, a new commission was appointed in Montana to amend and improve the code. This version was not adopted at first, but the bar and the legal profession insisted that the need for codification was so great as to recommend adoption of the codes prior to their amendment. This request was granted by the legislature, with one newspaper declaring that the codes had been bolted down like

205 For an overview of the codification process in Montana, see Robert G. Natelson, "Running with the Land in Montana", 51 *Montana Law Review* 1990, pp. 17–93.

206 "The Enabling Act" [Approved February 22, 1889], in *Laws passed at the second Legislature of the State of South Dakota,* Pierre: Free Press & Co. Publishing, 1891, p. ix.

207 Andrew P. Morriss, Scott J. Burnham, and Hon. James C. Nelson, "Debating the Field Civil Code 105 years late", 371 *Montana Law Review* 2000, p. 376.

208 *Ibid.*

209 *Ibid,* p. 377.

a "dose of castor oil".[210] Unlike what occurred in New York, but similar to what happened in the Dakota Territory, the bar supported and promoted codification. They saw it as a way to have a single source of law and a way to give this young state a place in modernity.[211]

The Montana codification process was implemented after it obtained statehood in 1889. The same year, the governor, in his inaugural message, called for the codification of the law. His call was received positively, and a quickly appointed commission would complete all its work in only two and a half years. The commission based its work on the Californian model rather than that of New York. There are several explanations for this choice. The most convincing is that it followed the evolving path of codification nationwide, much like its neighbor, the Dakota Territory, a few years prior. As a starting point, Montana used the most recent code and the one that was considered to be an improved version of the Field Civil Code. What is certain is that the model used was not officially justified by the commissioners, making their reasoning a matter of conjecture. The codes were presented for the first time to the legislature in 1892 and were rejected. They did not find them to be complete enough to supplant the common law.[212] The idea of codification was nevertheless not abandoned. After a revision, the codes were adopted three years later at the fourth state legislature in 1895. The Civil Code of Montana[213] consisted of 4,673 articles, having 1,130 more articles than the Civil Code of California, a fact justified by the state's particular needs.

This brief history of the nineteenth-century US civil codes demonstrates that, in each case, different motivations and circumstances drove codification. All of them are representative of the particular circumstances of given states, and each appears at the end of a long history of legal change. Though developed for different purposes, each of these codes had a similar goal: to improve the condition of the law in their respective states.

---

210 "Code Bill passes", *Daily Independent*, January 26, 1895.

211 Andrew P. Morriss, "'This State will soon have Plenty of Laws'—Lessons from one hundred Years of Codification in Montana", 56 *Montana Law Review* 1995, pp. 362–363.

212 *Ibid*, p. 384.

213 *MT C. & Stat. 1895*.

Bibliography

Barbé-Marbois, M.: *Histoire de la Louisiane et de la Cession de cette Colonie par la France aux États-Unis de l'Amérique septentrionale*, Paris: Imprimerie de Firmin Didot, Imprimeur du Roi, 1829.

Barham, Mack E.: "La Méthodologie du Droit civil de l'État de Louisiane", 27 *Revue internationale de Droit comparé* 1975, pp. 797–816.

Batiza, Rodolfo: "Origins of modern Codification of the Civil Law: The French Experiences and its Implications for Louisiana Law", 56 *Tulane Law Review* 1981, pp. 477–601.

Bennett, Estelline: *Old Deadwood Days*, Santa Barbara: The Narrative Press, 2001.

Bergan, Philip J; Fiss, Owen M.; McCurdy, Charles W.: *The Fields and the Law: Essays*, New York (NY): Federal Bar Council, 1986.

Billings, Warren M.: "Law in colonial America: The Reassessment of early American Legal History", 81 *Michigan Law Review* 1983, pp. 953–962.

Billings, Warren M.: "Louisiana Legal History and its Sources: Needs, Opportunities, and Approaches", in *Louisiana's Legal Heritage*, ed. Edward F. Haas, Pensacola (FL): The Perdido Bay Press, 1983.

Blackburn, William: "A History of Dakota", 1897.

Brown, Everett Somerville: *The Constitutional History of the Louisiana Purchase 1803–1812*, Union (NJ): The Lawbook Exchange, 2000.

Cairns, John W.: *Codification, Transplants and History. Law Reform in Louisiana (1808) and Quebec (1866)*, Clark (NJ): Talbot Publishing, 2015.

Carter, Clarence Edwin: *The Territorial Papers of the United States. Volume IX. The Territory of Orleans 1803–1812*, Washington: United States Government Printing Office, 1940.

Carter, James C.: "The Ideal and the Actual in the Law", in *Thirteenth Annual Meeting, August 21, 1890*, ed. American Bar Association, Philadelphia: Dando Printing and Publishing Company, 1890.

Carter, James C.: *Argument of James C. Carter in Opposition to the Bill to Establish a Civil Code before the Senate Judiciary Committee*, Albany: Senate Judiciary Committee, 1887.

Carter, James C.: *Law: Its Origin, Growth and Function*, New York (NY): Putnam's Sons, 1907.

Carter, James C.: *The proposed Codification of our Common Law*, New York (NY): Evening Post Job Printing Office, 1884.

Carter, James C.: *The Provinces of the written and unwritten Law*, New York (NY): Banks & Brothers, Law Publishers, 1889.

Clark, Richard H.: "The History of the first Georgia Code", in *Report of the Seventh Annual Meeting of the Georgia Bar Association*, ed. unknown, Atlanta (GA): Jas. P. Harrison & Co., 1890.

Clarke, R. Floyd: "The Science of Law and Lawmaking", 1898.

Coe, Mildred V.; Morse, Lewis W.: "Chronology of the Development of the David Dudley Field Code", 27 *Cornell Law Quarterly* 1942, pp. 238–245.

Coleman, Kenneth: *A History of Georgia*, 2nd ed., Athens (GA): University of Georgia Press, 1991.

Cook, Charles M.: *The American Codification Movement: A Study of Antebellum Legal Reform* (*Contributions in Legal Studies*), Westport (CT): Greenwood Press, 1981.

Dargo, George: *Jefferson's Louisiana: Politics and the Clash of Legal Traditions*, Clark (NJ): The Lawbook Exchange, 2009.

Davis, Archibald Hunt: *An Analysis of the Law of Georgia since the Code of 1882*, Atlanta (GA): Constitution Publishing Company, 1888.

Davis, Jefferson James: "The Georgia Code of 1863: America's first comprehensive Code", 4 *Journal of Southern Legal History* 1995, pp. 1–44.

de la Harpe, Bernard: *Journal historique de l'Établissement des Français à la Louisiane*, New Orleans: Paul Renouard, 1831.

Debouchel, Victor: *Histoire de la Louisiane: Depuis les premières Découvertes jusqu'en 1840*, New Orleans: J. F. Leleivre, 1841.

Dillon, John F.: "Codification", 20 *American Law Review* 1886, pp. 29–47.

Fabre-Surveyer, Edouard: "The Civil Law in Québec and Louisiana", 1 *Louisiana Law Review* 1939.

Fanebust, Wayne: *Outlaw Dakota: The murderous Times and criminal Trials of Frontier Judge Peter C. Shannon*, Sioux Falls: The Center for Western Studies, 2016.

Field, David Dudley: "A short Response to a long Discourse: An answer to Mr. James C. Carter's Pamphlet on the proposed Codification of our Common Law", 1884.

Field, David Dudley: "Codification in the United States", 1 *The Juridical Review* 1889, pp. 18–25.

Field, David Dudley: "Codification", 20 American Law Review 1886, pp. 1–7.

Field, David Dudley: "Codification—Mr. Field's Answer to Mr. Carter", 14 *Virginia Law Journal* 1890, pp. 1–9.

Field, David Dudley: *Codification: An Address delivered before the Law Academy of Philadelphia, April 18, 1886*, Philadelphia: Printed for the Law Academy, 1886.

Field, David Dudley: *Speeches, Arguments, and miscellaneous Papers*, New York (NY): D. Appleton & Co., 1884.

Field, David Dudley: *The Civil Code for the State of New York: Reported complete by the Commissioners of the Code*, Albany: Weed, Parsons & Co., 1865.

Fisch, William B.: "The Dakota Civil Code: More Notes for an uncelebrated Centennial", 45 *North Dakota Law Review* 1967, pp. 9–55.

Fontenot, H. Ward: "The Louisiana Judicial System and the Fusion of Cultures", 63 *Louisiana Law Review* 2002, pp. 1149–1160.

Fowler, Ludlow: *Codification in the State of New York*, 2nd ed., New York (NY): Martin B. Brown, 1884.

Friedman, Lawrence M.: *A History of American Law*, 3rd ed., New York (NY): Simon & Schuster, 2005.

Frost, John: *History of the State of California, from the Period of the Conquest by Spain, to her Occupation by the United States of America*, Auburn: Derby and Miller, 1853.

Funk, Kellen: *The Lawyer's Code: The Transformation of American Legal Practice, 1828–1938*, Princeton: Princeton University, 2018.

Gayarré, Charles: *Histoire de la Louisiane*, New Orleans: Imprimé par Magne & Weisse, 1846.

Green, Thos F.: "Georgia's next Code", 2 *Georgia Bar Association Journal* 1939, p. 16.

Grossman, Lewis: "'From Savigny through Sir Henry Maine': Roscoe Pound's flawed Portrait of James Coolidge Carter's Historical Jurisprudence", 21 *WCL Research Paper Series* 2009, pp. 1–50.

Grossman, Lewis: "Codification and the California Mentality", 45 *Hastings Law Journal* 1994, pp. 617–639.

Grossman, Lewis: "James Coolidge Carter and Mugwump Jurisprudence", 20 *Law and History Review* 2002, pp. 577–629.

Gruning, David: "Bayou State Bijuralism: Common Law and Civil Law in Louisiana", 81 *University of Detroit Mercy Law Review* 2003, pp. 437–464.

Gruning, David: "Mapping Society through Law: Louisiana Civil Law recodified", 26 *Lex Electronica* 2021, pp. 34–77.

Herman, Shael: "The Fate and the Future of Codification in America", 40 *The American Journal of Legal History* 1996, pp. 407–437.

Hoadly, George: "Codification of the Common Law: Address at the Convention of the American Bar Association", 1888.

Hoadly, George: *Codification in the United States: An Address delivered before the Graduating Class at the Sixtieth Anniversary of the Yale Law School on June 24, 1884*, New Haven: Published by the Law Department of Yale College, 1884.

Hood Jr., John T.: "The History and Development of the Louisiana Civil Code", 19 *Louisiana Law Review* 1958, pp. 18–33.

Hornblower, William: "Is Codification of the Law expedient? An Address delivered before the American Social Science Association", 1888.

Hornblower, William: "Report of the Committee on the Amendment of the Law upon the proposed Civil Codes, Association of the Bar of the City of New York", 1881.

Ingersoll, Thomas N.: "Slave Codes and Judicial Practice in New Orleans, 1718–1807", 13 *Law and History Review* 1995, pp. 23–62.

Jones, Leonard A.: "Uniformity of Laws through National and Interstate Codification", 28 *American Law Review* 1894, pp. 547–567.

Kammen, Michael G.: *Colonial New York: A History* (*A History of the American Colonies*), New York (NY): Scribner, 1975.

King Frederick II of Prussia: *Œuvres Philosophiques de Frédéric II, Roi de Prusse*, 2nd vol., Berlin: Rodolphe Decker, Imprimeur du Roi, 1848.

Kingsbury, George W.: *History of Dakota Territory*, 1st vol., Chicago: S. J. Clarke Publishing Co., 1915.

Klein, Milton M.: *The Empire State: A History of New York*, Ithaca (NY): Cornell University Press, 2005.

Kleps, Ralph N.: "The Revision and Codification of California Statutes", 42 *California Law Review* 1954, pp. 766–802.

Lamar, Howard Roberts: *Dakota Territory 1861–1889: A Study of Frontier Politics*, New Haven and London: Yale University Press, 1956.

Lang, Maurice Eugen: *Codification in the British Empire and America*, Clark (NJ): The Lawbook Exchange, 2005.

Levasseur, Alain A.: "A 'Civil Law' Lawyer: Louis Casimir Elisabeth Moreau Lislet", 42 *Loyola Law Review* 1996, pp. 203–263.

Levasseur, Alain A.: "The major Periods of Louisiana Legal History", 41 *Loyola Law Review* 1995, pp. 585–628.

Levasseur, Alain A.: *Louis Casimir Elisabeth Moreau-Lislet: Foster Father of Louisiana Civil Code*, Baton Rouge: LSU Law Center Publications Institute, 1996.

Lewis, William Draper: *Great American Lawyers: The Lives and Influence of Judges and Lawyers who have acquired permanent national Reputation, and have developed Jurisprudence of the United States*, 5th vol., Philadelphia: John C. Winston Co., 1908.

Lincoln, Charles: *Messages from the Governors, comprising executive Communications to the Legislature and other Papers relating to Legislation from the Organization of the first Colonial Assembly in 1683 to and including the Year 1906, with Notes*, Albany: J. B. Lyon Company, State Printers, 1909.

Lincoln, Charles: *The Constitutional History of New York from the Beginning of the colonial Period to the Year 1905: Showing the Origin, Development, and Judicial Construction of the Constitution*, Rochester: The Lawyers co-operative Pub. Co., 1906.

Lovett, John A.: "On the Principle of Legal Certainty in the Louisiana Civil Law Tradition: From the Manifesto to the Great Repealing Act and Beyond", 63 *Louisiana Law Review* 2003, pp. 1397–1448.

Lumpkin, Joseph: "Law Reform in Georgia—Judge Lumpkin's Report on Law Reform", 7 *Western Law Journal* 1850, pp. 383–391.

Martin, François-Xavier: *The History of Louisiana from the Earliest Period*, New Orleans: Lyman and Beardslee, 1827.

Masferrer, Aniceto: "Defense of the Common Law against postbellum American Codification: Reasonable and fallacious Argumentation", 50 *The American Journal of Legal History* 2008, pp. 355–430.

Masferrer, Aniceto: "The passionate Discussion among Common Law Lawyers about postbellum American Codification: An Approach to its legal Argumentation", 40 *Arizona State Law Journal* 2008, pp. 173–256.

Mathews, Albert: "Thoughts on Codification of the Common Law", 1887.

McCall, Hugh: *History of Georgia, containing brief Sketches of the most remarkable Events, up to the present Day*, Savannah (GA): William T. Williams, 1811.

Miller, Samuel F.: "Codification", 20 *American Law Review* 1886, pp. 315–322.

Moreau-Lislet, Louis; Carleton, Henry: *Digeste général des Actes de la Législature de la Louisiane passés depuis l'Année 1804 jusqu'en 1827, inclusivement, en force de Loi à cette dernière Époque: Suivi d'un Appendix et d'une Table de Matières*, 1st vol., New Orleans: Benjamin Levy, 1828.

Moreau-Lislet, Louis; Carleton, Henry: *The Laws of Las Siete Partidas which are still in Force in the State of Louisiana*, 1st vol., New Orleans: James McKaraher, 1820.

Moréteau, Olivier: "De Revolutionibus: The Place of the Civil Code in Louisiana and in the Legal Universe", 5 *Journal of Civil Law Studies* 2012, pp. 31–66.

Moréteau, Olivier: "Les Codes Civils de Louisiana dans leurs Ordre naturel", 7 *Les Cahiers Portalis* 2020, pp. 207–223.

Moréteau, Olivier: "The Future of Civil Codes in France and Louisiana", 2 *Journal of Civil Law Studies* 2009, pp. 39–60.

Moréteau, Olivier; Parise, Agustín: "Recodification in Louisiana and Latin America", 83 *Tulane Law Review* 2009, pp. 1103–1162.

Morriss, Andrew P.: "'This State will soon have Plenty of Laws'—Lessons from one hundred Years of Codification in Montana", 56 *Montana Law Review* 1995, pp. 359–450.

Morriss, Andrew P.; Burnham, Scott J.; Nelson, Hon. James C.: "Debating the Field Civil Code 105 years late", 371 *Montana Law Review* 2000, pp. 371–405.

Natelson, Robert G.: "Running with the Land in Montana", 51 *Montana Law Review* 1990, pp. 17–93.

Ostroukh, Asya: The Mystery of the Mixité around the Title of the Louisiana Digest of the Civil Laws of 1808", 62 *Loyola Law Review* 2016, pp. 725–748.

Palmer, Vernon Valentine: "The French Connection and the Spanish Perception: Historical and contemporary Debates Evaluation of French Influence in Louisiana Civil Law", 63 *Louisiana Law Review* 2003, pp. 1067–1126.

Palmer, Vernon Valentine: "The Origins and Authors of the Code Noir", 56 *Louisiana Law Review* 1996, pp. 363–407.

Palmer, Vernon Valentine: "The Quest to implant the Civilian Method in Louisiana: Tracing the Origins of judicial Methodology", 73 *Louisiana Law Review* 2013, pp. 793–819.

Palmer, Vernon Valentine: *The lost Translators of 1808 and the Birth of Civil Law in Louisiana*, Athens (GA): University of Georgia Press, 2021.

Parise, Agustín: "A Translator's Toolbox: The Law, Moreau-Lislet's Library, and the Presence of multilingual Dictionaries in nineteenth-century Louisiana", 76 *Louisiana Law Review* 2016, pp. 1163–1184.

Parise, Agustín: "Codification of the Law in Louisiana: Early nineteenth-century Oscillation between Continental European System and Common Law Systems", 27 *Tulane European & Civil Law Forum* 2012, pp. 133–164.

Parise, Agustín: "Private Law in Louisiana: An Account of Civil Codes, Heritage, and Law Reform", in *The Scope and Structure of Civil Codes* (*Ius Gentium, 32nd vol.*), ed. Julio César Rivera, Dordrecht: Springer, 2013.

Pomeroy, John Norton: *The "Civil Code" in California*, New York (NY): West Coast Reporter, 1885.

Pomeroy, John Norton: *The true Method of Interpreting the Civil Code*, San Francisco: Bancroft, 1884.

Ray, John: "Report to the Joint Committee on the Revision of the Civil Code, dated December 27, 1869", in *The Civil Code of the State of Louisiana*, ed. John Ray, Monroe (LA): Office of the 'Louisiana Intelligencer', 1869.

Reese, Trevor Richard: *Colonial Georgia: A Study in British Imperial Policy in the eighteenth Century*, Athens (GA): University of Georgia Press, 2010.

Reimann, Mathias: "The historical School against Codification: Savigny, Carter, and the defeat of the New York Civil Code", 37 *The American Journal of Comparative Law* 1989, pp. 95–119.

Reimann, Mathias: *Historische Schule und Common Law. Die deutsche Rechtswissenschaft des 19. Jahrhunderts im amerikanischen Rechtsdenken* (*Comparative Studies in Continental and Anglo-American Legal History, 4th vol.*), Berlin: Duncker & Humblot, 1993.

Rolston, Arthur: "An Uncommon Common Law: Codification and the Development of California Law 1849–1874", 2 *California Legal History Journal* 2007, pp. 143–163.

Royce, Josiah: *The Letters of Josiah Royce*, ed. John Clendenning, Chicago and London: University of Chicago Press, 1970.

Russel, W. H. H.: "California System of Codes", 2 *Michigan Law Journal* 1893, pp. 279–295.

Sherman, William C.; Thorson, Playford V.; Henke, Warren A.: *Plainsfolk: North Dakota's ethnic History* (*North Dakota centennial Heritage Series*), Fargo (ND): North Dakota Institute for Regional Studies at North Dakota State University, 1986.

Sullivan, Buddy: *Georgia: A State History*, Mount Pleasant (SC): Arcadia Publishing, 2010.

Surrency, Erwin J.: "The Georgia Code of 1863 and its Place in the Codification Movement", 11 *Journal of Southern Legal History* 2003, pp. 81–106.

Tuthill, Franklin: *History of California*, San Francisco: H. H. Bancroft & Co., 1866.

Vanderlinden, Jacques: "Origins of the French Legal Culture in North America", 2 *LSU Law Center Journal of Civil Law Studies* 2008, pp. 1–38.

Wall, Bennett H.: *Louisiana: A History*, 6th ed., Hoboken (NJ): Wiley-Blackwell, 2013.

Weiss, Gunther A.: "The Enchantment of Codification in the Common-Law World", 25 *Yale Journal of International Law* 2000, pp. 435–532.

Wigmore, John H.: "Louisiana: The Story of its Legal System", 1 *Southern Law Quarterly* 1916, p. 1, reprinted in 90 *Tulane Law Review* 2016, p. 529.

Yiannopoulos, A. N.: "Requiem for a Civil Code: A commemorative Essay", 78 *Tulane Law Review* 2003, pp. 379–410.

Yiannopoulos, A. N.: "The Civil Codes of Louisiana", 1 *Civil Law Commentaries* 2008, pp. 1–23.

Yiannopoulos, A. N.: "Two critical Years in the Life of the Louisiana Civil Code: 1870 and 1913", 53 *Louisiana Law Review* 1992, pp. 5–33.

PART 2

CHAPTER 3

Creating a Fertile Ground for Codification

Codification is the culmination of willful determination by important actors and the coalescing of certain key conditions. All codes are the result of a variety of explicit and implicit influences. An examination of the conditions and multiple influences that undergirded the different civil codes allows for a better understanding of the elements necessary to create fertile grounds for codification.

Codification theorists have worked for years to define the necessary conditions and elements driving codification. In addition to empirical studies, they developed theories about how and when successful codification efforts might take place. For example, John Head, in his article *Code, Culture, Chaos, and Champion*,[1] considers that in order for codification to be implemented in a given country, there needs to be a high regard for written law, a high concentration of political power, and an individual prepared to act as a champion for codification.[2] For Remi Cabrillac in *Les Codifications*,[3] codification can only occur when there is a context of socioeconomic transformation coupled with discontent with the law and political power strong enough to allow for legal transformation. For Bruno Oppetit,[4] codification initiatives tend to occur after a societal crisis. As a result, some authors describe codification as a sort of social contract.[5] These are just a few examples of the numerous factors that researchers throughout the centuries have identified as being the necessary

1 John W. Head, "Codes, Cultures, Chaos and Champions: Common Features of legal Codification Experiences in China, Europe, and North America", 13 *Duke Journal of Comparative & International Law* 2003, p. 11.

2 *Ibid*, p. 7.

3 Rémy Cabrillac, *Les Codifications* (*Droit, Éthique, Société*), Paris: Presses Universitaires de France, 2002, p. 63.

4 Bruno Oppetit, *Essai sur la Codification* (*Droit, Éthique, Société*), Paris: Presses Universitaires de France, 1998.

5 Helmut Coing, *Europäisches Privatrecht*, 2nd vol., Munich: C. H. Beck, 1989, pp. 7–9; Franz Wieacker, *Privatrechtsgeschichte der Neuzeit unter besonderer Berücksichtigung der deutschen Entwicklung* (*Jurisprudenz in Einzeldarstellungen, 7th vol.*), 3rd ed., Göttingen: Vandenhoeck & Ruprecht, 2016, p. 322. For an overview of these theories in codification, see Ingo Kroppenberg and Nikolaus Linder, "Coding the Nation. Codification History from a (Post-)Global Perspective", in *Entanglements in Legal History: Conceptual Approaches* (*Global Perspectives on Legal History, 1st vol.*), ed. Thomas Duve, Frankfurt am Main: Max Planck Institute for European Legal History, 2014, pp. 67–100.

 | DOI:10.1163/9789004689978_006

drivers of codification. However, the question here is that of the elements which created a fertile ground for the codification of private law in the United States.

The most important factors influencing the codification of private law are processes of social and economic change which, in turn, foment legal transformation. Economic and social development within states tends to increase the need for legal certainty and, thus, to positively influence codification. In the US case, most of the codes were implemented after the Civil War, in other words, after society had been transformed to its core, and after the country had been split between North and South. The Civil War was a time of upheaval, and it forced adaptation to a new social reality—the abolition of slavery. Given this fundamental change, some states felt compelled to legislate, and, for some, this meant a civil code. The introduction of a code in a society, "which might have seemed necessary to establish new social rules of the game",[6] is not exclusive to North America. This response to social upheaval has occurred from ancient times to the present day, with a pre-eminent example being the French Civil Code itself which, "after the extreme upheavals and confrontations of the revolutionary period, intended to promote a new social order".[7]

To examine the US cases, this chapter starts with the official legal justifications for codification (3.1). The study then turns to the possible influence of state institutions (3.2), but also human factors such as the impact of immigration or railways (3.3). Finally, the chapter examines what seems to have been the decisive element driving codification in the states, individual jurists. These were not just any jurists, as but men—they were all men—who were devoted to an idea and used their networks and connections to enact it (3.4). The combination of these factors made some states perfect crucibles for efforts to codify private and common law.

3.1 Official Legal Justification behind Codification

Before examining the factors that created suitable ground for codification, it is useful to explore the arguments state officials gave in favor of codification projects. The motivations for codification were generally set forth in the

6 Bruno Oppetit, *Essai sur la Codification* (*Droit, Éthique, Société*), Paris: Presses Universitaires de France, 1998, p. 11. "laquelle il a pu paraitre necessaire de fixer de Nouvelles règles du jeu sociales."

7 *Ibid*, p. 12. "après les bouleversements et affrontements extremes de la période révolutionnaire, a entendu proumouvir un nouvel ordre social."

preliminary reports and prefaces to the codes. First and foremost, the codes were formally listed as a legal solution to previously identified legal problems. One parallel can be drawn here between official justifications and the legal issues pinpointed by the American codification movement. Even if earlier debates over the desirability of codification were not explicitly cited or mentioned, official explanations of codification clearly drew on earlier arguments by pro-codification discussants.

At the terminological level, code commissioners were clear that they had written a "code".[8] By using this term, they clearly indicated their aim to codify common law tradition, rejecting definitions of their projects as mere revisions of statutory law. However, what were their intentions for the codes they produced? Surprisingly, none of them tried to define the concept of code or codification, as if the name itself was not worth a definition or already had a prior meaning accepted by all. In reality it seems that by not defining the term code, they left some room for interpretation of the term. Codification in a nineteenth century common law country was a term which could reference the Justinian Digest as much as the Napoleonic Code, and which could reference a compilation of the law as much as a revision of the law. Not giving a definition in this case allowed the advocates of codification to rally reluctant believers, moderates and radicals alike in favor of their project. While the final results were presented as codes, in their subsequent writing the term "codification" was avoided as much as possible. Their endeavors were qualified instead as "written law" or "put(ting) into writing the law".[9] This idea of putting the law into a written form points to a loose definition of the word "code"—as a document in which the law is written. The rejection of the term codification was more than a practical precaution; the commissioners hoped to eschew ties with Jeremy Bentham and his overly theoretical conception of the term.

As to the necessity of a code, state officials justified their code as being "indispensable"[10] or a "remedy"[11] to legal issues. According to official logic, putting the law into written form was an urgent imperative pertaining to the very foundations of the law. The idea that codification was an indispensable remedy to legal problems arose from the view of codes as the ideal way to structure

8 *GA C. 1861*, p. IV; *NY Civ. C. 1865*, p. II; *DT Rev. C. 1877*, p. III; *ND Rev. C. 1895*, p. XI; *MT C. & Stat. 1895*, p. XVIII; *SD Rev. C. 1903*, p. I.

9 *LA Digest 1808*, p. 12; "Report of the Code Commissioners of the Code for the State of Georgia", in *GA C. 1861*, p. 29; *NY Civ. C. 1865*, p. 24.

10 *LA Digest 1808*, p. 13; "Promulgation Act for the New York Code Commission", in *NY Civ. C. 1865*, p. VII.

11 *LA Civ. C. 1825*, p. 9.

rules. Indeed, one constant justification found in all the civil codes is the question of "organization",[12] which meant that the common goal of all states was to arrange and harmoniously combine the law as a coherent whole, creating a unique source of law for all laws. Accordingly, for the commissioners, the primary purpose of the civil codes was more about form than content. As a structural tool, a code allows for the rearranging of the law according to a scientific method. In fact, since the Napoleonic Code, this process has been known as the rationalization of law. By combining legislation, common law, and various existing legal sources in one place, the code systemized the law thus providing a form of legal certainty. In a code, each provision is part of a coherent whole that is comprehensive and explanatory.[13] This organizational purpose of a code, as a tool for systematizing law, was not taken lightly. Jurists recognized that the endeavor posed, "considerable difficulty in placing the various subjects under their appropriate relative positions".[14] Through the codification process, proponents argued that the law would become more consistent, as texts were brought physically and intellectually closer to each other and no longer dispersed among multiple books.[15]

> The commissioners have endeavored to bring together and arrange in order, all the general rules known to our law upon the subjects contained within the scope of such a code.[16]

In the New York reports, the idea of codification as a compilation project predominates, with the authors expressing intent to organize the mass of laws into a coherent and logical form.[17] Yet, some states, among them Louisiana, Georgia, New York, California, and North Dakota, went further in their ventures, not only organizing the law as requested, but also "reducing" it in the process. Their codification processes aimed to "reduce the legislation into a document"[18] by suppressing irrelevant but still officially enforceable legislation

12 *LA Civ. C. 1825*, p. 10; *GA C. 1861*, p. 12; *NY Civ. C. 1865*, p. xv; *CA Civ. C. 1872*, p. v; *ND Rev. C. 1895*, p. x.

13 Rémy Cabrillac, *Les Codifications* (*Droit, Éthique, Société*), Paris: Presses Universitaires de France, 2002, p. 138.

14 "California Code Commission Reports", in *CA Civ. C. 1872*, p. 2.

15 Brigitte Basdevant and Jean Gaudemet, *Introduction historique au Droit* (*XIIIe–XXe Siècle*), 4th ed., Issy-les-Moulineaux: LGDJ, 2016, p. 373.

16 *NY Civ. C. 1865*, p. III.

17 *LA Digest 1808*, p. 2; *LA Civ. C. 1825*, p. VI; *GA C. 1861*, p. VII; *NY Civ. C. 1865*, p. X; *CA Civ. C. 1872*, p. 22; *ND Rev. C. 1895*, p. II.

18 *LA Rev. Civ. C. 1870*, p. II; *GA C. 1861*, p. VI; *CA Civ. C. 1872*, p. 12.

or laws, thus increasing the legal efficiency of the code. New York, California, and the Dakota Territory took the most ambitious steps in this direction, as their project aimed at the "removal of the common law".[19] Hence, the code's official purpose was to replace the common law by writing and selecting legislation to draft into the code. This aspiration to abolish the common law cannot be found in other states. After the Dakota Division, the resulting states recodified the law, which suggests that they shared the goals of their predecessor. As for Louisiana, this debate never occurred, for there had never been a common law tradition in the state. In contrast, in Georgia, it was made official from the start that the common law was not to be suppressed, but to be supplemented.

Aside from the organizational argument, codes were also justified and promoted as a way to modernize the law. In fact, the second strong explanation used by the commissioners in favor of their codifications was that the code, by selecting and adapting, made the law more modern and relevant to existing society. The codes were a means of adapting law to the new realities of the nineteenth century, whether it was independence, cultural transformation, or the abolition of slavery. Yet, the different codification endeavors did not achieve this goal in the same way. First, some saw the modernization of the law as a way to "settle legal disputes",[20] deciding between various court decisions or statutes on a subject and choosing which one would be enshrined in a code. The idea was to establish legal solutions with maximum permanence. The other way codification worked to modernize the law was to "remove old laws",[21] legal rules that were either no longer in use or obsolete. In Louisiana and North Dakota, modernization also meant creating "new rules"[22] more adapted to society and the principles that governed it, whereas in Georgia, the code,

> attempt[s] no change or alteration in any defined rule of law which had received legislative sanctions or judicial exposition, and to add no principle or policy.[23]

19 *NY Civ. C. 1865*, p. III; *DT Rev. C. 1877*, p. II.

20 *LA Rev. Civ. C. 1870*, p. II; *GA C. 1861*, p. V; *NY Civ. C. 1865*, p. IV; *CA Civ. C. 1872*, p. 15.

21 *LA Digest 1808*, p. VII; *LA Civ. C. 1825*, p. 7; *NY Civ. C. 1865*, p. XI; *CA Civ. C. 1872*, p. 6; *DT Rev. C. 1877*, p. V; *ND Rev. C. 1895*, p. XII; *MT C. & Stat. 1895*, p. 15; *SD Rev. C. 1903*, p. 8.

22 *LA Civ. C. 1825*, p. 4; *ND Rev. C. 1895*, p. X.

23 "Report of the Committee to the General Assembly of the State of Georgia", in *GA C. 1861*, pp. V–IX.

In requesting that the code attempt no change in any rules that had received some form of official sanction, the Georgia legislature intentionally reduced the code-writers ability to create new law. Even so, obsolete rules could still be removed. In Georgia, the idea of changing the law through codification remained unofficial and to see its impact one must read between the lines.

To summarize official justifications for codification, one could simply look at the national debate over codification. The codes provided an indispensable remedy to legal issues by organizing the law, by writing it, thus allowing it to be systematized, reduced, and modernized. While official justifications were fundamental, alone they were not enough to support the codes, and other elements were necessary to bring these ambitions to life.

3.2 State Institutions as Factors Influencing Codification

It is generally accepted among researchers that there is a connection between state institutions and codification.[24] Indeed, the laws established by the legislature are an expression of the political authority that, at some point, required new laws to reinforce its power.[25] One of the first keys to understanding the role of state institutions in US civil codification is contemporary politics. Two institutional questions were central to the outcome of nineteenth century codification projects: first, the question of the age of the states, meaning whether codifying states were young or "already established" (3.2.2). Second is the question of influence by one of the two traditional American political parties (3.2.3). In fact, the various examples of codification throughout the world have shown that a successful code generally begins as an item on a political party's agenda.

Before considering the states themselves, it is essential to briefly consider a possible trailblazing element, namely the impact of the former colonial tradition.

3.2.1 *The Impact of the Colonial Tradition*

What were the colonial legal legacies in the five different codifying territories, Louisiana, Georgia, New York, California, and the Dakotas? Is there a

---

24 Rémy Cabrillac, *Les Codifications* (*Droit, Éthique, Société*), Paris: Presses Universitaires de France, 2002, pp. 160–189; Aude Zaradny, *Codification et État de Droit*, Paris: Université Panthéon-Assas, 2011.

25 Ignazio Castellucci, "Law v. Lex: An Analysis of a Critical Relation in Roman and Civil Law", 8 *Global Jurist* 2008, pp. 1–32.

correlation between the colonial legacy and the codification of private law? A link does appear upon examination of the states' histories. In most cases, the codes were the result of deep historical foundations that had their roots in the colonial heritage of the state. By colonizing the territory, the colonizers brought with them a system of law that left its mark long after they were gone.[26]

The territory of the United States was mainly colonized by three European countries, England, France, and Spain,[27] one common law and two civil law traditions. Even though the thirteen original colonies of the United States came from a common law tradition, Roman law tradition was also found in the territory. Indeed, Spain and France had claimed a sizeable portion of American soil at the establishment of the thirteen colonies and they would remain North American territorial powers into the nineteenth century.

Louisiana[28] and the Dakota Territory,[29] which includes North Dakota, South Dakota, and Eastern Montana, are former French colonies. They all became part of the United States in 1803 through the Treaty of Paris,[30] also known as the Louisiana Purchase. These territories were subject to French law, namely the *Coutume de Paris* and royal legislation, and therefore were part of a civil law system. Among the territories of the American continent colonized by France, Québec—which falls outside the scope of this study—also adopted a civil code.[31] Even though the Dakota Territory was actually scarcely populated

26 *De l'Armorique a l'Amérique de l'indépendance. Deuxième partie du colloque du bicentenaire indépendance américaine 1796–1976 (Annales de Bretagne et des Pays de l'Ouest, 84th vol.)*, Rennes: Linarmor, 1977; Peter de Bolla, *The fourth of July and the Founding of America*, Woodstock (NY): Overlook Press, 2008.

27 Jaap Lintvelt, *Réal Ouellet, and Hub Hermans, Culture et Colonisation en Amérique de Nord: Canada, États-Unis, Mexique = Culture and Colonization in North America: Canada, United States, Mexico (Les Nouveaux Cahiers du CÉLAT)*, Sillery (Québec): Septentrion, 1994, p. 4.

28 For a complete history of colonial Louisiana, see Victor Debouchel, *Histoire de la Louisiane: Depuis les premières Découvertes jusqu'en 1840*, New Orleans: J. F. Leleivre, 1841; Charles Gayarré, *Histoire de la Louisiane*, New Orleans: Imprimé par Magne & Weisse, 1846; Bernard de la Harpe, *Journal historique de l'Établissement des Français à la Louisiane*, New Orleans: Paul Renouard, 1831; François-Xavier Martin, *The History of Louisiana from the Earliest Period*, New Orleans: Lyman and Beardslee, 1827; Bennett H. Wall, *Louisiana: A History*, 6th ed., Hoboken (NJ): Wiley-Blackwell, 2013.

29 William Blackburn, "A History of Dakota", 1897; Howard Roberts Lamar, *Dakota Territory 1861–1889: A Study of Frontier Politics*, New Haven and London: Yale University Press, 1956.

30 Peter J. Kastor and François Weil, *Empires of the Imagination: Transatlantic Histories of the Louisiana Purchase*, Charlottesville: University of Virginia Press, 2009.

31 Edouard L. de Bellefeuille, *Code Civil du Bas-Canada*, Montréal (Québec): C. O. Beauchemin & Valois, Éditeurs, 1866; Paul-André Crépeau, "Réflexions sur la Codification du Droit Privé", 38 *Osgoode Hall Law Journal* 2000, pp. 267–295; Brian J. Young, *The Politics of*

during the early settlement period, French law still found its way there. Fur traders and merchants came to the territory from Canada, whether for commercial reasons or as permanent immigrants, and the influence of the laws they brought with them cannot be denied. The archrival materials at the North Dakota State University (NDSU) on French settlements in the Dakota Territory also highlight the usage of French law and customs in everyday conflict resolution and an array of other legal matters.[32] Though the French community was small, it was not to be neglected. From the accounts of Father William "Bill" C. Sherman, who researched ethnic groups—especially the French—in North Dakota,

> French settlers from Trois Riviere in Québec settled near the junction of the Red River and the Wild Rice in what is now Cass Country. This early date represents a time well before the coming of the railroads and the establishment of any of the present-day North Dakota major towns. Only a handful of river-oriented people were in present day North Dakota. The early French settlers came, not by the cross Canada route for such railroads were non-existent, but rather though the United States via railroad and ultimately Red River cart caravan from St. Paul.[33]

His manuscripts as well as his entire collection of research materials, consisting of maps of French settlements, memoires, journal articles, and genealogies of French settlers, are preserved at the NDSU and demonstrate the location of French settlements and their importance for the region.

> The French in North Dakota have been a quiet people, yet they have every reason to be proud. It was their people who "opened up" the frontier, all the others came later. Their colorful way still brightens the lives of North Dakotas Turtle Mountain Metis residents. Their humble onion soup may not have the popularity of lefse, but it was the delicacy of the first pioneers.[34]

Codification: The lower Canadian Civil Code of 1866, Montréal (Québec): McGill-Queen's University Press, 1994.

32 William C. Sherman, *French Settlement in North Dakota Collection*, MS 335, Institute for Regional Studies, Fargo: North Dakota State University.

33 William C. Sherman, *French Settlement in North Dakota Collection*, MS 335, *Folder 005 Wild Rice*, Institute for Regional Studies, Fargo: North Dakota State University.

34 William C. Sherman, *French Settlement in North Dakota Collection*, MS 335, *Folder 004 Turtle Mountains*, Institute for Regional Studies, Fargo: North Dakota State University.

Aside from the French settlers, Dakota Territory was populated by German and German speaking people, known for their attachment to Roman and written law. No colonial laws were established to apply one tradition over the other, but the people did come with their knowledge, expectations, and customs.

Consequently, it seems that the former French colonies had a tendency towards codification. Overall, five of the eight US civil codes came from a territory with colonial heritage in French and Roman law.

The legacy of civil law is also found in the former Spanish territories that adopted a code.[35] During the colonial period, Georgia[36] saw the arrival of a small number of Spaniards in the sixteenth century,[37] after which it became a British colony. As much as Spaniards had occupied the territory, it can be fairly assumed that their tradition was not instrumental in the legal organization and sources within the territory. California,[38] meanwhile, was a Spanish colony before becoming part of Mexico. Finally, Louisiana was under Spanish dominion from 1763 to 1800. Accordingly, these colonies became accustomed to the workings of civil law.[39] Two of the eight codifying states became familiar with civil law through Spanish influence, which seemed to facilitate the later implementation of codification.

Not every territory that was colonized by France or Spain opted for codification, however. In some states, the tradition of the colonizer was rejected. Though the civil tradition did not necessarily lead to civil codes, however, it nonetheless appears that in most cases codification was drawn from the colonial legacy. Indeed, out of eight states with a civil code, six were former Roman

---

35 Fernando González Roa, *El Carácter de la Legislación colonial española en América (Del México actual, 8th vol.)*, Ciudad de México: Secretaría de Relaciones Exteriores, 1933; Manfred Kossok, *L'Espagne et son Empire d' Amérique: Histoire de Structures politiques, économiques et sociales, 1320–1824*, Paris: Ediciones Hispano Americanas, 1972.

36 For a complete history of the State of Georgia, see Kenneth Coleman, *A History of Georgia*, 2nd ed., Athens (GA): University of Georgia Press, 1991; Trevor Richard Reese, *Colonial Georgia: A Study in British Imperial Policy in the eighteenth Century*, Athens (GA): University of Georgia Press, 2010; Buddy Sullivan, *Georgia: A State History*, Mount Pleasant (SC): Arcadia Publishing, 2010.

37 John E. Worth, "Spanish Exploration", in *New Georgia Encyclopedia*, eds. John C. Inscoe, Edward Hatfield, and Stephanie Devine, Athens (GA): University of Georgia Press, 2020, available at »https://www.georgiaencyclopedia.org/articles/history-archaeology/spanish-exploration/« and last retrieved August 1, 2023.

38 John Frost, *History of the State of California, from the Period of the Conquest by Spain, to her Occupation by the United States of America*, Auburn: Derby and Miller, 1853, p. 102.

39 José María Castán Vázquez, "Reciprocal Influences between the Laws of Spain and Louisiana", 42 *Louisiana Law Review* 1981, pp. 1473–1484; Aniceto Masferrer, "Plurality of Laws, Legal Traditions and Codification in Spain", 4 *Journal of Civil Law Studies* 2011, pp. 419–448.

law colonies.[40] The influence of the colonial tradition is clearly important, especially considering that those states willingly chose codification. These conclusions must be drawn with caution, however, as colonial heritage is not explicitly recognized in any of the documents related to codes, except for in the case of Louisiana. Consequently, the effects of colonial influence remain a matter of interpretation by later historians.

The link between code and colonial tradition is also reflected in the history of codification in the two states with a common law tradition. Georgia has the only civil code which was based on a totally different approach from the other codes, namely that of no change in the law and the expectation that codification would integrate the common law, as well an array of other sources. This code was anathema to efforts to implement civil codification and was the only one never to circulate beyond state borders. While New York[41] was a British colony and was therefore accustomed from the start to common law traditions, it had never been governed by written law. Although a system opposed to the common law may have seemed appealing at times, it would have been hard to implement and required too many changes. This might partially explain why codification was blocked in the state. During the nineteenth century, two other common law states from among the original thirteen British colonies—Massachusetts and South Carolina[42]—studied the possibility of a codification, but in each state the project was rejected at the initial stage of the commission review. The link between colonial tradition and codification therefore seems evident, as only one common law state chose to carry out a codification of their private law.

Colonial heritage thus mattered, and the states that embarked on the path of codification did not do so completely by chance. In most cases, the written law was already a part of their cultural heritage. Since they had already known and lived under a civil law system, codification was less mysterious than it seemed to those who only knew the common law. This familiarity also gave these states greater awareness of the defects of common law, and arguments to support the implementation of a rationalized system of written law. In fact, among the

40 On the influence of Roman law on the American legal system, see José Luis Zamora Manzano, "La Influencia del Derecho romano en Estados Unidos en el ámbito académico y jurisprudencial", 17 *GLOSSAE. European Journal of Legal History* 2020, pp. 722–743.

41 Michael G. Kammen, *Colonial New York: A History* (*A History of the American Colonies*), New York (NY): Scribner, 1975, p. 142.

42 Charles M. Cook, *The American Codification Movement: A Study of Antebellum Legal Reform* (*Contributions in Legal Studies*), Westport (CT): Greenwood Press, 1981, pp. 73–181; George L. Haskins, "Codification of the Law in colonial Massachusetts: A Study in Comparative Law", 30 *Indiana Law Journal* 1954, pp. 1–17.

different states, a strong colonial tradition seems to have played a crucial role in driving codification forward. In Louisiana, it was colonial identity and the desire to preserve French tradition that provided the impetus for codification. In Georgia, it was the longstanding concerns for unity and accessibility of the law dating back to colonial times that drove the codification endeavors. For these two states tradition worked in favor of codes, while in the third state, New York, the old common law identity worked against them.

These colonial traditions also made it possible to distinguish between the codes and to classify them. The legal legacies behind the codes shaped them in terms of both content and form. In the case of the civil law codes, the only civil law codes found in the United States during the nineteenth century were in Louisiana. It is the only territory that, at the time of the adoption of its code, had never experienced any system other than the civil law, either during the French or the Spanish colonial period. Civil law codes are characterized by an application of the code as the sole or main source of law. Additionally, in a pure civil law code, the content of the code primarily follows civil law sources, in this case mainly the Napoleonic Code. Alongside the civil law codes were those of the common law tradition, including the Civil Codes of New York, the only state in this study that never experienced any other legal traditions, and the Code of Georgia. Those two states alone created two very distinct common law codification models. Finally, there were those states that had experienced both civil and common law traditions. These included California and the Dakota Territory as well as its subdivisions. The peculiarity of these states is that their codes were a hybrid between the two legal systems, with some aspects of their codes coming from the civil law tradition, while most of the content was intended to derive from common law.

These classifications are useful in trying to apprehend the nineteenth-century US civil codes, but the colonial tradition is only one factor amongst many others influencing the codification of private law. In other words, the colonial tradition is not sufficient on its own to explain the choice for codification.

3.2.2 *The Direct Link between Codification and the Age of the State*

Analysis of the date of statehood[43] and the adoption of codes allows us to determine whether codification tended to occur in long-established or younger states (Table 1). In "old" states, codes were often the result of discontentment

43 For more information on the obtainment of statehood, see Michael Grossberg and Christopher Tomlins, *The long nineteenth Century (1789–1920)*, Cambridge: Cambridge University Press, 2008.

TABLE 1 The Obtainment of Statehood and Adoption of Civil Code by State

State	Obtainment of Statehood	Adoption of Civil Code
Louisiana	1812	1808
New York	1788	1860
Georgia	1788	1860
California	1850	1872
Dakota Territory	Division of the Territory	1865 / 1877
North Dakota	1889	1895
Montana	1889	1895
South Dakota	1889	1903

with the law, while in the case of young states, codification was one choice amongst others during a formative period, and therefore represents a part of the process founding the state's basic governing structures.[44]

Examining dates of statehood shows that most codifying states were young and did not have a long-lasting legal tradition. This was true in all states, in fact, except for Georgia. This seems explainable by the fact that young states were in search of a state identity, or at least did not have a strong pre-existing identity that could block codification. Especially in the common law states, codifications appeared as a foundational and deliberate choice.

Further detailed examination also shows that two of the eight states codifying their private law—Louisiana and the Dakota Territory—adopted their codes before they were even granted statehood. In these cases, the code became a fundamental element of territorial identity. A territory could operate without a final determination of statehood; however, it could not function without law. In both places, one of the first battles fought by inhabitants concerned the choice of legal system. In the case of Louisiana, the result was more turbulent than in the Dakota Territory, where the adoption of the code went smoothly. It is notable that in these two territories the civil code was adopted even before the procedural codes, thus making it a fundamental part of the identity of the

44 Rémy Cabrillac, *Les Codifications* (*Droit, Éthique, Société*), Paris: Presses Universitaires de France, 2002, pp. 169–171.

territories. Further, it is striking that, in both cases, the code was drafted before a state constitution, evidence of its legal and symbolic influence.

As for the remaining six states, four of them—California, Montana, North Dakota, and South Dakota—were young states, less than fifteen years old, and still under construction. California adopted its code twelve years after obtaining statehood; for Montana and North Dakota, the code came after six years. Finally, in South Dakota, a state code was adopted fourteen years after obtaining statehood, although it had a civil code from the start—first that of the Dakota Territory and later that of North Dakota.

In North and South Dakota, where the population had already experienced a civil code before statehood as part of the Dakota Territory, the civil code—whether it arrived before or after statehood—became a seminal part of the state's founding. These codes were adopted during the creation phase of each states' institutions and laws, at a time when the legal system was flexible enough to adopt them. The creative outpouring that accompanies early growth in a young state seems to facilitate the implementation of new legal tools. This explains why some states turned to the civil law and therefore a code rather than or in addition to the common law. This choice was facilitated by the fact that these states had no stable and ancient institution that would block the choice of codification, as was the case in New York with the Bar Association of New York. Even though it created the most widely imitated civil code, the State of New York itself was never successful in adopting its own creation. This old state, one of the first in the United States, was blocked by its very own traditions and institutions.

However, every rule has exceptions, and one long-established state did adopt a civil code. Georgia's adoption of a code does not seem consistent with the other codes in terms of the age of the state, having adopted its code after 72 years of existence Indeed, this made it one of the oldest states with a civil code. This decision surprised many including one of the code's editors, who wrote that,

> When the legislature of 1858 made provision for a Code, and a Code that would be such an innovation, the whole state was surprised. Indeed, the legislature was itself taken by surprise.[45]

---

45 Richard H. Clark, "The History of the first Georgia Code", in *Report of the Seventh Annual Meeting of the Georgia Bar Association*, ed. unknown, Atlanta (GA): Jas. P. Harrison & Co., 1890, p. 1.

Despite this apparent surprise, the Code of Georgia was the culmination of concerns about the law that had circulated since the state's creation. Georgia's desire for a defined and clear state law took precedence over the age of the state and appears, in this case, to have been enough to justify the adoption of the code. As discussed in the section on Georgia's history, from the start, there was a strong concern within state institutions for unity and consistency in the law. For Georgian officials, the law had to be the same throughout the state to ensure the most perfect justice possible. Therefore, codification was a tool for the unification of law. The Georgian code might also be interpreted as an act of separation from both the Federal Government and the tradition of common law it had come to represent. Indeed, the Code of Georgia was adopted at the dawn of the Civil War, at a time of tension and separation between the Northern and Southern States.

Nevertheless, not all new states chose the process of codification, for if they had, all states, or at least most of them, would have adopted a civil code. Being a young state was undeniably a facilitating factor toward the implementation of codification, but again, this alone was not enough, necessitating other external factors and motives.

3.2.3 *Civil Codes and Political Parties*

The history of codification shows that, in order to be implemented, a code depends on the existence of a strong political power.[46] The content of draft codes has an inherently political function,[47] as legislation is often viewed as a means to implement a political agenda.[48] The role of politics in civil codification can be seen by looking at which political party was in power at the time of the adoption of a state's codes and at the moment of appointment and the political orientation of the commission. Were codes tied to the political project of one of the two major US political parties? If so, were they associated more regularly with one party than another?

During the nineteenth century, the political landscape of the United States developed from the very first party system, organized into Federalist and Democratic-Republican parties, to Jacksonian Democrats and Whigs and, finally, to the Democrat-Republican divide which emerged on the eve of the

46 Jean-Louis Halpérin, *L'impossible Code Civil* (*Histoires*), Paris: Presses Universitaires de France, 1992.

47 Rémy Cabrillac, "Les Enjeux de la Codification en France", 46 *Les Cahiers du Droit* 2005, pp. 533–545.

48 Catherine Skinner, "Codification and the Common Law", 11 *European Journal of Law Reform* 2009, p. 232.

Civil War and continues in the present.[49] Policies varied by party, however the Jacksonian Party was the only one explicitly involved in codification, with its members joining of the national debate over codification as advocates of codes. Growing out of the Jeffersonian Party and sometimes referred to as the Democratic-Republican party before simply becoming the Democratic party, the Jacksonian Party gained wild popularity across the national territory. Before the Civil War, the Democrats[50]were supporters of slavery and worked against the Federalists[51] but were also a party that welcomed new immigrants and opposed Federal Government programs such as national banking.[52] Until 1854, the United States had, at least on the surface, two parties opposed to each other, with the Democrats in power and the Whigs in opposition.[53] The Republican Party was created between 1854 and 1856, following the collapse of the Whigs.[54] The core of Republican party ideology during the antebellum period was sympathy for abolitionism as well as the protection of American businesses.[55] A rapid examination of these two political parties' doctrines shows that, following the decline of the Jacksonian Party, codification in the United States was not part of the agenda of a single party but rather received some support from both main parties. Actually, Democrats supported codification as it allowed the law to be subjected to democratic approval through the legislature, while Republicans supported it for its limitation of the courts' power to creatively interpret law.

Here I have assembled research data on the effect of political parties on codification. The data examines the political orientation of the three institutions that held influence over codes in individual states, namely, the Governor, the state House of Representatives, and the state Senate, in order

---

49 David M. Brady and Mathew D. McCubbins, *Party, Process, and Political Change in Congress: Further new Perspectives on the History of Congress (Social Science History)*, 2nd vol., Stanford (CA): Stanford University Press, 2007, p. 3.

50 For an overview of the history of the Democratic Party, see Jules Witcover, *Party of the People: A History of the Democrats*, 1st ed., New York (NY): Random House, 2003.

51 Marjorie Randon Hershey, *Party Politics in America*, 18th ed., New York (NY): Routledge, 2021, p. 40.

52 *Ibid*, p. 18.

53 Lewis L. Gould, *The Republicans: A History of the Grand Old Party*, Oxford and New York (NY): Oxford University Press, 2014, p. 10.

54 For an overview of the history of the Republican Party, see Eric Foner, *Free Soil, free Labor, free Men: The Ideology of the Republican Party before the Civil War*, Oxford and New York (NY): Oxford University Press, 1995; Lewis L. Gould, *The Republicans: A History of the Grand Old Party*, Oxford and New York (NY): Oxford University Press, 2014.

55 Lewis L. Gould, *The Republicans: A History of the Grand Old Party*, Oxford and New York (NY): Oxford University Press, 2014, p. 37.

to determine the political majority at work within each institution. The survey data reveals that, in cases where codification was proposed, the chambers always worked together, allowing to speak simply of the "legislature". Thus, on analysis, they were grouped under the term "legislature". The political orientation of the selected institutions for each state was examined first at the time of the commission appointment—which coincided with the moment the state decided to opt for the codification of private law. For Louisiana, this was 1806, 1822, and 1868.[56] For Georgia, it was 1858.[57] For New York, it was 1847, 1849, and 1857.[58] For California it was 1870.[59] For Montana, it was 1889.[60] For North Dakota, it was 1893.[61] Finally, for South Dakota it was

56 For a list of members of the Louisiana legislature, see *Membership in the Louisiana House of Representatives, 1812–2024*, Baton Rouge: Louisiana House of Representatives, 2022, available at »https://house.louisiana.gov/h_pdfdocs/housemembership_history_current.pdf« and last retrieved August 1, 2023; *Membership in the Louisiana State Senate, 1880–2024*, Baton Rouge: Louisiana State Senate, 2020, available at »https://senate.la.gov/documents/membership/1880membership.pdf« and last retrieved August 1, 2023. For a list of Louisiana governors, including their political affiliation and a short biographical entry, see the *Archives of the National Governors Association*, available at »https://www.nga.org/former-governors/louisiana/« and last retrieved August 1, 2023.

57 For information on the Georgia legislature, see the *Journals of the General Assembly*, provided by the Digital Library of Georgia, available at »https://dlg.usg.edu« and last retrieved August 1, 2023. For a list of Georgia governors, including their political affiliation and a short biographical entry, see the *Archives of the National Governors Association*, available at »https://www.nga.org/former-governors/georgia/« and last retrieved August 1, 2023.

58 For a list of members of the New York legislature, see S. C. Hutchins, *Civil List and Forms of Government of the Colony and State of New York, compiled from official and authentic Sources*, Albany: Weed, Parsons, & Co., 1868. For a list of New York governors, including their political affiliation and a short biographical entry, see the *Archives of the National Governors Association*, available at »https://www.nga.org/former-governors/new-york/« and last retrieved August 1, 2023.

59 For a list of members of the California legislature, see the *California State Assembly Journals*, provided by the California State Assembly, available at »https://clerk.assembly.ca.gov/archive-list/« and last retrieved August 1, 2023. For a list of California governors, including their political affiliation and a short biographical entry, see the *Archives of the National Governors Association*, available at »https://www.nga.org/former-governors/california/« and last retrieved August 1, 2023.

60 For the majority and minority party numbers of the Montana legislature, see the listing provided by the Montana State Legislature, available at »https://leg.mt.gov/civic-education/facts/party-control/« and last retrieved August 1, 2023. For a list of Montana governors, including their political affiliation and a short biographical entry, see the *Archives of the National Governors Association*, available at »https://www.nga.org/former-governors/montana/« and last retrieved August 1, 2023.

61 For information on the North Dakota legislature, see the listing of General Assemblies provided by the North Dakota Legislative Branch, available at »https://ndlegis.gov/assembly«

1901.[62] No data was collected for the appointment of a commission in the Dakota Territory, since the state directly adopted the Civil Code of New York in 1865. The only commission that existed in Dakota was created in 1877, and it worked towards revision of the code. As a result, it did not fully fulfill the same political role and agenda as commissions in the other states. The orientation of the same institutions was examined again at the moment the codes were adopted: 1808, 1825, and 1870 in Louisiana;[63] 1860 and 1865 in New York;[64] 1860 in Georgia;[65] 1872 in California;[66] 1877 in the Dakota Territory;[67] 1895 in

---

and last retrieved August 1, 2023. For a list of North Dakota governors, including their political affiliation and a short biographical entry, see the *Archives of the National Governors Association*, available at »https://www.nga.org/former-governors/north-dakota/« and last retrieved August 1, 2023.

62 For a list of members of the South Dakota legislature, see the listing provided by the South Dakota Research Council, available at »https://sdlegislature.gov/legislators/historical/« and last retrieved August 1, 2023. For a list of South Dakota governors, including their political affiliation and a short biographical entry, see the *Archives of the National Governors Association*, available at »https://www.nga.org/former-governors/south-dakota/« and last retrieved August 1, 2023.

63 *Laws, Memorials and Resolutions of the Territory of Dakota, passed at the fifth Session of the Legislative Assembly*, Yankton: G. W. Kingsbury, 1866, p. 361.

64 For a list of members of the Louisiana legislature, see *Membership in the Louisiana House of Representatives, 1812–2024*, Baton Rouge: Louisiana House of Representatives, 2022, available at »https://house.louisiana.gov/h_pdfdocs/housemembership_history_current.pdf« and last retrieved August 1, 2023; *Membership in the Louisiana State Senate, 1880–2024*, Baton Rouge: Louisiana State Senate, 2020, available at »https://senate.la.gov/documents/membership/1880membership.pdf« and last retrieved August 1, 2023. For a list of Louisiana governors, including their political affiliation and a short biographical entry, see the *Archives of the National Governors Association*, available at »https://www.nga.org/former-governors/louisiana/« and last retrieved August 1, 2023.

65 For information on the Georgia legislature, see the *Journals of the General Assembly*, provided by the Digital Library of Georgia, available at »https://dlg.usg.edu« and last retrieved August 1, 2023. For a list of Georgia governors, including their political affiliation and a short biographical entry, see the *Archives of the National Governors Association*, available at »https://www.nga.org/former-governors/georgia/« and last retrieved August 1, 2023.

66 For a list of members of the New York legislature, see S. C. Hutchins, *Civil List and Forms of Government of the Colony and State of New York, compiled from official and authentic Sources*, Albany: Weed, Parsons, & Co., 1868. For a list of New York governors, including their political affiliation and a short biographical entry, see the *Archives of the National Governors Association*, available at »https://www.nga.org/former-governors/new-york/« and last retrieved August 1, 2023.

67 For a list of members of the California legislature, see the *California State Assembly Journals*, provided by the California State Assembly, available at »https://clerk.assembly.ca.gov/archive-list/« and last retrieved August 1, 2023. For a list of California governors, including their political affiliation and a short biographical entry, see the *Archives*

Montana[68] and North Dakota;[69] and 1903 in South Dakota.[70] Comprehensive review of all the data gathered concerning the decision to codify, regardless of the code or period, has demonstrated a balance of political orientation, with no party emerging as the clear party of codification.

Study of state cases shows that, among governors supporting codification, 42% were Republicans, 36% were Democrats, and 21% belonged to the Democratic-Republican party.[71] However, this third party was found in Louisiana only in 1808 and 1825. For the legislatures, 52% were Republicans, 21% were Democrats, and 26% had a different political orientation.[72] Admittedly, 52% of the legislatures had a Republican majority. However, this remained a small percentage and did not mean that codification was a central part of the Republican agenda, especially considering the composition of the commissions appointed to draft the codes, which will be examined later. Consequently, the distribution of the political parties within institutions did not have clear consequences for the codification process. Here the case of New York is notable, as the code was adopted and blocked multiple times by Republican or Democratic legislatures and governors, with both parties adopting and rejecting codification at different moments.

---

of the National Governors Association, available at »https://www.nga.org/former-governors/california/« and last retrieved August 1, 2023.

68 For the majority and minority party numbers of the Montana legislature, see the listing provided by the Montana State Legislature, available at »https://leg.mt.gov/civic-education/facts/party-control/« and last retrieved August 1, 2023. For a list of Montana governors, including their political affiliation and a short biographical entry, see the *Archives of the National Governors Association*, available at »https://www.nga.org/former-governors/montana/« and last retrieved August 1, 2023.

69 For information on the North Dakota legislature, see the listing of General Assemblies provided by the North Dakota Legislative Branch, available at »https://ndlegis.gov/assembly« and last retrieved August 1, 2023. For a list of North Dakota governors, including their political affiliation and a short biographical entry, see the *Archives of the National Governors Association*, available at »https://www.nga.org/former-governors/north-dakota/« and last retrieved August 1, 2023.

70 For a list of members of the South Dakota legislature, see the listing provided by the South Dakota Research Council, available at »https://sdlegislature.gov/legislators/historical/« and last retrieved August 1, 2023. For a list of South Dakota governors, including their political affiliation and a short biographical entry, see the *Archives of the National Governors Association*, available at »https://www.nga.org/former-governors/south-dakota/« and last retrieved August 1, 2023.

71 See Appendices 1 and 2.

72 In Louisiana, the legislature was dominated by Democratic-Republicans, while in Montana, a coalition of Republicans and Democrats existed at the time.

Examination of political orientation at the moment of codification seems to confirm the preliminary observations. In summary, at the moment of adoption of codes, 65% of the institutions were Republican.[73] As for the appointment of commissions, the trend seemed to be reversed. With 44% of the institutions being Democratic and only 28% Republican. As for the remaining 28%, they were similar to the Democratic-Republicans in Louisiana and a coalition of Republicans and Democrats in Montana.

Even though there again appears to be a slight majority of Republican-led institutions, the numbers remain quite low and are not conclusive enough to declare codification a part of the Republican agenda. As evidenced by the different states, a variety of political orientations coexisted with interest in codification. Once again, the Code of Georgia differs from others, for it was the only code whose commission was appointed and adopted by a Democratic majority. This could perhaps explain why this civil code was not exported to the other states, or why it was that the code developed so differently from the other common law civil codes. It might even be possible to conclude that the Code of Georgia represented a Georgian Democratic doctrine of codification. To summarize the results of the study, it shows that neither of the two main US political parties was the party of codification. While statutes are considered an endorsement of the political will at a given moment and should thus be interpreted and applied as strictly as possible,[74] codes in the United States seem to escape this rule of being the tool of politics, functioning instead as tools for the improvement of law. This fact makes the US codes rather peculiar. They are the result more of a legal will, than of any specific political agency.

Confirming these findings, the last element this study examined was the political orientation of the commission, meaning the political orientation of the code commissioners. The study at this point revealed that the commissions did not have a predominant political orientation, nor was there a clear correlation between the political orientation of the commissioners and the political orientation of the institutions appointing them.[75] Indeed, a Republican majority did not necessarily designate Republicans to draft the code, and vice versa. Only the Louisiana commissions of 1808 and 1825 were perfectly in line with the institution's orientation. However, this can be easily explained by the situation in Louisiana as well as the state of development of political parties in the broader United States at that particular moment. When the code was adopted,

73 See Appendices 1 and 2.

74 Reinhard Zimmermann, "Statuta sunt stricte interpretanda? Statutes and the Common Law: A continental Perspective", 56 *The Cambridge Law Journal* 1977, p. 318.

75 See Appendices 1 and 3.

it was indeed a real battle to implement it. On the other end of the spectrum, the members of the commission sometimes were members of the party not in power. Such was the case in California, North Dakota, and Montana. In the States of Georgia, New York, Louisiana in 1870, as well as in South Dakota, commissions were representative of the various political orientations of the territory which also varied amongst members. Commissioners were therefore selected for their competence, not their political opinions. This lack of political harmony between commissions and institutions can be explained by the restricted number of competent and available candidates available to draft a code. The drafting of a civil code required a broad knowledge of the law of the territory, of the civil law tradition, and the mode of operation of a code in order to incorporate aspects of the common law. Even amongst the nineteenth century's cultured legal population, the number of persons with this vast knowledge in any given state was limited. Additionally, this mix of political affiliations amongst the commissioners allowed them to detach the code from a specific political party and thus give it some independence from the political institutions in power. This detachment between code and politics is not common and is one of the paradoxes of the codification of private law in the United States during the nineteenth century.

3.3 Population Migration Patterns and Civil Codes

The implementation of a civil code is defined by particular times and places. It is seen as the reflection of a particular society at a unique time.[76]

The growth of the population, particularly due to the development of new means of transportation, resulted in the exponential growth of injustice and conflict within states, facts which militated in favor of creating a set of laws that were written and easily accessible. Indeed, the codes acted as a unifying social element, creating a balance between the past, present, and future.

A comprehensive review of the history of the codes reveals that the codification of the private law in a territory generally coincided with the arrival of new inhabitants.[77] This migratory flow called for a code that would allow these new inhabitants to relate to their fellow residents under the aegis of

76 J. M. Milo, J. H. A. Lokin, and J. M. Smiths, *Tradition, Codification and Unification: Comparative-Historical Essays on the Development in Civil Law (Ius Commune Europeum)*, Cambridge: Intersentia, 2014, p. 4.

77 Richard L. Forstall, *Population of States and Counties of the United States: 1790–1990*, Washington: US Department of Commerce, Bureau of the Census, 1996.

one, unified law[78] and enable the creation of geographical unit. The massive influx of people was the result of settlement in new territories which seemed to unfold in similar ways, no matter the state. Pierre-Clément de Laussat,[79] a Frenchman in Louisiana, explained in his memoirs how such an influx of new inhabitants impacted an already existing territory:

> Wherever the Anglo-Americans touch, the land is fertilized, and progress is rapid. There is a class of them who make it their business to precede the population in the deserts of America by 50 leagues: they immigrate there first, clear the land, populate it, and then push forward without any other purpose or profession than to open the way for new settlers. Those who start in this way in unknown places are called *Black-Settlers*. They plant their huts, cut and burn trees, kill savages or are killed by them, and disappear from this land either by death, or by soon giving up to a more stable farmer the land that was beginning to be cleared. When a score of new settlers has thus agglomerated on a point, two printers arise, one federalist, the other anti-federalist; then the doctors; then the advocates, then the adventurers; one drinks toasts; one names a speaker, one erects a city; one conceives children at will. Finally, one displays vast territories for sale: one attracts and deceives the buyers as much as one can. One swells the population tables so that they arrive promptly at the number of sixty thousand souls, to which is acquired the right to form an independent state and to be represented in the congress ... And here is one more star in the flag of the United States.[80]

---

78 Rémy Cabrillac, *Les Codifications* (*Droit, Éthique, Société*), Paris: Presses Universitaires de France, 2002, p. 156.

79 Pierre-Clément de Laussat was a Frenchman who was nominated "Préfêt de Louisiana" in 1802 and moved to the territory at the time of its cession to Spain. He was later the French representative for Louisiana's cession to the United States. See Adolphe Robert and Gaston Cougny, "Pierre-Clément de Laussat", in *Dictionnaire des Parlamentaires Français 1889–1891*, eds. Adolphe Robert and Gaston Cougny, Paris: Bourleton, 1891, pp. 635–636.

80 Pierre-Clément de Laussat, *Memoires sur ma Vie a mon Fils*, Pau: E. Vignancour, 1831, p. 40. "Partout où les anglo-américains touchent, la terre se fertilise et les progress sont rapides. Il es tune classe d'entre eux qui fait métier de devancer sans cesse de 50 lieues, dans les deserts de l'Amerique, la population: ils y immigrant les premiers, y défrichent, y peuplent et d'encore en encore poussent en avant sans autre but ni profession que d'ouvrir la route de nouveaux colons. Ceux qui débutent ainsi dans des lieux inconnus s'appellent *Black-Settlers*. Ils plantent leurs baraques, coupent et brulent des arbres, tuent des sauvages ou en sont tués, et disparaissent de cette terre soit par le mort, sout en y cedant bientôt à un cultivateur plus stable celle qui commençait à être éclaircie. Quan d'une vingtaine de nouveux colons se sont ainsi agglomérés sur un point, deux imprimeurs surviennent, l'un féderaliste, l'autre antiféderaliste; puis les médicins; puis les advocats, puis les aventuriers;

The nineteenth century was certainly characterized by substantial movement of people within the US territory, and data from the states' population censuses indicates a major increase in population in the twenty years preceding the adoption of codes. Indeed, the population of California increased by 75.6% between 1850 and 1860, then by 32% between 1860 and 1870. In Georgia, the population increased by 23.7% between 1840 and 1850 and by 14% between 1850 and 1860. In Montana, it increased by 72% between 1880 and 1890. Finally, in North Dakota, the population grew by 40% between 1890 and 1900, and in South Dakota by 13% during the same period. As for New York, every ten years between 1820 to 1890, the population increased by 15% to 21%.[81] An analysis of the population data shows that the adoption of codes tended to coincide with both the stabilization of immigration flows and the consolidation of governing structures.

This increase in the population was sometimes the result of the admission of a new territory to the United States, like Louisiana, or the result of a discovery, such as the first gold nugget in California. It could also have resulted from developments in transportation, such as the railway extension to Dakota. Whatever the reason, the growth of a state's population called for clarification of the law. In addition, independently from the reason for the arrival of people within a territory, the wave of immigration meant the introduction of new ideas and new cultures. Consequently, a diverse intellectual frame was created within states that received large numbers of immigrants.[82] Population increase also led to new conflicts that required quick and expedient judicial resolutions. With a code in place, a newcomer was not able to claim ignorance of the law, as it was readily available in a fixed document. For example, the population of Louisiana at the moment of its incorporation into the United States counted

---

on boit des *toasts*; on nomme un *speaker*, on s'érige en cite; on engender des enfants à l'envi. On affice enfin de vastes territoires à vendre: on attire et on trompe tant qu'on peut les acheteurs. On enfle les tableaux de population pour qu'ils arrivent promptement au nombre de soixante mille âmes, auquel est acquis le droit de former un état independent et de se faire representer au congrès ... Et voilà une étoile de plus dans le pavillon des États-Unis." See also Seán Patrick Donlan, "Entangled up in Red, White, and Blue: Spanish West Florida and the American Territory of Orleans, 1803–1810", in *Entanglements in Legal History: Conceptual Approaches* (*Global Perspectives on Legal History, 1st vol.*), ed. Thomas Duve, Frankfurt am Main: Max Planck Institute for European Legal History, 2014, pp. 213–251.

81 See Appendix 4. Data calculated according to Richard L. Forstall, *Population of States and Counties of the United States: 1790–1990*, Washington: US Department of Commerce, Bureau of the Census, 1996.

82 Michael R. Haines and Richard H. Steckel, *A Population History of North America*, Cambridge and New York (NY): Cambridge University Press, 2000, p. 228.

about 72,000 inhabitants, half of whom were slaves. The other inhabitants mostly consisted of descendants of French and Spanish settlers. The population of New Orleans alone was greater than 10,000.[83] The acquisition of this territory by the United States was accompanied by a flow of foreign immigration into Louisiana. Among the new inhabitants, many were lawyers and traders who came to make their fortunes. Most of them did not master French or Spanish nor did they become familiar with the civil law tradition.[84] By 1820, outside arrivals had brought the population of the state up to 153,407,[85] generating a population increase of 46%. Antipathy to newcomers who adjusted too slowly to local conditions resulted in the adaptation of the code, partially as a means of resistance to these newcomers. From the perspective of new arrivals, however, this resistance was seen as foolish. As one historian wrote,

> [t]he Colonists in Louisiana had been for a century the spoiled children of France and Spain. Petted, protected, fed, paid, flattered, and given every liberty except the right of self-government, they liked Spain, and they loved France, but they did not love the English or the Americans.[86]

The advent of statehood in 1812 once again exponentially increased the number of inhabitants in the state and deepened the gap between already established and newly arrived populations. The civil code came to be seen as an emblem of Louisiana's original culture and a means of preserving independence from the intrusion of other US states. The situation was different for North Dakota, South Dakota, and Montana, as in these young states, the code was seen as a way to strengthen their law and to manage the conflicts that arose with the arrival of new inhabitants. The codes were not adopted as a tool of resistance by the local population, but as in Louisiana they provided a means of preserving earlier legal culture. In fact, the codes even underwent recodification by as the Civil Code of Dakota or that of California were retailored to fit the needs of new states. In California, the population saw an increase

83 John T. Hood Jr., "The History and Development of the Louisiana Civil Code", 19 *Louisiana Law Review* 1958, p. 19.

84 *Ibid*, pp. 19–20.

85 Richard L. Forstall, *Population of States and Counties of the United States: 1790–1990*, Washington: US Department of Commerce, Bureau of the Census, 1996, pp. 70–73.

86 Henry Adams, *History of the United States of America during the Administration of Thomas Jefferson and James Madison*, 1st vol., New York (NY): The Library of America, 1986, p. 808; Daniel Usner, "Between Creoles and Yankees: The discursive Representation of Colonial Louisiana in American History", in *French Colonial Louisiana and the Atlantic World*, ed. Bradley G. Bond, Baton Rouge: Louisiana State University Press, 2005, pp. 1–21.

of at least 200,000 new residents every ten years, starting in 1850, when the arrival of the forty-niners turned the state into a true melting pot. In fact, more than 300,000 people decided to immigrate to California after the discovery of gold.[87] In the Californian case, no legal tradition was culturally predominant, as the population was so large and diverse that no pre-existing law was able to dominate in the territory. The result was a hybrid legal system.[88] The civil code appeared the perfect solution as it offered the possibility of bridging heterogeneous legal traditions. The cases of Georgia and New York are different as, being older states, both experienced a much slower population increase, with steady growth every decade. Additionally, population growth in both places was due primarily to the arrival of immigrants from outside of the country instead of the movement of Americans within the country. The domestic or foreign origin of migrants influenced whether or not codes were adopted in specific states. Aside from population increases, the other common element between the states that adopted codes was that most of the new people were arriving from other states. This population expected to see laws similar to those of their states of origin. This expectation also worked in favor of codification, as the states had to find a middle ground between the new legal expectations and previously existing laws, with codes enabling them to bridge this gap. Whether it was to conserve a long tradition or to reflect a diverse reality, population expansion encouraged the implementation of civil codes, providing a way for states to meet the specific needs of a growing body of citizens.

Another factor that influenced these population flows was the development of transportation. Most of the population influx the states examined here was due to the achievement of statehood and, in parallel, the arrival of the railroad. Trains allowed for easier movement across the United States, enabling people and ideas to travel farther and more rapidly between states. The nineteenth century is indeed considered the golden age of railroads in the United States, with railway lines coming to connect major cities and allowing the United States to acquire a certain degree of prosperity (Figure 4 and Figure 5).[89] It was only after 1920 that the railway monopoly began to face competition from

87 Lawrence M. Friedman, *A History of American Law*, 3rd ed., New York (NY): Simon & Schuster, 2005, p. 113.

88 *Ibid.*

89 On the American railroads' history, see Robert Frey, *Railroads in the nineteenth Century* (*Encyclopedia of American Business History and Biography*), New York (NY): Facts on File, 1988; Derek Hayes, *Historical Atlas of the North American Railroad*, Berkeley (CA): University of California Press, 2010; H. Roger Grant, *Railroads and the American People*, Bloomington: Indiana University Press, 2012.

other means of transportation, such as the car or plane.[90] The expansion of rail lines to the West brought the Field Civil Code[91] from New York to California, and the lines between California and Dakota or New York and Dakota also allowed the code to arrive by train. The transcontinental railway, a railroad between New York, Chicago, and San Francisco, was built in just six years by workers of Central Pacific and Union Pacific railways and stretched for more than 2,000 miles. This endeavor began in 1853, but tensions in Congress and the outbreak of the American Civil War caused delays. The Pacific Railroad Act[92] was only adopted by the government on July 1, 1862, almost ten years after it was first presented. The project started in 1863 and ended on May 10, 1869, with the meeting of the West and East teams in Omaha, Nebraska.[93] This project increased California's population massively, as it offered plentiful employment opportunities and reduced the journey between New York and California from a few months to a few days. The line between Chicago, Nebraska, Wyoming, and South Dakota was also key to the spread of the codes. This line was inaugurated in the late 1860s and connected the Dakota Territory with the eastern US territory,[94] beginning in Nebraska and reaching the easternmost part of Dakota in 1879. Called the Cowboy Line, it enabled agriculture to develop in the territory due to increased immigrant flows to the state. Once this project was completed, it generated subsidiary roads that extended through the Dakotas and Montana, providing easier circulation of the population in these areas.[95] In addition, the railway companies distributed circulars throughout Europe to influence people to buy land along the railway. At times they went further, organizing entire colonies of emigrants.[96]

---

90 See Michael J. Del Vecchio, *Railroads Across America*, Ann Arbor (MI): Lowe & B. Hould Publishers, 1999.

91 *NY Civ. C. 1865*.

92 A digital version of the Pacific Railway Act of 1862 is provided by the *United States National Archives and Records Administration*, available at »https://www.archives.gov/milestone-documents/pacific-railway-act/« and last retrieved August 1, 2023. On the matter, see Xavier Duran, "The First US Transcontinental Railroad: Expected Profits and Government Intervention", 73 *The Journal of Economic History* 2013, pp. 177–200.

93 William Deverell, *Railroad Crossing: Californians and the Railroad, 1850–1910*, Berkeley (CA): University of California Press, 1994.

94 See James D. Drake, "A Divide to heal the Union: The Creation of the Continental Divide", 84 *Pacific Historical Review* 2015, pp. 409–447; Albert J. Churella, "The Pennsylvania Railroad in the Trans-Mississippi West", 208 *Railroad History* 2013, pp. 64–82. See also Mike Bartels, Bill Kratville, Rick Mills, and Jerry Penry, *The C&NW Cowboy Line*, David City (NE): South Platte Press, 1998.

95 *Ibid.*

96 Frederick C. Luebke, "Ethnic Group Settlement on the Great Plains", 8 *Western Historical Quarterly* 1977, p. 410.

FIGURE 4 Map exhibiting the several Pacific Railroads, 1883, Western United States
COURTESY OF THE LIBRARY OF CONGRESS, AVAILABLE AT »HTTPS://WWW.LOC.GOV/ITEM/GM71000841/« AND LAST RETRIEVED AUGUST 1, 2023

Such initiatives were promoted by railway companies because a population increase would guarantee the success of the rail companies' endeavors. The development of transportation thus allowed for a greater flow of ideas, projects, and enterprise to take place in the US territories.

FIGURE 5 Map exhibiting the several Pacific Railroads, 1883, Eastern United States
COURTESY OF THE LIBRARY OF CONGRESS, AVAILABLE AT »HTTPS://WWW.LOC.GOV/ITEM/GM71000841/« AND LAST RETRIEVED AUGUST 1, 2023

It is also striking that the adoption of codes in the territories of California and Dakota seemed to have clearly coincided with the train's arrival. It is undeniable that greater circulation of people influenced the implementation of an innovative idea such as codification, especially because it allowed model codes to circulate in the US territories. In this sense, technological progress brought innovation.

Theses migration patterns helped to create a fertile ground for codification, however they were not unique to the states that chose codification, as they were also present in other US states such as Florida and Texas, where they did not have the same effect. Hence, even coupled with the other factors we have looked at, they were not strong enough to constitute a singular explanation for codification. Indeed, even when all were present these factors required one final element—a codifier.

3.4 No Civil Code without a Man

In the nineteenth-century United States, codification and civil codes were not promoted by a national or statewide agency or institution. It was charismatic and devoted local figures who determined their fate. For instance, the Field Code—the Civil Code and Procedural Code of New York—was named after David Dudley Field. In addition to being an editor, Field was a promoter of the code and acquired notoriety as a codifier. By attaching the code to a single individual, he became a champion and representative for the code who could use his power and visibility to popularize it. Looking at all the nineteenth-century civil codes, two different patterns emerge in the relationship between individual codifiers and civil codes. In some cases, the issue of codification served as a battleground between influential jurists, all of them men. On the other hand, it was championed by individual jurists, again all men, who faced little, if any, resistance.

3.4.1 *The Civil Codes: a Fuel for Dispute between Influential Men*

Codification of private law was such a burning issue in some states that it fueled disputes between powerful men, who in turn fueled debate among the general public. In two states, codification added additional fuel to pre-existing resentment amongst competing individuals. Debates over codification served as a convenient forum for publicly airing disputes because the topic emphasized two opposite ways of seeing the law and society. This situation was particularly evident in the two states where lawyers came into open conflict—in Louisiana, between Livingston, Clark, and Claiborne, and in New York, between Carter and Field. The stories of these two virulent debates show how urgent the issue could become.

In Louisiana, the debate over whether the legal system must come from civil law or common law began with the arrival of the territory's first governor,

Claiborne, a lawyer and advocate of common law. Meanwhile, the opposition rapidly coalesced in the personas of Livingston and Clark, Louisiana natives who were strong supporters of the civil law system. At a time when Louisiana needed to decide which legal system it would use, the quarrel between these men quickly escalated into attacks ranging from the private and personal to the legal-intellectual. The fight became so heated that even the adoption of the code could not bring such quarrels to an end. Claiborne, for instance, spoke of Clark and Livingston as men "without principles" in his letters to the President of the United States, indicating that they were hostile to the US government[97] because of their opposition to the introduction of the common law. Claiborne went as far as to openly criticize how Livingston practiced his legal profession. He argued that, by accepting payment in land rather than money, Livingston abused his position and only took business that was financially advantageous for him.[98] As for Clark, a document entitled *Characterization of New Orleans Residents*, written for President Jefferson by one of Claiborne's friends, James Wilkinson, described him as someone who "possesses capacities to do more good or harm than any other individual in the province—He pants for power, and is mortified by disappointment".[99] Despite his strong position within the territory, to his dismay Claiborne depended on Livingston and Clark for their knowledge of the territory, language, and local population, even though they stood at opposite extremes on the issue of the law. In 1805, a duel was held between Claiborne and Clark. Claiborne accused Clark of being part of the Burr Conspiracy,[100] leading Clark to defend his honor by requesting a duel with his accuser. In the course of the duel, Claiborne was shot in the thigh—an injury that would make him limp for the rest of his life.[101] The dispute between

97 Letters of Governor Claiborne to the Secretary of State [James Madison], New Orleans, June 3, 1804; June 29, 1804; November 5, 1804; Letter of Governor Claiborne to the President [Thomas Jefferson], New Orleans, January 29, 1805. Clarence Edwin Carter, *The Territorial Papers of the United States. Volume IX. The Territory of Orleans 1803–1812*, Washington: United States Government Printing Office, 1940, pp. 242, 245, 320, 385.

98 Junius P. Rodriguez, *The Louisiana Purchase: A historical and geographical Encyclopedia*, Santa Barbara (CA): ABC-CLIO, 2002.

99 Characterization of New Orleans Residents, New Orleans, July 1, 1804. Clarence Edwin Carter, *The Territorial Papers of the United States. Volume IX. The Territory of Orleans 1803–1812*, Washington: United States Government Printing Office, 1940, pp. 248, 255.

100 The Burr Conspiracy, allegedly planned by Aaron Burr, former Vice President of the United States, was a supposed plot to create an independent nation in Central America. Burr was arrested in 1807 and acquitted for the lack of evidence. For the full history of the Burr Conspiracy, see James E. Lewis, *The Burr Conspiracy: Uncovering the Story of an early American Crisis*, Princeton: Princeton University Press, 2017.

101 John T. Hood Jr., "The History and Development of the Louisiana Civil Code", 19 *Louisiana Law Review* 1958, p. 21.

these men did not end there. During the appointment of the drafting committee for the code, Claiborne vetoed the nomination of Livingston, viewing him as unsuitable for the job and likely continuing a personal vendetta as well.[102] Indeed, before the veto, Brown, one of the 1808 Digest draftsmen, refers to Claiborne's attitude towards Livingston in a letter to Breckinridge: "The Council appear disposed to engage Mr. Livingston and myself to digest a code; but such is the unfortunate dislike of the Governor towards the only man in whom the Council seems disposed to confide as my assistant, that is believed the measure will fail."[103] The eventual implementation of the code in 1808 did not smooth the friction, and the three men continued to challenge each other until Clark's death in 1813. Through the years, the governors would call Livingston as someone "unprincipled" and "in exciting opposition to the General and local Administration".[104] The debates on the Civil Code of Louisiana therefore took place amid personal tensions between the major local political players in the codification process. Claiborne had to accept the code by force of circumstance, as demonstrated by the history "of the digest of civil laws currently in force in the Territory of Orleans".[105] After the legislature's requested code became the perfect focus for the three men's dispute, the Civil Code of Louisiana became the code of Louis Moreau-Lislet, its main author. In Louisiana the code was thus the work of three champions—two prior to and one during its publication.

The quarrel between James C. Carter and David Dudley Field in New York was as virulent as the conflict in Louisiana. The dispute ultimately scuttled codification, and researchers on this subject have concluded that it was Carter's efforts as the leader of the anti-codification movement[106] that prevented the adoption of the Civil Code of New York.[107]

102 *Ibid*, p. 20.

103 Vernon Valentine Palmer, *The lost Translators of 1808 and the Birth of Civil Law in Louisiana*, Athens (GA): University of Georgia Press, 2021, pp. 17–18; George Dargo, *Jefferson's Louisiana: Politics and the Clash of Legal Traditions*, Clark (NJ): The Lawbook Exchange, 2009, p. 203; John T. Hood Jr., "The History and Development of the Louisiana Civil Code", 19 *Louisiana Law Review* 1958, p. 26.

104 Vernon Valentine Palmer, *The lost Translators of 1808 and the Birth of Civil Law in Louisiana*, Athens (GA): University of Georgia Press, 2021, p. 18.

105 Louis Moreau-Lislet and Henry Carleton, *Digeste général des Actes de la Législature de la Louisiane passés depuis l'Année 1804 jusqu'en 1827, inclusivement, en force de Loi à cette dernière Époque: Suivi d'un Appendix et d'une Table de Matières*, 1st vol., New Orleans: Benjamin Levy, 1828, pp. 207–208.

106 For a detailed discussion of the conflict Field versus Carter, see Aniceto Masferrer, "The passionate Discussion among Common Law Lawyers about postbellum American Codification: An Approach to its legal Argumentation", 40 *Arizona State Law Journal* 2008, pp. 173–256.

107 *Ibid*, p. 176; George Whitney Martin, *Causes and Conflicts: The centennial History of the Association of the Bar of the City of New York, 1870–1970*, New York (NY): Fordham

Lawrence M. Friedman summarizes the infamous dispute as follows:

> The codification movement is one of the set pieces of American legal history. It has its hero, Field; its villain is James C. Carter of New York, who resisted the idea of codification with as much vigor as Field fought for it.[108]

James C. Carter (Figure 6) was a preeminent New York lawyer and the founder and five-time leader of the Bar Association of New York.[109] As for David Dudley Field, he was a prominent New York lawyer and the foremost defender of codification. The conflict between the two men took the form of articles published in a protracted back and forth.

From his position as the head of the New York group that opposed codification, Carter elaborated a core set of arguments drawing on the writings of the German jurist Friedrich Carl von Savigny.[110] Indeed, Carter relied heavily on Savigny's writings on the question of custom as a source of law and on the use of science in law.[111] The codification dispute began in 1884 with Carter's pamphlet against the Civil Code, *The Proposed Consolidation of Our Common Law*; followed by a pamphlet in 1889, *The Provinces of the Written and the Unwritten Law*, and then an article called *The Ideal and Actual in the Law*, presented to the American Bar Association in 1890.[112] Field responded to each of these directly, for example by publishing a pamphlet entitled *A Short Response to a*

University Press, 1997, p. 173; James Grafton Rogers, *American Bar Leaders: Biographies of the Presidents of the American Bar Association, 1878–1928*, Chicago: American Bar Association, 1932, pp. 80–85.

108 Lawrence M. Friedman, *A History of American Law*, 3rd ed., New York (NY): Simon & Schuster, 2005, p. 302.

109 David M. Rabban, *Law's History: American legal Thought and the transatlantic Turn to History (Cambridge Historical Studies in American Law and Society)*, Cambridge: Cambridge University Press, 2013, pp. 27–31.

110 *Ibid*, p. 31.

111 Aniceto Masferrer, "Defense of the Common Law against postbellum American Codification: Reasonable and fallacious Argumentation", 50 *The American Journal of Legal History* 2008, p. 417; Sylvain Soleil, "'On the Vocation of our Age for Codes.' Le Recours à Savigny lors de la Controverse anglo-américaine sur la Codification du Common Law (1820–1835)", 18 *Historia et Ius* 2020, pp. 1–31.

112 Maurice Eugen Lang, *Codification in the British Empire and America*, Clark (NJ): The Lawbook Exchange, 2005, p. 147; Aniceto Masferrer, "The passionate Discussion among

FIGURE 6 James Coolidge Carter
COURTESY OF THE LIBRARY OF CONGRESS, AVAILABLE AT »HTTPS://WWW.LOC.GOV/ITEM/2016645698/« AND LAST RETRIEVED AUGUST 1, 2023

Common Law Lawyers about postbellum American Codification: An Approach to its legal Argumentation", 40 *Arizona State Law Journal* 2008, p. 176.

long Discourse, in 1884 following Carter's first pamphlet.[113] Although competing views on codification drove the dispute, these were not the sole cause of the conflict. Tensions between the two lawyers had arisen before codification became a burning subject of debate, as they had found themselves in opposing camps on a range of earlier issues. The confrontation began with the *Erie Railroad* case,[114] in which Carter sat on the opposite side of the case from Field. This pushed Carter to organize the Bar Association of New York in 1869, in what he declared to be an attempt to moralize the state's legal profession against bad actors such as Field. The situation then escalated when the two men represented opposing litigants during the famous *Tweed Corruption* case of 1870—during which Carter acted as the lawyer for the city of New York, while Field defended William "Boss" Tweed, the infamous head of Tammany Hall accused of stealing millions from the city.[115] The conflict between the two men was a matter of public record: one *New York Times* article described a trial involving both men during which Carter accused Field of using "every device of technicality for the purpose of obstructing the progress of justice and leading to an erroneous result" while associating him with "the great frauds which have disgraced the civilization of our time" and of being the "person mainly and chiefly responsible for them".[116] Carter's words show that jurisprudential differences had spilled over into outright disrespect and even contempt between the men. It is perhaps unsurprising that when Field began to pose as a defender of codification, Carter immediately decided to oppose him. A review of the public polemic between these men[117] reveals a conflict in which both parties refused

---

113 David Dudley Field, "A short Response to a long Discourse, an Answer to Mr. James C. Carter's Pamphlet on the proposed Codification of our Law", 1884, p. 6.

114 John R. Vile, "James Coolidge Carter", in *Great American Lawyers: An Encyclopedia*, 1st vol., ed. John R. Vile, Santa Barbara (CA): ABC-CLIO, 2001, pp. 9–11.

115 John R. Vile, "David Dudley Field", in *Great American Lawyers: An Encyclopedia*, 1st vol., ed. John R. Vile, Santa Barbara (CA): ABC-CLIO, 2001, pp. 125–138.

116 "The Suit against Tweed", *New York Times*, March 8, 1876.

117 David Dudley Field, *The State of New York against the State of Louisiana, Argument of Mr. David Dudley Field replying for the State of New York*, New York (NY): John Polhemes, 1882; David Dudley Field, "Correspondence between the California Bar and Mr. David Dudley Field", 1870, p. 465; David Dudley Field, "A short Response to a long Discourse, an Answer to Mr. James C. Carter's Pamphlet on the proposed Codification of our Law", 1884; David Dudley Field, "A Third of a Century given to Law Reform", 1873; David Dudley Field, *An Address to the graduating Class of the Law School of the University of Albany, delivered on March 23, 1856*, Albany: W.C. Little & Co., 1856; David Dudley Field, *Answer to the Report of the New York City Bar Association against the Civil Code*, New York (NY): John Polhemes, 1881; David Dudley Field, *Centenary Essays: Celebrating One Hundred Years of Legal Reform*, New York (NY): Alison Reppy, 1949; David Dudley Field, *Codification: An Address delivered before the Law Academy of Philadelphia, April 18, 1886*, Philadelphia: Printed for the Law

to hear one another. One of the most glaring examples of this type of bad faith is illustrated by their exchange on their respective visions of a possible code, specifically its application. When Field explained that his code had to be consistent with the common law, Carter answered that he wanted to abrogate the common law and its contents entirely. When Field responded that his code could not and was not intended to cover all possible cases, Carter retorted that the code was indeed meant to provide guidance for all imaginable cases, a goal which is not feasible in practice.[118] These are just two examples of the polemical answers each gave to the other, often showing a lack of consideration for the others' points. The pre-existing hostility seems to have been too strong to allow for a reasoned and respectful discussion; instead, each steadfastly held to his ideas without listening to his opponent. Like the conflict in Louisiana, the debate on the Civil Code of New York provided an excuse for a public and political confrontation between leading figures. These conflicts were heated, in part, because of the existing rivalry between these men—but they gained additional intensity because codification often touched on the emotional subject of legal culture and identity.[119] In their own ways, each of these jurists were striving to protect their community—like Livingston in Louisiana or Carter in

---

Academy, 1886; David Dudley Field, "Codification—Mr. Field's Answer to Mr. Carter", 14 *Virginia Law Journal* 1890, pp. 1–9; David Dudley Field, *Speeches, Arguments, and miscellaneous Papers*, New York (NY): D. Appleton & Co., 1884; James C. Carter, *Argument of James C. Carter in Opposition to the Bill to establish a Civil Code before the Senate Judiciary Committee*, New York (NY): Senate Judiciary Committee, 1887; James C. Carter, *Law: Its Origin, Growth and Function*, New York (NY): Putnam's Sons, 1907; James C. Carter, *The proposed Codification of our Common Law*, New York (NY): Evening Post Job Printing Office, 1884; James C. Carter, *The Provinces of the written and unwritten Law*, New York (NY): Banks & Brothers, Law Publishers, 1889.

118 Aniceto Masferrer, "The passionate Discussion among Common Law Lawyers about postbellum American Codification: An Approach to its legal Argumentation", 40 *Arizona State Law Journal* 2008, pp. 194–199.

119 See Aniceto Masferrer, "Codification as Nationalisation or Denationalisation of Laws: The Spanish Case in comparative Perspective", 4 *Comparative Legal History* 2016, pp. 100–130. See also Ernst Levy, "The Reception of highly developed Legal Systems by People of different Culture", 25 *Washington Law Review* 1950, pp. 233–245; Christian Atias and Alain A. Levasseur, "American Legal Culture and traditional scholarly Order", 46 *Louisiana Law Review* 1986, pp. 1117–1136; Jaap Lintvelt, Réal Ouellet, and Hub Hermans, *Culture et Colonisation en Amérique de Nord: Canada, États-Unis, Mexique = Culture and Colonization in North America: Canada, United States, Mexico* (*Les Nouveaux Cahiers du* CÉLAT), Sillery (Québec): Septentrion, 1994, p. 84; John W. Head, "Codes, Cultures, Chaos and Champions: Common Features of legal Codification Experiences in China, Europe, and North America", 13 *Duke Journal of Comparative & International Law* 2003, pp. 2–93; Nir Kedar, "Law, Culture and Civil Codification in a Mixed Legal System", 22 *Canadian Journal of Law and Society* 2007; Sheldon Leader, "Legal Theory and the Variety of Legal Cultures",

New York—from whatever their opponents—be it Field or Claiborne—sought to change so drastically. Unsurprisingly, the debate quickly became passionate, as it was not just about law but also about fundamental issues of feelings and identity.

From Louisiana or New York, these conflicts had the effect of putting the issue of codification center stage. Due to these very public and vitriolic conflicts, everyone, whether they were legal professionals or not, was invited to take a position. A subject of seemingly limited legal interest thus became a matter of widespread public concern.

3.4.2 *The Civil Codes, Legal Tools Advocated by Individual Men*

Where the issue of codification did not stir up broader social tensions, it was often spearheaded by individual men. These men used their reputations to advocate for and implement a civil code. A review of these cases shows that these figures were mostly judges, a fact which testifies to the strength of judicial power in common law states.

The Code of Georgia was pursued by two different champions, George A. Gordon, who first proposed the idea, and Thomas R. R. Cobb, who worked on the draft and the adoption of the code. Gordon, who was born in 1830 and died in 1872 of typhoid fever contracted during the war, was admitted as a lawyer to the Georgia Bar on January 19, 1852. He was later a member of the Senate and the House of Representatives. At twenty-eight, the young attorney "fell in love" with the Code of Alabama.[120] He discovered this code while in Huntsville, Alabama for his marriage, at a time when the Alabama legal profession was celebrating the code's adoption. Seduced by the idea of a code, Gordon strove for Georgia to adopt such a document. He went even further, however, arguing that unlike the Code of Alabama, the Code of Georgia should include all state law. It was Gordon, in his capacity as state representative, who pushed the legislature on November 9, 1858, to vote unanimously for codification.[121] This act was so easily approved because of the stature of the man himself, as this future general of the Confederate army was highly regarded by his contemporaries. He himself had carefully drafted the act, deciding on some of the specific characteristics that would distinguish the Code of Georgia from the other codes,[122]

---

3 *Journal of Civil Law Studies* 2010, pp. 99–110; Frédéric Audren and Jean-Louis Halpérin, *La Culture juridique française* (CNRS *Droit*), Issy-les-Moulineaux: LGDJ, 2014.

120 Richard H. Clark, "The History of the first Georgia Code", in *Report of the Seventh Annual Meeting of the Georgia Bar Association*, ed. unknown, Atlanta (GA): Jas. P. Harrison & Co., 1890, p. 151.

121 *Ibid*, pp. 150–151.

122 *Ibid*, p. 151.

such as its organization and the model that inspired it. Gordon used all his political power to drive home a vision backed by his firmest convictions.

After laying the foundations for the code, Gordon entrusted the commissioners with implementing the legal transformation. Once the act providing for a codification of the law was adopted, he left his contemporaries to make it a reality. Of the three members of the commission, two of them, Irwin and Clark, were judges, while Cobb, who was mainly in charge of the civil code, was a lawyer. They were responsible for publishing progress reports on their work, but they also took over the push to get the code adopted by the legislature. Crucially, they proposed that the code be voted on by section instead of by article[123] in order to move the adoption process along. Each man was responsible for a different code and for seeing it through to final approval by the legislature. Cobb, for instance, met with the different members of the legislature who advocated the civil code, published the report, and ensured its adoption.

In California, the man who brought codification to the territory was a judge, Justice Stephen Johnson Field (Figure 7), David Dudley Field's brother. Despite his codification work, he is best known by the legal profession for his work as Justice of the US Supreme Court. In fact, he held the position for a period of 12,614 days, making his tenure the second longest in Supreme Court history. He was nonetheless a major player in the codification effort in California. Having been a lawyer at his older brother's law firm for ten years before moving to California,[124] he arrived in San Francisco on December 29, 1849,[125] and began his career as a judge in Marysville,[126] while renting land he had previously acquired in the hopes of making a fortune.[127] At the end of his tenure in May 1850, he resumed his law practice before being elected to the legislature in January 1851.[128]

123 Marion Smith, "The first Codification of the substantive Common Law", 4 *Tulane Law Review* 1929, pp. 178–189.

124 Philip J. Bergan, Owen M. Fiss, and Charles W. McCurdy, *The Fields and the Law: Essays*, New York (NY): Federal Bar Council, 1986, p. 28.

125 Carl Brent Swisher, *Stephen J. Field: Craftsman of the Law*, Washington: The Brookings Institution, 1930, p. 26.

126 Stephen J. Field, "Personal Reminiscences of early Days in California", 1893, p. 19.

127 *Ibid*, p. 30. "To make a long story short, until I was superseded by officers under the United States government, I superintended municipal affairs and administered justice on Marysville with success. Whilst there was a large number of residents there of his character and culture, who would have done honor to any city, there were also unfortunately many desperate persons, gamblers, blacklegs, thieves, and cut-throats; yet the place was as orderly as a New England village. There were no disturbances at night, no riots, and no lynching. It was a model town of the whole country for peacefulness and respect for law."

128 Carl Brent Swisher, *Stephen J. Field: Craftsman of the Law*, Washington: The Brookings Institution, 1930, p. 48.

It was at that point that he became a member of the Judiciary Committee, which he headed and which worked towards the adoption of the civil procedure and criminal codes that his brother David had drafted for New York, while modifying them to suit the particular needs of California.[129]

It was the Field brothers' initiatives that brought codification to the Californian territory. Following the adoption of the procedural code, the Californian lawyers started to wonder about a further codification of substantive law. By this point Field had resumed his activities as a lawyer and was thus not involved in these later efforts. He was appointed as a judge of the California Supreme Court in 1857 and Justice of the US Supreme Court in 1863 by Abraham Lincoln. He did not abandon the codification effort entirely, however, and his early efforts long bore fruit: so thoroughly had he managed to implement the codes and the idea of codification in the territory, that there was virtually no resistance to the codes' adoption.

In the Dakota Territory, the champions of codification were judges of the Supreme Court. Founded in 1861, this court was made up of three men, Chief Justice Philemon Bliss, Associate Justice George P. Williston, and Associate Justice Joseph L. Williams, all appointed by Abraham Lincoln. Not many details are available about these men, as sources on the Dakota Territory during 1860 are inconsistent. However, in his 1915 book on the Dakota Territory's history, the historian George Kingsbury explains that the 1860 Draft Civil Code for the State of New York made its way up to the Dakota Territory where

> a printed copy of the report of the commission containing the civil and penal codes, and also the maritime code, came into the possession of the Supreme Court of the Territory of Dakota.[130]

Having this innovative document at their disposal, and being in the position to shape the state's structures at its inception, the Supreme Court judges seized the opportunity. They asked the legislature to adopt the Code of New York.[131] Seeing no reason to refuse this gift of a clear and up to date piece of law, in

129 Stephen J. Field, "Personal Reminiscences of early Days in California", 1893, p. 78. "I took up the Code of Civil Procedure, as reported by the commissioners in New York, remodeled it so as to adapt it to the different condition of things and the different organization of the courts in California, and secured its passage."

130 George W. Kingsbury, *History of Dakota Territory*, 1st vol., Chicago: S. J. Clarke Publishing Co., 1915, p. 430. "A printed copy of the postponement of the commission containing the Civil and Penal Codes, and the Maritime Code, came into the possession of the Supreme Court of the Territory of Dakota."

131 *Ibid*, p. 431.

FIGURE 7 Stephen Johnson Field
COURTESY OF THE LIBRARY OF CONGRESS, AVAILABLE AT »HTTPS://WWW.LOC.GOV/ITEM/2017893413/« AND LAST RETRIEVED AUGUST 1, 2023

1865 the legislature adopted the code without any changes or revisions. Unfortunately, no records of the discussions that led to the decision have been preserved, so we cannot know the legislators' precise reasoning.

The issue of a civil code was, in all the states, advocated by men who used their political power and fought strongly either for or against it. Judges, meanwhile, did not stand by idly, instead getting involved in every state, either in opposition, as in New York where judges actively opposed the code, or as advocates as was the case in other states. Even in Louisiana, where judges did not intervene at the origins of the code, they spearheaded the 1825 Civil Code revision. In other states—Georgia, California, and Dakota—judges were active supporters and instigators of civil codes. They were invested positively from the beginning in committees and were even at times the codes' original promoters.

3.4.3 *The Field Network*

One of the questions this research raised was linked to the appearance of a civil code in the Dakota Territory. Why was the 1860 Draft of a Civil Code for the State of New York sent to this barely populated place and not to other states? And why was it sent to the Supreme Court judge when, in New York, most of the magistrates opposed it? The examination of some of the protagonists brings an answer to these questions while also shedding some new light on the actor's driving codification in the United States during the nineteenth century. The answer points to the Chief Justice of the Dakota Territory Supreme Court, Philemon Bliss (Figure 8).[132] Genealogical research showed that Bliss was a distant cousin of the Field brothers, though the documentation is silent on whether the two branches of the family knew one another. However, they were born in the same state, Connecticut, and David[133] and Philemon[134] both did their legal studies in the same city, New York, in 1820. The third element that allows one to suppose they knew or met each other is that both personally knew

132 Bliss's genealogy shows that his great-great-grandmother was the sister of the great-grandfather of David Dudley Field. Indeed, Lydia Field, Zechariah Field's sister, married John Bliss I. Hence, this lineage link shows that there is a family connection between the Field and the Bliss families which made David and Stephen Field distant cousins by marriage to the Dakota Territory's Supreme Court judge Philemon Bliss. See Appendix 5. For the Bliss family's genealogy, see John Homer Bliss, *Genealogies of the Bliss Family in America, from about the Year 1550–1880*, Boston: John Homer Bliss, 1881.

133 For David Dudley Field's life history, see Henry Field, *The Life of David Dudley Field*, New York (NY): Charles Scribner's Sons, 1898.

134 For Philemon Bliss's life history, see John Homer Bliss, *Genealogies of the Bliss Family in America, from about the Year 1550–1880*, Boston: John Homer Bliss, 1881.

Abraham Lincoln.[135] Therefore, it is not unlikely that these cousins knew each other, as they circulated in the same circles. This is an especially compelling assumption given the fact that the 1860 Draft of a Civil Code for the State of New York was sent to Bliss in the Dakota Territory. These hypothetical relationships might explain the arrival of a copy of the civil code so early and quickly to the Dakota Territory. The fact that a draft—not the final code—was sent makes the event even more unusual and further points towards a personal connection of some sort. The link between Field and Bliss is a connection that is key in the history of US civil codes, as it explains the arrival of an essential document in a sparsely populated and distant territory. This family connection also sheds new light on the how the different codes inspired one another, as family relations appear to be at the heart of the codes' circulation. While no organization had been created to promote codification in the US territory, it seems that codes tended to circulate and influence one another in states and territories linked by circles of family and friendship. At the nexus of these circles was David Dudley Field. Indeed, during his year drafting the Code of New York, Field engaged in profuse correspondence with Livingston in Louisiana; his brother then became the Californian advocate for codification, and finally the code arrived in Dakota, likely after having been sent to their cousin.

The nineteenth-century US civil codes are thus the result of a network of educated men. History seems to show that David Dudley Field was the key individual behind codification in the United States. He is certainly the person who most actively promoted the circulation of his codes thanks to his connections, whether private or familial, to other jurists. However, he was not alone as a defender of codification in the United States. There could not have been so many codes in the United States without powerful men in different states. Gordon, Bliss, Moreau-Lislet, Livingston, as well as Stephen Johnson Field, were also leading figures in the push for codification. But codification in the United States was more a matter of men than state agencies, or perhaps even the result of a collective effort of Field and his men.

3.5 Concluding Remarks

To summarize, the factors that explain the codification of private law in the United States are shared across a number of states, but no single factor seems

135 John Homer Bliss, *Genealogies of the Bliss Family in America, from about the Year 1550–1880*, Boston: John Homer Bliss, 1881; Philip J. Bergan, Owen M. Fiss, and Charles W. McCurdy, *The Fields and the Law: Essays*, New York (NY): Federal Bar Council, 1986.

FIGURE 8 Philemon Bliss

COURTESY OF THE LIBRARY OF CONGRESS, AVAILABLE AT »HTTPS://WWW.LOC.GOV/ITEM/2010649345/« AND LAST RETRIEVED AUGUST 1, 2023

determinant. Most of the codifying states were young states experiencing their formative years. It does not seem as if there was one political party that pushed for codification, even if a slight majority of those who pushed for or agreed to codes were Republican. Most states experienced an influx of inhabitants during the years preceding the adoption of the code and / or the arrival of new railways. However, among all of the factors studied, some common elements were found across the states that adopted codes that influenced codification endeavors in similar ways. All the codifying states justified their endeavors as efforts to organize and modernize the law, all had a civil law colonial legacy, and all used the same procedure to codify the law. Each, finally, had a champion in the form of a powerful man who promoted the civil code. To conclude, one of the main factors that drove codification in the different states was the availability of an already existing model, a factor which was closely tied to the circulation of David Dudley Field's model code within his networks.

Finally, looking at all the codifying states on a map, one final point becomes clear: all the codifying states are peripheral states, also called border states, which means that all the states that adopted a civil code lie on one of the US borders. This fact to date defies explanation. Was a state's location on the border of the United States significant? Perhaps they benefited from more legal freedom being further from central political power. Or maybe being a possible point of entry for outsiders increased the population flux—and the diversity of legal ideas—compared to central states. These border states were also points of entry for businesses arriving in the US territory; through ports or border accesses they were centers of circulation and exchange, a factor which, as established previously, facilitates the circulation of ideas.

Bibliography

Adams, Henry: *History of the United States of America during the Administration of Thomas Jefferson and James Madison*, 1st vol., New York (NY): The Library of America, 1986.

Atias, Christian; Levasseur, Alain A.: "American Legal Culture and traditional scholarly Order", 46 *Louisiana Law Review* 1986, pp. 1117–1136.

Audren, Frédéric; Halpérin, Jean-Louis: *La Culture juridique française* (*CNRS Droit*), Issy-les-Moulineaux: LGDJ, 2014.

Bartels, Mike; Kratville, Bill; Mills, Rick; Penry, Jerry: *The C&NW Cowboy Line*, David City (NE): South Platte Press, 1998.

Basdevant, Brigitte; Gaudemet, Jean: *Introduction historique au Droit* (*XIIIe–XXe Siècle*), 4th ed., Issy-les-Moulineaux: LGDJ, 2016.

Bliss, John Homer: *Genealogies of the Bliss Family in America, from about the Year 1550–1880*, Boston: John Homer Bliss, 1881.

Brady, David M.; McCubbins, Mathew D.: *Party, Process, and Political Change in Congress: Further new Perspectives on the History of Congress* (*Social Science History*), 2nd vol., Stanford (CA): Stanford University Press, 2007.

Cabrillac, Rémy: "Les Enjeux de la Codification en France", 46 *Les Cahiers du Droit* 2005, pp. 533–545.

Cabrillac, Rémy: *Les Codifications* (*Droit, Éthique, Société*), Paris: Presses Universitaires de France, 2002.

Carter, James C.: *Argument of James C. Carter in Opposition to the Bill to establish a Civil Code before the Senate Judiciary Committee*, New York (NY): Senate Judiciary Committee, 1887.

Carter, James C.: *Law: Its Origin, Growth and Function*, New York (NY): Putnam's Sons, 1907.

Carter, James C.: *The proposed Codification of our Common Law*, New York (NY): Evening Post Job Printing Office, 1884.

Carter, James C.: *The Provinces of the written and unwritten Law*, New York (NY): Banks & Brothers, Law Publishers, 1889.

Castán Vázquez, José María: "Reciprocal Influences between the Laws of Spain and Louisiana", 42 *Louisiana Law Review* 1981, pp. 1473–1484.

Castellucci, Ignazio: "Law v. Lex: An Analysis of a Critical Relation in Roman and Civil Law", 8 *Global Jurist* 2008, pp. 1–32.

Churella, Albert J.: "The Pennsylvania Railroad in the Trans-Mississippi West", 208 *Railroad History* 2013, pp. 64–82.

Coing, Helmut: *Europäisches Privatrecht*, 2nd vol., Munich: C. H. Beck, 1989.

Coleman, Kenneth: *A History of Georgia*, 2nd ed., Athens (GA): University of Georgia Press, 1991.

Cook, Charles M.: *The American Codification Movement: A Study of Antebellum Legal Reform* (*Contributions in Legal Studies*), Westport (CT): Greenwood Press, 1981.

Crépeau, Paul-André: "Réflexions sur la Codification du Droit Privé", 38 *Osgoode Hall Law Journal* 2000, pp. 267–295.

Dargo, George: *Jefferson's Louisiana: Politics and the Clash of Legal Traditions*, Clark (NJ): The Lawbook Exchange, 2009.

de Bellefeuille, Edouard L.: *Code Civil du Bas-Canada*, Montréal (Québec): C. O. Beauchemin & Valois, Éditeurs, 1866.

de Bolla, Peter: *The fourth of July and the Founding of America*, Woodstock (NY): Overlook Press, 2008.

de la Harpe, Bernard: *Journal historique de l'Établissement des Français à la Louisiane*, New Orleans: Paul Renouard, 1831.

de Laussat, Pierre-Clément: *Memoires sur ma Vie a mon Fils*, Pau: E. Vignancour, 1831.

Debouchel, Victor: *Histoire de la Louisiane: Depuis les premières Découvertes jusqu'en 1840*, New Orleans: J. F. Leleivre, 1841.

Del Vecchio, Michael J.: *Railroads Across America*, Ann Arbor (MI): Lowe & B. Hould Publishers, 1999.

Donlan, Seán Patrick: "Entangled up in Red, White, and Blue: Spanish West Florida and the American Territory of Orleans, 1803–1810", in *Entanglements in Legal History: Conceptual Approaches (Global Perspectives on Legal History, 1st vol.)*, ed. Thomas Duve, Frankfurt am Main: Max Planck Institute for European Legal History, 2014.

Drake, James D.: "A Divide to heal the Union: The Creation of the Continental Divide", 84 *Pacific Historical Review* 2015, pp. 409–447.

Duran, Xavier: "The First US Transcontinental Railroad: Expected Profits and Government Intervention", 73 *The Journal of Economic History* 2013, pp. 177–200.

Field, David Dudley: "A short Response to a long Discourse, an Answer to Mr. James C. Carter's Pamphlet on the proposed Codification of our Law", 1884.

Field, David Dudley: "A Third of a Century given to Law Reform", 1873.

Field, David Dudley: "Codification—Mr. Field's Answer to Mr. Carter", 14 *Virginia Law Journal* 1890, pp. 1–9.

Field, David Dudley: "Correspondence between the California Bar and Mr. David Dudley Field", 1870.

Field, David Dudley: *An Address to the graduating Class of the Law School of the University of Albany, delivered on March 23, 1856*, Albany: W.C. Little & Co., 1856.

Field, David Dudley: *Answer to the Report of the New York City Bar Association against the Civil Code*, New York (NY): John Polhemes, 1881.

Field, David Dudley: *Centenary Essays: Celebrating One Hundred Years of Legal Reform*, New York (NY): Alison Reppy, 1949.

Field, David Dudley: *Codification: An Address delivered before the Law Academy of Philadelphia, April 18, 1886*, Philadelphia: Printed for the Law Academy, 1886.

Field, David Dudley: *Speeches, Arguments, and miscellaneous Papers*, New York (NY): D. Appleton & Co., 1884.

Field, David Dudley: *The State of New York against the State of Louisiana, Argument of Mr. David Dudley Field replying for the State of New York*, New York (NY): John Polhemes, 1882.

Field, Henry: *The Life of David Dudley Field*, New York (NY): Charles Scribner's Sons, 1898.

Field, Stephen J.: "Personal Reminiscences of early Days in California", 1893.

Foner, Eric: *Free Soil, free Labor, free Men: The Ideology of the Republican Party before the Civil War*, Oxford and New York (NY): Oxford University Press, 1995.

Forstall, Richard L.: *Population of States and Counties of the United States: 1790–1990*, Washington: US Department of Commerce, Bureau of the Census, 1996.

Frey, Robert: *Railroads in the nineteenth Century (Encyclopedia of American Business History and Biography)*, New York (NY): Facts on File, 1988.

Friedman, Lawrence M.: *A History of American Law*, 3rd ed., New York (NY): Simon & Schuster, 2005.

Frost, John: *History of the State of California, from the Period of the Conquest by Spain, to her Occupation by the United States of America*, Auburn: Derby and Miller, 1853.

Gayarré, Charles: *Histoire de la Louisiane*, New Orleans: Imprimé par Magne & Weisse, 1846.

Gould, Lewis L.: *The Republicans: A History of the Grand Old Party*, Oxford and New York (NY): Oxford University Press, 2014.

Grant, H. Roger: *Railroads and the American People*, Bloomington: Indiana University Press, 2012.

Grossberg, Michael; Tomlins, Christopher: *The long nineteenth Century (1789–1920)*, Cambridge: Cambridge University Press, 2008.

Haines, Michael R.; Steckel, Richard H.: *A Population History of North America*, Cambridge and New York (NY): Cambridge University Press, 2000.

Halpérin, Jean-Louis: *L'impossible Code Civil (Histoires)*, Paris: Presses Universitaires de France, 1992.

Haskins, George L.: "Codification of the Law in colonial Massachusetts: A Study in Comparative Law", 30 *Indiana Law Journal* 1954, pp. 1–17.

Hayes, Derek: *Historical Atlas of the North American Railroad*, Berkeley (CA): University of California Press, 2010.

Head, John W.: "Codes, Cultures, Chaos and Champions: Common Features of legal Codification Experiences in China, Europe, and North America", 13 *Duke Journal of Comparative & International Law* 2003, pp. 2–93.

Hershey, Marjorie Randon: *Party Politics in America*, 18th ed., New York (NY): Routledge, 2021.

Hood Jr., John T.: "The History and Development of the Louisiana Civil Code", 19 *Louisiana Law Review* 1958, pp. 18–33.

Kammen, Michael G.: *Colonial New York: A History (A History of the American Colonies)*, New York (NY): Scribner, 1975.

Kastor, Peter J.; Weil, François: *Empires of the Imagination: Transatlantic Histories of the Louisiana Purchase*, Charlottesville: University of Virginia Press, 2009.

Kedar, Nir: "Law, Culture and Civil Codification in a Mixed Legal System", 22 *Canadian Journal of Law and Society* 2007.

Kossok, Manfred: *L'Espagne et son Empire d' Amérique: Histoire de Structures politiques, économiques et sociales, 1320–1824*, Paris: Ediciones Hispano Americanas, 1972.

Kroppenberg, Ingo; Linder, Nikolaus: "Coding the Nation. Codification History from a (Post-) Global Perspective", in *Entanglements in Legal History: Conceptual*

Approaches (*Global Perspectives on Legal History, 1st vol.*), ed. Thomas Duve, Frankfurt am Main: Max Planck Institute for European Legal History, 2014.

Leader, Sheldon: "Legal Theory and the Variety of Legal Cultures", 3 *Journal of Civil Law Studies* 2010, pp. 99–110.

Levy, Ernst: "The Reception of highly developed Legal Systems by People of different Culture", 25 *Washington Law Review* 1950, pp. 233–245.

Lewis, James E.: *The Burr Conspiracy: Uncovering the Story of an early American Crisis*, Princeton: Princeton University Press, 2017.

Lintvelt, Jaap; Ouellet, Réal; Hermans, Hub: *Culture et Colonisation en Amérique de Nord: Canada, États-Unis, Mexique = Culture and Colonization in North America: Canada, United States, Mexico* (*Les Nouveaux Cahiers du* CÉLAT), Sillery (Québec): Septentrion, 1994.

Luebke, Frederick C.: "Ethnic Group Settlement on the Great Plains", 8 *Western Historical Quarterly* 1977, pp. 405–430.

Martin, François-Xavier: *The History of Louisiana from the Earliest Period*, New Orleans: Lyman and Beardslee, 1827.

Martin, George Whitney: *Causes and Conflicts: The centennial History of the Association of the Bar of the City of New York, 1870–1970*, New York (NY): Fordham University Press, 1997.

Masferrer, Aniceto: "Codification as Nationalisation or Denationalisation of Laws: The Spanish Case in comparative Perspective", 4 *Comparative Legal History* 2016, pp. 100–130.

Masferrer, Aniceto: "Plurality of Laws, Legal Traditions and Codification in Spain", 4 *Journal of Civil Law Studies* 2011, pp. 419–448.

Masferrer, Aniceto: "The passionate Discussion among Common Law Lawyers about postbellum American Codification: An Approach to its legal Argumentation", 40 *Arizona State Law Journal* 2008, pp. 173–256.

Milo, J.M.; Lokin, J.H.A.; Smiths, J.M.: *Tradition, Codification and Unification: Comparative-Historical Essays on the Development in Civil Law* (*Ius Commune Europeum*), Cambridge: Intersentia, 2014.

Oppetit, Bruno: *Essai sur la Codification* (*Droit, Éthique, Société*), Paris: Presses Universitaires de France, 1998.

Palmer, Vernon Valentine: *The lost Translators of 1808 and the Birth of Civil Law in Louisiana*, Athens (GA): University of Georgia Press, 2021.

Rabban, David M.: *Law's History: American legal Thought and the transatlantic Turn to History* (*Cambridge Historical Studies in American Law and Society*), Cambridge: Cambridge University Press, 2013.

Reese, Trevor Richard: *Colonial Georgia: A Study in British Imperial Policy in the eighteenth Century*, Athens (GA): University of Georgia Press, 2010.

Roa, Fernando González: *El Carácter de la Legislación colonial Española en América* (*Del México actual, 8th vol.*), Ciudad de México: Secretaría de Relaciones Exteriores, 1933.
Robert, Adolphe; Cougny, Gaston: "Pierre-Clément de Laussat", in *Dictionnaire des Parlamentaires Français 1889–1891*, eds. Adolphe Robert and Gaston Cougny, Paris: Bourleton, 1891.
Rodriguez, Junius P.: *The Louisiana Purchase: A historical and geographical Encyclopedia*, Santa Barbara (CA): ABC-CLIO, 2002.
Rogers, James Grafton: *American Bar Leaders: Biographies of the Presidents of the American Bar Association, 1878–1928*, Chicago: American Bar Association, 1932.
Skinner, Catherine: "Codification and the Common Law", 11 *European Journal of Law Reform* 2009, pp. 225–258.
Smith, Marion: "The first Codification of the substantive Common Law", 4 *Tulane Law Review* 1929, pp. 178–189.
Soleil, Sylvain: "'On the Vocation of our Age for Codes.' Le Recours à Savigny lors de la Controverse anglo-américaine sur la Codification du Common Law (1820–1835)", 18 *Historia et Ius* 2020, pp. 1–31.
Sullivan, Buddy: *Georgia: A State History*, Mount Pleasant (SC): Arcadia Publishing, 2010.
Swisher, Carl Brent: *Stephen J. Field: Craftsman of the Law*, Washington: The Brookings Institution, 1930.
Usner, Daniel: "Between Creoles and Yankees: The discursive Representation of Colonial Louisiana in American History", in *French Colonial Louisiana and the Atlantic World*, ed. Bradley G. Bond, Baton Rouge: Louisiana State University Press, 2005.
Vile, John R.: "David Dudley Field", in *Great American Lawyers: An Encyclopedia*, 1st vol., ed. John R. Vile, Santa Barbara (CA): ABC-CLIO, 2001.
Vile, John R.: "James Coolidge Carter", in *Great American Lawyers: An Encyclopedia*, 1st vol., ed. John R. Vile, Santa Barbara (CA): ABC-CLIO, 2001.
Wall, Bennett H.: *Louisiana: A History*, 6th ed., Hoboken (NJ): Wiley-Blackwell, 2013.
Wieacker, Franz: *Privatrechtsgeschichte der Neuzeit unter besonderer Berücksichtigung der deutschen Entwicklung* (*Jurisprudenz in Einzeldarstellungen, 7th vol.*), 3rd ed., Göttingen: Vandenhoeck & Ruprecht, 2016.
Witcover, Jules: *Party of the People: A History of the Democrats*, 1st ed., New York (NY): Random House, 2003.
Young, Brian J.: *The Politics of Codification: The lower Canadian Civil Code of 1866*, Montréal (Québec): McGill-Queen's University Press, 1994.
Zamora Manzano, José Luis: "La Influencia del Derecho romano en Estados Unidos en el ámbito académico y jurisprudencial", 17 *GLOSSAE. European Journal of Legal History* 2020, pp. 722–743.
Zaradny, Aude: *Codification et État de Droit*, Paris: Université Panthéon-Assas, 2011.
Zimmermann, Reinhard: "Statuta sunt stricte interpretanda? Statutes and the Common Law: A continental Perspective", 56 *The Cambridge Law Journal* 1977, pp. 315–328.

CHAPTER 4

Inside the US Civil Codes

Civil codes in the United States are the result of implantation and transplantation.[1] In both the selection of sources and the code's final form, the drafting process showed the influence of prior circulation and borrowing. Here I first examine the sources, asking about the origins of the laws contained in each code. Studying the sources of the civil codes allows to know which part of the state's cultural identity was enshrined in the code and which new cultural elements were introduced through the code. The second element assessed is the form of the civil codes, referring to the organization of their legal notions and principles. Which of these are chosen for inclusion in the civil codes and how are they ordered in relation to one other? Here we can see how the drafters of the nineteenth-century US civil codes understood codification as an idea. The study of the civil codes' form also involves analysis of the choices made with regard to the written features of the codes' articles. These elements combined provide insight into what I argue was a specifically US definition of civil codes that shaped code-writing in the nineteenth century.

4.1 The Sources of Nineteenth-Century US Civil Codes

The nineteenth-century US civil codes are based on multiple sources, all of them very different from a geographical and institutional point of view. The sources take many forms and come from all over the world. My analysis showed that four types of sources can be identified in each civil code: legal, statutory, doctrinal sources, and, finally, other codes. These different sources come from several geographic areas, namely Ancient Rome, the United States, England, France, Spain, and Mexico, and cover an extensive chronological scope. The identification of the sources of a code allows us to apprehend the origin of the laws contained in each newly adopted code, which can in turn be divided into

1 Alan Watson, *Legal Transplants: An Approach to Comparative Literature*, 2nd ed., Athens (GA) and London: University of Georgia Press, 1993; Agustín Parise, *Ownership Paradigms in American Civil Law Jurisdictions: Manifestations of the Shifts in the Legislation of Louisiana, Chile, and Argentina (16th–20th Centuries)*, Leiden and Boston: Brill Nijhoff, 2017; Olivier Moréteau, Aniceto Masferrer, and Kjell Å. Modéer, *Comparative Legal History (Research Handbooks in Comparative Law)*, Cheltenham: Edward Elgar Publishing, 2019.

 | DOI:10.1163/9789004689978_007

laws that are local, on the one hand, and those that are a transposition of foreign or out-of-state law on the other. As Aniceto Masferrer writes, "the fact that national parliaments enacted codes whose content had been highly influenced by foreign codes reveals that codification also contributed to the denationalization of law".[2] In the case of the United States, however, this tendency towards incorporation of foreign sources also contributed to a nationwide unification of the law. I identified the sources for the different codes in two ways: first, the civil codes generally included a list of their sources in the codifying commission's reports or introductions to the code. Secondly, lists of material sources were often included by commissioners in the code's specific articles. The identification of sources following specific articles appeared for the first time in the Civil Code of New York and was replicated in those codes that were inspired by it. Examination of the sources of the codes was conducted first state by state, then comparatively, allowing evaluation of the different types of sources used as well as visualization of the patterns that emerge in the use of sources by the various nineteenth-century civil codes.

4.1.1 *The Civil Codes of Louisiana*

The Civil Code of Louisiana[3] was sometimes referred to as "a Spanish girl in a French dress",[4] to emphasize the Spanish content of some of its articles, which persisted despite a powerful French influence. The legacy of Louisiana's colonial tradition is found in the code's two main sources and naturally comes from French and Spanish law. The identification and study of the material sources of the 1808 Digest is facilitated by a wide range of available sources, in particular a copy of the 1808 Digest[5] with handwritten annotations by Louis Moreau-Lislet, the code's principal author. In this copy, he identifies and lists the sources of the various articles of the code. He also explains his approach to the 1808 Digest:

2 Aniceto Masferrer, "Codification as Nationalisation or Denationalisation of Laws: The Spanish Case in comparative Perspective", 4 *Comparative Legal History* 2016, p. 100.

3 LA *Digest 1808*; LA *Civ. C. 1825*; LA *Rev. Civ. C. 1870*.

4 Robert A. Pascal, "Of the Civil Code and Us", 59 *Louisiana Law Review* 1998, pp. 301–324.

5 Louis Moreau-Lislet, *A Reprint of Moreau-Lislet's Copy of 'A Digest of the Civil Laws now in force in the Territory of Orleans' (1808)—'The de la Vergne Volume'*, Baton Rouge: The Louisiana State University Law School and the Tulane University School of Law, 1968. See also Joseph Dainow, "Moreau-Lislet's Notes on Sources of Louisiana Civil Code of 1808", 19 *Louisiana Law Review* 1958, pp. 43–51; Robert A. Pascal, "A recent Discovery: A Copy of the 'Digest of the Civil Laws' of 1808 with marginal Source References in Moreau-Lislet's Hand", 7 *Louisiana History: The Journal of the Louisiana Historical Association* 1966, pp. 249–251; Mitchell Franklin, "Libraries of Edward Livingston and of Moreau-Lislet", 15 *Tulane Law Review* 1940, pp. 401–414.

> The goal of this publication is to make known through written notes on blank pages attached to the digest of the laws of this state, what are the texts of civil and Spanish laws who report to those articles. […] We did not merely cite the laws that have some connection with the various articles of the digest [nor did we] only mark which ones contain similar provisions; we also added the ones that treat the same subject but prescribe or contain exceptions to the general principles set out there.[6]

This document offers a comprehensive list of sources for the 1808 Digest, which include the Justinian Code, Roman law, Jean Domat and Robert-Joseph Pothier, the French Civil Code, the *Siete Partidas*, the *Fuero Real*, the *Libreria de Escribanos de Febrero* and the *Curia Philipica of Don Juan Hevia Bolanos*, canon law, the canon and civil law class of Pedro Murillo Velarde, the works of Antonio Gomez, the *Fuero Juzgo*, and the *Fuero Viejo*, the laws of Toro, the recompilation of Castile as well as the *Autos Acordados*.[7] This handwritten annotated copy of the 1808 Digest added to the extensive literature on the subject of sources makes the question of sources one of the most debated points about the Civil Codes of Louisiana. The goal in this work is not to undertake an extensive study of the usage of these sources, as this has already been done,[8] but

6 *Ibid*, pp. i-xx. "Le but de cet ouvrage est de faire connaitre par des notes écrites sur des pages en blanc attaché au Digeste des lois de cet état, quel sont les textes des lois civiles et espagnoles qui y ont quelques rapports. […] On ne s'est pas borne en citant les lois qui ont quelques rapports avec les divers articles de Digeste de marquer seulement celle qui contiennent des dispositions semblables; mais on y a ajouté celles qui, sur la même matière, offrent des différences dans ce qu'elles prescrivent ou qui contiennent des exceptions aux principles généraux qui y sont éconcés."

7 *Ibid.*

8 Rodolfo Batiza, "The Louisiana Civil Code of 1808: Its actual Sources and present Relevance", 46 *Tulane Law Review* 1971, pp. 4–165; Rodolfo Batiza, "Sources of the Civil Code of 1808, Facts and Speculation: A Rejoinder", 46 *Tulane Law Review* 1971, pp. 628–652; Rodolfo Batiza, "Justinian's Institute and the Louisiana Civil Code of 1808", 69 *Tulane Law Review* 1994, pp. 1639–1648; Rodolfo Batiza, "Roman Law in the French and Louisiana Civil Codes: A comparative textual Survey", 69 *Tulane Law Review* 1994, pp. 1601–1630; Robert A. Pascal, "Sources of the Digest of 1808: A Reply to Professor Batiza", 46 *Tulane Law Review* 1971, pp. 603–627. For a summary of this debate, see Joseph Modeste Sweeney, "Tournament of Scholars over the Sources of the Civil Code of 1808", 46 *Tulane Law Review* 1972, pp. 585–602. For other contributions written on the subject, see also Louis Baudouin, "The Influence of the Code Napoléon", 33 *Tulane Law Review* 1958, pp. 21–28; Olivier Moréteau, "Louisiana 1812–2012: 200 Years of Statehood and 300 Years of French Law Influence, 59 *Louisiana Bar Journal* 2012, pp. 325–326; Seth S. Brostoff, "The Encyclopedist Code: 'Ancien Droit' Legal Encyclopedias and their verbatim Influence on the Louisiana Digest of 1808", 13 *Journal of Civil Law Studies* 2020, pp. 33–86.

to present the main sources of the Civil Codes of Louisiana. In 1971, Rodolfo Batiza carried out the main study of the sources of the 1808 Digest, identifying the sources of each of its articles. According to Batiza, 85% of the articles of the code were influenced by, derived from, or an exact replica of the Napoleonic Code. This preeminence given to French sources generated significant controversy, especially given that Spanish law was in force at the time of acquisition by the United States. In response to Batiza's claim, Robert A. Pascal argued that both Spanish and French law were derived from Roman law, and that it was thus dangerous to describe certain articles as being inherited from the French when they might just as well come from Spanish law.[9] Pascal also explained that, at the time of codification in Louisiana, Spanish law was predominant in the Louisiana courts. Other studies of the legal foundations of Louisiana jurisprudence over the period 1803 to 1828 show that the codes, customs, and laws of Spain were cited four times more than their French counterparts in legally justifying court decisions.[10] Nevertheless, the sheer volume of articles produced by Batiza and Pascal prompted Joseph Modeste Sweeney to call their controversy a "tournament of scholars" in 1973.[11] Not surprisingly, this controversy continues, and debate continues today over the French or Spanish nature of the code.[12] Controversy aside, France and Spain were not the only sources of the 1825 Civil Code of Louisiana. Indeed, both authors revealed a surprising source of the 1808 Digest: William Blackstone.[13] Specifically, in the preliminary

9 Robert A. Pascal, "Sources of the Digest of 1808: A Reply to Professor Batiza", 46 *Tulane Law Review* 1971, pp. 603–608.

10 Raphael J. Rabalais, "The Influence of Spanish Laws and Treatises on the Jurisprudence of Louisiana; 1762–1828", 42 *Louisiana Law Review* 1982, pp. 1485–1508.

11 Joseph Modeste Sweeney, "Tournament of Scholars over the Sources of the Civil Code of 1808", 46 *Tulane Law Review* 1972, pp. 585–602.

12 Alain A. Levasseur, "The Louisiana Civil Code: A Vademecum", 82 *Louisiana Law Review* 2022, pp. 1109–1141; Agustín Parise, "A Translator's Toolbox: The Law, Moreau-Lislet's Library, and the Presence of multilingual Dictionaries in nineteenth-century Louisiana", 76 *Louisiana Law Review* 2016, pp. 1163–1184; John W. Cairns, "Spanish Law, the 'Teatro de la legislaciòn universal de España e Indias', and the Background to the Drafting of the Digest of Orleans of 1808", 31 / 32 *Tulane European & Civil Law Forum* 2017, pp. 79–120; Vernon Valentine Palmer, "Sounding the Retreat: The Exit of Spanish Law in Early Louisiana 1805–1808", 31 / 32 *Tulane European & Civil Law Forum* 2017, pp. 121–147; Gail S. Stephenson, "Custom as a Source of Law in Louisiana", 79 *Louisiana Law Review* 2019, pp. 1046–1070; Seth S. Brostoff, "The Encyclopedist Code: 'Ancien Droit' Legal Encyclopedias and their verbatim Influence on the Louisiana Digest of 1808", 13 *Journal of Civil Law Studies* 2020, pp. 33–86.

13 Stephen M. Sheppard, "Legal Jambalaya: A Commentary on John Cairns' 'Blackstone on the Bayous', in *Re-interpreting Blackstone's Commentaries: A Seminal Text in national and international Contexts*, ed. Wilfried Prest, Oxford: Hart Publishing, 2014.

TABLE 2 The Similarities between the 1808 Digest and the *Blackstone Commentaries*

1808 Digest of Louisiana	***Blackstone Commentaries*, French translation**
Article 14 Les termes d'une loi doivent être généralement entendus dans leur signification la plus connue et la plus usitée, sans s'attacher autant aux raffinements des règles de la grammaire, qu'à leur acceptation générale et vulgaire.	*N 3, Vol 1, 86* Les mots doivent être entendus dans le sens le plus connus & le plus usité; c'est à dire, en faisant plus d'attention à l'usage général & populaire, qu'à la propriété grammaticale.
Article 18 Le moyen enfin le plus universel et le plus efficace pour découvrir le véritable sens d'une loi, lorsque les expressions en sont douteuses, est de considérer la raison et l'esprit de cette loi, ou la cause qui a détermine la Législature à la rendre.	*N 3, Vol 1, 88* Le moyen enfin le plus universel & le plus efficace pour découvrir le véritable sens d'une loi, lorsque les mots sont douteux, est d'en considérer la raison & l'esprit; c'est-à-dire, le motif qui l'a fait faire.

title,[14] two articles are versions of those found in the famous *Blackstone Commentaries* (Table 2).[15]

14 See also James C. Carter, *The proposed Codification of our Common Law*, New York (NY): Evening Post Job Printing Office, 1884, p. 65. In an assessment of the Civil Code of Louisiana, he observed that the drafters were "largely imbued with the principles and methods of the English common law, they have looked to that body of jurisprudence, so far as the code permitted them, as containing the real sources of the law, and have fully adopted its maxim of stare decisis. Nothing is more observable than the extent to which the English and American reports and textbooks are cited as authoritative in that state."

15 Stephen M. Sheppard, "Legal Jambalaya: A Commentary on John Cairns' 'Blackstone on the Bayous', in *Re-interpreting Blackstone's Commentaries: A Seminal Text in national and international Contexts*, ed. Wilfried Prest, Oxford: Hart Publishing, 2014.

The Blackstone articles show a limited introduction of the common law tradition into the heart of the 1825 Civil Code of Louisiana, perhaps a premonition of the evolution of Louisiana law throughout the following centuries. Blackstone is not only found in some parts of the 1808 Digest, but is also key to its English translation because these articles introduced terminology understood by any English-speaking lawyer. Blackstone was studied and known by all and also of great influence in Louisiana. The *Blackstone Commentaries* were frequently cited in court, whether in civil or criminal cases. Moreau-Lislet had no less than two sets of them in his personal library, one in French and one in English.[16] As a result, this fundamental reference, part of the everyday practice of law, could not be ignored in the process of drafting the civil code.

Otherwise the code did not change dramatically over time. The 1825 Civil Code of Louisiana looks very similar to the 1808 Digest, but with the addition of a few chapters and several specific changes at the article level. Batiza studied the sources of the Civil Code of Louisiana much as he did for the 1808 Digest, tracing the origin of the additions to the code to the Roman *Corpus Juris Civilis*, the *Siete Partidas*, and the 1800 Draft of the French Civil Code, as well as to various works by authors such as Blackstone, Pothier, and Domat, as well as Josef Febrero, Jacques Maleville, and Charles Touiller.[17] Additions to the 1825 Civil Code of Louisiana were inspired in large part by Spanish law, mainly because this version of the code was created to include the remaining legislation which was not present in the 1808 Digest. Thus, the 1825 Civil Code of Louisiana differs more from the Napoleonic Code than its predecessor due to the more direct incorporation of Spanish law, which also brought its number of articles up to 3,556 compared to the 2,281 for the French Civil Code. It is because of this revision that the 1825 Civil Code of Louisiana gained its nickname, "a Spanish girl in a French dress". As for the 1870 Revised Civil Code of Louisiana, there was no change in or addition to the sources of the code. It simply adapted the civil code to the aftermath of the Civil War, mainly by suppressing all articles about or including slavery. Examining the three Civil Codes of Louisiana, it becomes clear that most of their sources arose from French or Spanish law and came from the civil law tradition. Hence, the codes were based on legislation and doctrine with hardly to no common law content.

16 Vernon Valentine Palmer, *The lost Translators of 1808 and the Birth of Civil Law in Louisiana*, Athens (GA): University of Georgia Press, 2021, pp. 75–78.

17 Rodolfo Batiza, "The actual Sources of the Louisiana Project of 1823: A general analytical Survey", 47 *Tulane Law Review* 1972, p. 3.

4.1.2 *The Sources of a Code Like No Other, the Code of Georgia*

The Code of Georgia does not explicitly state the different sources it used, and it does not provide the sources underlying each section. Nor does there seem to be a document that lists the sources by article. In 1951, Almand Bond speculated that the lack of source justification was intentional, "because the Commissioners did not want the legislature to really know how much new law they had written into the code".[18] However, if the quantity and variety of sources was not made explicit, the General Assembly of Georgia's December 9, 1858 act appointing the commission for the codification of the law did, at least, indicate the sources that should be used to write the Code of Georgia. These included the law of Georgia, whether it was derived from the constitution, the statutes, or common law, or the decisions of the Supreme Court. The next logical source were the English statutes applicable within the territory.[19] The latter were defined by William Schley,[20] who was appointed in 1826 to compile the English law in use in Georgia.[21] In consequence, the legislature gave an exhaustive list of legal sources for the code, rather than allowing the commissioners room to select from all the possible material sources. In this way, the legislature isolated a precise list of sources and thereby gained control over the contents of the code. The General Assembly's 1858 act also set out the specific model that the code was to follow, indicating that the layout of the code should emulate that of the Code of Alabama.[22] Even if the Code of Georgia does not use the content of the Code of Alabama, the latter is still to be considered a source which dictated the Code of Georgia's organization and form. This is also why the organization of legal concepts in the Code of Georgia is very different from that of the Napoleonic Code.[23]

---

18 Bond Almand, "The Preparation and Adoption of the Code of 1863", 14 *Georgia Bar Journal* 1951, pp. 161–167; Richard H. Clark, "The History of the first Georgia Code", in *Report of the Seventh Annual Meeting of the Georgia Bar Association*, ed. unknown, Atlanta (GA): Jas. P. Harrison & Co., 1890, p. 159.

19 *1858 Georgia Laws No. 95*. "a code, which shall as near as practicable, embrace in a condensed form, the laws of Georgia, whether derived from the common law, the constitution of the state, the statutes of the state, the decisions of the Supreme Court, or the statutes of England of force in this state."

20 Erwin J. Surrency, "The Georgia Code of 1863 and its Place in the Codification Movement", 11 *Journal of Southern Legal History* 2003, p. 91.

21 *GA C. 1861*, pp. iii–iv.

22 *1858 Georgia Laws No. 95*. "and shall be modeled, if practicable, upon the present Code of Alabama."

23 Jefferson James Davis, "The Georgia Code of 1863: America's first comprehensive Code", 4 *Journal of Southern Legal History* 1995, p. 14.

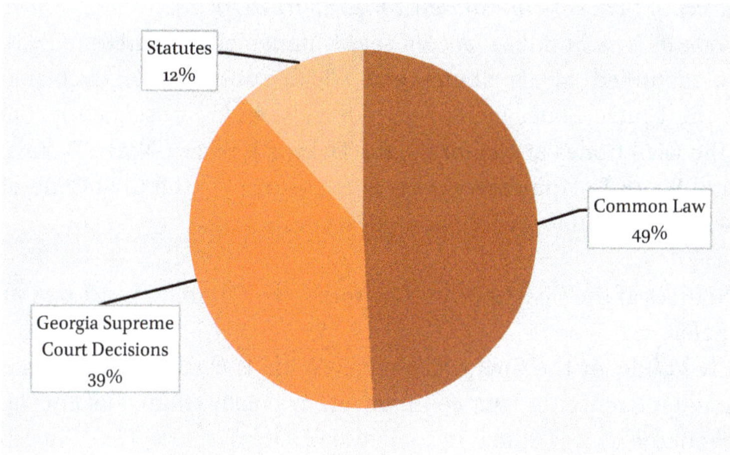

DIAGRAM 1 The Sources of the Code of Georgia Articles on Contract, Torts, and Equity

No full study exists of the code's sources. Jefferson James Davis' 1996 study of the Code of Georgia examines all the sources of the 482 articles (of the 1,575 articles in the code) related to contracts, tort, and equity, corresponding to three titles (of nine) in the code. His study showed that 56 articles were derived from state statute, 188 from decisions of the Georgia Supreme Court, and the remaining 238 from the common law, including the different legal texts that shaped it (Diagram 1).[24]

Though this study certainly did not analyze the entire code, it nonetheless attests to the fact that the code seems to follow the sources laid out by the legislature. One of the discoveries concerning the sources of the Code of Georgia is that at no point did the code's authors seem to have drawn on sources from the civil law tradition. Even if this study is partial and the official list of sources came before the code, it only listed common law sources.

The lack of civil law sources, such as the Napoleonic Code or even the Civil Code of Louisiana, can be interpreted as a willful rejection of civil law sources, and explains why this code is so different from the others. Even if some similarities may appear with the aforementioned civil codes, the Georgian legislature and commissioners never recognized or admitted any civil law influence, thus rendering the Code of Georgia an exclusively common law civil code.

24 *Ibid*, p. 22.

4.1.3 *Sources of the Civil Code of New York and Its Heirs*

The Civil Code of New York has its own set of fundamental sources (4.1.3.1), which were identified by its drafter and which subsequently circulated throughout the United States along with the code itself. Consequently, the sources of the Civil Codes of California, the Dakota Territory, North Dakota, Montana, and South Dakota draw on the same sources as the Civil Code of New York, with the addition, of course, of local law (4.1.3.2).

4.1.3.1 Sources of the Civil Code of New York—the Common Law Code Reference

The Field Civil Code, or the Civil Code of New York, is considered the main example of and reference for later common law civil codes due to its circulation throughout the United States. Its main writer, David Dudley Field, identified the sources of his code and had them printed in its official version. Indeed, the author placed the source identification under each article of the code, creating a precise system which at times went so far as to mention the exact common law decisions undergirding specific legal principles. The jurisprudence, statute, doctrine, or other sources at the origin of each rule within the code can thus be perfectly traced in cases where they are listed. Field referenced the sources this way in about two thirds of the code.[25] When looking for the sources of the articles of the Field Civil Code, three types of cases thus arise. The first case is the absence of source references, usually occurring with articles pertaining to a well-established rule that does not need to be traced, such as Article 75.[26] The second case consists of articles containing the following statement: "This provision is new, but manifestly just, under the present state of the law".[27] For instance, this occurs in Article 83.[28] The statement indicates the creation of a new legal rule justified not by earlier written codes or laws but by the contemporary state of the law or society. In consequence, these provisions represent pure societal legislation. Finally, the third case, making up two thirds of the code's articles, appears as follows:

25 Rodolfo Batiza, "Sources of the Field Civil Code: The Civil Law Influences on a Common Law Code", 60 *Tulane Law Review* 1986, pp. 799–819.

26 *NY Civ. C. 1865*, § 75. "Husband and wife contract towards each other obligations of mutual respect, fidelity, and support."

27 *NY Civ. C. 1865*, § 83. "This provision is new, but manifestly just, under the present state of the laws."

28 *NY Civ. C. 1865*, § 83. "Neither husband nor wife, as such, is answerable for the acts of the other."

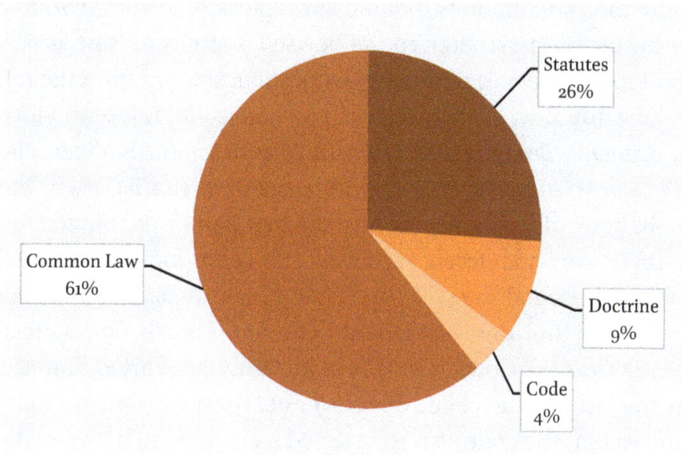

DIAGRAM 2 The Sources of the Civil Code of New York (Field Civil Code)

> If the wife abandons the husband, he is not liable for her support[1] until she offers to return,[2] unless she was justified, by his misconduct, in abandoning him.
>
> 1 *Blowers v. Sturtevant, 4 Denio*, 46, and cases there cited.
>
> 2 *McGahay v. Williams*, 12 *Johns*, 293.

Article 85 of the Field Civil Code shows how precisely the code commissioners justified and explained their sources, going into detail and highlighting the common law origins of each part of the articles. Attention to detail was also a way to demonstrate how much the commissioners had mastered the common law, and to prove that the code did not necessarily mean a change within the content of the law. We can also assume that such detail was intended for educational purposes serving to introduce the legal profession to the origins of codified law.

The Civil Code of New York consists of 2,034 articles, with 1,376 of them including an explicit list of sources written by Field himself. In addition to his studies of the Civil Codes of Louisiana, Rodolfo Batiza[29] has explored the Civil Code of New York's sources, dividing them into four categories: statutory, judicial, doctrinal, and other codes. He finds that 700 references arose from judicial sources, specifically, from English, national, and local courts,

29 Rodolfo Batiza, "Sources of the Field Civil Code: The Civil Law Influences on a Common Law Code", 60 *Tulane Law Review* 1986, pp. 799–819.

and based on more than 50 different common law reports.[30] 300 of the source references were to statues, most often to the Revised Statutes of New York.[31] Slightly more than 100 references pertained to doctrinal sources from the following authors: Edward Coke, William Blackstone, James Kent, Joseph Story, Thomas Lewin, *Branch's*, *Broom's*, and *Francis's Maxims*, John Bouvier, and Robert-Joseph Pothier.[32] These sources vary in terms of territorial origin but represent the main body of legal references in the first half of the nineteenth century. Finally, there were 50 references to five prior codes from three different places: the 1808 Digest and the 1825 Civil Code of Louisiana, the Justinian Code of Ancient Rome, and the Napoleonic Code and French Commercial Code (Diagram 2).[33] The Civil Code of New York was truly an effort to draft the common law, as the latter is the code's direct source. However, Batiza's study of the sources shows that the code also established a connection between the common law and civil law traditions. Indeed, geographically, the sources of the Field Civil Code come from five locations around the world and two different traditions, which it attempts to bridge. However, numerically, there is a clear imbalance in favor of the common law tradition, as references to common law sources correspond respectively to 700 references of common law rules and 300 references of statutory laws. This makes up 1,000 articles with references to common law sources out of the 1,376 articles with identified sources in the code. This number does not even include references to doctrinal sources from the common law tradition. It is therefore safe to say that the common law is the main source of the Civil Code of New York and that this code incorporates only a limited amount of the civil law tradition.[34]

4.1.3.2 The Sources of the Descendants of the Civil Code of New York

The heirs of the Field Civil Code all have some peculiarities, as each code added the state's own laws to the code's basic structure. The goal of this section is to determine the extent to which the inclusion of the local law changed the content of the Civil Code of New York.

30 *Ibid*, p. 804.

31 *Ibid*, pp. 799–819.

32 *Ibid.*

33 *Ibid.*

34 *Draft of a Civil Code for the State of New York; prepared by the Commissioners of the Code and submitted to the Judges and others for Examination, Prior to Revision by the Commissioners*, ed. unknown, Albany: Weed, Parsons & Co., 1862, p. viii.

Adopted in 1872, the Civil Code of California is, in reality, the 1860 Draft of a Civil Code for the State of New York adapted to Californian law.[35] The civil code's editors chose to base their work on the 1860 draft rather than on the final 1865 Civil Code of New York. This choice is probably due to the greater availability of the draft. The Civil Code of California contains 3,543 articles, 1,509 more than the Civil Code of New York. It includes 385 articles on social questions and hydraulic rights,[36] corresponding to 25% of new articles. These additions included provisions specific to conditions in California. The sources of California's civil code were, first, those of the Civil Code of New York, namely English, US, and New York common law and statutes, plus the Roman, French, and Louisianan codes. To these sources, the Californian commissioners added Californian law, which is partly derived from Spanish and Mexican law.[37] The Californian laws in themselves are the statutes and the common law of the State of California. Indeed, 1,361 of the 3,543 articles of the code cite a statute of the State of California as their source, which corresponds to just over 38% of the articles in the code. However, the code does not only include the statutes of the state, but also its common law. As the revision commission stated in 1874, "Codes collect the principles established in a series of cases, and reduce them into maxims or general formula".[38]

Regarding the sources of the Civil Code of the Dakota Territory, its original version from 1865 is the 1860 Draft of a Civil Code for the State of New York adopted without any alteration. Hence, the code's sources did not vary from the Civil Code of New York. The Dakotan drafters did not even include local laws, simply adopting the code as it was. This changed with the 1877 revision:

> It is well known to the profession that our codes are for the most part transcripts from the New York Code and the California Code, completed by the leading local decision in the state.[39]

The Civil Code of the Dakota Territory subsequently became more than just the Field Civil Code. The revision translated the evolution of the territory's

35 Maurice E. Harrison, "First half-century of the California Civil Code", 185 *California Law Review* 1922, p. 187; Arthur Rolston, "An Uncommon Common Law: Codification and the Development of California Law 1849–1874", 2 *California Legal History Journal* 2007, p. 159.

36 CA *Civ. C. 1872*, §§ 283–653, 1410–1425.

37 Arthur Rolston, "An Uncommon Common Law: Codification and the Development of California Law 1849–1874", 2 *California Legal History Journal* 2007, pp. 149–151.

38 "California Code Commission Reports", in CA *Civ. C. 1872*, p. 22.

39 DT *Rev. C. 1877*, p. III.

civil code model, consequently creating a transposition of the Civil Code of California adapted to the local law in the form of the Revised Civil Code of the Dakota Territory. In the wake of this revision, the law of the Dakota Territory—its common law and statutes—was added to the sources described previously, namely the Field Civil Code and of the Civil Code of California and English, US, and New York common law and statutes, in addition to the Roman, French, and Louisianan codes, followed by Spanish and Mexican law.

The Revised Civil Code of the Dakota Territory, like its predecessors, displays its sources by article. It does this, however, to a lesser extent than its predecessor. Specifically, 1,770 of the 2,133 articles of the code contain references to origins, which corresponds to slightly more than 50% of the articles of the code. Three types of sources are found among the code references: the 1872 Civil Code of California, local jurisprudence, and the statutes of the Dakota Territory. Each article's cited sources contain a reference to the relevant 1872 Civil Code of California article from which it was derived. The second main source is local court decisions. More precisely, 542 articles cite references to the Dakota Territory courts of law, divided into three different published court reports: the *Northwestern Reporter*, the *Dakota Reporter*, and the *Minnesota Reporter*. The final source referenced in the code is from the statutes of the Dakota Territory—the Laws of Dakota—which can be found in 114 articles. Local Dakota law, meaning common law plus the statutes, is cited in 645 articles, representing 31% of the articles of the code. The number of provisions from local law in the Revised Civil Code of the Dakota Territory seems quite low compared to the other codes, but it was a market increase over the earlier version which included no local law. It is important to note, however, that most of the references to Dakota Territory laws are to common law or statutes that date between the first civil code and the start of the civil code revision process.

After the Dakota Division, three different codes were written, each an attempt to adjust the law to the new political reality of the two resulting states. In the case of the Civil Code of North Dakota, the sources are the same as those of the Revised Civil Code of the Dakota Territory—as enumerated above, English, US, and New York common law and statutes, plus Roman, French, and Louisianan codes, followed by Spanish and Mexican law—which became Californian common law and statutes—as well as the Dakota Territory's common law and statutes. The idea of this code was not to implement significant changes but to keep the same code and sources, though with a few tweaks. In fact, the code even displays the numeration of the former Civil Code of the Dakota Territory to allow for swift location of the original article, and it only mentions the source of the article if there has been a change from the original version. Hence, it appears that only 322 articles (13%) of the 2,476 included in the code are different from the former Civil Code of the Dakota Territory. It can therefore be safely assumed that the intent of this code was not to change the law, but to maintain legal continuity during the transition to statehood. In addition, all of the altered articles contained a reference to the Dakota Territory or North Dakota's local common law and statutes.

A different system was used for the Civil Code of Montana. Only 164 articles out of the 1,291 have a small paragraph explaining specific clauses with reference to a statute (10 articles) and / or to case law (159 articles). This information allows us to connect these parts of the Civil Code of Montana to the local law. For the rest, no sources were listed. However, examination of the unreferenced articles shows that they were derived word-for-word from those of the Revised Civil Code of the Dakota Territory, and they can thus be similarly traced to the sources enumerated in the paragraph above, again English, US, and New York common law and statutes, plus the Roman, French, and Louisianan codes, followed by Spanish and Mexican law.

Finally, the Civil Code of South Dakota does not mention the sources of its articles at all. However, we can suppose that it has also been adapted to the local law, as evidenced by the fact that the code's introduction recognizes the Civil Code of North Dakota as inspiration and partial transliteration. Secondly, adaptation to local law is reflected in changes to the number of articles in the code compared to its model. The Civil Code of South Dakota consists of 2,477 articles, 212 less than the Civil Code of North Dakota. Some articles were omitted for being inefficient or inapplicable within the state, while others were removed and replaced by a different law. In each case, the code was adapted to the state. Local peculiarities are evident in these alterations although there is no account of the reasons for or the origin of the changes.

4.1.4 *Comparative Study of the Use of Different Sources within the US Civil Codes*

As evidenced by the previous sections, the sources of the US civil codes[40] were as varied as the codes themselves. The following graph (Diagram 3) visualizes the use of the various sources within the different codes. Putting all the codes together, there are eighteen sources that codifiers drew from.

Comparative analysis of the source's usage shows that the most common source for the codes was English doctrine. However, even as English doctrine makes up 11% of the total sources, it is not that far ahead of the 9% representing

40 *LA Digest 1808; LA Civ. C. 1825; LA Rev. Civ. C. 1870; GA C. 1861; NY Civ. C. 1865; DT Rev. C. 1877; ND Rev. C. 1895; MT C. & Stat 1895; SD Rev. C. 1903.*

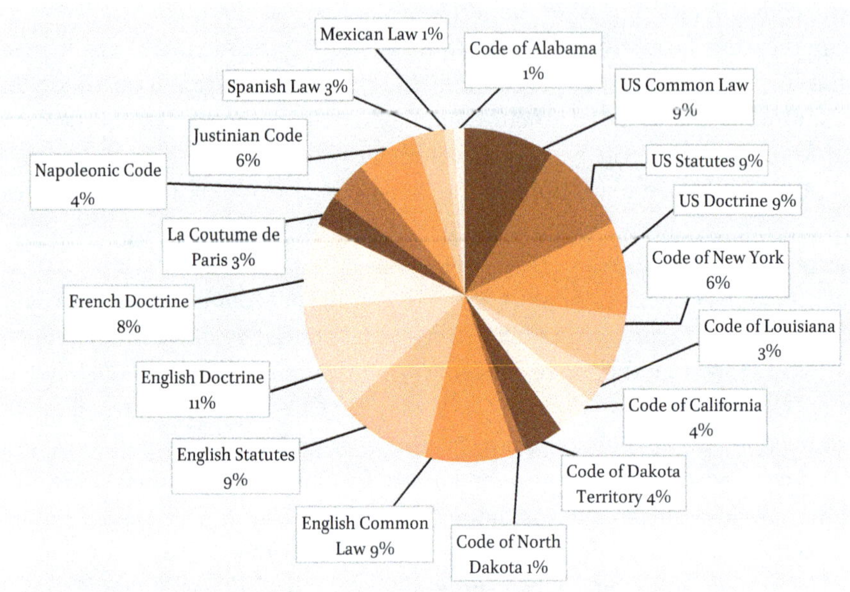

DIAGRAM 3 The Sources of US Civil Codes

both US common law, statutes, and doctrine, as well as English common law and statutes. Hence, preliminary observation of the sources of nineteenth-century civil codes shows that common law sources predominated. This aligns with the fact that all the US civil codes except one, the Civil Code of Louisiana, are common law codes. A more detailed comparative study of the sources of the codes can be undertaken through two different analytic approaches. First, the sources can be studied according to their countries of origin and, second, allowing the identification of a predominant influence from a country over the nineteenth-century US civil codes. Secondly, the sources can be examined according to their legal type, in order to understand whether one type of legal document was used more than others in the drafting of the codes. The different numbers and percentages in the following charts are based solely on the main sources of the code, identified by the code commissioners as the direct source used to create a code's different legal rules. Other sources, what might be described as unintentional sources, are present through the reworking of articles from other codes. These indirect sources are not shown in the chart and were not included in the calculation of the usage of particular sources in the codes. These indirect sources are the sources of the code's model, but they had to be excluded from this calculation, whose goal was to reveal the draftsmen's intentions.

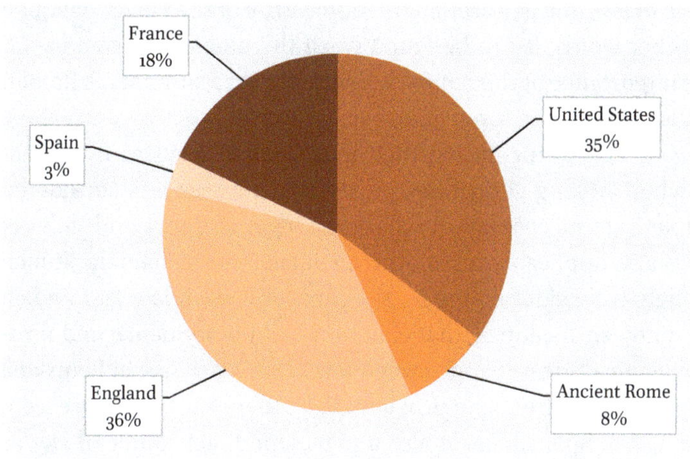

DIAGRAM 4 The Sources of US Civil Codes by Country of Origin

While they are still technically secondary sources, their inclusion was not necessarily intentional. For example, by adopting the Civil Code of California in the Dakota Territory, the code's drafters included some Mexican law in the sources of the new codes, but it is impossible to know whether the legislature knew and willingly decided to add those laws to the state's legal corpus in adopting the code. It can be assumed that these new legal sources were included incidentally, in some cases without lawmakers realizing they were doing so. The secondary sources are still mentioned, however, for they often help explain key aspects of the codes, such as how a law foreign to a state's legal culture man-aged to appear in the code. This is how, for example, some Spanish and Mexican laws can be found in the Dakota Territory, a place never under Spanish or Mexican dominion.

The study of the sources according to their country of origin (Diagram 4) shows that the most common sources are from common law tradition countries—England and the United States—which together correspond to 71% of the direct sources of the nineteenth-century US civil codes. This is hardly surprising, considering common law was the applicable legal tradition in the majority of the states that codified their private law as well as the fact that most of the codes on US territory are common law codes, most derived from the Field Civil Code. Indeed, English and US law, whether common law or statutes, is a source present in all the codes except that of Louisiana, although even there the common law maintained a slight influence through Blackstone. Nevertheless, one civil law source—Roman law—can be found in all the codes, albeit as an indirect influence. It is present in Louisiana, Georgia, and New York as a direct source of law, and as a secondary source in all of the Field Civil Code successors. In other words, it can be found in all the nineteenth-century US civil codes. The importance of this source is definitely not a surprise, as Roman law is used as a legal reference throughout the world.

Roman law was and is highly regarded and is often used as a preeminent example when looking at civil law, most likely because it is considered the "first" complete set of civil laws.[41] The same logic of direct and indirect sources of law is also applicable for another civil law source, namely, French law. Unsurprisingly—considering the high regard for French law and French authors in the nineteenth century that compounded the influence and prestige of the Napoleonic Code—it appears as a direct source of law in Louisiana and New York and as an indirect source of law in all other codes with the exception of Georgia. Lastly, Spanish law is also a notable indirect source of law, as it is a main source of law in both Louisiana and California and thus an indirect source in the Civil Code of the Dakota Territory and its successors (North Dakota, Montana, and South Dakota). The case of Spanish law demonstrates how the circulation of codes could transplant a particular legal tradition into a state with no link to its country of origin, its history, and by consequence, its law. Hence, some legal traditions deeply rooted in a foreign and unfamiliar culture were introduced and implemented without significant awareness or consideration. An example is the provision allowing for prescription as a means of acquiring private property. Prescription was defined in Louisiana and California—under similar influences from Spanish law—and then introduced in the Dakota Territory through direct adoption of the article from the Civil Code of California.[42]

Accordingly, geographical analysis of the sources of law illustrates that common law was the main source of the codes, while the civil law was a secondary influence for all the codes, except for in Louisiana, where the order of sources was reversed. What is also striking is that, out of the three main civil codes (Louisiana, New York and Georgia), two (Louisiana and New York) had civil law sources as the direct sources of law. This fact shows the importance of the civil

41 Fritz Schulz, *History of Roman Legal Science*, Oxford: Clarendon Press, 1946; Patrick Vassart, *Manuel de Droit romain*, Bruxelles: Bruylant, 2015; Ignazio Castellucci, "Law v. Lex: An Analysis of a Critical Relation in Roman and Civil Law", 8 *Global Jurist* 2008, pp. 1–32; Timothy G. Kearly, "From Rome to the Restatement: S. P. Scott, Fred Blume, Clyde Pharr, and Roman Law in early twentieth-century America", 108 *Law Library Journal* 2016, pp. 55–77.

42 LA *Digest 1808*; LA *Civ. C. 1825*, Article 866; LA *Rev. Civ. C. 1870*, Article 870; CA *Civ. C. 1872*, §§ 1000–1001; DT *Rev. C. 1877*, §§ 580–582.

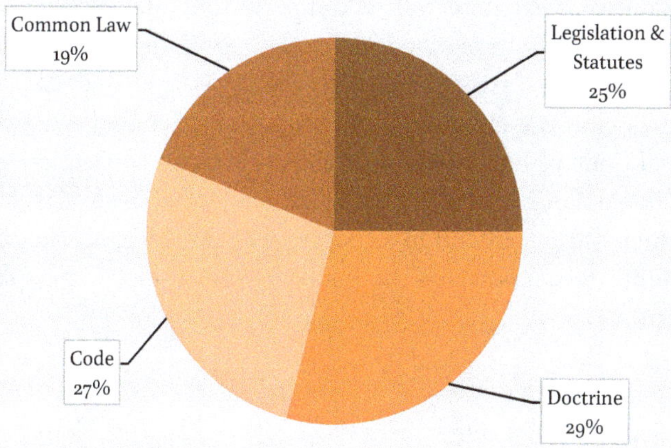

DIAGRAM 5 The Sources of US Civil Codes by Type

law tradition in the codification process. Moreover, examination of the sources shows that when they turned to civil law, common law lawyers privileged the Napoleonic Code over other European codes.[43] As Masferrer writes, the "standard of code is the continental Napoleonic [...] Code", and consequently, "for the English the model of a code is the Code Napoléon". Indeed, "[m]any common law lawyers cannot envisage the possibility of codifying without Napoleon in mind".[44]

The second way of analyzing the sources of the codes is according to their types, that is, according to the type of legal document that they are (Diagram 5). Most common law codes drew from the same types of sources, although the different codes privileged different sources. Indeed, it should be noted that the least represented source in the comparative analysis was case law. Even though it is the main source for all of the common law codes, case law was not used at all in the Civil Codes of Louisiana, a fact which tipped the balance and made it less important overall. It is also explained by the fact that even if it is found in most of the codes as the principal source, case law competes with all the other sources of law, such as statutes and doctrine. Indeed, the study here looks only at what sources were used, and not to what extent each source was used in the codes, for there are vast differences from one code to another, as earlier

43 Aniceto Masferrer, "French Codification and Codiphobia in Common Law Traditions", 34 *Tulane European & Civil Law Forum* 2019, p. 5.

44 *Ibid*, p. 6.

code studies have shown. The circulation and mutual influence of the codes also meant the appearance of unplanned, undesired, or unidentified sources in many of them. This was the case for all the successors of the Field Civil Code. Indeed, the influence and the circulation of the New York model—drawing as it did on the Civil Code of Louisiana—had the unforeseen consequence of making the Civil Code of Louisiana a source of all the common law codes, even for those states which did not intend to adopt its laws. As a result, a key element of the US codification model was the acculturation and legal transplantation into new territories.

4.2 The Shape of US Civil Codes

Particularly in those states accustomed to common law, the question of how to organize a civil code was central to the debates preceding the codes. Indeed, each local debate grappled with how to introduce changes to the law, and with how to phrase and to organize legal provisions in the form of a code. Of particular interest was the question of how to enshrine common law in writing, thereby changing its form without, it was hoped, changing its content. To support their endeavor, the code's drafters used the Napoleonic Code and the Civil Codes of Louisiana as models. The Napoleonic Code—a code rooted in rationalization of the law—was used, for instance, to illustrate the formal aspects of codification.

Here the goal is to identify whether there is a nineteenth-century US civil code model that was common to all of the codifying states. To this end, I have analyzed the form of each code by studying aspects of the code's written form, such as syntax, then by looking at its language, and finally by doing a comparative analysis of the organization of the nineteenth-century civil codes.

4.2.1 *Analysis of the Form of Civil Code Articles: Syntax and Type of Provisions*

The shape or form of an article is defined by how it is written, which fundamentally determines the way it is read and understood. It is form that allows a message to be transmitted or, in some cases, to be imposed. For this exact reason, one of the most emblematic features of a civil code is its writing style. For instance, the Napoleonic Code's iconic writing style and features are represented worldwide, and have become a symbol of codification. It is by its particular style that a section of a code acquires its identity and strength. This style is characterized, first, by a code's unique syntax, and second, by the duality between mandatory and discretionary provisions.

4.2.1.1 The Civil Code Articles, an Iconic Syntax

The grammatical and syntactical choices made in writing an article have a direct impact on the law. Indeed, depending on how the article is written, it can also restructure certain aspects of the legislation or attempt to predict or control the future.[45] One of the first characteristics of a code section or article inspired by the Napoleonic Code is the austerity of the text, meaning that the law is expressed soberly without images or ornamentation. The contents are clearly stated without color or romance in,[46] in a style that departs from the accretion of facts and precedents characteristic of the common law. Today, this objective and way of phrasing legal pronouncements is called the legislative style, and is also referred to as neutral language. It allows the code editor to make a timeless and universal legislative provision.[47]

The strength of the legislative style (Table 3) is the use of clear, short sentences, written succinctly, highlighting the inherent logic of the content of the provision and, consequently, promoting the rationalization of law. The law is not a matter of ornamentation, but an elementary subject whose form should not divert attention from its content.[48] Writing a code in legislative style increases the accuracy of the legal rule and provides the greatest possible clarity. This feature is usually enhanced by the usage of the third person, which creates a sense of universality. The purpose "of modern legislation is to have nothing left to the imagination".[49] Specialized vocabulary and precise definition of the terms used in specific articles also defines legal language,[50] which is quite different from ordinary language. Legal language is characterized by accuracy, precision, conciseness, and simplicity of terms,[51] and it is directly linked to the characteristic austerity of civil codes. In legal language words sometimes do not have the same meaning as in common usage. Moreover, the law, through legal language, must be serious without becoming so solemn as to alienate the reader.[52]

---

45 Olivier Moréteau, "Les Frontières de la Langue et du Droit: Vers une Méthodologie de la Traduction juridique", 61 *Revue internationale de Droit comparé* 2009, pp. 695–713.

46 Jean Ray, *Essai sur la Structure logique du Code Civil français*, Paris: Librairie Felix Alcan, 1926, pp. 23–24.

47 Dennis R. Klinck, "The Language of Codification", 14 *Queen's Law Journal* 1989, p. 38.

48 *Ibid*, pp. 33–66.

49 Jean Ray, *Essai sur la Structure logique du Code Civil français*, Paris: Librairie Felix Alcan, 1926, p. 25.

50 Heikki E. S. Mattila and Christopher Goddard, *Comparative legal Linguistics: Language of Law, Latin and modern Lingua Francas*, 2nd ed., Farnham: Ashgate Publishing, 2013, p. 201.

51 Paul-André Crépeau, "Réflexions sur la Codification du Droit Privé", 38 *Osgoode Hall Law Journal* 2000, p. 286.

52 Heikki E. S. Mattila and Christopher Goddard, *Comparative legal Linguistics: Language of Law, Latin and modern Lingua Francas*, 2nd ed., Farnham: Ashgate Publishing, 2013, p. 54.

TABLE 3 The "Legislative Style" in the French Civil Code and the US Civil Codes

	Examples of Articles
France	*FR C. Civ. 1804*, Article 2. "The law only states for the future: she has no retroactive effect."
Louisiana	*LA Civ. C. 1825*, Article 1. "Law is a solemn expression of legislative will, upon a subject of general interest and interior regulation."
Georgia	*GA C. 1861*, § 1652. "Marriage is encouraged by the law, and very effort to restrain or discourage marriage by contract, condition limitations or otherwise is invalid and void."
New York	*NY Civ. C. 1865*, § 1884. "Law is a rule of property and of conduct prescribed by the sovereign power of the state."
California	*CA Civ. C. 1872*, Section 3. "No part of it is retroactive unless expressly so declared."
Dakota Territory	*DT Rev. C. 1877*, Section 2. "Law is a rule of property and of conduct prescribed by the sovereign power."
North Dakota	*ND Rev. C. 1895*, § 2763. "Husband and wife contract toward each other obligations of mutual respect, fidelity, and support."
Montana	*MT C. & Stat. 1895*, § 1. "This act shall be known as the Civil Code of the State of Montana."
South Dakota	*SD Rev. C. 1903*, § 2. "Law is the rule of property and of conduct prescribed by the sovereign power."

In the case of codes the use of legal terms meant a legal revolution, as the meanings of the terms were both precisely defined and set in stone for subsequent generations. This was an important change for the common law tradition especially, which is characterized by the constant evolution of legal language.

The example of articles selected randomly from the US civil codes shows the famous legislative style in action. Whatever the code, the articles are all written in a clear and precise style without any figurative speech. Furthermore, all are grammatically composed in the same manner, demonstrating the rationalization and standardization of the law.

The civil codes use a simpler language, which fulfills its goal of accessibility and comprehensibility to all. In this way, civil law also moves further away from the traditional writing of the common law. Hence, even in cases where the common law formed the main source for the code, codes went beyond merely recording the common law, engaging instead in a substantive rewriting. The implementation of the legislative style by the civil codes allowed a theory of law to develop and enabled the creation of numerous definitions of legal concepts that did not explicitly exist before but were deduced from case law. By never mentioning precise facts, civil codes instituted an inversion of legal reasoning: the facts now had to be fitted to legislative solutions, and not the other way around. Moreover, in cases where a word requires a definition that is not found in or created by the code, the law requires the reader to refer to the statutes and the common law that the rules come from, also known in civil law tradition as the spirit of the law. Another characteristic and symbolic feature of a code article is its tense. Codes are primarily written in the present tense. The present tense is used to report on something, here the law, and state a fact or principle, which is the purpose of a code; for example, to state the applicable law in a territory. It also helps to make the law in the code mature and unchanging, applicable both at the time of writing and in the future. By being short and written in present tense, the articles in a civil code reach a level of universality that allows any relevant fact to be adapted to them. These features of a code's writing allow its articles to become timeless rather than temporary.

4.2.1.2 Mandatory and Discretionary Provisions

The distinction between mandatory (declarative) and discretionary dispositions is as old as the law itself. It dates back to Roman law with its distinction between *jus cogens*, which was imperative, and *jus dispositivum*, from which it was possible to depart by private contractual agreement. As illustrated in the table of articles below (Table 4 and Table 5),[53] the US civil codes follow the tradition of the Roman civil codes and resume this distinction.

53 The articles have been selected as mere examples and do not by themselves account for a unique vision of the codes.

Both types of dispositions are typical of civil law, helping to highlight the link between authority and citizens[54] and providing different levels of legal strength to the different articles of a code. This distinction has always existed in the civil law system and is a direct consequence of the principle of free will.[55] Articles 11 and 12 of the 1825 Civil Code of Louisiana[56] clearly explain this distinction:

Article 11	Individuals cannot, by their convention, derogate from the force of laws made for the preservation of public order or good morals. But in all cases in which it is not expressly or impliedly prohibited, they can renounce what the law has established in their favor, when the renunciation does not affect the rights of others, and it is not contrary to the public good.
Article 12	Whatever is done in convention of a prohibitory law is void, although the nullity is not formally directed.

Depending on the case, if the article is not related to public order or good morals, it is possible to derogate from it and to adapt the law to the circumstances. These articles represent free will and a flexibility in the law that can, in some particular cases, allow a range of individual options,[57] for instance the previously mentioned possibility of derogating from the discretionary provisions through a private contract. To implement this openness and possibility, discretionary articles were not written in the same way as the declarative ones. The written form of these articles had to show that a choice between different options was possible (as was the case, for example, in Article 1986 of the French Civil Code or Article 920 of the Civil Code of South Dakota). In this case, the codes provide an option granting more freedom to conduct business affairs, while allowing a separate and more specialized statute to deal with the issue in depth. The last way to write a discretionary provision is the use of a negative formula (such as Article 5024 of the Civil Code of North Dakota).

54 Dennis R. Klinck, "The Language of Codification", 14 *Queen's Law Journal* 1989, p. 43.

55 Alejandro M. Garro, "Codification Technique and the Problem of Imperative and Suppletive Laws", 41 *Louisiana Law Review* 1981, pp. 1007–1030.

56 *LA Civ. C. 1825*, Articles 11 and 12.

57 Alejandro M. Garro, "Codification Technique and the Problem of Imperative and Suppletive Laws", 41 *Louisiana Law Review* 1981, p. 1013.

TABLE 4 Provisions' Phrasing in the French Civil Code and the US Civil Codes, Part I

	Examples of declarative Provisions	**Examples of discretionary Provisions**
France	*FR C. Civ. 1804*, Article 214. "La femme est oblige de vivre avec son mari."	*FR C. Civ. 1804*, Article 1986. "Le mandat est gratuit, s'il n'y a pas de convention contraire."
Louisiana	*LA Civ. C. 1825*, Title II, Article 1. "The domicile of each citizen is in the parish wherein is situated his principal establishment."	*LA Civ. C. 1825*, Title XIII, Article 5. "The procuration is gratuitous, unless there has been a contrary agreement."
Georgia	*GA C. 1861*, § 2022. "Lawful interest in this state shall be at the rate of seven per cent, per annum."	*GA C. 1861*, § 1889. "A partnership may be created either by written or parole contract, or may arise from a joint ownership, use and enjoyment of the profits of undivided property, real or personal."
New York	*NY Civ. C. 1865*, § 15. "A minor cannot give a delegation of power."	*NY Civ. C. 1865*, § 128. "A guardian appointed by a court has no power over the person and property of the ward, unless otherwise ordered."
California	*CA Civ. C. 1872*, Section 236. "A guardian is a person appointed to take care of the person or property of another."	*CA Civ. C. 1872*, Section 70. "Marriage may be solemnized by either a Justice of the Supreme Court, District or County Judge, Justice of the Peace, mayor, priest, or minister of the gospel of any denomination."
Dakota Territory	*DT Rev. C. 1877*, Section 265. "The owner of the land in fee has the right to the surface, and to everything permanently situated beneath or above it."	*DT Rev. C. 1877*, Section 1432. "If no term is prescribed by agreement for its duration, a general partnership continues until dissolved by a partner or by operation of law."

TABLE 5 Provisions' Phrasing in the French Civil Code and the US Civil Codes, Part II

	Examples of declarative Provisions	Examples of discretionary Provisions
North Dakota	*ND Rev. C. 1895*, § 2776. "All children born in wedlock are presumed to be legitimate."	*ND Rev. C. 1895*, § 5024. "Except as otherwise provided in this article the specific performance of an obligation may be compelled."
Montana	*MT C. & Stat. 1895*, § 131. "The effect of a judgement of divorce is to restore the parties to the state of unmarried persons."	*MT C. & Stat. 1895*, § 2180. "A contract is either expressed or implied."
South Dakota	*SD Rev. C. 1903*, § 6. "In this state the Common Law is in force except where it conflicts with the codes or the constitution."	*SD Rev. C. 1903*, § 920. "A transfer may be made without writing in every case in which a writing is not expressly required by statute."

As for dispositions related to public order and good morals, these cannot be put aside with a private contract. These provisions are referred to as mandatory (declarative) provisions. They are usually identifiable by the choice of verbs, which, as the tables above show, are often descriptive verbs or verbs creating obligation. The declarative provisions can in turn be divided into two categories: explanatory and mandatory. The explanatory provisions explain a law or provide a definition, whereas the mandatory provisions impose a duty or an obligation. As the code's foundations, their main purpose is an educational and informative one.

A final editorial feature of civil codes must be pointed out, one that is specific to common law codes. Common law civil codes have an incomplete (often verb-less) sentence at the beginning of each article, explaining the main principle contained in the article. This nonverbal expression can have two forms, depending on the code. The Civil Codes of Georgia, California, the Dakota Territory, and North Dakota put this expression at the beginning of each provision, after the article number. For instance, Article 155 of the Civil Code of California[58] reads as follows:

> § 155. *Mutual obligations of husband and wife.* Husband and wife contract toward each other obligations of mutual respect, fidelity and support.[59]

In New York and South Dakota this expression is put on the side, in the margin of the code. For example, it can be seen in Article 37 of the Civil Code of South Dakota:

> *Consent must be present* § 37 — The consent to a marriage must be to one commencing instantly, and not to an agreement to marry afterwards.

This presentation in the codes demonstrates the didactic and pedagogical concern that animates the common law civil codes. By announcing the content and the rule of law of each article, the commissioners hoped to quickly inform the reader of its content. The annotations also reflect an interest in efficiency. Indeed, the codes were written to allow for easy and swift access to the law. The titles of these articles also remind us of the process of drafting statutes. This titling practice developed over time, and in Louisiana, Robert A. Pascal declared in his Memorandum that "comments and article titles are distractors that interrupt the flow of the reading and make each code article look like an isolated statute, departing from the logic of a code that should be regarded as a whole."[60]

4.2.2 *Bilingualism and the Special Case of Louisiana*

All the US civil codes were written in English, except for the 1808 Digest and the 1825 Civil Code of Louisiana, which were written in French and then translated into English.[61] Surprisingly, no Spanish translation was ordered. This raises

58 *CA Civ. C. 1872*, § 155.

59 *CA Civ. C. 1872*, § 155.

60 Olivier Moréteau, "Introduction to Robert A. Pascal's Memorandum: The Code as a Textbook and a Rule Book", 13 *Journal of Civil Law Studies* 2020, pp. 435–439.

61 Dominique Garreau and Enrica Bracchi, *Codes, Termes et Traductions: Enjeux transdisciplinaires. Actes du Colloque international des 22 et 23 Janvier 2015*, Milano: Giuffrè, 2017, pp. 107–119.

the question of the influence of language and translation on the final form of the codes. It is not surprising that the first codes in Louisiana were written in French; in the first years of being a US territory, the people of Louisiana did not speak English, but rather French and were so against changing their language that English only became the official state language after the Civil War. This fact was reflected in the state's civil codes throughout the nineteenth century. The resolution appointing the commissioners to draft the 1808 Digest did not specify the language to be used for writing it.[62] The editors therefore drafted the 1808 Digest in French, their preferred language, and the official language of the state at that time. However, with Louisiana becoming part of the United States, they had to have the code translated into English. Two men were commissioned by the legislature for this task,[63] and the code was ultimately published in both English and French. The men who completed the translation were Nugent and Davezac.[64] Henry Paul Nugent was an Irishman who moved to the United States in 1873 and lived a nomadic life, traveling and settling all over the United States. Nugent was a dance teacher, but also a language teacher, and worked for several newspapers. In Louisiana, he operated his own private school where he taught "English, French, Spanish, Latin and Greek, Writing, Arithmetic, Geography, and the use of the globes", being a translator between French and English. He had no legal training, but worked as a sworn interpreter at the Superior Court in New Orleans.[65] Auguste Davezac de Castera came from a prominent family in Saint Domingue. He relocated to the United States after the slave rebellion and first settled in North Carolina, where he studied medicine. He moved to New Orleans in 1805 or 1806 to join his sister, who married Edward Livingston soon after Davezac began his lawyer apprenticeship in the latter's office. Livingston quickly became his friend, protector, and mentor. Davezac became a lawyer in 1808.[66] As Vernon Valentine Palmer notices in his book on the translators, "they [the translators] made no private or public comment during their lifetime on the subject of their sources and their interactions."[67] Indeed, given the reception of the translation work as a badly executed one, they never even acknowledge it as being their own work.

62 John T. Hood Jr., "The History and Development of the Louisiana Civil Code", 19 *Louisiana Law Review* 1958, p. 26.

63 *Acts passed at the second Session of the first Legislature of the Territory of Orleans*, New Orleans: Bradford & Anderson, Printers to the Territory, 1807, pp. 190–192.

64 Vernon Valentine Palmer, *The lost Translators of 1808 and the Birth of Civil Law in Louisiana*, Athens (GA): University of Georgia Press, 2021.

65 *Ibid*, pp. 20–39.

66 *Ibid*, pp. 40–45.

67 *Ibid*, p. 49.

As a result of the translation, a rule was included in the enactment of the 1808 Digest establishing the shared authority of both codes (English and French):

> Section 5. If in any of the provisions made in this digest, there is some obscurities or ambiguities, or some mistakes or omissions, both English and French texts will be consulted to interpret each other.[68]

In consequence, both versions of the code had the same interpretive strength and were used to explain one another other in turn. In cases of doubt, one code could then be used to help elucidate the other. The legislature, aware of the state's bilingualism, decided that in order to avoid any linguistic confusions, neither code, nor therefore either of the two languages, would prevail over the other.[69] The choice to give the English version as much strength as to the French demonstrates a willingness to be included in the United States. However, even if both versions were supposed to have the same strength, the English version was a translation of the code originally written in French, and had many shortcomings as the result of the nature of the translation. By simply translating words as quickly as possible without thinking of the intention of the law or its meaning (the English version appeared only several weeks after the French version), the authors of the English translation included a number of translation errors. As a result, both lawyers and prevailing doctrine tended to privilege the French version in practice, legal parity notwithstanding. Indeed, they often used the French version without even looking at the English one. In cases where the English version was used, the judge usually enforced the intended meaning of an article as contained in the French version.[70] This was known as the "French-preference rule". The English translation was directed primarily toward common law-trained lawyers who were not necessarily familiar with civil law and civil law concepts. Hence, the approach of substituting civil law legal

68 Louis Moreau-Lislet and Henry Carleton, *Digeste général des Actes de la Législature de la Louisiane passés depuis l'Année 1804 jusqu'en 1827, inclusivement, en force de Loi à cette dernière Époque: Suivi d'un Appendix et d'une Table de Matières*, 1st vol., New Orleans: Benjamin Levy, 1828, pp. 207–208. "Section 5. Si dans quelqu'une des dispositions contenues dans ledit digest, il se trouve quelques obscurités ou ambiguïtés, ou quelques fautes ou omissions, les deux textes anglaise et français seront consultés pour s'interpréter mutuellement."

69 Olivier Moréteau, "The Louisiana Civil Code in French: Translation and Retranslation", 9 *Journal of Civil Law Studies* 2016, pp. 223–258.

70 "Preliminary Reports of the Code Commissioners, Project of the Civil Code of 1825", 1 *Louisiana Legal Archives* 1937.

terms for common law ones which, whether it was successful or not, "makes the translation an interesting mixed-jurisdiction artifact."[71]

The 1825 Civil Code made no change on the issue of the code's bilingualism. Similar to the 1808 Digest, the 1825 Civil Code was prepared in French and then translated into English.[72] The legislature, by an act approved on April 12, 1824, provided for the publication and implementation of the Civil Code of Louisiana according to the following procedure:

> Section 2. This Code as it was amended will be printed neatly on good paper, in the English and French languages, with both texts titled "Civil Code of the State of Louisiana".[73]

This task fell to the "lawyers responsible for drafting the amendments" and was performed as follows: the text in its final form was written in French on one page with its English equivalent on the other side so as to simplify the understanding for all.[74] This unique bilingual layout was an attempt to resolve the problems that arose during the translation of the articles. Printing the two versions side by side was also an attempt to ensure effective equality between the different versions of the code and to allow each version to more easily clarify the other. As the English language became increasingly dominant due to immigration, the English version of the code slowly came to be viewed as the primary point of reference in interpreting the 1825 Civil Code of Louisiana.[75] However, attachment to the state's French heritage prevented the French version from falling into disuse, at least until the American Civil War. It was only after the Civil War that the problem of bilingualism was resolved, when English became the only official language of the state with the adoption of the 1868 Constitution. After this point, the new civil code was written in

71 Vernon Valentine Palmer, *The lost Translators of 1808 and the Birth of Civil Law in Louisiana*, Athens (GA): University of Georgia Press, 2021, p. 57.

72 John T. Hood Jr., "The History and Development of the Louisiana Civil Code", 19 *Louisiana Law Review* 1958, pp. 28–32.

73 Louis Moreau-Lislet and Henry Carleton, *Digeste général des Actes de la Législature de la Louisiane passés depuis l'Année 1804 jusqu'en 1827, inclusivement, en force de Loi à cette dernière Époque: Suivi d'un Appendix et d'une Table de Matières*, 1st vol., New Orleans: Benjamin Levy, 1828, pp. 210–212. "Section 2. Ledit Code tel qu'il a été amendé sera imprimé proprement et sur du bon papier, dans les langues anglaise et française, avec les deux textes en regard sous le titre de 'Code Civil de l'État de la Louisiane'."

74 *Ibid.*

75 Olivier Moréteau, "The Louisiana Civil Code in French: Translation and Retranslation", 9 *Journal of Civil Law Studies* 2016, p. 252.

English only, including the articles inherited from the 1800 Draft of the French Civil Code. The articles of the 1825 Civil Code were once more translated into English, though this time very carefully. In consequence, a single version of the code now came into force. This was the 1870 Revised Civil Code of Louisiana, written in English only. The issue of the language of the code and the evolution of the "preferred version" adds even more proof to the fact that a civil code has to be considered as a cultural byproduct. In the Louisianan case, the code was a cultural artifact that evolved with the transformation of the state and its population. The French version disappeared as Louisiana integrated more fully into the United States.

4.2.3 *The Structure of the Civil Codes: an Assertion of US Uniqueness*

The structure of a civil code is the organization of legal concepts, but also how they are articulated among themselves. The uniqueness of the US civil codes is to be found in their unique structural vocabulary and in organizational particularities resulting from their position as a bridge between the common law and civil law traditions.

4.2.3.1 A Unique Structural Vocabulary for a Civil Code

Common law codes, that is to say all US civil codes except those of Louisiana, have a unique structural feature, namely, they do not use the same vocabulary traditionally found in codes such as the Napoleonic Code or Roman civil law codes. Nevertheless, even though the vocabulary differs, the US civil codes retain the same level of organization and division of legal concepts (Table 6). The Napoleonic Code and the civil law tradition codes are organized as follows: books, titles, chapters, sometimes sections, paragraphs, and finally articles. By contrast, common law codes are divided into divisions, parts, titles, articles, and sections.

The codes therefore used a completely different vocabulary but nonetheless maintain analogous structural levels. Moreover, a review of the content of civil and common law civil codes shows that the difference is one of vocabulary alone. The books of a civil law code correspond, for instance, to the divisions in the common law codes. Titles become parts, chapters become titles. A section turns into an article. Finally, the civil law tradition articles become sections in common law codes and are marked by the sign "§". This structural equivalence between the codes from the civil law tradition and common law codes raises the question of why a different vocabulary was selected by the American commissioners—a vocabulary that is also found in the later common law codes like the Uniform Commercial Code. It is possible that the shift was simply due to mistranslation. However, considering the predominance and

TABLE 6 The Organization of the French Civil Code and the Common Law Civil Codes

French Civil Code	Common Law Civil Codes
Books	Divisions
Titles	Parts
Chapters	Titles
Sections	Articles
Articles	Sections

notoriety of French law during the nineteenth century, errors in translation are highly unlikely. The second hypothesis is a willful desire to retain a more familiar vocabulary and adapt it to the form of a code. The organization into divisions, parts, titles, articles, and section was already found in statutes. The conservation of the statutory division likely allowed for a sense of tradition and security to be retained by using a known vocabulary. At the same time, retaining this vocabulary followed the common law tradition and honored the content of the codes. Finally, the retention of the earlier organizational terminology allowed the US civil codes to show their uniqueness and distinguish themselves from codes stemming from the civil law tradition.

The common law codes could be divided in three possible ways. The first method was the book[76] or division[77] structure, found most often in the US civil codes. In this case, the civil code is a single document with the highest structural level being that of a book or a division. The second type of structure is the title style used in Georgia. The third structure is the chapter style used in the Dakota Territory. The peculiarity of the Code of Georgia and the Civil Code of the Dakota Territory compared to the others is that the top structural level, namely the division, does not exist. The difference between the three types of structures is therefore primarily a question of vocabulary.

4.2.3.2 The Organizational Peculiarities of the Civil Codes

The organization of the legal concepts within a given code is fundamental, as it helps to show its exclusivity and strength as a source of law.

Looking at each document as a whole, there is some difference between these organizational aspects. Noticeably, for Georgia, the Dakota Territory,

76 LA *Digest 1808*; LA *Civ. C. 1825*; LA *Rev. Civ. C. 1870*.

77 NY *Civ. C. 1865*; CA *Civ. C. 1872*; DT *Rev. C. 1877*; MT *C. & Stat. 1895*; SD *Rev. C. 1903*.

North and South Dakota, and Montana, the civil codes were not the only code within the document. This fact is evidenced by the titles of the codes. Not named "Civil Code of" but "Code of", the titles indicate that, within each code, there is a criminal code, a procedural code, a public code, a governmental organization code, and an array of other codes which exist alongside the civil code itself. Hence, the civil code was understood in these cases as part of a wider codification endeavor. The civil code was distinguished in content and parts from the other codes, but was nevertheless to be found in the same document. To give one example: the Code of Georgia was divided into four parts: Part 1, "The Political and Public Organization of the State", Part 2, "The Civil Code", Part 3, "The Code of Practice", and Part 4, "The Penal Laws". The same organization was applied in the Dakota Territory, North Dakota, South Dakota, and Montana. These peculiarities, which did not change the content of the different codes, allow for the codes to be classified based on their format as single codes or as compendia of various codes put together. Solitary civil codes, such as the Civil Codes of Louisiana, New York, and California, can be placed on one side, while the combined Codes of Georgia, the Dakota Territory, North and South Dakota, and Montana can be placed on the other. The solitary codes were adopted on their own, without forming part of a larger document. The group codes, in contrast, were adopted as part of a whole codification document. This is probably why these codes are sometimes called statutes.

As to other organizational features, these vary by code in the US context. An important document, legal or not, usually starts with a table of contents. The goal of the table of contents is to allow the reader to be able quickly observe the document's contents and organization. In this regard, it is noteworthy that some codes have neither an index nor a table of contents, specifically, those of Montana and South Dakota. Though this choice may appear unusual, it was counterbalanced by the inclusion of an index of concepts organized alphabetically at the end of the code. This lack of a table of contents was clearly a choice, and not simply an editorial one, as it is found repeatedly, regardless of the editor of the civil code in question. There was also some variation among the codes concerning their preliminary titles. A preliminary title, as the name suggests, is placed at the beginning of a code. It is used to set forth the legal rules relating to the codes and their applications and all generic legislation that appears as essential, such as information on the promulgation of the code, its application,[78] its entry into effect,[79] and even the codifying committee's

78 See for example LA *Digest 1808*, Preliminary Title of Chapters II and IV.

79 See for example CA *Civ. C. 1872*, § 2.

chosen definition of law.[80] It generally contains the peripheral provisions. Most of the codes include a preliminary title except for three of them: those of Georgia, the Dakota Territory, and Montana. The Code of Georgia lacks a preliminary title but has a general preliminary division containing all the information necessary for the use and application of the codes in general. The 1877 Civil Code of the Dakota Territory and the Civil Code of Montana have no preliminary provisions whatsoever. One of the reasons for this might be the fact that these states were already accustomed to the functioning of a civil code. They may not have felt a need to give details on its workings, as its workings were already well-known.

Another aspect worth mentioning is the numbering of articles. The writers of the code had to decide whether the code's articles would be continuously numbered, or if the numbering would start at one at the beginning of each new level of organization. The traditional numbering style for a code is successive numbering which starts from the first article and continues to the last article of the code. This type of numbering simplifies understanding of the document and avoids confusion, as it renders the code into a coherent whole. All codes except one used a successive and consecutive numbering style for the code articles. Only the 1808 Digest came with a numbering style that restarts with each title of the code. This numbering can be found in some nineteenth-century European codes, such as the Prussian Code of 1794, titled "Allgemeines Landrecht", though no link has been found between the two codes. However, it is quite possible that a copy of the Prussian Code of 1794 was imported to the New World. Likely in recognition of the fact that this type of numbering was not the most efficient, the revision of the 1808 Digest changed the numbering style to successive numbering.

One last aspect of the numbering of articles is the numbering of the combined codes—different codes within a document containing more than one code. This question arose in the case of the Code of Georgia and the Civil Codes of the Dakota Territory, North Dakota, South Dakota, and Montana. In these cases, there were two options. The first option was that the article's numbering be continuous from the beginning of the document to the end, despite the change of codes. This style was selected in the Code of Georgia. Therefore, the first article of the Code of Georgia starts at number 1,582. The second option is seen in the Civil Codes of the Dakota Territory and its subdivisions, North Dakota, South Dakota, and Montana. In these cases, the numbering starts over

80 See for example *NY Civ. C. 1865*, § 2.

at the start of each separate code contained in the general code. This option allowed the codes to be more independent from each other.

The other peculiarity in the organization of the US codes is in the structure of the codes' provisions. According to Roman law, the use of a plan to organize different ideas is the perfect way to reach didactic clarity. The study of the organization of codes helps to assess the level of rationalization of the law in general and within each code. It can also help to clarify the choices made by the commissioners regarding the meaning and scope of civil law. The overall structure and organization of ideas among the common law codes inspired by the Civil Code of New York is not new. Indeed, the Civil Code of New York's four-part organization—persons, property, obligations, and general provisions—was previously found in the *Kent Commentaries*.[81] The Napoleonic Code, on the other hand, had a tripartite structure[82]—persons, property, and the different ways of acquiring property. The Napoleonic Code's structure is now considered traditional. Experts explain the structure of the Napoleonic Code in reference to Napoleon's effort to grant pre-eminence to property rights, which he perceived to be among the most fundamental in the world.[83] Some authors have gone even further, stating that the first book of the Napoleonic Code is an introduction to the two others.[84] Others have argued that this division comes from the Roman institutes, which were divided into three parts: people, things, and actions.[85] The 1800 Draft of the French Civil Code, whatever its origins, uses the following reasoning: the individual has their own rights (book one) and rights over things (book two), and these rights can be granted, modified, or lost by various means (book three).

In the case of the US codes, surprisingly little discussion took place regarding their organization, focusing more on content instead. This was probably because American jurists were not used to reflecting on such elements. At the structural level, only the Civil Codes of Louisiana used the French tripartite organization.[86] Other US civil codes are divided into a four-part structure.

81 Rodolfo Batiza, "Sources of the Field Civil Code: The Civil Law Influences on a Common Law Code", 60 *Tulane Law Review* 1986, p. 807.

82 For more information on the French choice for a tripartite structure, see André-Jean Arnaud, *Les Origines doctrinales du Code Civil français*, Paris: LGDJ, 1969.

83 René Savatier, *L'Art de faire les Lois: Bonaparte et le Code Civil*, Paris: Dalloz, 1927, p. 302.

84 On this matter, see François Ewald, *Naissance du Code Civil: La Raison du Législateur*, 2nd ed., Paris: Flammarion, 2014.

85 Gaius, *The Institutes of Gaius* (*Texts in Roman Law*), eds. W. M. Gordon and O. F. Robinson, London: Duckworth, 1988, Book I, § 8, at pp. 22–23. "Omne autem ius, que utimir, uel ad personas pertinet uel ad res uel ad actiones."

86 Alain A. Levasseur, "On the Structure of a Civil Code", 44 *Tulane Law Review* 1970, pp. 694–695.

David Dudley Field and the commissioners of the Civil Code of New York explained this choice as follows:

> The civil code was required to embrace the law of personal rights and relations, of property and of obligation. It has four general divisions: the first relating to persons, the second to property, the third to obligations, and the fourth containing general provisions relating to these different subjects.[87]

Despite this four-part organization, the link between the civil law tradition codes, such as the Napoleonic Code, and the US civil codes, is visible. Indeed, Field himself explained that he was greatly inspired by the 1808 Digest of Louisiana and, consequently, the Napoleonic Code when he wrote the Civil Code of New York.[88] The main difference between the French and American organization of codes, then, is the addition of a fourth part on general provisions. The reason for this new part in the common law codes seems simple. American lawyers unaccustomed to the civil code tradition chose to create a "miscellaneous" category. This fourth part allowed for the inclusion of all the legal provisions the writers intended for the code, even when the optimal location for these provisions was unclear, as was the case for the famous maxims of jurisprudence derived from Roman law. In addition, this fourth part acted as a safeguard, allowing room to add new or forgotten elements without having to revise the code wholesale.

A final short remark on the organization of the codes regards the array of legal concepts they cover. Codes from the civil law tradition usually contain all the legal concepts and institutions of traditional private law, such as personal relations, marriage, family relations, relationships, private property, obligations, contracts, and so on. However, the common law codes—all US civil codes except those of Louisiana—went further. These codes added provisions relating to corporations. One of the major innovations of the US private law codes was that they included the laws relating to corporations and by consequence extended the field of civil law.

In sum, the organizational features of the nineteenth-century US civil codes are quite in line with the tradition of the nineteenth-century civil codification. However, two main US particularities were created: the structural vocabulary and the four-part division of a civil code.

---

87 *NY Civ. C. 1865*, p. v.

88 Rodolfo Batiza, "Sources of the Field Civil Code: The Civil Law Influences on a Common Law Code", 60 *Tulane Law Review* 1986, pp. 799–819.

Bibliography

Almand, Bond: "The Preparation and Adoption of the Code of 1863", 14 *Georgia Bar Journal* 1951, pp. 161–167.

Arnaud, André-Jean: *Les Origines doctrinales du Code Civil français*, Paris: LGDJ, 1969.

Batiza, Rodolfo: "Justinian's Institute and the Louisiana Civil Code of 1808", 69 *Tulane Law Review* 1994, pp. 1639–1648.

Batiza, Rodolfo: "Roman Law in the French and Louisiana Civil Codes: A comparative textual Survey", 69 *Tulane Law Review* 1994, pp. 1601–1630.

Batiza, Rodolfo: "Sources of the Civil Code of 1808, Facts and Speculation: A Rejoinder", 46 *Tulane Law Review* 1971, pp. 628–652.

Batiza, Rodolfo: "Sources of the Field Civil Code: The Civil Law Influences on a Common Law Code", 60 *Tulane Law Review* 1986, pp. 799–820.

Batiza, Rodolfo: "The actual Sources of the Louisiana Project of 1823: A general analytical Survey", 47 *Tulane Law Review* 1972, pp. 1–115.

Batiza, Rodolfo: "The Louisiana Civil Code of 1808: Its actual Sources and present Relevance", 46 *Tulane Law Review* 1971, pp. 4–165.

Baudouin, Louis: "The Influence of the Code Napoléon", 33 *Tulane Law Review* 1958, pp. 21–28.

Brostoff, Seth S.: "The Encyclopedist Code: 'Ancien Droit' Legal Encyclopedias and their verbatim Influence on the Louisiana Digest of 1808", 13 *Journal of Civil Law Studies* 2020, pp. 33–86.

Cairns, John W.: "Spanish Law, the 'Teatro de la legislaciòn universal de España e Indias', and the Background to the Drafting of the Digest of Orleans of 1808", 31 / 32 *Tulane European & Civil Law Forum* 2017, pp. 79–120.

Carter, James C.: *The proposed Codification of our Common Law*, New York (NY): Evening Post Job Printing Office, 1884.

Castellucci, Ignazio: "Law v. Lex: An Analysis of a Critical Relation in Roman and Civil Law", 8 *Global Jurist* 2008, pp. 1–32.

Clark, Richard H.: "The History of the first Georgia Code", in *Report of the Seventh Annual Meeting of the Georgia Bar Association*, ed. unknown, Atlanta (GA): Jas. P. Harrison & Co., 1890.

Crépeau, Paul-André: "Réflexions sur la Codification du Droit Privé", 38 *Osgoode Hall Law Journal* 2000, pp. 267–295.

Dainow, Joseph: "Moreau-Lislet's Notes on Sources of Louisiana Civil Code of 1808", 19 *Louisiana Law Review* 1958, pp 43–51.

Davis, Jefferson James: "The Georgia Code of 1863: America's first comprehensive Code", 4 *Journal of Southern Legal History* 1995, pp. 1–44.

Ewald, François: *Naissance du Code Civil: La Raison du Législateur*, 2nd ed., Paris: Flammarion, 2014.

Franklin, Mitchell: “Libraries of Edward Livingston and of Moreau-Lislet”, 15 *Tulane Law Review* 1940, pp. 401–414.

Gaius *The Institutes of Gaius* (*Texts in Roman Law*), eds. W. M. Gordon and O. F. Robinson, London: Duckworth, 1988.

Garreau, Dominique; Bracchi, Enrica: *Codes, Termes et Traductions: Enjeux transdisciplinaires. Actes du Colloque international des 22 et 23 Janvier 2015*, Milano: Giuffrè, 2017.

Garro, Alejandro M.: “Codification Technique and the Problem of Imperative and Suppletive Laws”, 41 *Louisiana Law Review* 1981, pp. 1007–1030.

Harrison, Maurice E.: “First half-century of the California Civil Code”, 185 *California Law Review* 1922, pp. 185–201.

Hood Jr., John T.: “The History and Development of the Louisiana Civil Code”, 19 *Louisiana Law Review* 1958, pp. 18–33.

Kearly, Timothy G.: “From Rome to the Restatement: S. P. Scott, Fred Blume, Clyde Pharr, and Roman Law in early twentieth-century America”, 108 *Law Library Journal* 2016, pp. 55–77.

Klinck, Dennis R.: “The Language of Codification”, 14 *Queen's Law Journal* 1989, pp. 33–66.

Levasseur, Alain A.: “On the Structure of a Civil Code”, 44 *Tulane Law Review* 1970, pp. 693–703.

Levasseur, Alain A.: “The Louisiana Civil Code: A Vademecum”, 82 *Louisiana Law Review* 2022, pp. 1109–1141.

Masferrer, Aniceto: “Codification as Nationalisation or Denationalisation of Laws: The Spanish Case in comparative Perspective”, 4 *Comparative Legal History* 2016, pp. 100–130.

Masferrer, Aniceto: “French Codification and Codiphobia in Common Law Traditions”, 34 *Tulane European & Civil Law Forum* 2019, pp. 1–31.

Mattila, Heikki E. S.; Goddard, Christopher: *Comparative legal Linguistics: Language of Law, Latin and modern Lingua Francas*, 2nd ed., Farnham: Ashgate Publishing, 2013.

Moreau-Lislet, Louis: *A Reprint of Moreau-Lislet's Copy of 'A Digest of the Civil Laws now in force in the Territory of Orleans' (1808)—'The de la Vergne Volume'*, Baton Rouge: The Louisiana State University Law School and the Tulane University School of Law, 1968.

Moreau-Lislet, Louis; Carleton, Henry: *Digeste général des Actes de la Législature de la Louisiane passés depuis l'Année 1804 jusqu'en 1827, inclusivement, en force de Loi à cette dernière Époque: Suivi d'un Appendix et d'une Table de Matières*, 1st vol., New Orleans: Benjamin Levy, 1828.

Moréteau, Olivier: “Introduction to Robert A. Pascal's Memorandum: The Code as a Textbook and a Rule Book”, 13 *Journal of Civil Law Studies* 2020, pp. 435–439.

Moréteau, Olivier: “Les Frontières de la Langue et du Droit: Vers une Méthodologie de la Traduction juridique”, 61 *Revue internationale de Droit comparé* 2009, pp. 695–713.

Moréteau, Olivier: "Louisiana 1812–2012: 200 Years of Statehood and 300 Years of French Law Influence, 59 *Louisiana Bar Journal* 2012, pp. 325–326.

Moréteau, Olivier: "The Louisiana Civil Code in French: Translation and Retranslation", 9 *Journal of Civil Law Studies* 2016, pp. 223–258.

Moréteau, Olivier; Masferrer, Aniceto; Modéer, Kjell Å.: *Comparative Legal History* (*Research Handbooks in Comparative Law*), Cheltenham: Edward Elgar Publishing, 2019.

Palmer, Vernon Valentine: "Sounding the Retreat: The Exit of Spanish Law in Early Louisiana 1805–1808", 31 / 32 *Tulane European & Civil Law Forum* 2017, pp. 121–147.

Palmer, Vernon Valentine: *The lost Translators of 1808 and the Birth of Civil Law in Louisiana*, Athens (GA): University of Georgia Press, 2021.

Parise, Agustín: "A Translator's Toolbox: The Law, Moreau-Lislet's Library, and the Presence of multilingual Dictionaries in nineteenth-century Louisiana", 76 *Louisiana Law Review* 2016, pp. 1163–1184.

Parise, Agustín: *Ownership Paradigms in American Civil Law Jurisdictions: Manifestations of the Shifts in the Legislation of Louisiana, Chile, and Argentina (16th–20th Centuries)*, Leiden and Boston: Brill Nijhoff, 2017.

Pascal, Robert A.: "A recent Discovery: A Copy of the 'Digest of the Civil Laws' of 1808 with marginal Source References in Moreau-Lislet's Hand", 7 *Louisiana History: The Journal of the Louisiana Historical Association* 1966, pp. 249–251.

Pascal, Robert A.: "Of the Civil Code and Us", 59 *Louisiana Law Review* 1998, pp. 301–324.

Pascal, Robert A.: "Sources of the Digest of 1808: A Reply to Professor Batiza", 46 *Tulane Law Review* 1971, pp. 603–627.

Rabalais, Raphael J.: "The Influence of Spanish Laws and Treatises on the Jurisprudence of Louisiana; 1762–1828", 42 *Louisiana Law Review* 1982, pp. 1485–1508.

Ray, Jean: *Essai sur la Structure logique du Code Civil français*, Paris: Librairie Felix Alcan, 1926.

Rolston, Arthur: "An Uncommon Common Law: Codification and the Development of California Law 1849–1874", 2 *California Legal History Journal* 2007, pp. 143–163.

Savatier, René: *L'Art de faire les Lois: Bonaparte et le Code Civil*, Paris: Dalloz, 1927.

Schulz, Fritz: *History of Roman Legal Science*, Oxford: Clarendon Press, 1946.

Sheppard, Stephen M.: "Legal Jambalaya: A Commentary on John Cairns' 'Blackstone on the Bayous', in *Re-interpreting Blackstone's Commentaries: A Seminal Text in national and international Contexts*, ed. Wilfried Prest, Oxford: Hart Publishing, 2014.

Stephenson, Gail S.: "Custom as a Source of Law in Louisiana", 79 *Louisiana Law Review* 2019, pp. 1046–1070.

Surrency, Erwin J.: "The Georgia Code of 1863 and its Place in the Codification Movement", 11 *Journal of Southern Legal History* 2003, pp. 81–106.

Sweeney, Joseph Modeste: "Tournament of Scholars over the Sources of the Civil Code of 1808", 46 *Tulane Law Review* 1972, pp. 585–602.
Vassart, Patrick: *Manuel de Droit romain*, Bruxelles: Bruylant, 2015.
Watson, Alan: *Legal Transplants: An Approach to Comparative Literature*, 2nd ed., Athens (GA) and London: University of Georgia Press, 1993.

PART 3

CHAPTER 5

One Nation, Distinct Conceptions of Codification

What makes the nineteenth-century US civil codes so unique is that, even as they circulated and drew from one another to create a distinctive pattern of codification, the civil codes also represent different conceptions of codification. As Portalis remarks, codification is nothing less than the "spirit of method applied to the law".[1] The term "codification", according to its etymology and Latin origin, is the action of making a code.[2] The accepted definition of codification varies according to different theories and depending on location and time. Visions of codification in Ancient Rome,[3] in the canon law of the Middle Ages,[4] and in the Napoleonic era[5] are vastly different from each other. Even today, there is no universally accepted definition of codification, as the books and articles on this topic are numerous and are situated across a broad definitional spectrum.[6] Furthermore, the basic elements that make up a code vary from one accepted definition to another, and from one theory to another: exclusivity of legal sources, style of writing and structural organization, usage of the code, legal philosophy, subjects covered—many elements can be considered fundamental.[7] Though finding a universal definition seems to be an impossible mission, it is nevertheless possible to look at nineteenth-century US civil codes and see whether they conformed to existing models or created a new understanding of what codification is.

Analysis of the factors driving codification has already highlighted a possible classification of the codes based on the colonial past of the codifying state. In the US case, we must ask not only about the method of codification, but

1 Jean-Marie Portalis, "Discours préliminaire du premier Projet de Code Civil", 1801.

2 Csaba Varga, *Codification as a socio-historical Phenomenon*, Budapest: Szent István Társulat, 2011, p. 9.

3 Patrick Vassart, *Manuel de Droit romain*, Bruxelles: Bruylant, 2015, pp. 61–62.

4 Fernando della Rocca, *Manual of Canon Law*, London: Bruce Publishing, 1959.

5 On this matter, see Jean-Louis Halpérin, *Le Code Civil* (*Connaissance du Droit*), Paris: Dalloz, 1996.

6 For an overview of the evolution of codification, see the Introduction to this book.

7 Jacques Vanderlinden, *Le Concept de Code en Europe Occidentale du XIIe au XIXe Siècle: Essai de Définition*, Bruxelles: Éditions de l'Institut de Sociologie de l'Université libre de Bruxelles, 1967; John W. Head, "Codes, Cultures, Chaos and Champions: Common Features of legal Codification Experiences in China, Europe, and North America", 13 *Duke Journal of Comparative & International Law* 2003, pp. 2–93.

 DOI:10.1163/9789004689978_008

also about whether a given code represented novelty or imitation of an earlier colonial model. These two questions allow to divide the codes according to the classical codification classification theories. Additionally, the study of the US notion of codification could not be exhaustive without looking at one of the fundamental legal tools for a lawyer, the legal dictionary. Dictionaries set in time the meaning of a legal notion. Through the legal dictionary, the evolution of the definition of codification and the impact of the civil codes are also set in stone.

5.1 US Civil Codes: Compilation, Innovation, and Recodification

The nineteenth-century US civil codes are all substantive codifications, in the sense that, even when they compile the common law, they group all sources of law within one legal field, private law, while unifying and adjusting it to the particular social moment in which the code is written. However, unification and adjustment were more intensive in some states than in others. In terms of classifying different styles of codification, one of the established distinctions is between innovation, compilation, and recodification.[8] The notion of innovation through codification appeared in the years following the introduction of the Napoleonic Code, and referred to a codification characterized by the creation of a legal document containing the various legal materials related to a subject, which produces a shift or a change in the law. Thus, innovation is characterized by two elements: the formal aspect of reducing the law into one document, and the creation of new legal rules. It is this second aspect that defines a particular codification effort as an innovation. In contrast, compilation codification is more formal. It corresponds mainly to a formal arrangement of the various legal materials in one legal field in one document. In theory, codification compilation does not entail a shift in the law, focusing on its rationalization and organization. The final distinction is recodification,[9] with the term already suggesting that, in this particular case, the code is recodified, or reworked, and updated either in terms of organizational features or content.

8 Rémy Cabrillac, *Les Codifications* (*Droit, Éthique, Société*), Paris: Presses Universitaires de France, 2002; Csaba Varga, *Codification as a socio-historical Phenomenon*, Budapest: Szent István Társulat, 2011; Paul-André Crépeau, "Réflexions sur la Codification du Droit Privé", 38 *Osgoode Hall Law Journal* 2000, pp. 267–295.

9 Jean Pineau, "A very brief History of Recodification and its Problems", 88 *Canadian Bar Review* 2009, pp. 223–230.

In the US case, two codes specifically identify their choice for codification innovation: the Civil Codes of Louisiana and the Code of New York. In the report of the commission for the revision of the 1808 Digest in 1825, the commissioners clearly explain that they were not going to pursue a simple recodification of the 1808 Digest, instead declaring that, "it is our first duty to comprise in the several codes we were directed to prepare, all the rules we deem necessary for stating and defining the rights of individuals".[10] The idea was, therefore, to codify the existing law, whether or not it was contained in the 1808 Digest, and to include the legal provisions that were previously excluded from it. Regarding the Field Civil Code in 1865, the initial report by the commissioners explained that their job was "to reduce into a written and systematic code the whole body of the laws of this state, or so much and such parts thereof as shall seem to them practicable and expedient".[11] The idea of a simple compilation of law was rejected in New York, with the goal instead being to overhaul and modify the law to make it as efficient as possible.

The case of California is less direct than that of Louisiana and New York. The examination of the code clearly shows that the civil code was a codification-innovation, even though the commissioners' report did not mention this fact or provide any information on it. The intention to create new legal rules is made clear and based on the governor's address to the legislature for the years 1869 to 1870:

> Such commission shall proceed to revise all the statutes of this state, [...] and correct verbal errors and omissions, and suggest such improvements as will introduce precision and clearness into the wording of the statutes, [...] and prepare substitutes therefore when necessary; to recommend all such enactments as shall, in the judgment of the commission, be necessary to supply the defects of and give completeness to the existing legislation of the state.[12]

10 *LA Civ. C. 1825*, p. 12. "It is our first duty to comprise in the several codes we were directed to prepare, all the rules we deem necessary for stating and defining the rights of individuals in their personal relations to each other, for giving force and effect to the different mode of acquiring, preserving and transferring property and rights, and for seeking civil redress for any injury offered to either."

11 *NY Civ. C. 1865*, p. x.

12 Ralph N. Kleps, "The Revision and Codification of California Statutes", 42 *California Law Review* 1954, pp. 766–802.

This discourse does not seem to highlight a codification project, but rather to present a revision of statutes. Nevertheless, since the legislature had not given explicit permission for the commission to innovate, it was the commission itself that decided to take the path of innovation, extending their own mandate to rewrite the law in the 1872 Civil Code of California. One of the commissioners, Charles Lindley, noted that the commission went "a little beyond" the powers given by the legislature. In light of these facts, it is quite clear that California's civil code was one which embraced innovation. In the Dakota Territory, no documentary account of the codification process has been located to this day. We know that the first code was a direct adoption of the 1860 Draft of a Civil Code for the State of New York, which did not pass through a commission prior to being approved. The only document available on the code in the Dakota Territory is the act of adoption, which simply states that the code "provides for the revision and codification of the laws of Dakota Territory".[13] However, examination of the existing common law in the territory[14] shows that the code brought significant legal change to the state. Indeed, by bringing an entirely new legal code to the state, it created a new legal order at the stroke of a pen, thus constituting a form of codificatory innovation.

The existing scholarship has tended to describe the US codes as compilations, but the facts above show that the majority of US civil codes undertook codificatory innovation. Only one US civil code was a compilation, the Code of Georgia. More precisely, this code was in fact a restatement of the law. What distinguishes a codification compilation from a revision of a statute is, first, the inclusion of all legal sources and not just legislative ones like in statutes. Secondly, it is the rationalization of the law, meaning that the law in a compilation code is organized in accordance with a thematic and content frame rather than an alphabetical or chronological order. This rejection of innovation in Georgia was clearly exposed in the commissioners' reports, where their work and the fundamental principles are explained:

> This principle was, to attempt no change or alteration in any defined rule of law which had received legislative sanctions or judicial exposition, and to add no principle or policy which had received the condemnation of the former or was antagonistic to the settled decisions of the latter.[15]

---

13 *DT Rev C. 1877*, p. XXI.

14 Howard Roberts Lamar, *Dakota Territory 1861–1889: A Study of Frontier Politics*, New Haven and London: Yale University Press, 1956.

15 *GA C. 1861*, p. v.

As a result, the Code of Georgia was a compilation that gathered recognized legal principles and offered no additions. However, in the rare event that a new legal rule was required, the commissioners explained that the hypothetical new principle should not disagree with any already established legal rule. This gave them some room to maneuver to bring necessary change within the content of the law.

Finally, codes in the category of recodification are quite common in the United States. The nineteenth century was a period of great territorial change. Territories received statehood, borders between states changed, and new states carved out of larger territorial units. The Dakota Territory—and the states that emerged from its division—is one of these cases. Following the Division of the Dakota Territory, recodification took place in Montana, North Dakota, and South Dakota.[16] Two of the states chose recodification directly: Montana and North Dakota. The third, South Dakota, took until the early 1900s to recodify its law. Another famous act of recodification is the 1870 Civil Code of Louisiana, which updated the code to reflect the end of slavery after the American Civil War, while leaving the majority of its provisions intact.[17]

Looking at the nineteenth-century US civil codes, there is clear diversity in the types of civil codes states and territories chose. Hence, there is no linear nor national US understanding or adaptation of the concept of a civil code, at least according to those chosen criteria of classification.

5.2 The Circulation of the Civil Codes and the Snowball Effect

The law is by definition a moving target. Therefore, it is not surprising that the US civil codes circulated throughout the territory. Indeed, since its birth, the legal field has been an arena of circulation, migration and exchange. As Azzedine Kettani explains,

> one of the qualities of the law is its dynamism. The law evolves, the law changes, the law circulates, it migrates, it spreads, it is imitated, it scores, it inspires other law: these are phenomena to which the lawyer cannot be indifferent.[18]

16 *LA Civ. C. 1825*, p. 20; *LA Rev. Civ. C. 1870*, p. xv; *ND Rev. C. 1895*, p. xx; *MT C. & Stat. 1895*, p. 22; *SD Rev. C. 1903*, p. 10.

17 A. N. Yiannopoulos, "Two critical Years in the Life of the Louisiana Civil Code: 1870 and 1913", 53 *Louisiana Law Review* 1992, pp. 5–33.

18 Azzedine Kettani, *Indépendance nationale et Système juridique au Maroc. Actes du Colloque des 26 et 27 Mars 1998*, Grenoble: Presses universitaires de Grenoble, 2000, p. 31.

Mutual influence, importation, transformation, and transposition are at the heart of law. This is the fundamental nature of the field. Taking such exchange seriously adds another possible method of classifying codification based on whether the code is a consolidation of state law or an imitation of another code.[19] This mode of classification, which attends to the sources of the law, allows one a full picture of patterns of codification within the states and territories. In fact, most states undertook codification because they had a local model to use, though they often obscured these influences. The prefaces to most codes declare themselves the first to undertake such an effort, and they often fail to recognize the codes that influenced them, even when the latter are used as sources of law. The Codes of New York,[20] California,[21] Georgia,[22] and the Dakota Territory[23] all proclaim to have been the first to codify private law, even if it is impossible for all of them to actually be the first. Chronologically, the first civil code to appear in the US territory was the 1808 Digest of Louisiana's laws. While the Digest of Louisiana was the chronological first in the United States, other codes might claim vanguard status based on other criteria. The Code of Georgia can claim the title of the first code, but it would be the first common law civil code. The Civil Code of the Dakota Territory can also be given this title, because it was the first territory to adopt the Civil Code of New York.[24] Following that logic, the Civil Code of California is also a first, as California was the first state to adopt a revised version of the Civil Code of New York.

The succession of civil codes in the United States adheres to a pattern. After the 1808 Digest of Louisiana, a revised civil code came to be in 1825, with both codes modeled after the Napoleonic Code.[25] Twenty years later, when New York decided to undertake a codification of its private law, commissioners

---

"L'une des qualités du droit est son dynamism. Le droit évolve, le droit change, le droit circule, il migre, il se diffuse, il est imité, il marque, il inspire d'autres droits: autant de phénomènes auxquels le jurist ne peut être indifferent."

19 Bruno Oppetit, *Essai sur la Codification (Droit, Éthique, Société)*, Paris: Presses Universitaires de France, 1998, p. 17.

20 *NY Civ. C. 1865*, p. XIII. "The first common law code."

21 "California Code Commission Reports", in *CA Civ. C. 1872*, p. 33. "That California has been the first of this class to enact a complete code [...]. It will be the boast of California that first of English-speaking states, she set the example of written law as the necessary complement of a written constitution for free people."

22 *GA C. 1861*, p. II. "The first comprehensive code of common law."

23 *ND Rev. C. 1895*, p. 4. "The Territory of Dakota was the first English community to adopt a codification of substantive law."

24 Robert Vogel, "Looking back on a Century of complete Codification of the Law", 53 *North Dakota Law Review* 1976, pp. 225–237.

25 *LA Civ. C. 1825*, p. 9.

TABLE 7 The Genealogy of US Civil Codes

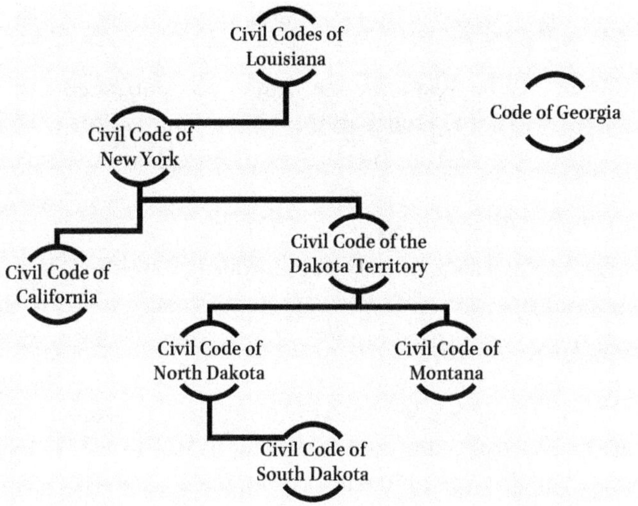

naturally turned to the Civil Code of Louisiana for inspiration and as a source of law. After its creation, the Civil Code of New York became the main vector of private law codification in the US territories and subsequently replaced the Civil Code of Louisiana as the primary point of inspiration. This likely happened because, unlike the Civil Code of Louisiana, its content was imbued with common law, not civil law. This Code of New York was then adopted "as is" in the Dakota Territory, and later adapted to local conditions in California. The Dakota Territory meanwhile revised its civil code, this time basing its work on the slightly modified Californian version. The Revised Civil Code of the Dakota Territory was therefore adopted and adapted after the territory's division. Next, North Dakota and Montana revised the code to create their own version. The version of the code in North Dakota was again adopted and revised years later in South Dakota. Hence, excluding the Code of Georgia, the civil codes are all interrelated (Table 7).[26] In 1889 David Dudley Field commented on the fact that the Code of Georgia had failed to circulate northward during the New York codification experiment:

> Before the New York commissioners had finished their labors, the State of Georgia enacted a civil code for that state which, though not so full as

26 See Appendix 7.

> the New York Codes, was drawn up with care and precision, and is now in force, and, according to all accounts, is working well.
>
> The preparation of this last-named code, which was published I think about the year 1861, was not known to the New York commissioners while they were engaged in their labors, owing, it is supposed, to the breaking out of the Civil War.[27]

However, the code was not exported to Georgian border states either, suggesting that something more than the Civil War was at work. Was this due to a strong attachment to the common law in the Southern States, or simply to the pre-eminence of other concerns during the Civil War? The lack of circulation of the Code of Georgia might indeed be due to the fact that codes are an object imbued with a state's culture and are therefore inapplicable to other states. One final consideration might explain the lack of circulation of such an innovative document. At the time, very few copies of the code had been printed due to paper rationing. Indeed, the process of printing of the code was greatly hindered by the Civil War and the various economic embargoes against the South, which made it at times impossible to find paper, among other key goods. To ensure the printing of the code, the printers had to rely on paper from another state, North Carolina. Due to delays, the task of printing was given to eleven printers simultaneously in an effort to produce the code more quickly.[28] Only 5,000 copies of the civil code were printed, making them rare commodities. It was thus almost impossible for precious copies to be sent to other states.[29]

Understanding the codes as interdependent and influencing each other has many consequences. The fact that the states reproduced and adopted each other's codes means that the law experienced a process of acculturation: states with vastly different cultures adopted and enforced laws rooted in the culture of other states and territories. These adoptions and adaptations created changes in the law and promoted evolution in the law, at times beyond the culture of a given state.

In view of the different elements of US civil codes that have been analyzed here, as well as the circulation patterns demonstrated earlier, the answer to whether US codification was primarily imitation or consolidation of existing

27 David Dudley Field, "Codification in the United States", 1 *The Juridical Review* 1889, pp. 18–19.

28 Erwin J. Surrency, "The Georgia Code of 1863 and its Place in the Codification Movement", 11 *Journal of Southern Legal History* 2003, p. 96.

29 Jefferson James Davis, "The Georgia Code of 1863: America's first comprehensive Code", 4 *Journal of Southern Legal History* 1995, pp. 25–26.

state law, seems clear. All US civil codes are imitations or transplants of others. In fact, it is quite difficult for a code to be a pure consolidation of state law alone. This conclusion includes even the Code of Georgia, which used another code, the Code of Alabama, as a model in establishing its final form. In fact, the Code of Georgia clearly stated in its preface that the code was written to "embody the great fundamental principles of our jurisprudence from whatsoever source derived, together with such legislative enactments of the state, as the wants and circumstances of our people had from time to time, shown to be necessary and proper",[30] while also recognizing the use of the Code of Alabama as a primary model. This methodology of imitation is clearly illustrated when observing the content of the codes. For example, the definitions of marriage within the different codes show cross-state unity of states while maintaining particularism. Marriage in the United States was mostly understood as a civil contract rather than a sacrament—a reality which shows in the civil codes.[31] The Civil Code of Louisiana defines marriage following the provisions on marriage in Articles 1 and 2 of the Napoleonic Code.[32] The Napoleonic vision defined marriage as a civil contract, a rule which originated in the revolutionary period. This culturally specific rule was then taken up in Louisiana. The culturally understood framework of marriage as a civil contract is also visible in the Civil Codes of New York, California, and the Dakota Territory, which all adopted the Napoleonic—or in this case Louisiana—definition of marriage nearly verbatim as a result of their imitation of the Code of New York. Articles 34 and 35 of the Civil Code of New York are found word for word in Article 55 of the Civil Code of California and in Article 34 of the Civil Code of the Dakota Territory. These articles state that marriage is a relationship between people arising from a civil contract, and that as a result the consent of capable individuals is fundamental.[33] In these cases, imitation is pushed to its limit with word

---

30 *GA C. 1861*, p. iv. "Embody the great fundamental principles of our jurisprudence from whatsoever source derived, together with such legislative enactments of the state, as the wants and circumstances of our people had from time to time, shown to be necessary and proper."

31 Roderick Phillips, *Putting Asunder. A History of Divorce in Western Society*, Cambridge: Cambridge University Press, 1988, p. 134.

32 *LA Digest 1808*, Articles 1 and 2. "Article 1: The law considers marriage as a civil contract. Article 2: Marriage is a contract which, in its origin, is intended to last until death of one of the contracting parties, however, the contract can be dissolved before the death of either spouse for reasons determined by law."

33 *NY Civ. C. 1865*, §§ 34–35; *CA Civ. C. 1872*, § 55; *DT Rev. C. 1877*, § 34. "Marriage is a personal relationship arising out of a civil contract, to which the consent of the parties able of making that contract is considered. Consent alone will not constitute wedding; it must be followed by a solemnization authorized by this code."

for word reproduction of articles from the original code. However, the codes are not identical on all points, as they retain some peculiarities—such as a different minimum age for marriage—despite imitation. One remaining question is whether the Civil Code of New York was a consolidation of state law or an imitation. In drafting the common law in the form of a code, the Civil Code of New York engaged in a classic act of consolidation. At the same time, the code proposed many changes in the law drawn, most often, from the Napoleonic Code, the Civil Code of Louisiana, and Roman law.[34] Hence, it seems that the Civil Code of New York was a hybrid of imitation and consolidation, trying to join Louisiana in creating a mixed-tradition legal monument.

5.3 The American Dictionaries and Codification

During the nineteenth century, the development of legal dictionaries advanced in parallel to changes in the law. This raises the question of how and if the definition of codification evolved with the creation of American legal dictionaries. Here I examine one particular dictionary, *Bouvier's Law Dictionary,* to gain insight into the impact of codes on US legal theory. First appearing in 1839, *Bouvier's Law Dictionary* was the first American legal dictionary published, and it continued to be produced during subsequent centuries. John Bouvier justified the task of drafting a legal dictionary by noting that, "to find among the reports and the various treatises on the law the object of inquiry was a difficult task: a labyrinth without a guide".[35] He also explained that the lack of an American legal dictionary obliged the American legal profession to refer to English legal dictionaries, parts of which had become obsolete as US law moved further away from its English roots. Indeed, the dictionary appeared during the formative period of US law. In the preface to the first edition of his dictionary, Bouvier explains his methodology for drafting the various notices, "in the first place, [it] defined and explained that various words and phrases, by giving their most enlarged meaning and then all the shades of signification".[36] He also explains that the different definitions are derived from federal and state statutes, judicial decisions, customs, and constitutions.[37]

34 Rodolfo Batiza, "Sources of the Field Civil Code: The Civil Law Influences on a Common Law Code", 60 *Tulane Law Review* 1986, pp. 799–819.

35 John Bouvier, *Law Dictionary and concise Encyclopedia*, Kansas City: Vernon Law Book Co., 1839, p. i.

36 *Ibid*, p. iv.

37 *Ibid*, p. vii.

The first edition of *Bouvier's Law Dictionary* defined a code as, "legislation, [which] signifies in general a collection of law. It's the name given by way of eminence to a collection of such laws made by the legislature".[38] The entry goes on to list the existing codes: canonical collections, the Justinian Code, the Austrian Civil Code of 1811, and the Napoleonic Code. This definition remained unchanged until 1891. Thus, despite the evolution and transposition of the concept of a code and its new usages in the United States, this definition stayed the same for most of the century without taking into consideration US reality. The definition denied US codification to such a degree that the Civil Code of Louisiana did not appear in the list of codes. For fifty-two years, the US states and territories subsisted with a broad definition and empirical examples of codes taken from outside their own experience. As for the origins of this definition, its inspiration is found in one of the most famous dictionaries in the world, the *Encyclopédie* by Denis Diderot.[39] There, a code is defined as a "collection of laws", and the entry includes a list of the major existing codes throughout history. There are several possible reasons for such an imprecise definition in *Bouvier's Law Dictionary*. Chronologically, and taking into consideration the national debate over the possibility of codification, it can be assume that this broad and generic definition was meant to grant wide latitude to the ongoing debate, leaving room for later adaptation to reflect the debate's outcome. The reality is likely more mundane, namely that at the time of the dictionary's publication, US law and US legal theory were under construction making it expedient to keep the definition broad and to center ideas from the European context. Moreover, after the question of codes and codification lost its appeal, it is likely that the idea of changing the definition lost priority status. The lack of evolution of the definition showcases, at least on a national level, loss and lack of interest in codification.

As regards the definition itself, several points are notable. First, a code is defined as a "collection of laws". This definition reduces codification generally to what we have described as compilation. Here there is no mention of changes to the law. Accordingly, the question of bringing together different sources of law within one document, and the notion of the code as exhaustive, are also ignored. What is also striking is that, from the start, private codifications are

38 *Ibid*, p. v.

39 Denis Diderot, *Encyclopédie ou Dictionnaire raisonné des Sciences, des Arts et des Métiers, par une Sociètè de Gens de Lettres*, 1st ed., 3rd vol., Paris: Briasson, David, Le Breton, Durand, 1751, Entry "Code"; Seth S. Brostoff, "The Encyclopedist Code: 'Ancien Droit' Legal Encyclopedias and their verbatim Influence on the Louisiana Digest of 1808", 13 *Journal of Civil Law Studies* 2020, pp. 33–86.

excluded entirely from this definition, with a key qualification for codification being receipt of an official seal. The definition seems to take into account changes brought to the notion of codification from the different codification endeavors in eighteen-century and nineteenth-century Europe, where codes came to be understood as more than a compilation or collection of the law, also being rational products. Moreover, it seems to stay a definition of everyday life, without going into the legal specificities and the theory surrounding the concept.

The definition of a code finally evolved with publication of the 1891 edition of the dictionary. The new definition described a code as "a body of law established by the legislative authority of the state, and designed to regulate completely, so far as a statute may, the subject to which it relates".[40] The definition was followed by a new list of important examples of existing codes worldwide. This time, the new list included the Codes of New York, particularly the Civil Code of New York and the Code of Civil Procedure, and the Civil Codes of Louisiana. It is only from 1891 onwards that the codes appear to have enough impact to be worth mentioning in a national reference guide. What is also new to this definition is its inclusion of limits on the applicability of codes. A code only regulates the law "so far as a statute may", meaning that the code has to be strictly applied by judges and only for those cases specifically mentioned. With the formulation, "so far as a statute may", the definition thus provides a means for the common law to be a substitute for the code and, if desired, to remain hierarchically above it.[41] With the 1891 definition, then, the legal dictionary was brought into line with the new legal reality in the United States created by the codes and their rule of interpretation of codification. Whether civil or procedural, the codes now acted as a supplement the common law. Finally, this definition is important because it would come to be the main definition of codification in subsequent American legal dictionaries and because this definition is so distinctive that it cannot be found in other countries of the world, especially in civil law countries. The US definition of codification is so attached to the specificities of the country that it cannot travel to other places.

To complete this brief overview of the concept of code in legal dictionaries, it is worth looking at a few other American legal dictionaries. Doing so shows significant agreement on the American legal definition of a code. One of the first editions of the *Burrill's Law Dictionary* of 1851, for instance, defines a code

40 John Bouvier, *Law Dictionary and concise Encyclopedia*, Kansas City: Vernon Law Book Co., 1891.

41 Reinhard Zimmermann, "Statuta sunt stricte interpretanda? Statutes and the Common Law: A continental Perspective", 56 *The Cambridge Law Journal* 1977, p. 315.

as "a body of laws: a collection or compilation of laws, by public authority".[42] This definition is also worth mentioning because it departs from the *Bouvier's Law Dictionary* definition, noting that,

> a code may be either a mere compilation of existing laws (though this is more properly a digest) or a new system of laws founded on new fundamental principles.[43]

Doing so shows significant agreement on the American legal definition of a code, particularly as it pertained to the necessity of public sanction and the subservience of the code to common law. Yet other dictionaries also show evolution over time. The entry then continues with the familiar list of various codes considered to be important worldwide, with the list being the same as in the first edition of *Bouvier's Law Dictionary*. In other words, the Civil Code of Louisiana is not listed. This definition is maintained in the different editions of the *Burrill's Law Dictionary* throughout the century and the beginning of the next. What is fundamental with this definition is that for the first time in the United States, the theoretical distinction between codification, compilation, and innovation is rendered official. This definition goes more in depth in the legal theory of codification. As for why this distinction was added, it could be due to the particular education and influences that shaped the writer of the entry, the influence of other countries, particularly of European countries, the influence of the American codification movement, or the influence of the Civil Code of Louisiana, though it would be difficult to know for sure. Finally, it is necessary to mention the definition provided by a third dictionary, the *Black Legal Dictionary*, particularly in its 1891 edition. This version defined a code as "a collection or compendium of laws. A complete system of positive law, scientifically arranged, and promulgated by legislative authority".[44] As in *Burrill's Law Dictionary*, the entry distinguishes the different types of codes—innovation and compilation.[45] The novelty in this definition is that, contrary to

42 Alexander Burrill, *A Law Dictionary and Glossary*, New York (NY): Baker, Voorhis & Co., 1851, p. 224.

43 *Ibid.*

44 Henry Campbell Black, *Black's Law Dictionary*, 1st ed., Clark (NJ): The Lawbook Exchange, 1991, p. 215.

45 *Ibid.* "The collection of laws and constitution made by order of the Emperor Justinian is distinguished by the appellation of the code, by way of eminence. See Code of Justinian. A body of law established by the legislative authority, and intended to set forth, in generalized and systematic form, the principles of the entire law, whether written or unwritten, positive or customary, derived from enactment or from precedent. A code is to be

the others, it does not provide a list of codes. Consequently, this definition puts the emphasis on the scientific method and the rationalization of the law more than on its physical manifestation, a theoretical approach that appears closer to that of the European civil law tradition.[46]

To conclude this brief analysis of the evolution of the definition of code through dictionaries, it is clear that the received definition evolved over the course of the nineteenth century, coming more and more into line with legal reality in the United States. However, it is impossible to know whether this evolution the fruit of the development of US legal theory or of the development of the codes themselves. Most likely, the answer lies somewhere in the middle.

Bibliography

Batiza, Rodolfo: "Sources of the Field Civil Code: The Civil Law Influences on a Common Law Code", 60 *Tulane Law Review* 1986, pp. 799–820.

Black, Henry Campbell: *Black's Law Dictionary*, 1st ed., Clark (NJ): The Lawbook Exchange, 1991.

Bouvier, John: *Law Dictionary and concise Encyclopedia*, Kansas City: Vernon Law Book Co., 1839.

Bouvier, John: *Law Dictionary and concise Encyclopedia*, Kansas City: Vernon Law Book Co., 1891.

Brostoff, Seth S.: "The Encyclopedist Code: 'Ancien Droit' Legal Encyclopedias and their verbatim Influence on the Louisiana Digest of 1808", 13 *Journal of Civil Law Studies* 2020, pp. 33–86.

Burrill, Alexander: *A Law Dictionary and Glossary*, New York (NY): Baker, Voorhis & Co., 1851.

Cabrillac, Rémy: *Les Codifications* (*Droit, Éthique, Société*), Paris: Presses Universitaires de France, 2002.

Crépeau, Paul-André: "Réflexions sur la Codification du Droit Privé", 38 *Osgoode Hall Law Journal* 2000, pp. 267–295.

distinguished from a digest. The subject matter of the latter is usually reported decisions of the courts. These consist of an orderly collection and classification of the existing statutes of a state or nation, while a code is promulgated as one new law covering the whole field of jurisprudence."

46 Agustín Parise, "A Translator's Toolbox: The Law, Moreau-Lislet's Library, and the Presence of multilingual Dictionaries in nineteenth-century Louisiana", 76 *Louisiana Law Review* 2016, pp. 1163–1184.

Davis, Jefferson James: "The Georgia Code of 1863: America's first comprehensive Code", 4 *Journal of Southern Legal History* 1995, pp. 1–44.

della Rocca, Fernando: *Manual of Canon Law*, London: Bruce Publishing, 1959.

Field, David Dudley: "Codification in the United States", 1 *The Juridical Review* 1889, pp. 18–25.

Halpérin, Jean-Louis: *Le Code Civil* (*Connaissance du Droit*), Paris: Dalloz, 1996.

Head, John W.: "Codes, Cultures, Chaos and Champions: Common Features of legal Codification Experiences in China, Europe, and North America", 13 *Duke Journal of Comparative & International Law* 2003, pp. 2–93.

Kettani, Azzedine: *Indépendance nationale et Système juridique au Maroc. Actes du Colloque des 26 et 27 Mars 1998*, Grenoble: Presses universitaires de Grenoble, 2000.

Kleps, Ralph N.: "The Revision and Codification of California Statutes", 42 *California Law Review* 1954, pp. 766–802.

Lamar, Howard Roberts: *Dakota Territory 1861–1889: A Study of Frontier Politics*, New Haven and London: Yale University Press, 1956.

Oppetit, Bruno: *Essai sur la Codification (Droit, Éthique, Société)*, Paris: Presses Universitaires de France, 1998.

Parise, Agustín: "A Translator's Toolbox: The Law, Moreau-Lislet's Library, and the Presence of multilingual Dictionaries in nineteenth-century Louisiana", 76 *Louisiana Law Review* 2016, pp. 1163–1184.

Phillips, Roderick: *Putting Asunder. A History of Divorce in Western Society*, Cambridge: Cambridge University Press, 1988.

Pineau, Jean: "A very brief History of Recodification and its Problems", 88 *Canadian Bar Review* 2009, pp. 223–230.

Portalis, Jean-Marie: "Discours préliminaire du premier Projet de Code Civil", 1801.

Surrency, Erwin J.: "The Georgia Code of 1863 and its Place in the Codification Movement", 11 *Journal of Southern Legal History* 2003, pp. 81–106.

Vanderlinden, Jacques: *Le Concept de Code en Europe Occidentale du XIIe au XIXe Siècle: Essai de Définition*, Bruxelles: Éditions de l'Institut de Sociologie de l'Université libre de Bruxelles, 1967.

Varga, Csaba: *Codification as a socio-historical Phenomenon*, Budapest: Szent István Társulat, 2011.

Vassart, Patrick: *Manuel de Droit romain*, Bruxelles: Bruylant, 2015.

Vogel, Robert: "Looking back on a Century of complete Codification of the Law", 53 *North Dakota Law Review* 1976, pp. 225–237.

Yiannopoulos, A. N.: "Two critical Years in the Life of the Louisiana Civil Code: 1870 and 1913", 53 *Louisiana Law Review* 1992, pp. 5–33.

Zimmermann, Reinhard: "Statuta sunt stricte interpretanda? Statutes and the Common Law: A continental Perspective", 56 *The Cambridge Law Journal* 1977, pp. 315–328.

CHAPTER 6

The Civil Codes in Action

As we have seen, the history of the codes differs from one state to another, as each civil code resulted from a unique context and disparate conjunctural forces. What remains is the question of what happened following the adoption of the codes: how did they work in practice? What was the fate of the codes beyond the letter of the law, in the domain of usage? This question is answered by looking at the process of adopting the codes, which turns out to have been similar across the states. As for the application of the different codes, examining their peripheral articles and the application of each code's rules demonstrates a gap between intent and reality.

6.1 The Codification Process within the States, a Legal Turn

When looking at the civil codes there is a clear point of institutional convergence between all the codes: the codification process itself. In general, the creation of a civil code tends to allow for the assertion of power by state legislatures.[1] In the US case, each code's institutional origin story was similar, driven by the same institutional mechanisms, including the commission structure and shared adoption procedures.

6.1.1 *The institutional Mechanics of Codification*

Whether driven by the judiciary, the bar, or the general population, all the codes come from a decision of the legislature to authorize codification or revision of the law. This is one of the main innovations of codification in the US context. US law, especially private law, was a predominantly judicial creation. With the creation of a code, the legislature and its elected members become the source of law, and thus the law was brought into the democratic sphere. Indeed, it transfers the law as a whole to the democratic institutions, not only specific legal questions. In theory, codes could have been created by order of a governor, the holder of the state executive power, or through the constitutional route. However, in all of the cases here, the legislature was the only body

1 Rémy Cabrillac, *Les Codifications* (*Droit, Éthique, Société*), Paris: Presses Universitaires de France, 2002, p. 72.

 | DOI:10.1163/9789004689978_009

deemed competent for this task. Some states also took the constitutional path, even while continuing to work through the legislature, perhaps to give more legitimacy to their codification endeavors. This was the case for three of the eight codifying states: Louisiana, Georgia, and New York, though each took a different approach—two after the adoption of their code, and one before. In Louisiana, the 1845 Constitution and its successors refer to codes in their titles on the general provisions.

> The legislature shall never adopt any system or code of laws by general reference to such system or code of laws, but in all cases shall specify the several provisions of the laws it may enact.[2]

Here the concept of a code appears even though the constitution does not expressly set out a procedure for codifying laws, nor does it mandate a choice for common or civil law. This can be explained by the fact that the constitution of this state was written post-codification. By mentioning the code in its constitution, Louisiana recognized codes as an integral part of the legal system. The constitution's authors appear to have perceived the need to constitutionally define and limit the powers of the legislature as they pertained to codification. Accordingly, in Louisiana a comprehensive code cannot be adopted without specifying its scope. In Georgia, the constitution refers to codes in terms of the state's legal hierarchy, specifying the code's place among other sources of law. Article v, Section 5 of the 1865 Constitution states that the laws in force in the state are organized according to the following hierarchy: 1. United States Constitution, federal law, and treaties; 2. The Constitution of the State of Georgia; and 3. The Code of Georgia with its amendments, the common law, English statutes in force in the territory, and the state common law not expressly repealed by the code, "as is not expressly superseded, by, nor inconsistent with said Code, though not embodied therein".[3] The hierarchy of norms in Georgia therefore expressly states that the code and the common law are equal in strength. In this state, too, the date of the constitution is quite important, as it was also written after the adoption of the code. Fortified by the first two years of application of the code, this article only confirms a fact without altering existing legal structure. This provision demonstrates, nevertheless, a concern for the proper implementation of the law and a certain rigidity in

2 *Constitution of the State of Louisiana*, 1845, Article 120; *Constitution of the State of Louisiana*, 1852, Article 117; *Constitution of the State of Louisiana*, 1868, Article 116; *Constitution of the State of Louisiana*, 1879, Article 31; *Constitution of the State of Louisiana*, 1898, Article 33.

3 *Constitution of the State of Georgia*, 1865.

its application. In New York, it was the 1846 Constitution that brought a real innovation. Paragraph 17, Article 1 of that constitution declared clearly that the common law would be maintained, but that a codification commission must be appointed at the first session following the adoption of the constitution. The commission would be composed of three commissioners whose duties would be,

> to reduce into a written and systematic code the whole body of the law of this state, or so much and such parts thereof as to the said commissioners shall seem practicable and expedient.[4]

The commission was thus created by the highest legal authority at the state level. In the constitution, there is also another provision mandating the creation of a commission tasked with the codification of procedural law, though it did not commit to adopting the resulting code.[5] In fact, it left the choice of commissioners, the extent of their powers, the timeframe, and the adoption of the code in the hands of the legislature, a task the latter never completed. This constitutional provision recalls another in a different country that also did not carry a code to adoption. Title 1 of the French Constitution of September 3, 1791, holds that "a code of civil laws common to all the Kingdom shall be created".[6] These two examples had the same consequence—non-implementation—though whether this is simply coincidence is unclear. As for the other states with a civil code—California, the Dakota Territory, North Dakota, South Dakota, and Montana—codification, codes, or the choice between common and civil law were not addressed. One can only hypothesize as to why the constitutions' drafters chose not to address these concerns. It might be the fact that the code was created after the constitution, or that, while revising the constitution, drafters did not think it relevant to give this kind of permanency to a code. When constitutions endorse private law codification, it is a strong indication that the codification endeavor forms part of an overall policy perspective

---

4 *Constitution of the State of New York*, 1846, Article 1 Section 17, "to reduce into a written and systematic code the whole body of the law of this state, or so much and such parts thereof as to the said commissioners shall seem practicable and expedient."

5 *Constitution of the State of New York*, 1846, Article 5, Section 24, "The Legislature, at its first session after the adoption of this constitution, shall provide for the appointment of three commissioners, whose duty it shall be to revise, reform, simplify, and abridge the rules of practice, pleadings, forms and proceedings of the courts of record of this state, and to report thereon to the legislature, subject to their adoption and modification from time to time."

6 "Il sera fait un code des lois civiles communes à tout le Royaume", *La Constitution française du 3 Septembre 1791*, Paris: L'Imprimerie Nationale, 1791.

on state law. It also gives greater legitimacy to the code, as it is confirmed by the first and most fundamental legal document, an especially important fact given the high regard for the constitution in common law states.

Returning to codification procedures, in each case the formal proceedings of codification began during a legislative session. An act proposing a codification of the law would be put forward, and the legislature would then choose one of three options. They could accept or reject the motion outright or, in some rare cases, they could select a third option which involved appointing a commission to study the feasibility of codification and the possibility of enforcing a future code. In this third case, in the United States, codification usually never happened. It was the outcome in Massachusetts and South Carolina, where the codification process died while the commission thought about it.[7] In cases where legislatures voted for codification, the act would go on to define the field of action for the commission. Usually, the commission had a clear and limited scope defined by the legislature, with a clear framework to follow regarding their work. For example, after appointing James Brown and Louis Moreau-Lislet to create Louisiana's 1808 Digest, the legislative act approved on June 7, 1806, instructed the codifiers to "base the codification on the civil law which governs the territory".[8] In this case, the framework was rigid, and the commissioners could not draw upon any other source of law. In addition to having a strict framework, the act also set a maximum timeframe for finishing the work. The process could extend between one and three years initially, and could take up to five more years if the commissioners called for it.

6.1.2 *The Code Commission and Commissioners*

The commissions were composed of a variety of individuals appointed by the legislature based on their legal abilities.[9] Commissioners were not elected officials, and in none of the cases examined here were commissioners members of the legislature. This decision once again helped to isolate the code from political factions, political pressure, and lobbying. The downside of this choice was that it also placed commissioners outside of the democratic process. As a result, the codes appeared to some as law written by men lacking popular support.

All the commissions were appointed by the legislature, apart from in Montana where the commission was appointed by the governor.[10] In terms of

7 Charles M. Cook, *The American Codification Movement: A Study of Antebellum Legal Reform* (*Contributions in Legal Studies*), Westport (CT): Greenwood Press, 1981, pp. 73–81, 121–131.

8 A. N. Yiannopoulos, "The Civil Codes of Louisiana", 1 *Civil Law Commentaries* 2008, pp. 1–23.

9 See Appendix 3.

10 See Appendix 3.

structure, each state decided to go with a collegial commission. Teamwork was therefore preferred to encourage the exchange of ideas and avoid domination by a single individual. Collegiality in code commissions was a legacy of other great codifications, such as the Roman *Corpus Juris Civilis*,[11] and the Napoleonic Code.[12] Despite the formal requirement of collegiality, however, history generally identifies each code with a single individual,[13] like Louis Moreau-Lislet for Louisiana or David Dudley Field for New York. Examination of the various legislative acts appointing the commissions provides valuable information on the composition of each commission, all of which I have analyzed here except for that of South Dakota, for which there was no available information.[14] For New York, I have only examined the commission that drafted the civil code in 1860. Most of the commissions were composed of three members, except in Louisiana in 1808, where only two members were appointed, and in New York, where the commission was comprised of four members. Hence, most of the commissions have an odd number of members to avoid a stalemate due to discordant opinions. Regarding these members, most of them were from the legal profession. Specifically, most commissioners were lawyers or judges. Hence, the US civil codes—as well as their European counterparts, like the French and German Civil Codes—were written by practitioners of law and not by academics.[15] The training of the lawyers on the commissions was relatively traditional for the nineteenth century. Among the twenty-three lawyers who together made up the codifying commissions, seventeen were trained through apprenticeship in a law firm, at the time the most common way to become a member of the legal profession. The remaining six did not have this form of legal training. Five were trained in law schools, including three at the School of Law of the University of Paris, one at Yale Law School and one at Albany Law School. The last one, Frederick W. Cole, a member of the Montana commission,

---

11 Rémy Cabrillac, *Les Codifications* (*Droit, Éthique, Société*), Paris: Presses Universitaires de France, 2002, p. 212.

12 On this matter, see Jean-Louis Halpérin, *L'impossible Code Civil* (*Histoires*), Paris: Presses Universitaires de France, 1992.

13 Rémy Cabrillac, *Les Codifications* (*Droit, Éthique, Société*), Paris: Presses Universitaires de France, 2002, p. 211.

14 See Appendix 3.

15 Wienczyslaw J. Wagner, "Codification of Law in Europe and the Codification Movement in the Middle of the nineteenth Century in the United States", 2 *Saint Louis University Law Journal* 1952, p. 337. For an overview of the creation process of the 1900 German Civil Code (Bürgerliches Gesetzbuch), see Franz Wieacker, *Privatrechtsgeschichte der Neuzeit unter besonderer Berücksichtigung der deutschen Entwicklung* (*Jurisprudenz in Einzeldarstellungen, 7th vol.*), 3rd ed., Göttingen: Vandenhoeck & Ruprecht, 2016, pp. 468–474.

was a self-taught lawyer. Of the twenty-seven members of the nine commissions, only two were non-lawyers. The first non-lawyer was a commissioner in Louisiana during the writing of the 1808 Digest, James Brown. He was the former governor of Virginia and former US ambassador to France. Even though he did not practice law, he had legal training and had completed an apprenticeship in a law office in Kentucky.[16] The second non-lawyer was Colonel F. A. Hall (also a commissioner in Louisiana, but in 1870), who had only completed military training. He worked as one of the assistants to the revision.

Even though these men did not practice law, they interacted with it regularly in the course of their work. Including a non-lawyer who was nonetheless accustomed to the law must have seemed a logical choice for the legislatures, as these individuals knew the law but were not necessarily conditioned by it. The hope was to create a more accessible and understandable law through the code, one that would allow non-lawyers to better understand the law. Who better to attest to the intelligibility of the code's provisions than someone from outside of the legal profession? The professions of the commissioners are thus not surprising, and appear in line with the composition of code commissions in earlier cases. Indeed, to take the example of the Napoleonic Code, the members of the code's commissions were "Tronchet, President of the Tribunal de Cassation, Bigot-Préameneu, government commissioner of that court, and Portalis, commissioner of the Conseil des Prises".[17] All of these men were lawyers who trained in, practiced, and wrote about law regularly. As for the commissioners' salaries, they varied from one state to another and ranged between 800 dollars and 4,000 dollars for the entire job. Nowadays, this would correspond to a salary between around 31,000 and 157,000 dollars. There was no standard remuneration for these works. Nonetheless, being a code commissioner was never one's main job. It was more of a moonlight post, as all of the commissioners continued to exercise their main professions during the drafting period. The commissions usually worked over a period of 24 months—Louisiana in 1808 and 1870, as well as in Georgia, California, the Dakota Territory, and Montana. However, the duration could be up to three years, as was the case in Louisiana in 1825, or five years, like in New York. Nevertheless, the average duration for drafting a code was two years. This is a relatively reasonable amount of time taking into consideration the amount of

16 John T. Hood Jr., "The History and Development of the Louisiana Civil Code", 19 *Louisiana Law Review* 1958, p. 8.

17 *Arrête des Consuls du 24 Thermidor an VIII*, "Tronchet, président du tribunal de cassation, Bigot-Préameneu, commissaire du gouvernment près de ce tribunal, et Portalis, commissaire au conseil des prises."

work, the fact that the members continued their regular jobs in parallel, and that most of them were not trained in civil law.

6.1.3 *The Submission of Codes and Their Possible Adoption*

The adoption procedure for the civil codes consisted of several steps. First, the commissioners wrote a report to send to the legislature, explaining what they had accomplished, the changes they had made to the law, and their methods. In some cases, such as in New York or California, the commission submitted annual progress reports. The code was then subjected to the approval of the legislature which met either jointly or separately, with the House and Senate engaging in parallel deliberations. The goal was to pass the drafted code with a majority of votes. If the code was adopted by the legislature, then a legislative act was voted to implement it. This act contained information such as the printing procedure, the distribution process, the date the code would go into effect, the code's final name, and its effect on the existing law and the common law. All of this occurred in the simpler cases, meaning if everything went as smoothly, as it did in the Dakota Territory and California. Nevertheless, roadblocks could arise. One roadblock could occur if a member of the chamber voted for the code, but the others did not. Another roadblock could arise if the code did not reach the required majority in both chambers. In these cases, several options were still available. The project could be postponed and voted on again later. If there was discontent over the specifics of the code, the legislature could ask the same commission, or appoint a new commission, to rework the drafted code. The last option was to totally abandon the code. The roadblocks described here are not mere conjecture: for instance, all of them appeared at one point or another during writing of the 1860 Draft of a Civil Code for the State of New York. The New York case showcases another possible procedural difficulty: the code could be adopted by the legislature, but the project could then be blocked by the governor's veto. This scenario occurred three times in New York in 1878, 1879, and 1882. Each time, the code was adopted by the legislature, yet it was prevented from going into effect. In this case, the only option was to try to have the code readopted in the next legislature or to appoint a new commission to rework the code. In the absence of a veto, the code could then become law and the procedure would follow its normal course. A small parenthesis is in order here to mention the Procedural Code of New York, and those of the other states. Those codes followed the exact legal institutional patterns of the civil code in all states, suggesting that this procedure had become the norm within the states.

The civil codes were meant to be a major innovation in the states that adopted them, and yet an equally significant innovation followed in their wake, namely, a change in the source of the law. Although, prior to the codes, legislation appeared in statutes, it did not have the same strength that proponents hoped a code would provide. The statutes are only very specific laws, with limited and clearly defined applicability,[18] whereas the codes cover a full legal field and allow for broad interpretation. Indeed, the use of legislation fully transformed the conception of the law within the states. The law was no longer set partially by common law, but was instead established by the legislature.

6.2 The Peripheral Articles of the Codes

The peripheral articles, or even sections of the codes are parts of a code that identify and define other parts of the code. These elements include title, implementation date, definitions, impact on other laws, and so forth. They are fundamental, providing crucial information about how the code should work. Generally situated at the beginning of the codes within the preliminary provisions, or, in rarer cases, among the last articles of the code, peripheral sections provide guidance on using a code, preserving its vision and legislative intent. The analysis of these articles showed that there are two main types of peripheral articles. The first category corresponds to the rules of construction for the articles, the establishment of their scope, and the definition of concepts used within the code. The second category corresponds to repeal provisions in cases of conflict between the code and other sources of law.

6.2.1 *The Establishment of the Interpretation of the Code*

How should civil codes be interpreted? How extensive are the vocabulary and principles present in the code? Does the "spirit of the law" matter?[19] This concept first appeared in Montesquieu's book *L'ésprit des Lois*, which theorized a separation of powers, with one body drafting the law, one executing it, and one charged with its application. The "spirit of the law" is the search for the will of the legislator in case of doubt regarding the application of a law or, in this case, within an article of a code.[20] This idea of legislative intent appeared in the codes of two states, Louisiana and New York.[21] In his *Discours Prélimianire au*

18 Ignazio Castellucci, "Law v. Lex: An Analysis of a Critical Relation in Roman and Civil Law", 8 *Global Jurist* 2008, p. 12.

19 Jean-Marie Carbasse, *Manuel d'Introdiction historique au Droit*, 4th ed., Paris: Presses Universitaires de France, 2011, p. 227.

20 René Sève, *Philosophie et Théorie du Droit*, 2nd ed., Paris: Dalloz, 2016, pp. 171–209.

21 LA *Digest 1808*, Articles 18 and 16; LA *Civ. C. 1825*, Articles 17 and 15; LA *Rev. Civ. C. 1870*, Articles 17 and 15, NY *Civ. C. 1865*, § 1998.

Code Civil des Français, Portalis explains how the search for the spirit of the law is supposed to work, declaring that it is, "the magistrate and lawyer, imbued with the general spirit of the legislation, who directs its application".[22] He goes on to note that,

> [t]here is a science for legislators, as there is for judges, and one is not like the other. The science of the legislator is to find in each subject the most favorable principle for the common good; the science of the magistrate is to put these principles into action, to explore their ramifications, to expand them through a wise and reasoned application of received hypotheses, to study the spirit of the law when the letter kills, and to avoid the risk of being either enslaved or of disobeying the law through a spirit of servitude.[23]

The two functions—legislator and judge—are separated in the civil law tradition. This separation was challenging to apply to the American legal profession, considering that in the common law tradition, the two can be the same office and person. Hence, writers of the US civil codes decided that, in the case where a section of the code appeared uncertain or insufficient, the judge could refer to maxims, customs, and the intention of the legislature to interpret and apply it to a case. The addition of this rule of interpretation of articles, allowing interpretation in line with the spirit of the law, was a major shift for US states. It cemented the fact that the judge was no longer a legislator nor the creator of law, as he had previously been in the common law tradition.[24] The judge's role was here reduced to that of interpreting the will of the legislature. Aware of the difficulty of introducing this new judicial role, legislators specified that, if in doubt, the judge must refer to "the best known and most used meaning",[25] except in cases where "technical expressions and phrases should

22 Jean-Marie Portalis, "Discours préliminaire du premier Projet de Code Civil", 1801, p. 17. "C'est au magistrat et au jurisconsulte, pénétrés de l'esprit général des lois, à en diriger l'application."

23 *Ibid*, p. 20. "Il y a une science pour les législateurs, comme il y en a pour les magistrats, et l'une ne ressemble pas à l'autre. La science du législateur consiste à trouver dans chaque matière les principles les plus favorables au bien commun; la science du magistrat est de mettre ces principes en action, des les ramifier, de les étendre par une application sage et raisonnée aux hypotheses prévues, d'étudier l'esprit de la loi quand la letter tue, et de ne pas s'exposer aux risques d'être tour esclave et de désobéir par esprit de servitude."

24 Granville Munsom, "Does the Court make or interpret the Law?", 58 *University of Pennsylvania Law Review* 1909, pp. 365–375.

25 *LA Digest 1808*, Article 14. "Les termes d'une loi doivent être généralement entendus dans leur signification la plus connue et la plus usitée, sans s'attacher autant aux raffinements

be interpreted according to the meaning and sense given to them by persons skilled in each of these arts, crafts or professions".[26] The common law tradition, however, did not disappear in favor of the civil law, a fact established directly in some of the peripheral articles. Indeed, it is difficult to remove at the stroke of a pen so many years of practice, particularly in the specialized work of drafting legislation. Uncertain of how to write a general code, the editors of the civil codes thus referred to and used the legislative techniques they already knew to draft the new tool. In fact, the civil codes—except the Louisiana ones—appear to be written in the style of a special statute, which tended to establish legal rules precisely and to focus narrowly on a specific topic.[27] To ensure its smooth operation and proper application, the legislator specifies the meaning of the terminology used in the statute. This method of precisely defining terminology is partly found within the codes. Thus, even as some articles state that the vocabulary must be understood in its generally accepted meaning, these articles also imbue the general meaning of certain terms with specialized clarifications. The articles go as far as they can to ensure the widest possible application[28] and the most precise comprehension of the code's articles. Such explanations and clarifications are numerous and common in the US civil codes, except in Louisiana, as it had the only code arising from a strong civil law tradition, according to which a code must retain a sufficient level of generality.[29] As for terminological definitions, Article 5 of the Code of Georgia and Article 14 of the Civil Code of California provide excellent examples. For instance, both codes include a section clarifying that:

> Words used in this code in the present tense include the future as well as the present; words used in the masculine gender include the feminine

des règles de la grammaire, qu'à leur acception générale et vulgaire." *NY Civ. C. 1865*, § 1999. "Words used in this code are to be understood in their ordinary sense except when a contrary intention plainly appears, and except also that the words hereinafter explained are to be understood as thus explained."

26 *LA Digest 1808*, Article 15; *CA Civ. C. 1872*, § 13. "Words and phrases, how construed. Words and phrases are construed according to the context and the approved usage of the language; but technical words and phrases, and such others as may have acquired a peculiar and appropriate meaning-in-law, or are defined in the succeeding section, are to be construed according to such peculiar and appropriate meaning or definition."

27 Reinhard Zimmermann, "Statuta sunt stricte interpretanda? Statutes and the Common Law: A continental Perspective", 56 *The Cambridge Law Journal* 1977, pp. 315–328.

28 *NY Civ. C. 1865*, §§ 2000–2032; *CA Civ. C. 1872*, § 4 and § 14; *GA C. 1861*, § 6.

29 Jean-Marie Carbasse, *Manuel d'Introdiction historique au Droit*, 4th ed., Paris: Presses Universitaires de France, 2011, p. 261.

> and neuter; the singular number includes the plural, and the plural the singular.[30]

The article continues by explaining the meaning of different terms such as person, property, month, will or section, among others.[31] The definitions list is quite extensive in order to cover as much ground as possible. The need to explain vocabulary shows that the code commissioners and likely users of the code were not accustomed to writing generic legislation in the civil law sense. There was, therefore, a need for precision that might appear excessive in a civil law country or according to the civil law tradition. The idea, however, was to make the code as clear as possible. These explanations of vocabulary are also found in the civil codes with similar articles.

A quick detour has to be made to point out the link between the Code of Georgia and the Civil Code of California. Both codes followed the same development path, with peripheral articles written in exactly the same way. However, the Code of Georgia is not proven to have traveled outside the state, nor was it recognized as an influence on the Civil Code of California. And yet, given that the same article is found word-for-word in both, it would be safe to assume that the California commissioners probably had access to the Code of Georgia, and were inspired by it at least in the case of these particular provisions. Further evidence is available in the fact that this article in particular did not follow the Codes of New York. The purpose of these definitional articles was to enable the broadest application of the code, and to avoid potential problems regarding its scope. Though, in the words of Portalis, "forecasting everything is an impossible goal",[32] the commissioners of the codes were nonetheless trying to

---

30 CA *Civ. C. 1872*, § 14; GA *C. 1861*, § 5 and § 6.

31 *Ibid.* "The word person includes a corporation as well as a natural person, country includes city and country; writing includes printing and typewriting, oath includes affirmation or declaration, and every mode of oral statement, under oath or affirmation is embraced by the term testify, and every written one in the term depose, signature or subscription includes mark, when the person cannot write, his name being written near it, by a person who writes his own name as a witness; provided that when the signature is by mark it must in order that the same may be acknowledged or may serve as the signature to any sworn statement be witnessed by two persons who must subscribe their own names as witness thereto. The following words have in this code the signification attached to them in this section unless otherwise apparent from the context: "1. The word 'property' includes property real and personal; 2. The word 'real property' is coextensive with lands, tenements, and hereditaments; 3. The word 'personal property' includes money, goods, chattels, things in action, and evidence of debt; 4. The word 'month' means a calendar month, unless otherwise expressed; 5. The word 'will' include codicil."

32 Jean-Marie Portalis, "Discours préliminaire du premier Projet de Code Civil", 1801, p. 8. "Tout prévoir est un but impossible à atteindre."

protect themselves against the inapplicability of a provision due to vocabulary issues. Hence, one of the goals of the definitional articles was to avoid having a matter be regarded as sitting outside the scope of the code due to a technicality. In addition, for a user accustomed to the common law, such articles and information would appear relatively familiar, as evidenced by the statutes of building regulations still applied today. In fact, by writing the code in this way, the commissioners were in effect writing a special statute according to the common law tradition, one which had to follow pre-existing rules. The "Rules for Construction of Statutes" issued by the Supreme Court serve as a guide here, and they also establish the principle that judges should not interpret law but rather refer to the intention of the legislature, also known as the "spirit of the law". In an attempt to avoid the situation where a judge has to interpret a statute, the statute must define any terms that might be confusing, as well as the statute's scope, and all the information considered necessary to avoid judicial interpretation. The influence of the Supreme Court's rules is clear in the construction of the peripheral clauses.

6.2.2 *The Abrogative Articles in the Civil Codes*

Among the peripheral articles, there was another type of special articles—the abrogative ones. The aim of these articles is to clarify the relationship between the different sources of law, especially between the code and the other sources of law. These articles, in consequence, highlight the strength the legislature wanted to give to a code. Most of them provided the code with an abrogative power, making it superior to the other sources of law. In Louisiana, the question of abrogation of the other sources of law was covered in the act passed on March 31, 1808, which adopted Article 2 of the code:

> Section 2. All that in former civil laws of this territory, or in the territorial status, are contrary to the provisions contained in the digest, or incompatible with them, are repealed by this.[33]

This legal phrasing was not new. Indeed, it is the same as Article 7 of *La Loi du 30 Ventose An XII*, which gathered existing private law into the French Civil

33 Louis Moreau-Lislet and Henry Carleton, *Digeste général des Actes de la Législature de la Louisiane passés depuis l'Année 1804 jusqu'en 1827, inclusivement, en force de Loi à cette dernière Époque: Suivi d'un Appendix et d'une Table de Matières*, 1st vol., New Orleans: Benjamin Levy, 1828, pp. 207–208. "Section 2. Tout ce qui dans les anciennes lois civiles de ce territoire, ou dans le statut territorial, se trouve contraire aux dispositions contenues dans ledit digest, ou incompatible avec ells, est et demeure abrogé par le present."

Code[34] and established the relationship between the civil code and the other sources of law. Thus, in continuity with the tradition of the Napoleonic Code, the Civil Code of Louisiana was adopted to become the only source of private law in the state. For the Codes of New York and their successors—all common law codes except the Code of Georgia—the common law was officially abolished in favor of the civil code.

> In this state / territory there is no common law in any case where the law is declared by the five codes / the code.[35]

The content of this article reflects the desire of the legislature to make the civil code the only source of private law. In consequence, all legal or jurisprudential provisions relating to a field covered by the civil code were repealed in favor of the code, unless the code explicitly stated otherwise. The idea was to avoid half-measures: for the drafters, the code should not interact or compete with previous iterations and other sources of law, instead replacing all of them. In this line of thinking, § 2033 of the Civil Code of New York and Article 20 of the Civil Code of California precisely explained the intent of each code. By stating that all statutes, laws, or rules inconsistent with the provisions of the civil code would be repealed unless otherwise provided for in the code.[36] The other states with a version of the Civil Code of New York did not repeat this type of article but maintained general abolition of the common law. In these cases, the code was therefore the new standard and the only representative of the law. On this point, it seems that the codes were intended to become the main sources of law, thereby following the civil law tradition. The code was meant

34 *Loi du 30 Ventose An XII, sur la Réunion des Lois civiles en un seul corps, sous le Titre de Code Civil des Français*. "Article 7. À compter du jour où ces lois sonst exécutoires, les lois romaines, les ordinnances, les coutumes générales ou locales, les statutes, les règlements cessent d'avoir force de loi générale ou particulières dans les matières qui sont l'objet desdites lois composant le present code."

35 *NY Civ. C. 1865*, § 6; *CA Civ. C. 1872*, § 5; *DT Rev. C. 1877*, § 6; *ND Rev. C. 1895*, § 2696; *SD Rev. C. 1903*, § 6; *MT C. & Stat. 1895*, § 5.

36 *NY Civ. C. 1865*, § 2033. "All statutes, laws and rules heretofore in force in this state, inconsistent with the provisions of this code, are hereby repealed or abrogated; but such repeal or abrogation does not revive any former law heretofore repealed, nor does it affect any rights already existing or accrued, or any proceeding already taken, excepting as in this code provided." *CA Civ. C. 1872*, § 20. "No statute, law, or rule is continued in force because it is consistent with the provisions of this code on the same subject; but in all cases provided for this code, all statutes, laws, and rules heretofore in force in this state, whether consistent or not with the provisions of this code, unless expressly continued in force by it, are repealed or abrogated."

to wipe the slate clean and start fresh, while also maintaining a number of carefully selected laws which became a bridge between the past and the future.

Only the Code of Georgia differs from other US codes, as it was based on a different philosophy. Article 1 of the Code of Georgia[37] outlines the hierarchy of the different legal sources of private law, a hierarchy later confirmed by Article v, Section 5 of the 1865 Constitution.[38] The laws in force within the State of Georgia were ordered in the following descending hierarchy: 1. United States Constitution, federal law, and treaties; 2. The Constitution of the State of Georgia; and 3. The Code of Georgia with its amendments, the common

37 *GA C. 1861*, § 1. "The law of this state shall be thus graduated in reference to their obligations: *First.* The Constitution of the United States [changed at the printing to Confederate State]. *Second.* Treatises entered into by the Federal Government within the scope of their power. *Third.* Laws of the United States [changed at the printing to Confederate State] made in pursuance of the constitution. *Fourth.* The constitution of this state. *Fifth.* The statutes of this state including this code. *Sixth.* Such portions of the common, civil, canon, and statute laws of England, as were usually in force in the Province of Georgia prior to May 14, 1776, which were applicable to the condition and habits of the people so far as the same are consonant with our form of government, and are not repealed, modified, or superseded by the provisions of this code. *Seventh.* The customs of any business or trade shall be binding only when it is such universal practice as to justify the conclusion, that it became, by implication, a part of contract."

38 *Constitution of the State of Georgia*, 1865, Article 5, Section v. "The laws of general operation now of force in this state, are 1st, as the supreme law, the Constitution of the United States, the laws of the United States in pursuance thereof, and all treaties made under the authority of the United States; 2d, as next in authority thereto, this constitution; 3d, in subordination to the foregoing, all laws declared of force by an act of the General Assembly of this state, assented to December 9, 1860, entitled 'An act to approve, adopt, and make of force in the State of Georgia, a revised code of laws, prepared under the direction and by authority of the General Assembly thereof, and for other purposes therewith connected', an act of the General Assembly aforesaid, assented to December 16, 1861, amendatory to the foregoing, and an act of the General Assembly, aforesaid, assented December 13, 1862, entitled 'An act to settle the conflicts between the code and the legislation of this General Assembly', also, all acts of the General Assembly aforesaid, passed since the date last written, altering, amending, repealing, or adding to any portion of law hereinbefore mentioned (the latter enactment having preference in case of conflict); and also, so much of the common and statute law of England, and of the statute law of this state, of force in Georgia in the year eighteen hundred and sixty, as is not expressly superseded, by, nor inconsistent with said code, though not embodied therein, except so much of the law aforesaid as may violate the supreme law, herein recognized, or may conflict with this constitution, and except to so much thereof as refers to persons held in slavery, which excepted laws shall henceforth be inoperative and void and any future General Assembly of this state shall be competent to alter, amend, or repeal any portion of the law declared to be of force, the word 'Confederate' occurs before the word 'States', such law is hereby amended by substituting the word 'United' for the word 'Confederate'."

law, English statutes in force in the territory, and the state common law not expressly repealed by the code. Accordingly, the common law and the code are at the same level, complementing rather than superseding one another. Here the code is designed as a companion to the common law rather than being its superior. In fact, the two main sources of private law, common law, and the civil code, were supposed to run in parallel and work together to define the private law of the state. Furthermore, the Code of Georgia was understood as a continuation of the common law[39] and as a way of bringing, "shape and order, system and efficiency, to the sometimes crude and often ill expressed, sovereign will of the state".[40]

The civil codes are well-defined and carefully planned projects, but the reality of the application of the codes departed from the original plan, at least in most cases. However, setting aside the question of their application, the abrogative articles in the codes show a strong desire by the commissioners and the legislature to make the code the exclusive source of private law within each state.

6.3 The Application of the US Civil Codes

The gap between the legislative vision of the code and the reality of its application can be a universe. The civil law model was indeed more difficult to apply in the states than expected. Whereas, in Louisiana, the civil code rapidly became the main source of private law (6.3.1), the common law civil codes quickly became subsidiary sources of private law. The codes were sometimes even forgotten in order to give power back to the common law (6.3.2).

6.3.1 *A Civil Code: the Main and Exclusive Source of Private Law in Louisiana*

The debate over the application of the Civil Code of Louisiana was not one that was easily settled. The question of how to use the 1808 Digest was a source of conflict from the start. The trouble started in July 1817, nine years after the adoption of the 1808 Digest, when the Louisiana Supreme Court, composed of Pierre Derbigny, George Mathews, and François-Xavier Martin,[41] issued its decision in *Cottin v. Cottin*. With this decision, the Louisiana Supreme Court

39 *GA C. 1861*, p. VIII.

40 *Ibid*, p. ix.

41 Mack E. Barham, "La Méthodologie du Droit civil de l'État de Louisiane", 27 *Revue internationale de Droit comparé* 1975, p. 800.

held that the enactment of the 1808 Digest repealed only those laws contrary to the code, thus confirming Section 2 of the code.[42] This voluntary confirmation by the Louisiana Supreme Court had an effect that the code draftsmen had not foreseen: all legal provisions not contrary to the code, particularly Spanish law, would remain applicable. In consequence, this decision reprised the previous state of confusion, which the 1808 Digest was supposed to be the remedy. This decision was then used to bolster the common practice of treating the 1808 Digest as an incomplete body of laws.[43] The idea behind the 1808 Digest was the formalization of Louisiana's civil law inheritance and the creation of a single source of private law. At the very least, the process was supposed to make the code the main source of law, meaning that the Louisiana Supreme Court's ruling did not correspond to the intended philosophy behind the code. This *de facto* limitation of the codes status pushed the legislature to adopt a resolution on March 14, 1822 appointing Edward Livingston, Louis Moreau-Lislet, and Pierre Derbigny[44] "to revise the Civil Code by amending the same in such manner as they will deem it advisable, and by adding unto [...] [it] [...] such of the laws that are still in force and not included therein."[45] To prevent the same issues that arose with the 1808 Digest, a provision of the new code declared that all legislation related to the subject but not present in the code was no longer enforceable:

> Article 3521.—From the date of enactment of this code, the Spanish, French and Roman laws that were in force in this state, when Louisiana was ceded to the United States, and the acts of the Conseil Législatif, of the Territory of Orleans, and Louisiana state legislation, are and remain abrogated in all cases to be filled within the code; and they cannot be

42 LA *Digest 1808*, Article 2. "It must not be a lost sight that our civil code is a digest of the civil laws, which were in force in this country when it was adopted; that laws must be considered as untouched, whenever the alterations and amendments, introduced in the digest, do not reach them."

43 A. N. Yiannopoulos, "The Civil Codes of Louisiana", 1 *Civil Law Commentaries* 2008, pp. 11–14.

44 Alain A. Levasseur, *Louis Casimir Elisabeth Moreau-Lislet: Foster Father of Louisiana Civil Code*, Baton Rouge: LSU Law Center Publications Institute, 1996, p. 140. Among those offering their service for the writing of the Code the votes were distributed as follows: 43 votes for Moreau-Lislet, 25 votes each for Livingston and Derbigny, 23 votes for Workman, 22 votes for Mazureau, 3 votes for Smith, 2 votes each for Morel and Carleton.

45 "Preliminary Reports of the Code Commissioners, Project of the Civil Code of 1825", 1 *Louisiana Legal Archives* 1937, p. 29.

invoked as laws, even under the pretext that their provisions are not contrary to this code.[46]

The objective of the Louisiana officials in 1825 is clear: to repeal all previous laws related to any subject treated in the code or not included in it, with the goal of making the code the only legal source in the field of private law.[47] Finally, they wanted to ensure the effective and official establishment of the civil law system through the civil code. The Louisiana Supreme Court, however, did not share the same opinion as the legislature. In 1827, the court ignored Article 3521 in its decision in *Fowler v. Griffith*[48] and in *Lacroix v. Coquet*.[49] With these decisions, the Louisiana Supreme Court declared that all civil laws, whether within the code or not, were still enforceable within the state. An example was the Spanish law, which was not included in the 1825 Civil Code, as well as all articles of the 1808 Digest that were not included in the 1825 Civil Code. This opposition by the Louisiana Supreme Court has various possible explanations. Apart from the desire to retain certain provisions not included in the code, the court seemed to be using these decisions as opportunities to assert the same power that a common law state supreme court would have. Indeed, following the integration of Louisiana into the United States, the courts sought to follow the practices of common law. As in the common law tradition, rulings were signed by their authors, who gave their opinion on the legal issue at hand, and decisions are brief and concise.[50] Based on this model, the Louisiana Supreme Court had therefore been trying to detach itself from the civil law tradition since the adoption of the code. This would enable the court to gain the creative power that a common law court possessed, at the risk of jeopardizing the civil code. This desire on the part of the Louisiana Supreme Court was not new. In the case of *Orleans Navigation Co. v. New Orleans* in 1812, one of the judges,

46 *LA Civ. C. 1825*, Article 3521. "À dater de la promulgation de ce code, les lois espagnoles, romaines et françaises, qui étaient en force dans cet état, lorsque la Louisiane fut cédée aux États-Unis, et les actes du Conseil Législativ, de la législature du Territoire d'Orléans, et de la legislature de l'état de Louisiane, sont et demeurent abrogés, dans tous les cas auxquels il est pourvu spécialement dans ce code; et ells ne pourront pas être invoquées comme lois, même sous le prétexte que leurs dispositions n'en sont pas contraires à celle de ce code."

47 On the innovation of old laws in another form in France, see Marie-F. Renoux-Zagamé, "Additionnel ou innovative? Débats et Solutions des premières Décennies de Mise en Œuvre du Code Civil", 41 *Droits* 2005, pp. 19–36.

48 *Fowler v. Griffith*, 6 Mart. (n.s.) 89 (1827).

49 *Lacroix v. Coquet*, 5 Mart. (n.s.) 527 (1827).

50 Mack E. Barham, "La Méthodologie du Droit civil de l'État de Louisiane", 27 *Revue internationale de Droit comparé* 1975, pp. 801–802.

Justice Mathews, considered the distinction between common law and civil system as superfluous. He wrote that:

> The solutions are the same in both legal systems, why ask if they were established by an edict of the Roman Praetor, or an emperor, or defined by a distinguished English jurist.[51]

To this, Justice Martin replied that:

> The common law of England is not recognized by the party as rules of conduct; and in this case the civil law rule is the only one enforceable within the state and different totally on this point that it has pleased the Court to pronounce.[52]

This example reveals the distinct visions and disagreements between the Louisiana judges concerning the common law, the workings of the common law court, and the desire by some judges to acquire the interpretive prerogatives of a common law judge. Of distinct interest to these judges was the ability to create laws. Faced with deadlock at the court, the legislature had to intervene this time by adopting two acts.[53] One of these was the Great Repealing Act of 1828,[54] which stated that, except for Title 10[55] of the 1808 Digest, all provisions outside of the 1825 Civil Code and the 1808 Digest were now repealed. The following year, 1829, the Louisiana Supreme Court reprised its ambitions. A compromise was found in an agreement that certain principles not present in the code, but accepted by all, had always been and would remain in force within the state. As a result of this decision, there are some colonial Spanish

51 *Orleans Navigation Co. v. New Orleans*, 2 Mart. 214 (1812), “Les solutions étant mêmes dans les deux systems de droit, pourquoi se demander si ells ont été établies par un édit du préteur romain, ou un empereur, ou définies par un eminent juriste anglaise.”

52 *Orleans Navigation Co. v. New Orleans*, 2 Mart. 214 (1812), “Que la *common law* d'Angleterre n'est past reconnue par les parties comme règles de conduite, et qu'en l'espèce, la règle de droit civil, seul applicable dans l'état diffère totalement sur ce point de celle qu'il a plu à la cour de prononcer.”

53 John T. Hood Jr., “The History and Development of the Louisiana Civil Code”, 19 *Louisiana Law Review* 1958, pp. 32–33.

54 John A. Lovett, “On the Principle of Legal Certainty in the Louisiana Civil Law Tradition: From the Manifesto to the Great Repealing Act and Beyond”, 63 *Louisiana Law Review* 2003, pp. 1397–1448.

55 Title 10 being the title that focuses on Communities or Corporations.

laws enforceable in Louisiana to this day.[56] In addition, over the years, the Louisiana Supreme Court has justified some of its decisions on the writings of English lawyers and some common law principles, while maintaining that the civil code is the main source of law in the state. These decisions created Louisiana's famous hybrid system.[57]

6.3.2 *The Common Law Codes as Subsidiary Sources of Law*

With the exception of Louisiana, the practical implementation of all the US civil codes was full of surprises. Even where a code's peripheral articles acted as replacements for the common law, the implementation of these articles did not go as intended. This is true of all the common law codes with the exception of the Code of Georgia, which from the start was considered to be a bulwark of the common law. In the cases discussed in this section—the Codes of California, the Dakotas, and Montana—application of the code did not go as planned. The first years in which the Civil Code of California was in effect provide an excellent example of the gap between intention and reality.

Shortly after the adoption of the Civil Code of California, John Norton Pomeroy[58] developed a rule for its implementation that was rapidly accepted. This rule subsequently became the rule of implementation for the civil code in all the states that had adopted a version of the Civil Code of New York. John Norton Pomeroy was born in 1828 and died in 1885. His father was a judge in Rochester, and Pomeroy himself was admitted to the New York Bar in 1851.[59] He then practiced law until 1861, when he moved from Rochester to New York City to become headmaster of the Kingston Academy. It was during this period that he wrote his first book on municipal law. This book allowed him to obtain a professorship at New York University Law School, which he held from 1864 to 1871. He was chosen as the law school's dean in 1865, a post he held until he left the university. Due to health problems, he abandoned his post and returned to his hometown to become a full-time writer. In 1878, he moved to California

---

56 *Reynolds v. Swain*, 13 La. 193 (1839); *Hugh v. New Orleans & Carrollton Railroad*, 6 La. Ann. 485 (1851); *Moulin v. Monteleone*, 115 La. So. 447 (1927). On the matter, see A. N. Yiannopoulos, "The Civil Codes of Louisiana", 1 *Civil Law Commentaries* 2008, pp. 1–23; John A. Lovett, "On the Principle of Legal Certainty in the Louisiana Civil Law Tradition: From the Manifesto to the Great Repealing Act and Beyond", 63 *Louisiana Law Review* 2003, pp. 1414–1416.

57 Mack E. Barham, "La Méthodologie du Droit civil de l'État de Louisiane", 27 *Revue internationale de Droit comparé* 1975, pp. 802–805.

58 John C. Leary, "John Norton Pomeroy, 1825–1885", 47 *Law Library Journal* 1954, pp. 38–44.

59 David M. Rabban, *Law's History: American legal Thought and the transatlantic Turn to History (Cambridge Historical Studies in American Law and Society)*, Cambridge: Cambridge University Press, 2013, pp. 32–35.

after obtaining a position in the Hastings College of Law, the first law school established in the western state. He taught there for three years while continuing to write books on subjects related to the law. Pomeroy was initially a fervent defender of codification in California. Moreover, in his inaugural address to the faculty in 1878, he praised Californian achievements in the field of law, in particular regarding the state's codification's endeavors.

> The work which California has thus accomplished will certainly be imitated by other states [...] and spread with ever-increasing rapidity, until its effect shall be shown throughout the entire extent of our common country.[60]

He was convinced that a code would be a positive step for the law, provided that it includes both statutory and common law,[61] exactly what California appeared to have done. However, in the years following the implementation of the civil code, Pomeroy's enthusiasm declined precipitously. He declared the civil code dead in a set of articles on the implementation of the code and its rules of interpretation.[62] He passionately enumerated the code's many insurmountable defects. One of the code's greatest sins, his articles explained, was that it had generated more uncertainty in the law than had previously existed, because of the legal language used and the inefficiency of its organization.

> No reader of the code can feel certain that any given title or chapter relating to a particular subject matter contains all the rules which have been enacted concerning that subject matter, and which affect the private rights, duties and relations of persons. Additional rules, often of the very highest importance, are found in wholly different and unconnected portions of the same code, or even in the other codes—the political code or the code of procedure—in portions where no ordinary reader would have expected to find them.[63]

Due to these inherent flaws within the code, especially its lack of exclusivity and completeness, it was impossible for Pomeroy to think of California's code

60 John Norton Pomeroy, *The Hastings Law Department of the University of California: Inaugural Address*, San Francisco: Bancroft, 1878, p. 11.

61 John C. Leary, "John Norton Pomeroy, 1825–1885", 47 *Law Library Journal* 1954, p. 41.

62 John Norton Pomeroy, *The "Civil Code" of California, originally published as 'The true Method of Interpreting the Civil Code'*, San Francisco: California Bar Association, 1885.

63 *Ibid*, p. 12.

as sharing the European usage of codification. This meant that it was impossible to make the code the primary source of private law. Indeed, in his opinion, the Civil Code of California lacked many key dispositions concerning subjects central to the field of private law. For Pomeroy, the code required interpretation and elucidation by a court of law[64] to be efficient. The flaws Pomeroy identified existed at all levels of the code, from its content, as explained previously, to its organization.[65] There were even issues in the way the articles were written, many of which he found unclear and obscure.[66] In addition to issues of clarity and completeness, Pomeroy considered the European vision of a source of law purely based on code to be inapplicable to the US territory due to its common law tradition. Therefore, he argued, a code should be applied and used as a complement to the common law.[67] Accordingly, early in the discussion, Pomeroy insisted that, to avoid confusion and instability within the law related to the code, specific rules on the interpretation of the civil code had to be established. Consequently, he offered the following rule of interpretation and implementation of the code.

> Except in the comparatively few instances where the language is so clear and unequivocal as to leave no doubt of an intention to depart from, alter, or abrogate the common law rule concerning the subject matter, the courts should avowedly adopt and follow without deviation the uniform principle of interpreting all the definitions, statements of doctrines, and rules contained in the code in complete conformity with the common law definitions, doctrines, and rules, and as to all the subordinate effects resulting from such interpretation.[68]

64 *Ibid*, pp. 6–7, "Our civil code, regarded as a comprehensive system of statutory legislation, covering the entire private jurisprudence of the state, as a scientific or practical arrangement and statement of principles, doctrine and rules constituting that jurisprudence—in other words, as an example for true codification—is even in the estimation of its original authors, full of defects, imperfections and omissions and even inconsistencies, which must, so far as possible, be supplied, removed and harmonized by the courts."

65 John Norton Pomeroy, *The true Method of Interpreting the Civil Code*, San Francisco: Bancroft, 1884, p. 13. "It is a defect of arrangement. No reader of the code can feel certain that any given title or chapter, relating to a particular subject matter contains all the rules which have been enacted concerning a subject matter."

66 *Ibid*, p. 31. "I have thus given some striking instances of the uncertainty which must result from the adoption of new phraseology in the place of what was familiar and settled in its meaning and effect."

67 *Ibid*, pp. 52–56.

68 *Ibid*, p. 51.

This means that, except in cases where the code clearly expressed an intent to repeal or amend the provisions of the common law, the common law applies and is superior to the civil code, thus making the latter a subsidiary, or at best a secondary source of law. In California, the code subsequently became a piece of law used to illuminate the common law, a form of explanatory statute for the common law. This proposed rule of interpretation was discussed and expressly adopted by the California Supreme Court in *Shannon v. Shannon* in 1888, three years after the publication of Pomeroy's articles. This delay is unsurprising as three years was the usual amount of time for a case to go to the state supreme court. In addition, this rule of interpretation and implementation of the code was embraced by supporters of common law, who viewed it as a way to correct the rigidity of the code and to maintain the adaptability of common law. To common law's defenders, this rule was proof of the imperfection of codification and of common law's superiority. This rule was then readopted and applied multiple times over. For instance, in the judgment of the District Court of Appeals for the Third District in *Siminoff v. Goodman Bank* in 1912, the court decided in favor of the complainant on the grounds that, even if the literal provisions of the code seemed to cover the case, they were never intended to alter the common law liability. Hence, the common law rule was applied.[69] In contrast, when the code clearly intended to change the law, the will of the commissioners and legislature was respected. An example of this is found in the article of the code regarding ownership and future interests. The article arose directly from the Field Civil Code and was adopted with the intent to change the existing law on the subject. In this case, then, the rules of the code prevailed over the rules of the prior common law. To some extent, then, the will of the codifiers was respected. At the same time, however, a full substitution of the common law by codification was impossible. For members of the legal profession, this arrangement likely appeared the best of both worlds. Codification offered certainty, while common law allowed for an evolutive adaptation of the law over time. The code remained relevant and dominant in the event that it settled a legal dispute or improved the law. In all other cases, the common law took precedence. The view that the code is subsidiary unless there is no disposition in the preexisting law or a will to change it, is not unique to the United States. In Spain,[70] "the implementation of the civil code is merely subsidiary, that is, when regional laws do not contain a legal rule applicable to solve a legal

69 Maurice E. Harrison, "First half-century of the California Civil Code", 185 *California Law Review* 1922, p. 190.

70 The Spanish Civil Code (Código Civil) was adopted in 1889.

dispute".[71] This idea of using the civil code as a subsidiary source of law seems to be a solution used in cases where there is already a strong preexisting legal tradition to which a population is attached. Therefore, even if the Napoleonic Code is the source of inspiration for codification worldwide, the trajectory of different codes shows that the French idea of codification can be adopted and used in different ways. If the modern idea of the code linked the Napoleonic Code, this model has taken different shapes according to different local circumstances. The examples of Spain and the United States also show that a code does not need to be the primary source of law to be an effective, relevant, and useful source of law. A code, whatever its shape, cannot be reduced to its comparative importance with other sources of law. A model is just a model, and the Napoleonic Code was just one possible format for codification.

One of the problems created by this rule of interpretation and adoption can be seen in cases where the commissioners voluntarily intended to change the law. In such cases, the *Shannon v. Shannon* decision held that the court had to refer to the annotations of the code commissioners and to Field's note on his code to determine if the change was intended or not.[72] Perhaps coincidentally, this process returns to the concept of the spirit of the law already evident in the peripheral articles. The adoption of Pomeroy's rule of interpretation was heavily criticized by defenders of the code because they considered that the rule prevented the code from reaching its full potential in terms of change of and within the law.[73] This is why, for many, Pomeroy is the man who killed the Civil Code of California, for his rule kept it heavily constrained by common law.

Why did Pomeroy shift from advocate to opponent of codification and decide to undertake serious action to destroy the civil code? Officially, his articles suggested that his change of mind was due to the numerous defects of the code. It was his duty and mission as a law professor to right the wrong.[74]

---

71 Aniceto Masferrer, "Codification as Nationalisation or Denationalisation of Laws: The Spanish Case in comparative Perspective", 4 *Comparative Legal History* 2016, p. 101.

72 Maurice E. Harrison, "First half-century of the California Civil Code", 185 *California Law Review* 1922, pp. 194–195.

73 *Ibid*, pp. 197–198.

74 John Norton Pomeroy, *The "Civil Code" of California, originally published as 'The true Method of Interpreting the Civil Code'*, San Francisco: California Bar Association, 1885, pp. 5–6. "My position as a teacher of law, compelled to deal with the code as a whole and with all of its separate parts, to examine, compare, contrast and expound all of its material sections as constitution element of a complete system—this duty I say perhaps enables me to perceive more clearly than the practicing lawyer, the defect and imperfections of the code, and to appreciate the imperative necessity of adopting some uniform method or principle in its construction and interpretation."

However, if the problem was just a matter of error or misleading provisions, then the various revisions that followed the adoption of the code would have solved the issues. But this was not the only problem. We can suppose that his initial enthusiasm for codification decreased as the code came into effect, especially as judges, practitioners, and law professors like himself must have realized that using a code required a completely new legal education, legal understanding, and usage of the law. Content with the changes but puzzled by how to implement the code and irritated by the numerous broad definitions inserted in the code,[75] Pomeroy likely sought a solution that would maintain the code's changes to the law while allowing common law to remain paramount. Pomeroy's rule of application and interpretation of the civil code did not remain in California. As the code traveled to the Dakota Territory, his rule followed and remained even after the Dakota Division. Pomeroy could not have foreseen that his proposed rule of application for the civil code would become, with time and transposition of this legal feature, the rule of application and interpretation of all the common law civil codes. Nor could he have foreseen that he would in effect create an entirely new tradition of civil codification.

By looking at the implementation of the nineteenth-century civil codes, three categories can be distinguished, corresponding to the three possible applications of the code. In the first kind of implementation, the civil code is the main source of private law. An example is the Civil Code of Louisiana, the United States' most famous civil code (perhaps because of this feature in particular). Indeed, a code is usually considered a *true codification* when it becomes the main source of law, but as the case of the United States shows, the civil code can be a subsidiary or complementary source of law. This organization can occur whether it was intended, like in Georgia, or due to the reality of the code's enforcement and interpretation, as was the case for the Civil Codes of California, the Dakota Territory, North Dakota, South Dakota, and Montana. Surprisingly, the common law civil codes are routinely considered to be less effective than "real" civil codes, and at times they are not considered real codes at all. This happens especially in cases where the civil codes are not the only or even the principal source of law. This raises the question of whether a code needs to be the main source of law of a legal field to be an effective, or even a "real" civil code. Is the implementation of the code an essential, definitional part of its status as a code? Looking at the US civil codes, it would appear that the way the code is applied is not fundamental, even if this is quite contrary to the definition of codification arising from the Napoleonic Code. We might

75 *Ibid*, pp. 40–45.

say that the application of the code may be an element of definition, but it depends on the definition chosen, especially the importance the definition gives to the code's supremacy vis a vis other sources of law. As discussed above, there is no international definition of a civil code and codification. As a result, some scholars refuse to define the common law codes as civil codes and deny that a hybrid legal system exists capable of affecting either decisions or the law.[76] To these observers, the codes simply become "immersed in the sod of common law".[77] For a code to be effective, it needs to be both law and a source of law, though not the only source. This aspect seems to be a bonus, and not one of the essential points to qualify a document as a civil code. From the different sources related to the nineteenth-century US civil codes, it even appears that the code commissioners in several states never intended for their code to be enforceable as the main or sole source of law, as civil codes are in Europe. In fact, they knew such a structure would not work given the peculiarities of the American context. Therefore, it made sense that the commissioners believed it possible to have a true code regardless of how it was implemented. Behind these arguments the reality is that most of the states adopting civil codes could not change years of legal training and understanding of the law by making a new civil code the primary source of law. Indeed, they sometimes did not even seem to desire to enact this change. However, as noted in our working definition of codification,[78] all states undertook the process of codification because they wanted to create a better understanding of the law. Finally, given that the idea of a civil code can cover a broad number of possibilities, from the canonical French case to the American model, there seems to be no reason to restrict it.

---

76 Izhak Englard, "Li v. Yellow Cab. Co.—A belated and inglorious centennial of the California Civil Code", 65 *California Law Review* 1977, pp. 4–27; Joseph L. Lewinsohn, "Mutual Assent in Contract under the Civil Code of California", 2 *California Law Review* 1914, pp. 345–366; Mark D. Rosen, "What has happened to the Common Law? Recent American Codification, and their Impact on Judicial Practice and the Law's subsequent Development", 1119 *Wisconsin Law Review* 1994, pp. 1119–1286.

77 Izhak Englard, "Li v. Yellow Cab. Co.—A belated and inglorious centennial of the California Civil Code", 65 *California Law Review* 1977, p. 15.

78 Jacques Vanderlinden, *Le Concept de Code en Europe Occidentale du XIIe au XIXe Siècle: Essai de Définition*, Bruxelles: Éditions de l'Institut de Sociologie de l'Université libre de Bruxelles, 1967, pp. 15–16.

Bibliography

Barham, Mack E.: "La Méthodologie du Droit civil de l'État de Louisiane", 27 *Revue internationale de Droit comparé* 1975, pp. 797–816.

Cabrillac, Rémy: *Les Codifications* (*Droit, Éthique, Société*), Paris: Presses Universitaires de France, 2002.

Carbasse, Jean-Marie: *Manuel d'Introdiction historique au Droit*, 4th ed., Paris: Presses Universitaires de France, 2011.

Castellucci, Ignazio: "Law v. Lex: An Analysis of a Critical Relation in Roman and Civil Law", 8 *Global Jurist* 2008, pp. 1–32.

Cook, Charles M.: *The American Codification Movement: A Study of Antebellum Legal Reform* (*Contributions in Legal Studies*), Westport (CT): Greenwood Press, 1981.

Englard, Izhak: "Li v. Yellow Cab. Co.—A Belated and Inglorious Centennial of the California Civil Code", 65 *California Law Review* 1977, pp. 4–27.

Halpérin, Jean-Louis: *L'impossible Code Civil* (*Histoires*), Paris: Presses Universitaires de France, 1992.

Harrison, Maurice E.: "First Half-Century of the California Civil Code", 185 *California Law Review* 1922, pp. 185–201.

Hood Jr., John T.: "The History and Development of the Louisiana Civil Code", 19 *Louisiana Law Review* 1958, pp. 18–33.

Leary, John C.: "John Norton Pomeroy, 1825–1885", 47 *Law Library Journal* 1954, pp. 38–44.

Levasseur, Alain A.: *Louis Casimir Elisabeth Moreau-Lislet: Foster Father of Louisiana Civil Code*, Baton Rouge: LSU Law Center Publications Institute, 1996.

Lewinsohn, Joseph L.: "Mutual Assent in Contract under the Civil Code of California", 2 *California Law Review* 1914, pp. 345–366.

Lovett, John A.: "On the Principle of Legal Certainty in the Louisiana Civil Law Tradition: From the Manifesto to the Great Repealing Act and Beyond", 63 *Louisiana Law Review* 2003, pp. 1397–1448.

Masferrer, Aniceto: "Codification as Nationalisation or Denationalisation of Laws: The Spanish Case in comparative Perspective", 4 *Comparative Legal History* 2016, pp. 100–130.

Munsom, Granville: "Does the Court Make or Interpret the Law?", 58 *University of Pennsylvania Law Review* 1909, pp. 365–375.

Pomeroy, John Norton: *The "Civil Code" of California, originally published as 'The true Method of Interpreting the Civil Code'*, San Francisco: California Bar Association, 1885.

Pomeroy, John Norton: *The Hastings Law Department of the University of California: Inaugural Address*, San Francisco: Bancroft, 1878.

Pomeroy, John Norton: *The true Method of Interpreting the Civil Code*, San Francisco: Bancroft, 1884.

Portalis, Jean-Marie: "Discours préliminaire du premier Projet de Code Civil", 1801.

Rabban, David M.: *Law's History: American legal Thought and the transatlantic Turn to History* (*Cambridge Historical Studies in American Law and Society*), Cambridge: Cambridge University Press, 2013.

Renoux-Zagamé, Marie-F.: "Additionnel ou innovative? Débats et Solutions des premières Décennies de Mise en Œuvre du Code Civil", 41 *Droits* 2005, pp. 19–36.

Rosen, Mark D.: "What has happened to the Common Law? Recent American Codification, and their Impact on Judicial Practice and the Law's subsequent Development", 1119 *Wisconsin Law Review* 1994, pp. 1119–1286.

Sève, René: *Philosophie et Théorie du Droit*, 2nd ed., Paris: Dalloz, 2016.

Vanderlinden, Jacques: *Le Concept de Code en Europe Occidentale du XIIe au XIXe Siècle: Essai de Définition*, Bruxelles: Éditions de l'Institut de Sociologie de l'Université libre de Bruxelles, 1967.

Wagner, Wienczyslaw J.: "Codification of Law in Europe and the Codification Movement in the Middle of the Nineteenth Century in the United States", 2 *Saint Louis University Law Journal* 1952, pp. 335–359.

Wieacker, Franz: *Privatrechtsgeschichte der Neuzeit unter besonderer Berücksichtigung der deutschen Entwicklung* (*Jurisprudenz in Einzeldarstellungen, 7th vol.*), 3rd ed., Göttingen: Vandenhoeck & Ruprecht, 2016.

Yiannopoulos, A. N.: "The Civil Codes of Louisiana", 1 *Civil Law Commentaries* 2008, pp. 1–23.

Zimmermann, Reinhard: "Statuta sunt stricte interpretanda? Statutes and the Common Law: A continental Perspective", 56 *The Cambridge Law Journal* 1977, pp. 315–328.

Conclusion

The study of the genesis of the nineteenth-century US civil codes is, above all, a study in versatility—both of the concept of codification and of the United States itself. The 1808 and 1825 Civil Codes of Louisiana; the 1860 Draft of a Civil Code for the State of New York; the 1862 Code of Georgia; the 1866 Civil Code of the Dakota Territory; the 1870 Revised Civil Code of Louisiana; the 1872 Civil Code of California; the 1895 Revised Code of North Dakota; the 1895 Civil Code of Montana; and the 1903 Revised Code of South Dakota, are all a written testimonies to the particularities of their time and place.

These codes were all the products of clearly stated intentions. Inasmuch as they were controversial, codes were treasured as a tool of clarity. The codes were all written with the intention of structuring and harmoniously combining the law into a coherent whole. As such, they were a product of the broader nineteenth-century drive for rationalization. As codifiers themselves said, codes were meant to permit, "a better understanding of the law", legal instruments designed to more accurately reflect the political, social and economic reality of given places. Despite their diverse histories, the nineteenth-century civil codes also reflected the broader history of the United States in the sense that they are the product of the states laying their foundations.

Unveiling the civil codes' history allows one to distinguish them from the other existing "codes". All of the states have collected their statutes into compilations called "codes", but the civil codes went further. They are not merely lists of statutes organized by topic, but aim instead at rationalization and exhaustivity. Drafting them involved gathering all the sources of law, whether judicial, customary or legislative, and then organizing them according to a specific thematic and rational organization. Most of the content might not be revolutionary, but a process which resulted in applying Louisiana principles in New York law, then New York law in California, or Californian law in Dakota seems revolutionary enough not to be ignored.

Partially driven by their colonial legacy, most of the states that adopted a civil code—except Georgia—were young and in their formative years. Each also saw an important increase in population in the years preceding the codes and, after the adoption of their codes, the number of inhabitants within each of these states became stable. For the Dakota Territory and California, the arrival of codification also coincided with the arrival of the railway. As much as these elements could induce codification, they were not enough on their own. In fact, if these factors were sufficient, all the states would have had a civil code. Therefore, the codifying states had to have an extra element that drove

 | DOI:10.1163/9789004689978_010

them to codification: a network of codifiers. During the nineteenth century, neither the national debate on codification nor individual state endeavors, were led by any national or federal agency. Even the two main political parties did not make codification their panacea. Codification in the United States was fully detached from organizations and was primarily the product of the initiative of individual jurists. When researching the presence and influence of individuals championing codification, it was astonishing to find how closely they were all linked to each other. More precisely, they all gravitated around David Dudley Field, with the notable exception of the authors of the Code of Georgia. Indeed, during the year in which he drafted his code, Field engaged in profuse correspondence with Livingston in Louisiana. Field's brother then became the Californian advocate for codification, and the code arrived in Dakota because Field's cousin was Chief Justice of the Dakota Territory Supreme Court. All the main actors in codification were privately connected with each other, and the development of the civil codes in the United States during the nineteenth century is a testament to the strength of this network.

The codifiers were also driven by personal convictions and individual experiences. Indeed, Sampson and Field became defenders of codification because they stayed in France for personal reasons and witnessed the Napoleonic Code in action. As for Georgia, it was during his wedding in Alabama that the Georgian code's main supporter fell in love with the idea of a code. Private connections aside, the codification process also had a strong effect on the men's interactions. Codification was a heated subject, and it became the fuel for disputes between law practitioners in Louisiana and New York. Where personal conflicts did not arise, as in the remaining states, codification was an endeavor which brought unity. The network of codifiers was also supported by the circulation and availability of an already existing model of a civil code. The Civil Code of Louisiana influenced the Civil Code of New York, which shaped the Civil Code of California and the first Civil Code of the Dakota Territory. Then, the Civil Code of California influenced the Revised Civil Code of the Dakota Territory, which in turn influenced the Civil Codes of North Dakota and Montana. Finally, the Civil Code of North Dakota influenced the Civil Code of South Dakota. The nineteenth-century civil codes are thus part of a common lineage. The only code outside of this circulation pattern is, again, the Code of Georgia. Yet, some of its dispositions can be found in the Civil Code of California, testifying to a hidden influence by the latter. The circulation pattern of the codes reveals that all the codes are interlinked and work together, creating a certain cohesion to private law codification within the US territory.

Whether it was due to influence, driving factors, lineage, form, application, or content, one code stood apart from the others during this research. The

Code of Georgia was the only code adopted by an old state, and by institutions dominated by Democrats. It is also the only code with a structure based on the Code of Alabama. But most importantly the Code of Georgia was the only code written to supplement the common law and not replace it, all while never intending to introduce any changes to the content of the law. As for why this code stood apart, the answer seems to lie in the very networks the united the other codes. George A. Gordon, the individual most closely linked to the code, had no connections with the other codifiers, which explains why the variations introduced by this code were believed to be the next step for the Code of Alabama.

Examining the drafting process showed that the codes were based on two main legal sources. The direct sources had an intentional influence, and the indirect sources were those arising from an appropriation of another code's model. The common law civil codes were transplants from other codes and brought new and unexpected legal content to the places they traveled, for example introducing elements of Spanish law in the Dakota Territory. The most common primary source for the nineteenth-century US civil codes was the common law, while the most common secondary source that could be found in all the codes was civil law. More precisely it was Roman law, followed by French law, and finally Spanish law. The use of these two sources allowed the US civil codes to bridge the two main legal traditions. This hybrid quality is especially visible in the final shape these codes took.

The adoption mechanisms of the civil codes were the same in all the states. Legislatures first voted on the idea of codification, and appointed commissioners based on their abilities, and then voted later on the code itself and its implementation. The centrality of the legislature to this process brought the field of private law into the democratic arena. The nineteenth-century US civil codes have two categories of sources in terms of content. The codes were also written with the purpose of becoming the main source of law within each state. However, due to the creation of the rule of application by John Norton Pomeroy and the strength of the common law tradition, the common law civil codes ended up becoming a subsidiary source of law that only existed to complete the common law.

Bringing light to the nineteenth-century US civil codes opens the door to a new set of research opportunities, as many questions are left unanswered. The civil codes were a response to a changing society,[1] and they reflected their

1 David M. Rabban, *Law's History: American legal Thought and the transatlantic Turn to History* (*Cambridge Historical Studies in American Law and Society*), Cambridge: Cambridge University Press, 2013, p. 5.

time and place and were heirs to specific cultures. This study of the genesis of the civil codes provides a foundation for a comparative approach to the content of the code's legal institutions, so as to finally develop a full picture of US codification. For instance, preliminary research examining the evolution of divorce through the civil codes—while also looking at their judicial usage on the question—already showcases some novel findings. Divorcing in a civil code state during the nineteenth century was not particularly different from divorcing in a common law state. Like in any state, there were some specificities and peculiarities, but overall, the civil codes were just an enforcement of previous law, and the codes did not create a revolution in the field of divorce law. However, the civil codes had a unifying effect on divorce law in uniting the law of California with that of the broader West. In fact, the code dispositions regarding divorce in the Dakotas and Montana were similar in organization, but also in content to the Civil Code of California, which was, in fact, their original source. Examination of the legal basis of Supreme Court decisions after the adoption of the codes shows the degree to which they were used as legal foundations. Indeed, the civil codes were almost always cited in the Supreme Court case law examined here. To give one example, 80% of the Georgia cases quoted the code to justify their rulings. For the other codes—those of Louisiana, Dakota Territory, the Dakotas, Montana, and California—all divorce jurisprudence after 1887 cited the provisions of their respective civil codes. This finding was astonishing, considering the rule of interpretation of the common law codes (all except Louisiana) as a subsidiary source of law or secondary to the common law in force in the state. This small example is proof that the civil codes have many surprises in store for us.

To conclude, the nineteenth-century US civil codes are an essential but forgotten part of US legal history. With them, the history of codification has a new stone to build on and grow.

Timetable

1626 New Netherland is founded as Dutch Colony.
1664 New Netherland is conquered by the British and becomes New York.
1674 New York is reaffirmed as British Colony by the Treaty of Westminster.
1681 Louisiana is founded by Robert Cavalier de la Salle.
1685 New York becomes a British Royal Colony.
1752 Georgia becomes a British Royal Colony.
1762 Louisiana is ceded to Spain by the Treaty of Fontainebleau.
1765 California becomes a Spanish Colony.
1769 Louisiana is being taken possession of by Spain.
1779 Marshall-Wythe School of Law, the first US Law School, is founded.
1788 Georgia and New York ratify the US Constitution and become the fourth and eleventh States of the Union.
1790 The Capital of the United States is moved from New York to Philadelphia.
1792 The Democratic Party is founded.
1800 Louisiana is retroceded to France by the Treaty of San Ildefonso.
1803 Louisiana is ceded to the United States by the Treaty of Paris.
1806 Manifesto of June 3 against the Governor of Louisiana.
1806 Act of June 7 allowing the Drafting of a Civil Code for Louisiana.
1808 Adoption of the *Digest of Louisiana* on March 31.
1811 *Orleans Navigation Co. v. New Orleans* before the Louisiana Supreme Court.
1812 Louisiana passes a Constitution and is granted Statehood.
1817 *Cottin v. Cottin* before the Louisiana Supreme Court.
1817 Harvard School of Law is founded.
1820 Begin of the American Codification Movement.
1821 Alta California becomes Mexico.
1822 Appointment of a Commission for the Revision of the *Digest of Louisiana.*
1824 Adoption of the *Code of Legal Practice of Louisiana.*
1825 Adoption of the *Civil Code of Louisiana* on June 20.
1827 *Fowler v. Griffith* before the Louisiana Supreme Court.
1827 *Lacroix v. Coquet* before the Louisiana Supreme Court.
1828 Passing of the *Great Repealing Act* in Louisiana.

1846 New York passes a Constitution which contains the Article on Codification.
1847 Appointment of a Commission for the Codification of the Law in New York on April 8.
1848 Adoption of the *Code of Civil Procedure of New York.*
1848 California is ceded to the United States by the Treaty of Guadeloupe Hidalgo.
1849 Appointment of a new Commission for the Codification of the Law in New York.
1850 California adopts the Common Law and is granted Statehood.
1851 The Number of Law Schools in the United States reaches 19.
1852 Adoption of the *Code of Alabama.*
1852 The Republican Party is founded.
1857 Appointment of a new Commission for the Codification of the Law in New York.
1858 Act of November 9 allowing the Drafting of a Civil Code in Georgia.
1860 End of the Codification Movement.
1861 Georgia leaves the Union.
1861 First Presentation of the *Civil Code of New York* and subsequent Adoption
by the Legislature as well as Veto by the Governor of New York.
1862 Adoption of the *Code of Georgia.*
1862 Passing of the *Pacific Railroad Act.*
1862 Extension of the Schedule for the Commission for the Codification of the Law in New York.
1863 Adoption of the *Code of Georgia.*
1864 Creation of the Montana Territory.
1865 Adoption of the *Field Civil Code* in the Dakota Territory.
1865 Second Presentation of the *Civil Code of New York* and subsequent Adoption
by the Legislature as well as Veto by the Governor of New York.
1867 Revision of the *Code of Georgia.*
1868 Louisiana passes a Constitution after the End of the Civil War.
1868 Act of October 21 allowing the Revision of the *Civil Code of Louisiana* and the *Code of Legal Practice of Louisiana.*
1870 Appointment of a Commission for the Drafting of a Civil Code in California.
1870 Adoption of the *Revised Civil Code of Louisiana* on March 14.
1872 Adoption of the *Civil Code of California.*

1873	Revision of the *Code of Georgia.*
1878	Third Presentation of the *Civil Code of New York* and subsequent Adoption by the Legislature as well as Veto by the Governor of New York.
1879	End of the Cowboy Railroad Line.
1893	Appointment of a Commission for the Revision of the *Code of North Dakota.*
1895	Adoption of the *Code of North Dakota.*
1895	Adoption of the *Code of Montana.*
1901	Appointment of a Commission for the Revision of the *Code of South Dakota.*
1903	Adoption of the *Code of South Dakota.*

Appendix

State	Nomination of the Code Commission: Governor	Chamber	Senate	Adoption of the Codes: Governor	Chamber	Senate
Louisiana	1806	1806	1806	1808	1808	1808
Louisiana	1822	1822	1822	1825	1825	1825
Louisiana	1868	1868	1868	1870	1870	1870
Georgia	1858	1858*	1858	1860	1860	1860
New York	1860–1865	1860–1865	1860–1865	1860–1865	1860–1865	1860–1865
California	1870	1870	1870	1872	1872	1872
Dakota Territory	Direct Adoption of the Field Civil Code			1877	1877	1877
North Dakota	1893	1893	1893	1895	1895	1895
Montana	1889	1889	1889	1893	1893	1895
South Dakota	1901	1901	1901	1903	1903	1903

Democratic Party — Democratic Republican Party — Republican Party — Others

APPENDIX 1 The Political Parties in regard to the US Civil Code's Milestones by Year

 | DOI:10.1163/9789004689978_011

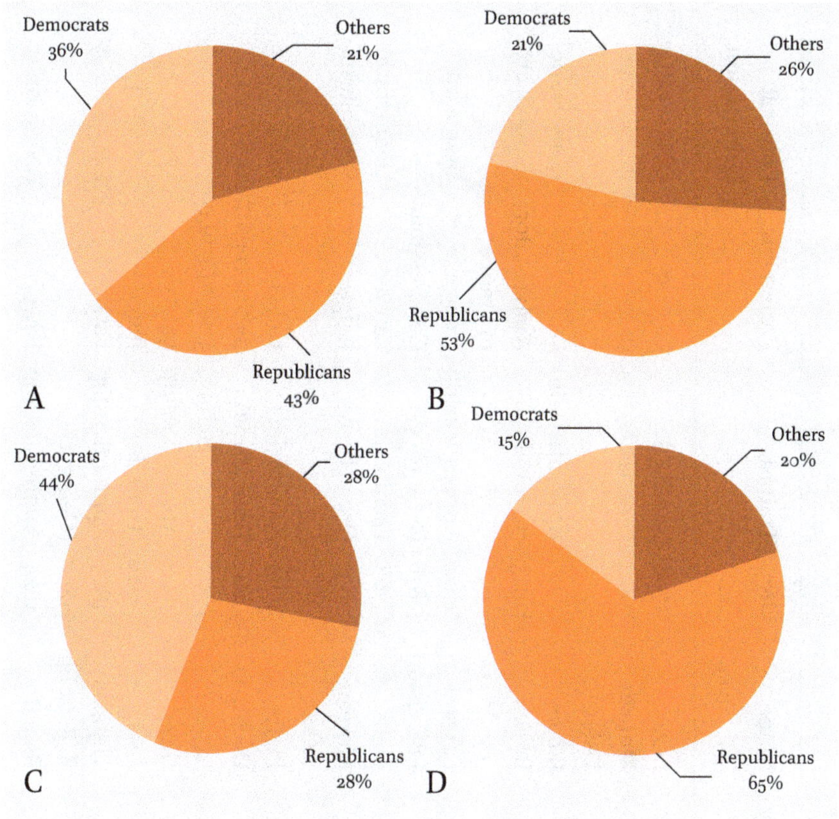

APPENDIX 2 The Political Orientation of Governors and the Legislatures
The Political Orientation of Governors (A) and the Legislatures (B) in general, as well as at the Time of the Commissioners' Nomination (C) and at the Time of the US Civil Code's Adoption (D) in total.

APPENDIX 3 The Commissions of the US Civil Codes and their Members

State	Date	Nomination	Duration	Salary	Name	Life	Training	Profession	Political Orientation
Louisiana C. Commission	1808	Legislature	2 yrs.	2,000 $	Louis Moreau-Lislet	*1768 †1832	Faculté de Droit (Paris)	Lawyer Judge	Democratic-Republican
					James Brown	*1766 †1825	Apprenticeship (Kentucky)	VA Governor Ambassador to France	Democratic-Republican
Louisiana Rev. Commission	1825	Legislature	3 yrs.	1,000 $	Edward Livingston	*1764 †1836	Apprenticeship (New York)	Lawyer Congressman	Democrat
					Louis Moreau-Lislet	*1768 †1832	Faculté de Droit (Paris)	Lawyer Judge	Democratic-Republican
					Pierre Derbigny	*1769 †1829	Faculté de Droit (Paris)	Lawyer LA Supreme Court Justice	Whig
Georgia C. Commission	1860	Legislature	2 yrs.	4,000 $	David Irwin	*1807 †1886	Apprenticeship (Georgia)	Lawyer Judge	Whig Unionist
					Thomas R. R. Cobb	*1823 †1886	Apprenticeship (Georgia)	Lawyer	Secessionist
					Richard H. Clark	*1824 †1896	Apprenticeship (Georgia)	Lawyer GA University Founder	Secessionist

State	Date	Nomination	Duration	Salary	Name	Life	Training	Profession	Political Orientation
New York C. Commission	1860	Legislature	5 yrs.	None	William C. Noyes	*1805 †1864	Apprenticeship (New York)	Lawyer	Republican
					Alexander Bradford	*1815 †1867	Apprenticeship (New York)	Lawyer	?
					David Dudley Field	*1805 †1894	University Apprenticeship (New York)	Lawyer	Democratic-Republican Liberal
Louisiana Rev. Commission	1870	Legislature	2 yrs.	15,000 $ (Ray)	John Ray (Main Writer)	*1816 †1888	Apprenticeship (Louisiana)	Lawyer Landowner	Republican
					Isaiah Garrett (Assistant)	*1845 †1897	Apprenticeship (Louisiana)	Lawyer Soldier	Democrat
					Franklin Garrett (Assistant)	*1840 †1896	Apprenticeship (Louisiana)	Lawyer Soldier	Democrat
					F. A. Hall	?	?	Colonel	?

APPENDIX 3 The Commissions of the US Civil Codes and their Members (*cont.*)

State	Date	Nomination	Duration	Salary	Name	Life	Training	Profession	Political Orientation
California Rev. Commission	1870	Legislature	2 yrs.	3,000 $	Creed Haymond	*1836 †1893	Apprenticeship (California)	Lawyer Soldier	Republican
					John C. Burch	*1826 †1885	Apprenticeship (Missouri)	Lawyer Miner CA Senator	Democrat
					Charles Lindley	*1822 †1882	Yale Law School	Lawyer Judge	Republican
Dakota Territory Rev. Commission	1877	Governor	2 yrs.	800$	Peter C. Shannon	*1821 †1899	Apprenticeship (Pennsylvania)	Lawyer PA Supreme Court Justice	Democrat Republican
					Granville Bennett	*1833 †1910	Self-taught (Iowa)	Soldier IA Senator	Republican
					Bartlett Tripp	*1839 †1911	Albany Law School	Lawyer	Democrat
North Dakota C. Commission	1893	Legislature	?	?	Burke Corbett	*1855 †1934	Apprenticeship (Pennsylvania)	Lawyer	Democrat
					George W. Newton	*1838 †1927	?	Businessman Poet	?
					Charles F. Amidon	*1856 †1937	Apprenticeship (Dakota)	Lawyer Judge	Democrat

State	Date	Nomination	Duration	Salary	Name	Life	Training	Profession	Political Orientation
Montana C. Commission	1895	Governor	2 yrs.	4,000 $	Decius S. Wade	*1835 †1905	Apprenticeship (Ohio)	Lawyer Judge	Republican
					Frederick W. Cole	*1837 †1895	Self-taught (New York)	Lawyer Judge	Democrat
					B. Platt Carpenter	*1837 †1921	Apprenticeship (New York)	Lawyer MT Senator	Republican

APPENDIX 4 Chart of the Population Evolution in the codifying States, 1800–1900

State	1800	1820	1840	1850	1860	1870	1880	1890	1900
Louisiana		153,407	352,411	517,762	708,002	726,915	939,946	1,118,588	1,381,625
Georgia	162,685	340,989	691,392	906,185	1,057,266	1,184,109	1,542,180	1,837,353	2,216,331
New York	589,051	1,372,812	2,428,921	3,097,394	3,380,735	4,382,759	5,082,871	6,003,174	7,268,894
California				92,597	379,994	560,247	864,694	1,213,398	1,485,053
North Dakota						2,405	36,909	190,983	319,146
Montana						20,595	39,159	142,924	243,329
South Dakota					4,837	11,776	98,268	348,600	401,570

APPENDIX 5 Field/Bliss Genealogy Tree

Main Source
Secondary Source

	Louisiana	Georgia	New York	Dakota Territory	California	North Dakota	Montana	South Dakota
US Common Law		M	M	S	S	S	S	S
US Statutes		M	M	S	S	S	S	S
US Doctrine		M	M	S	S	S	S	S
English Doctrine	M	M	M	S	S	S	S	S
English Statutes		M	M	S	S	S	S	S
English Common Law		M	M	S	S	S	S	S
French Doctrine			M	S	S	S	S	S
Local Laws	M	M	M	M	M	M	M	M
La Coutume de Paris	M		M	S	S	S	S	
Justinian Code	M	M	M	S	S	S	S	
Napoleonic Code	M		M	S	S	S	S	
Spanish Law	M				M			
Mexican Law					M	S	S	S
Code of New York				M	M	S	S	S
Code of Louisiana			M	S	S	S	S	
Code of California				M		S	S	S
Code of Dakota Territory						M	M	S
Code of North Dakota								M
Code of Alabama		M						

APPENDIX 6 The main Sources and secondary Sources of the US Civil Codes

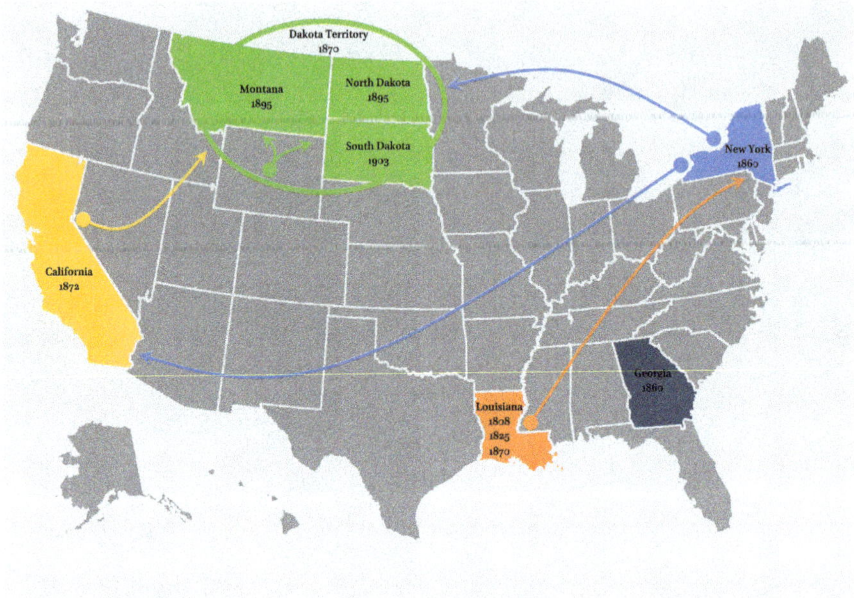

APPENDIX 7 The Circulation of US Civil Codes between the codifying States, 1808–1903

Index

www.ingramcontent.com/pod-product-compliance
Lightning Source LLC
Chambersburg PA
CBHW071324230926
51849CB00002B/310
9789004689961